Penguin Reference Books

A Dictionary of Challenging Words

Norman W. Schur, a Harvard B A, *summa cum laude*, in Latin and Italian literature, attended the University of Rome and the Sorbonne as a Harvard Sheldon Fellow and returned to the United States to study law at Harvard and Columbia law schools. He has now retired from law practice. Norman Schur is the author of the highly successful *British Self-Taught*, and of the subsequent revisions of this book, *English English* and *British English, A To Zed*. His other works include *1000 Most Practical Words* and *1000 Most Important Words*. He is now working on a young persons' *Thesaurus*.

Norman Schur is married and divides his time between Weston, Connecticut, and Kent, England.

A Dictionary of Challenging Words

Norman W. Schur

PENGUIN BOOKS

PENGUIN BOOKS

Published by the Penguin Group
27 Wrights Lane, London W8 5TZ, England
Viking Penguin Inc., 40 West 23rd Street, New York, New York 10010, USA
Penguin Books Australia Ltd, Ringwood, Victoria, Australia
Penguin Books Canada Ltd, 2801 John Street, Markham, Ontario, Canada L3R 1B4
Penguin Books (NZ) Ltd, 182–190 Wairau Road, Auckland 10, New Zealand

Penguin Books Ltd, Registered Offices: Harmondsworth, Middlesex, England

First published in the USA by Facts on File, Inc. 1987
Published in Penguin Books 1989
1 3 5 7 9 10 8 6 4 2

Printed and bound in Great Britain by
Cox & Wyman Ltd, Reading

For Marjorie

Latine is now of equal use become
To Englishmen, as was the Greek to Rome:
It guides our language, nothing is exprest
Gracefull or true but by the Roman test.
—DRYDEN

These are the opening lines of a poem signed "J. Drydon" (a contemporary spelling of *Dryden*), one of two poems prefacing a 17-century manuscript Latin grammar by Lewis Maidwell (1650–1715), a schoolteacher and minor author. The poem, forty lines long, goes on to praise Maidwell, through whose work

Grammer, which was before the ungratefull part
Of our green yeares, is made a pleasing Art . . .

and

. . . as it teaches words it moulds the mind.

. . . .

Beside, 'tis known he could speak Greek
As naturally as pigs squeak:
That Latin was no more difficile,
Than to a black-bird 'tis to whistle.
—SAMUEL BUTLER *(Hudibras)*

(Note: *Difficile* has to be pronounced *dih FIS uhl* to rhyme with *whistle*.)

. . . .

He Greek and Latin speaks with greater ease
Than hogs eat acorns, and tame pigeons peas.
—LIONEL CRANFIELD, Earl of Middlesex
(Panegyric on Tom Coriate)

(Note: Cranfield's couplet preceded Butler's *Hudibras* by a good many years.)

And to any who may object to the plenitude of space devoted to derivation, remember that none other than Dr. Johnson defined *lexicographer* as "a harmless drudge, that busies himself in *tracing the original*, and detailing the signification of words."

Preface

"Americans today," says Bryan A. Garner in volume X, No. 3, of *Verbatim, The Language Quarterly*, "are as averse as any nation to unfamiliar words, which seem to proclaim intellectual pretension, flaunted knowledge, or cultural snobbery—and this if they are used well! Yet hard words have a reputable literary tradition . . . But sesquipedalophobia ('hatred or fear of big words') has prevailed, even among men of learning . . ." (See **sesquipedalian.**)

There are more than 400,000 words in today's unabridged dictionaries, and supplements appear from time to time. They include entries like *you, me, it, is, to, how, why,* etc.—words that are part of every English-speaking person's vocabulary—and others like *abelmosk, benzophenone, holoblastic, leptoprosopic, mylohyoideus, zingiberaceous,* words that, a thousand to one, you'll never run into except perhaps in word games, and can live without. In between, there is a third lot: words not in common use, but ones you may well run into.

Within this third lot, there are certain groupings: words based on the names of people, real *(Lucullan, gerrymander, jeremiad, Roscian)* or fictional *(Gargantuan, Pantagruelian, rodomontade),* or on place names, geographical *(brummagem)* or literary *(Brobdingnagian, Lilliputian);* others that have been taken over intact from foreign languages *(a cappella, bivouac, bravura, chiaroscuro, legerdemain, louche, nous, tzigane, Zeitgeist).* The majority by far, though they owe their origin in the main to classical Latin and Greek, are perfectly good English words that might lurk around any corner of literature, waiting to jump out and perhaps puzzle you, and therefore challenge you. Hence the title of this book.

Compilations of difficult words are nothing new. Philetas of Cos in ancient Greece (b.c. 320 B.C.) produced such a work, known in English as "Miscellaneous Difficult Words," consisting of a collection explaining rare words found in Homer and certain dialects, and technical terms. His pupil, Zenodotus of Ephesus (b.c. 325 B.C.), the first head of the celebrated Library of Alexandria, wrote a Homeric glossary, known in English as "Difficult Words." He was responsible for a great innovation: he listed his entries in alphabetical order! Aristophanes of Byzantium (c. 257–180 B.C.— not to be confused with the earlier Aristophanes, c. 445–c. 385 B.C., the foremost writer of Greek comedy) became head of the great library c. 194 B.C., and followed up with an exhaustive compilation bearing the simple title "Words" that included, in addition to obscure terms from poetry, difficult words from prose writings as well. This book follows a tradition established a very long time ago.

Pronunciation is indicated in parentheses immediately following the headword.

"a"	for "a" as in "hat"
"ay" or "a——e"	for "a" as in "hate"
"ah"	for "a" as in "bah," "o" as in gone
"air"	for "a" as in "dare," "ai" as in "air"
"ar"	for "a" as in "art"
"aw"	for "a" as in "awe," "ou" as in "ought"
"e" or "eh"	for "e" as in "met"
"ee"	for "ee" as in "meet"
"i" or "ih"	for "i" as in "bit"
"(e)ye" or "i——e"	for "i" as in "bite"
"o"	for "o" as in "got"
"oh" or "o——e"	for "o" as in "go"
"oo"	for "oo" as in "look"
"ooh"	for "oo" as in "boot," "u" as in "lute"
"or"	for "o" as in "or"
"oy"	for "o" as in "boy" or "void"
"ou"	for "ou" as in "out"
"u" or "uh"	for "u" as in "but," and for schwa (an indefinite "uh?" sound of an unaccented syllable, like the "a" in "woman," the "i" in "pencil," the "u" in "focus," etc.)
"u(r)"	for "u" as in "fur"

In demonstrating meaning by example, I have at times seen fit to amplify my own concoctions with quotations from literature, with the dual purpose of showing such exquisitely apposite and dramatic choices of words by great writers as might serve to fix their meanings in the mind, and that of introducing readers to the masters and their writings in the hope that closer acquaintance might be sought. Foreign authors are, of course, quoted in translation, and here it is the translators whose choice of words is the model.

Wherever *Fowler* is quoted or mentioned in the text, I refer to *Fowler's Modern English Usage* (Second Edition Revised by Sir Ernest Gowers, Oxford University Press). *Latin* and *Greek* in the text mean the classical forms; *Late Latin* is that of A.D. 300–700; *Middle Latin* or *Medieval Latin* that of A.D. 700–1500; *New Latin* that which came into use circa 1500. *Old English* is the English of A.D. 450–1150; *Middle English* that of 1150–1475. *Old French* is the French of A.D. 1000–1400; *Middle French* that of 1500–1700.

Parts of speech are abbreviated thus: *n.* noun; *vb.* verb; *adj.* adjective; *adv.* adverb; *conj.* conjunction; *pl.* plural.

My criteria in the selection of the 1000 words have necessarily been subjective. They are, without exception, words that I have come across myself, words that have challenged me by giving me pause or somehow exciting my interest and inviting investigation. I have not resorted to plucking words out of dictionaries.

Any "challenging" word that appears in the explanatory comment under another entry is set in boldface. If you find an unfamiliar word set in ordinary type, look for it in my *1000 Most Important Words* or *1000 Most Practical Words*. If that doesn't work, find it in your unabridged and meet the challenge head on!

Norman W. Schur
Hawkhurst, Kent, England
Weston, Connecticut, U.S.A

■■■■

a fortiori (ay for shee OR eye) *adj, adv.* This Latin phrase meaning, literally, "from the stronger [point]" is used quite frequently in English to introduce a statement that, assuming a previous statement is accepted as true, must *all the more so* be true. What *a fortiori* really means, in arguing a point, is "all the more so." If statement A is true, then *a fortiori*, i.e., all the more so, statement B must be true. If a certain job can't be done by a certain crew in a week, *a fortiori* a similar job can't be done by a similar crew in five days. If a man isn't rich enough to stay a night at a second-rate hotel, *a fortiori* he can't afford to put up at the Ritz. This is a useful expression in arguing, to prove a weaker point from a stronger one—i.e., *a fortiori*.

a posteriori,   see **a priori**

a priori   (ay pree OR eye) *adj., adv.*; **a posteriori** (ay poh steer ee OR eye) (The vowels can be pronounced in different ways depending on one's system of pronunciation of Latin.) *adj., adv.* Both these expressions are Latin but are freely used in English, especially in argument. They mean, literally and respectively, "from the one before" and "from the one behind," and apply as follows: An *a priori* conclusion or judgment is one reached by reference to self-evident truths, deductively, not based on prior examination, experimentation or analysis. Thus, the American critic and editor Norman Cousins (born 1912) spoke of the "*a priori* acceptance of the greatness of a book," reasoning not from an examination of its merits but from deductions based on surrounding circumstances, such as the greatness of its author and the influence the book has had. In *a priori* reasoning, one works from a known premise or premises to an effect. An *a posteriori* conclusion is one reached by

1

examination and analysis of the specific facts, as happens in a science laboratory, where one reasons inductively from actual observation of data and derives a conclusion or theory from the observed facts. In short, an *a priori* conclusion is based upon presumptions; an *a posteriori* conclusion is based upon observations. Fowler ingeniously gives *God's in his heaven—all's right with the world* as either an *a priori* inference if it means: "We know there is a god; therefore the state of the world must be right," or an *a posteriori* inference if it means: "The world is so right that there must be a god in heaven."

abatis (AB uh tee, -tis, uh BAT ee, -is) *n.* A term describing a primitive form of military barricade; an obstruction against the foe consisting of felled trees with sharpened branches, sometimes interlaced with barbed wire. In these days of extremely long-range artillery, to say nothing of bombers (shall we remain silent about the A- and H- variety?), the *abatis* seems as naive as the classical military phalanx, but in its day the *abatis* was very effective. Incidentally, the hedges of today that serve to mark land boundaries, embellish landscapes, or provide residential privacy are descendants of another piece of old-time military construction, a defense used by the Roman army: its military hedges (*saepes* or *saepimenta*), as thick as 30 feet, very tall, a line of living trees with their branches interwoven, were quite impenetrable by the enemy. The noun *abatis* was taken from the French, a variant of *abattis*, the word used generally to denote any materials thrown down, based on the verb *abbatre* (throw down), but more specifically the label given to felled trees used as a barricade. You won't find *abatis* in today's military dispatches, but there are always those 1,184–page historical novels.

abecedarian (ay bee see DAIR ee un) *n.*, *adj.* This amusing word, obviously based on the first four letters of the alphabet (*abecedarianus* in Middle Latin, *abecedarius* in Late Latin), applies to a beginner, anyone learning the rudiments in any field of learning. The "ABC" or "ABCs" of anything is a term denoting the rudiments of that subject. The Russian physiologist Ivan Petrovich Pavlov (1849–1936) told the youth of his country who were going into science to "learn the ABC of science before you try to ascend its summit." As an adjective, *abecedarian*, apart from its literal use to describe anything pertaining to the alphabet or arranged in alphabetical order, means "rudimentary, elementary." The Wright brothers (Orville, 1871–1948, and Wilbur, 1867–1912) were the *abecedarians* of aeronautics. Spelt with an upper case *A*, *Abecedarian* was the title of an Anabaptist sect founded in 1520 that rejected human learning as a hindrance, on the ground that only the guidance of the Holy Spirit was needed for the interpretation of the Bible. (It wasn't so long ago that evolution was a taboo subject in the schools of certain American states.)

a-biblion, see **bibliopole**

abigail   (AB uh gale) *n.* We are familiar with *Abigail* as a girl's given name, quite popular in past generations, like so many other Biblical names. Abigail was the wife of Nabal, and later one of David's wives (1 Samuel 25); her name in Hebrew meant "My father is joy." When she first met David, she "fell at his feet" and called herself "thine handmaid." So it came to pass that when Beaumont and Fletcher (Francis Beaumont, 1584–1616, and John Fletcher, 1575–1625, who collaborated on a number of comedies) wrote a part for a "waiting gentlewoman" in their 1620 play *The Scornful Lady*, they named her *Abigail*. Whence, with a lower case *a*, the proper noun became a common noun for "lady's maid." There aren't many *Abigails* or *abigails* around these days, but at least now you know what they mean.

abiosis   (ab ee OH sis, ay bye-) *n. Abiosis* is the absence of life; the related adjective *abiotic* (ay by OT ik) describes any state or condition marked by the absence of life. Extensive tests were made by a satellite controlled from earth to determine whether life existed on Mars. It was found that that planet was characterized by *abiosis*. The moon has likewise been found to be *abiotic*. *Abiosis* is formed from the Greek prefix *a-* (the "alpha privative," indicating negation, as in *apolitical, asymmetrical, asexual*) plus *bio-* (the Greek prefix meaning "life," as in *biography, biology—bios* is the Greek word for *life*) plus *-sis* (the Greek suffix used to form nouns denoting state or condition, as in *paralysis, peristalsis, stasis*). The condition of Pompeii and Herculaneum after the eruption of Mt. Vesuvius in A.D. 79 was one of complete destruction of life and resulting *abiosis*. The defoliation program of the American forces

3

in Vietnam, to deprive the foe of cover, resulted in botanical *abiosis* over wide areas of the jungle. When, in office elevators, stony-faced passengers seem not to dare even look at one another, *abiosis* seems to have set in.

abjure (ab JOOHR) *vb.* To *abjure* something is to renounce it, retract, repudiate, forswear it. *Abjure* comes from the Latin verb *abjurare* (to deny under oath); *abjuration* from Late Latin *abjuratio* (recantation); both are based on *ab-* (away) plus *jurare* (to swear). Reformed sinners *abjure* the errors of their ways. A number of American communists *abjured* their allegiance to the Communist Party and informed on their former colleagues. The noun *abjuration* (ab joo RAY shuhn) implies renunciation upon oath, or at least some measure of solemnity and formality, something more than a mere change of mind. Born again Christians *abjure* their former unbelief. The English poet John Donne (1572–1631) wrote:

> The heavens rejoice in motion, why should I
> *Abjure* my so much loved variety?

In *Paradise Lost*, the English poet John Milton (1608–1674) says:

> I waked
> To find her, or for ever to deplore
> Her loss, and other pleasures all *abjure*.

ablation (ab LAY shun) *n.* *Ablation* has several usages. In surgery, *ablation* is the removal of growths from the body. In meteorology, *ablation* is the reduction of snow or ice through melting or evaporation. In rocketry, *ablation* is the falling off of parts of a nose cone melted away by the heat generated in reentry. It will be seen that, whatever the context, *ablation* involves the removal or taking away of something. There is a verb, to *ablate* (a BLATE), that covers all these senses. Both noun and verb are derived from Latin *ablatus*, past participle of *auferre* (to carry away). Do not confuse *ablation* with **ablution**, which has an entirely different derivation and meaning. *Ablation* is etymologically related to *ablative* (A bluh tiv), a grammatical case (in Latin and other inflected languages) involving changes in noun endings to indicate (inter alia) "place from which," i.e., removal.

ablaut (AB lout) *n*. In philology and grammar, *ablaut* is the term for vowel changes in related words and suffixes, especially in indicating a change in tense, part of speech or other grammatical function. Examples: *get, got; bid, bade* or *bad; ride, rode, ridden; sing, sang, sung, song; choose, chose. Ablaut* is from the German, based on the prefix *ab-* (off) plus *laut* (sound). It is synonymous with *apophony* (uh POF uh nee), based on the Greek prefix *apo-* (away, different from) plus, suffix *phone*, combining form of *phone* (sound).

ablution (ab LOOH shun, uh BLOOH-) *n*. *Ablution* is the washing of one's hands or body. To perform one's *ablutions* is to cleanse oneself. The British use "have a wash" as a polite euphemism for *urinate*, and jocularly speak of "attending to their *ablutions*" in the same connection. Fowler has some strong words to say on this subject: "Pedantic Humour . . ." is the "only fitting place outside religious ceremonial" for *ablutions*. "[We] do not need monstrosities like *ablution facilities, ablution cubicles*, and *mobile ablution centres*." *Ablution*, in religious terminology, is the ritual cleansing of the body, as in a *mikvah*, the public bathing establishment where orthodox Jews go for purification on certain occasions (notably, the bride, prior to the wedding). The English poet John Keats (1795– 1821) used the term *ablution* in a special poetic sense in his sonnet *Bright Star*, writing of

> The moving waters at their priestlike task
> Of pure *ablution* round earth's human shores.

This sonnet was found written on a blank page in Keats' copy of Shakespeare's *Poems*. The word comes from the Latin *ablutio*, related to *ablutus*, the past participle of the verb *abluere*, based on the prefix *ab-* (away) and the verb *luere* (to wash). Do not confuse *ablution* with **ablation**, which is a very different story.

aborticide (uh BOR tih side) *n*. *Aborticide* is defined as the destruction of the fetus in the womb. *Feticide* (FEE tih side) is given as a synonym. *Aborticide* can also be used of a drug or other substance that produces abortion; in this sense, it is a synonym of *abortifacient* (uh bor tuh FAY shunt). *Aborticide* is a peculiar word and seems incorrectly formed. In the run of *-cide* words, derived

5

from Latin -*cida*, based on *caedere* (to kill), the -*cide* is attached to the victim, and the word denotes the killing of that victim, as well, in some cases, as the killer or destructive agent. In the following examples, the identification of the victim follows the -*cide* word in parentheses: *deicide* (god—must have been a rare occurrence and perpetrated by another god); *fratricide* (brother); *fungicide* (fungi); *genocide* (national or racial group); *germicide* (germs); *herbicide* (weeds); *homicide* (person); *infanticide* (infant); *mariticide* (spouse); *matricide* (mother); *parasiticide* (parasites); *parricide* (parent, close relative); *pediculicide* (lice); *regicide* (king); *sororicide* (sister); *spermatocide* or *spermicide* (spermatozoa); *suicide* (oneself); *tyrannicide* (tyrant); *uxoricide* (wife); *viricide* (viruses). Thus, under this system, *aborticide* would logically mean "killing of an abortion," which is what it doesn't mean. The logical form is *feticide*, the killing of a fetus. Kindly note that we have dealt exclusively with the linguistic side of this matter, carefully avoiding the physiological, medical, ethical, and religious aspects so much in the news these days.

abri (uh BREE, ah-) *n.* An *abri* is a place of shelter or refuge, especially a dugout. It is a word taken over intact from the French, who, the authorities say, got it from the Latin *apricum* (open place), that being the neuter form of the adjective *apricus* (open to the sun), related to the verb *aperire* (to lay bare, to expose). Somewhere along the etymological line, someone or something must have gone off the track, else how could *apricum* (open place), of all things, have given rise to *abri* (shelter)? It would seem that the last place one would repair to in flight from the foe, for shelter or refuge, would be an *apricum*!

abruption, see **aposiopesis**

abscission (ab SIZH uhn, -SISH-) *n.* An *abscission* is a cutting off, a sudden termination. The verb *abscind* (ab SIND) means "sever, cut off." These are general terms, but the related verb *abscise* (ab SIZE) is a botanical term, used, for example, in the separation of a leaf from its stem. *Abscission* would be resorted to in an advanced case of gangrene, where the patient's life could be saved only by *abscission* of the affected member. *Abscission* has a special use in rhetoric, as a figure of speech in which words that

6

would normally be demanded by the sense are left unspoken, the speaker suddenly stopping short. Example: War, when one thinks of its indescribable and endless horrors—! *Abscission* is from Latin *abscissio; abscind* from the related verb *abscindere* (to tear off) and *abscise* from *abscissus*, past participle of *abscidere* (to cut off). *Abscissio* and *abscindere* are based on prefix *ab-* (away) plus *scindere* (to cut) and its past participle *scissus*, which helps to explain the *c* in *scissors*. *Abscise* happens to come from a different Latin verb: *abscidere* (to cut off), based on prefix *abs-*, a variant of *ab-*, plus *caedere* (to cut), which changes its *-ae-* to *-i-* in combining form. Thus, *abscidere* and its past participle *abscissus* do not help to explain the *s* in *scissors*. In any event, *scissors* came by its *c* honestly.

absquatulate (ab SKWAH chuh late) *vb*. This amusing, vivid, and expressive word is a bit of jocular, contrived slang. To *absquatulate* is to decamp, to scram, to take off in a hell of a hurry like a fugitive heading into the woods; sometimes, to abscond, like a cashier running off with the contents of the till. The term, invented in America in the 1830s and adopted by the English in the 1870s, is an example of supposed derivation from factitious mock-Latin, based on a combination of parts of *abscond, squat, perambulate* and heaven knows what else. A certain J. Lamont, in an old book entitled *Seahorses*, wrote of a grizzled bull-walrus who "heard us, and lazily awakening, raised his head and prepared to *absquatulate*." You may not run across this little item nowadays, but it's a picturesque word whose revitalization should be encouraged, though it may be used to describe a practice that should be discouraged.

abulia (uh BYOOH lee uh) *n*. *Abulia* is a term used mostly in psychiatry to denote a type of mental disorder causing the loss of willpower or volition, or at least its serious weakening. The word comes, via New Latin, from the Greek noun *aboulia* (lack of resolution; *a-* is the Greek prefix signifying negation and *boule* is Greek for "will"); it is often spelt *aboulia*, closer to its Greek origin. Hamlet is probably the best known sufferer from *abulia*; the entire "To be or not to be" soliloquy is a study in that disorder.

The native hue of resolution
Is sicklied o'er with the pale cast of thought
And enterprises of great pith and moment . . .
lose the name of action. (Act III, Scene 1)

To depart from the sublime (but not to the ridiculous), there is also the memory of the late Jimmy Durante (1893–1980), ambivalent in the extreme, sitting at the piano and singing: "Didja evah have the feelin' that ya wanted to go, and yet had the feelin' ya wanted to stay, go, stay, go, stay," etc. With each "go" he grabbed his battered fedora off the piano and started up; with each "stay" he darted back and dumped it back on the piano. Poor Hamlet and Jimmy both suffered from *abulia*—and not a psychiatrist in sight.

academe   (AK uh deem) *n. Academe* (sometimes capitalized) is the equivalent of "school," any place where instruction is given, but it is more commonly used to denote college or university ambience or environment. College professors often choose their careers because they look forward to the alleged peace and quiet of *academe*, as a refuge from the hurly-burly of the marketplace, but they sometimes despair at the internecine rivalries that embitter life in *academe*. Capitalized, *Academe* is the name of the garden or grove in ancient Athens, open to the public, where the Greek philosopher Plato (427–347 B.C.) taught. The place was named for Akademos, a Greek who lived in the mountainous region of Arkadia (see **Arcadian**), on whose property the philosophers of Athens used to meet. The Roman poet Horace (65–8 B.C.) wrote, in his *Epistles*, of those who "seek for truth in the groves of *Academe*" (translation from the Latin), and the English poet John Milton (1608–1674) wrote, in *Paradise Regained*, of

> The olive grove of *Academe*,
> Plato's retirement, where the Attic bird
> Trills her thick-warbled notes the summer long.

Academe gave rise to the word *academic* (ak uh DEM ik), which, in its literal sense, describes anything or anyone having to do with higher education, but has been expanded to include the figurative meanings of "theoretical, not practical" (any discussion of man's travel to other galaxies is of *academic* interest only) and "conventional" (the impressionists got away from the *academic* school of

8

painting). *Academic* is sometimes used as a noun to signify a college teacher or student. In the opening speech of Shakespeare's *Love's Labour's Lost*, Ferdinand, King of Navarre, outlining his three-year plan of ascetic life and study at his court, says:

> Our court shall be a little *academe*,
> Still and contemplative in living art.

acarine, see **accipitrine**

acarophobia, see **acrophobia**

accidence (AK sih dens) *n. Accidence* has nothing (except derivation) to do with its **homophone** *accidents*. In grammar, it is the part that deals with inflection (variations in the forms of words, like *go, goes, going, gone, went* or *boys, boy's, boys'*) and word order. *Accidence* sets the rules that govern word order and inflection. We don't say "I goes" or "Go I," but "I go," using the rules of *accidence*. Children who grow up in literate families get these things right by imitation (no *me and my friend are hungry* or *between you and I*) and only later, in school, learn the rules of *accidence*. It comes from Latin *accidentia*, neuter plural of *accidens*, present participle of the verb *accidere* (to happen), based on prefix *ac-* (to or towards; a variant of *ad-* before *c*) plus *cadere* (to fall).

accipitrine (ak SIP ih trin, -trine) *adj*. This adjective, formed from the noun *accipiter* (ak SIP ih tuhr), which means "hawk," as it does in Latin, is applicable to the Accipitridae family, one that includes certain types of hawk and other birds of prey. Apart from its scientific meaning, it may be used figuratively as the equivalent of "predatory." There is a large group of adjectives ending in *-ine* that designate zoological or entomological families but are susceptible of figurative use as well, in certain cases. Thus, *bovine*, which in its literal sense means "of or pertaining to the ox family," is commonly applied to people or their behavior to mean "dull, stolid, listless," and is undoubtedly used more often in that sense than as a zoological term. In the same way, the technical meaning of *asinine* is "pertaining to the ass family," but its more frequent use is to describe people or their acts as stupid or inane. *Aquiline* (relating to eagles) is most often found as a description of noses, like Julius Caesar's who gave his name to a gynecological operation rather

9

than a nose; and *leonine* (pertaining to the lion family) is a favorite dramatic representation of massive heads, particularly those with sweeping hairdos, like Beethoven's. *Feline* (relating to cats) is used, quite unfairly, to describe sly, stealthy, and even treacherous persons and their behavior. *Elephantine* has been used as a vivid description of ponderous, clumsy movements of people, and has also been applied to awkward, insensitive humor. The use of *accipitrine* might well be extended to describe predatory people and their acts, evoking the image of a hawk swooping down on its prey. It is unlikely that secondary, figurative uses will be found for a good many of the *-ine* words mentioned below (items like *alectoridine*, *charadrine*, *herpestine*, *oscine*). But, for the benefit of those who may run into *-ine* adjectives new to them and, even more importantly, for those who may wish to invent figurative uses of some of them, we append a list (not exhaustive, and, for convenience, inclusive of some words already discussed), and leave it to the reader to dream up figurative, even fanciful uses and thus enrich our beautiful language.

	Relates to:
acarine	mites
accipitrine	hawks, eagles
alaudine	skylarks
alci(di)ne	auks, puffins
alectoridine	cranes, rails
anatine	ducks
anguine	snakes
anopheline	mosquitoes
anserine	geese
antelopine	antelopes
aquiline	eagles
asinine	asses
aspine	asps
avine	birds
bisontine	bisons
bombycine	silkworms
bubaline	antelopes, hartebeests
buteonine	buzzards
caballine	horses
cameline	camels
canine	dogs
capreoline	roe, deer
caprine	goats
cathartine	vultures

cervine	deer
charadrine	plovers
ciconi(i)ne	storks
colubrine	king-, gartersnakes
columbine	doves
corvine	crows
cricetine	hamsters
crocodiline	crocodiles
crotaline	rattlesnakes
cuculine	cuckoos
culicine	mosquitoes
cygnine	swans
cyprine	carp
dacelonine	kingfishers
delphi(ni)ne	dolphins
didelphine	opossums
didine	dodos
elephantine	elephants
equine	horses
falconine	falcons
feline	cats
formicine	ants
fringilline	finches
fulciline	coots
fuliguline	eider ducks
galline	domestic fowl
garruline	magpies, jays
gazelline	gazelles
giraffine	giraffes
herpestine	mongooses
hippopotamine	hippopotami
hippotigrine	zebras
hirudine	leeches
hirundine	swallows
homarine	lobsters
hominine	man
hyenine	hyenas
hylobatine	gibbons
hystricine	porcupines
ibidine	ibises
lacertine	lizards
lapine	rabbits
lari(di)ne	gulls
lemurine	lemurs
leonine	lions
leporine	hares
lumbricine	earthworms
lupine	wolves

11

lutrine	otters
lyncine	lynxes
macropine	kangaroos
macropodine	kangaroos, wallabies
manatine	manatees
megapterine	humpback whales
meleagrine	turkeys
mephitine	skunks
milvine	kites
moschine	musk deer
murine	mice, rats
musteline	weasel, mink
nestorine	keas, kakas
noctilionine	bats
octopine	octopi
oscine	songbirds
ostracine	oysters
ovibovine	musk ox
ovine	sheep
pantherine	panthers
pardine	leopards
passerine	songbirds
pavonine	peacocks
phasianine	pheasants
phocaenine	porpoises
phocine	seals
picine	woodpeckers
piscine	fish
porcine	pigs
procyonine	raccoons, kinkajous
psittacine	parrots
pteropine	bats
ralline	rails
rangiferine	caribous, reindeer
ranine	frogs
rhinocerine	rhinoceroses
rucervine	Indian swamp deer
rupicaprine	chamoix
sabelline	sables
salamandrine	salamanders
sciurine	squirrels
serpentine	serpents
soricine	shrews
strigine	screech-owls
sturnine	swallows
suilline	hogs
talpine	moles
tapirine	tapirs

taurine	bulls
tetraonine	grouse, ptarmigans
tigrine	tigers
tolypeutine	armadillos
tringine	sandpipers
trochili(di)ne	hummingbirds
turdine	thrushes
ursine	bears
vaccine	cows
vespine	wasps
viperine	vipers
vituline	calves
viverrine	civets
volucrine	birds
vulpine	foxes
vulturine	vultures
zebrine	zebras

accouterment (uh KOOH tuhr muhnt) *n. Accouterment* is equipment, outfit, trappings. This word, taken over from the French *accoutrement* (which is the way the British sometimes spell it), has a specific application in military circles, where it denotes a soldier's outfit, as in a line by the English poet and dramatist Ambrose Philips (1675–1749):

> How gay with all the *accouterments* of war!

In Shakespeare's *Taming of the Shrew* (Act III, Scene 2), Petruchio shows up for his wedding in unseemly clothes and is chided by Tranio about his "irreverent robes." Petruchio answers:

> To me she's married, not unto my clothes.
> Could I repair what she will wear in me
> As I can change these poor *accoutrements*,
> 'Twere well for Kate and better for myself.

The verb is *accouter* (uh KOOH tuhr). To *accouter* someone is to equip or outfit him. In *Julius Caesar* (Act I, Scene 2), Shakespeare has Cassius tell how he accepted Caesar's dare to jump into the raging Tiber with him:

> Upon the word
> *Accoutred* as I was, I plunged in.

In *The Merchant of Venice* (Act III, Scene 4), Portia boasts to Nerissa:

> When we are both *accoutred* like young men,
> I'll prove the prettier fellow of the two.

These are all quotations from works of many a yesterday, but there is no reason why we should abandon these expressive words, or why we can't *accouter* ourselves today in whatever *accouterments* we wish, and saunter on *accoutered* as we choose.

acedia (uh SEE dee uh) *n. Acedia* is sloth, one of the seven deadly sins. It is more commonly known as *laziness. Acedia* was taken intact from Middle Latin, which took it from the Greek *akedeia*, based on negative prefix *a-* plus *kedos* (care). A specialized meaning of *acedia* is "indifference" (i.e., no care or concern), particularly in matters of religion. This word can be found in another form, *accidie* (AK sih dee), Middle English taken from Middle Latin *accidia*, a variant of *acedia*. Sloth, or *acedia*, was considered deadly enough to be included among the seven deadly sins. In Proverbs 6:6 we read: "Go to the ant, thou sluggard; consider her ways, and be wise." Such was the Biblical condemnation of sloth, *acedia*, or *accidie*! In an engaging letter to *The Times* (London—issue of August 2, 1986), from the Rev. G. S. Luff, mention is made of *accidie*, and this sentence follows: "Hard to define it, it has been described as 'don't-care-ishness' and 'torpor,' though the latter is more appropriate to the time after lunch."

acronical (uh KRAHN ih kul) *adj.* Also *acronykal*. This adjective applies to phenomena occurring at sunset, as opposed to *cosmical* (KOZ mih kul), applicable to things that occur at or near sunrise. Both terms are used in astronomy with respect to the rising and setting of certain stars; but they can be used figuratively of other events, like the chirping of some birds and insects that become active and make their sounds as the sun rises or sets. *Acronical* is not synonymous with *vespertine* (VES puhr tin, -tine), but comes close: *vespertine*, like **crepuscular**, covers things that happen in the early evening, at dusk, just after sunset, and is used of birds and insects that fly, or flowers that open, or, like nicotiana (flowering tobacco), begin to give off their scent at that time. *Ves-*

14

pertine is a poetic word, especially in a phrase like *vespertine calm* or *stillness*. *Acronical* comes from Greek *akronychos* (at nightfall), based on *akros* (at the edge) plus *nyx* (night). *Cosmical*, a variant of *cosmic*, is based on Greek *kosmikos* (of the world), related to *kosmos* (world). *Vespertine* is from Latin *vespertinus*, based on *vesper* (evening), which gave us *Vesper*, evening star, particularly Venus, and *vespers* (evensong). *Vesper* is also called *Hesperus* (HES puhr uhs); based on Greek *hesperos* (evening).

acrophobia (ak ruh FOH bee uh) *n. Acrophobia* is morbid dread of heights. The word is taken from New Latin, based on two Greek words that do a lot of service in the formation of English words: *akros* (highest, topmost) and *phobos* (fearing). The prefix *acro-* shows up in words like *acrobat, acronym, acropolis;* the suffix *-phobia* is likewise common: *agrophobia, claustrophobia, xeno-phobia*. People who suffer from *acrophobia* shouldn't climb mountains or live in penthouses. They would make good **spelunkers** unless they were also claustrophobic. A psychiatrist friend of the author refers to patients in the arts who fear success as "acro-phobes," those who dread the dizzying heights of fame and the consequent exposure. The insertion of an *a* between the first two syllables of this word produces *acarophobia* (ak uh ruh FO bee uh), a morbid fear of skin parasites. Here we have the familiar *-phobia* attached to the combining form of *acaris* (AK uhr uhs), meaning "mite," from which we get *acarology* (ak uh ROL uh jee), the study of mites, ticks, and the like. It is quite possible to suffer from both these phobias (as well as others we have not sufficient space to enumerate).

acuity (uh KYOOH ih tee) *n. Acuity* is a synonym of *acuteness, keenness, sharpness*, whether the sharpness applies to a physical object such as a nail or a needle, or, more commonly, to keenness of mind, understanding, or the senses. The word comes from Middle Latin *acuitas*, based on Latin *acus* (needle) and *acuere* (to sharpen). We get *acute* from *acutus*, past participle of *acuere*. Our noun *acumen* was taken over intact from Latin, where it means "anything sharp," and figuratively, "sharpness of mind," as in English. *Visual acuity* is a term in ophthalmology denoting sharpness of vision with respect to one's ability to resolve detail. The main use of *acuity* is in the field of understanding and perception.

A person lucky enough to be endowed with *acuity* is quick to comprehend, to get the point. Getting back to *acus* (needle) for a moment: In *Rudens*, a play by the Roman comic poet and dramatist Plautus (254–184 B.C.), Gripus says to Labrax, "Then you are a beggar?" Labrax answers, "Tetegisti *acu*," literally "You've touched [it] with a needle" (*acu* being a form of *acus*), and freely translated: "You've hit the nail on the head."

adduce (uh DOOHS, -DYOOHS) *vb.* To *adduce* is to cite as proof, to present as an argument or as evidence in order to support one's point. *Adduce* is from Latin *adducere* (to bring or lead [a person] to [a place]). Lawyers *adduce* as much evidence and as many arguments as they can muster to persuade judge or jury. The authors of almanacs *adduce* past weather records to support their predictions for the coming year. Such theories or arguments as are considered pertinent are *adducible* (uh DOOHS uh bul, -DYOOHS-).

adeem, see **ademption**

ademption (uh DEMP shun) *n.* If someone leaves you a specific object (as opposed to a sum of money, or a share of the estate) in his will, and after he dies, it turns out that it no longer belongs to the estate (he gave it away, sold it or lost it), the bequest fails. This failure is called an *ademption*, from Latin *ademptio* (a taking away), based on *ademere* (to take away). A related verb is *adeem* (uh DEEM), to cancel a bequest not by changing the will but by selling or otherwise disposing of the thing bequeathed. A will is "ambulatory," which in law means "alterable" or "revocable" at will. (This is a special meaning of *ambulatory* having nothing to do with patients walking around in hospitals.) Since a will can "walk around," as it were, and "speaks" only as of the date of the testator's death, then any specific object the will may bequeath to you, if it's not to be found after the testator's death, has been *adeemed* and you have become the victim of an *ademption*. So don't count your Rembrandts or your Stradivariuses before they're hatched.

ad hoc (ad hok) *adj., adv.* This phrase, taken over intact from the Latin, means "for this special purpose" or "with respect to this particular subject or occasion.'' The Latin phrase *ad hoc* means, literally, "for this (thing)," *hoc* being the neuter form of the demonstrative adjective *hic* (this) here used as a noun, as neuters often are in Latin. *Ad hoc* can apply to a body, such as a committee, or to a decision or an argument, to limit general application. It can sometimes have the disparaging effect of implying hurried improvisation, but this is not its usual sense. The expression can be used adjectivally or adverbially: one can speak of an *ad hoc* committee, or a committee formed *ad hoc*. An *ad hoc* decision is one applicable to a particular problem or state of affairs, often an emergency, without setting a binding precedent. An *ad hoc* committee is one formed for the particular occasion requiring study or decision and action. Such a committee disbands as soon as its work is completed.

adiaphorous (ad ee AF ur us) *adj.* This is a term that describes anything that neither benefits nor harms, like a placebo that is medically neuter. In a more general sense, *adiaphorous* means "neutral," "indifferent," "neither right nor wrong." The word is from the Greek *adiaphoros* based on negative prefix *a-* plus *diaphoros* (different), i.e., making no difference, of no consequence. An *adiaphoron* (ad ee AF ur on), a word taken intact from the Greek, is a matter of indifference in morals or ethics or religion: to each his own, *de gustibus*, etc.—providing it doesn't affect anyone else. These words have nothing to do with *adiaphoresis* (uh dy uh for EE sis), meaning "absence of sweat," or *adiaphoretic* (uh dy uh for ET ik), sweat-preventing, like all those beautifully packaged underarm sprays and sticks for sale in drugstores. For *diaphoresis*, see **sudorific**.

adulate (AJ uh late) *vb.* To *adulate* someone is to fawn upon, exhibit an excess of devotion to, express one's admiration for obsequiously, or make a disproportionate fuss over him or her. An *adulator* (AJ uh lay tuhr) is a sycophant. *Adulation* (aj uh LAY shuhn) is the noun for "abject adoration." The verb is a back formation from the noun, which comes from Latin *adulatio* (fawning), related to *adulatus*, past participle of *adulari* (to fawn). *Adulatory* (AJ uh luh tor ee, -tohr-) is the adjective. Courtiers, in the old days, *adulated* their sovereigns to a sickening degree. When foreign heads of state meet, there is a tendency to exchange *adulatory* addresses, full of platitudes and insincerity. *Adulation* seems to be an essential ingredient in the introductions of guests on talk shows. "The man who . . ." is an inevitable cliché in *adulatory* introductions at political rallies and conventions. After an *adulatory* introduction by the chairperson at a women's club during a political campaign, the American politician Adlai Stevenson (1900–1965) rose and said (in effect): "After hearing all the wonderful things Mrs. Smith [?] has said about me, I can hardly wait to hear myself begin."

adumbrate (ad UM brate) *vb*. To *adumbrate* something is to foreshadow it, to give a hint of what is coming to pass. The activities of Hitler in the late 1930s *adumbrated* the coming of World War II. The facility and poise of the child Mozart *adumbrated* the majestic career to come. There is another sense of *adumbrate*: to "outline" or sketch," as when a faint indication of something is given. It is in this sense that the theologians say the invisible God is *adumbrated* in the vastness and richness of the visible world. The noun is *adumbration* (ad um BRAY shuhn), meaning "faint sketch" or "outline." The English prelate Samuel Horsley (1733–1806), a noted scientist who became a bishop, wrote of the visible phenomena of the universe as "elegant *adumbrations* of sacred truth." In a section entitled "Formal words," Fowler lists "adumbrate (outline)" as one of those words used by people subject to the "prevalent notion that the commoner synonyms . . . ought to be translated into them"; then, in the section headed "French words," he cautions the speaker against excessive care in producing the exact pronunciation of a French term in the middle of an English sentence, and says: ". . . there are some French sounds so obviously alien to the English mouth that words containing them . . . should either be eschewed by English speakers, or have these sounds *adumbrated* [i.e., suggested, or hinted at]." Fowler, in this instance, didn't follow his own advice, but we love him all the more for this sign of human frailty. *Adumbrate* and *adumbration* are from Latin *adumbratus* (sketched; by extension, shadowy, imperfect), past participle of *adumbrare* (to sketch, especially in words), based on prefix *ad-* (towards) plus *umbra* (shade, shadow), from which we get, among other things, *umbrella*.

adventitious (ad ven TISH uhs) *adj*. Anything described as *adventitious* (do not confuse with *advantageous*) is associated with something else as a matter of happenstance, not intentionally as an integral part; something accidental, fortuitous, extraneous, foreign to the main purpose. The word comes from Latin *adventicius* (extraneous). Narrow, winding lanes lend an *adventitious* charm to the English countryside. Stone walls and hedges have long been used in various parts of the world as boundary markers; their proliferation in rural areas affords *adventitious* variety to what might otherwise have been uninteresting terrain. The hurly-burly of large centers adds *adventitious* excitement to city life. The sudden hush as the lights dim just before the curtain goes up in the theater produces an *adventitious* thrill of anticipation. Many painstaking efforts (the most elaborate picnic preparations) go unrewarded and soon forgotten, while *adventitious* occurrences (sudden thunderstorms with pelting showers) often make the most memorable impressions and best-remembered experiences.

aeonian (ee OH nee uhn) *adj.* An *aeon* (EE uhn, -ahn) is an immeasurable period of time, an eternity. Anything described as *aeonian* is everlasting, eternal. The source of *aeon* is, via Latin *aeon*, the Greek noun *aion* (age, period of time); *aeonian* comes from the Greek *aionios*. *Eon* and *eonian* are variant spellings, as so often happens with *e* taking the place of the diphthong *ae* in English. Both *aeon* and *aeonian* can be used literally or metaphorically. The English poet Rudyard Kipling (1865–1936) used *aeon* figuratively and dramatically in his poem *When Earth's Last Picture*:

> When Earth's last picture is painted and the tubes are
> twisted and dried,
> When the oldest colours have faded, and the youngest
> critic has died,
> We shall rest, and, faith, we shall need it—lie down
> for an *aeon* or two,
> Till the Master of All Good Workmen shall put us to
> work anew.

Not one of Rudyard's best, and his *aeon* had to be figurative; you can't, literally, have more than one eternity. All he meant by *aeon* was *one helluva long time*, as in: "Where have you been, dear? I've been waiting here for *aeons*!" *Aeonian* is far from common;

19

one would not expect to hear: "My love for you is *aeonian*," but it might be a nice way to put it.

aerie, aery, eyrie (AIR ee, EER ee) *n.* Literally, an *aerie* is a nest built by a bird of prey, especially an eagle, but the term can be applied to the nest of any bird that builds high in the air. Figuratively, *aerie* is used to denote a human residence perched high on a hill or mountainside. Hitler's mountaintop house in Garmisch-Partenkirchen, often referred to as "Hitler's *aerie*," was blown up by the allied forces after the war. Wealthy owners or occupants of city penthouses, and the society columnists who celebrate such denizens of the metropolis, sometimes refer to those lofty dwellings as "*aeries*." *Aerie* is traced to Old French *aire*, origin unknown.

afflatus (uh FLATE us) *n.* An *afflatus* is an inspiration, especially a prophetic one coming from a divine source, imparting special knowledge or power. The word sometimes implies, as well, an overpowering supernatural impulse. *Afflation* (uh FLAY shuhn) is a variant, and *afflated* (uh FLAY tid) means "inspired," with all the connotations attached to the noun. *Afflatus* was taken over intact from Latin, where it means, literally, a "breathing on," based on prefix *ad-* (to, toward), plus *flatus*, past participle of *flare* (to breathe). The American writer Max Eastman (1883–1969), who in his younger days was the editor of radical periodicals like *New Masses* but later attacked communism (and was famous, also, for engaging in fisticuffs with the American writer Ernest Hemingway [1899–1961]), wrote: "We imagine that a great speech is caused by some mysterious *afflatus* that descends into a man from on high." The teachings of the great religious figures of the past—Moses, Jesus, Confucius, Mohammed—all issued from divine *afflatus*. There are more recent individuals who have laid claim to the same source—Father Divine (1882–1965), Billy Sunday (1863–1935), Aimee Semple McPherson (1890–1944)—to say nothing of certain present-day evangelists who shall remain nameless and dateless.

agape (ah GAH pay, AH guh pay, AG uh pay) *n. Agape*, however you pronounce it, taken over from the Greek, was the name given to a love-feast practiced by early Christians in connection with the Lord's Supper. It came to signify God's love of mankind, and then, in a more general sense, brotherly love without sexual implications, as opposed to *eros* (EER ohs, AIR ohs), meaning, with a lower case *e*, "sexual desire." (Eros, with an upper case *E*, was, as we all know, the ancient Greek god of love, whom we know also as *Cupid*.) While we're on the subject, *platonic love* is a purely spiritual relationship free from sexual desire, especially between a man and a woman. "We are just good friends" is often heard in media interviews. Plato (427–347 B.C.) was responsible for the concept of platonic love as a striving toward love of spiritual beauty.

agitprop (AJ it prop) *n. Agitprop* is, as the word suggests, the combined activities of *agit*ation (in the political sense) and *prop*aganda, particularly in the cause of communism. The USSR maintains an office with the rather frightening name of "Agitprop-byuro," based on Russian *agitatsiya* (agitation) plus *propaganda* (same word as ours) plus *byuro* (bureau). *Agit* is from Latin *agitatus*, past participle of *agitare* (to set in motion, stir up, shake—as in "Shake well before using"; *agit*, in doctors' prescriptions, means just that, and *stirring* is, of course, the business of *agitators*). *Prop* is short for *propaganda*, a form of the Latin verb *propagare* (to propagate, spread, disseminate), and means, literally, "things to be spread," like the joys of the workers' paradise. *Byuro* is simply a Russianization of *bureau*, taken, as we took it, from the French. In one way or another, we extol and propagandize the virtues of our system, and in one way or another, we (particularly the CIA) do a bit of agitating, but thus far we have avoided the formation of an official *byuro* combining the *agit* and the *prop*.

aglet (AG lit) *n*. Also *aiglet* (AY glit) and *aiguillette* (ay gwih LET) *n*. An *aglet* is the metal end of a lace, e.g., of a shoelace or of a piece of string. The term can also be applied to any metallic ornament of a dress. In the form *aiguillette*, it usually denotes the metal point of shoulder-braid on certain costumes or uniforms. *Aiguillette*, later shortened to *aglet* or *aiglet*, was taken over intact from the French, where it is the diminutive of *aiguille* (needle), from the Latin *acucula*, diminutive of *acus* (needle). In Shakespeare's *Taming of the Shrew* (Act I, Scene 2), Grumio, Petruchio's servant, tells the latter's friend Hortensio that his master will marry any woman for her money: " . . . why, give him gold enough and marry him to a puppet or an *aglet*-baby, or an old trot [crone] with ne'er a tooth in her head . . ." An *aglet-baby* was a small ornamental figure serving as the tag of a lace.

agnate (AG nate), *n.*, *adj.* An *agnate* is a relative on the paternal side. A *cognate* (KOG nate) is a relative descended from any common ancestor. An *enate* (EE nate) is a relative on the maternal side. All three words serve as adjectives as well. Your father's brother is your *agnate*, or an *agnate* uncle. Your mother's brother is an *enate*, or an *enate* uncle. Both are your *cognates*, or *cognate* uncles. These three words come from Latin: *agnatus*, *cognatus*, and *enatus*, all formed from prefixes plus *natus*, past participle of *nasci* (to be born). *Cognate* has a special meaning in philology: words in different languages descended from a common ancestor are *cognate* words, or *cognates*. English *father*, German *vater*, Latin *pater* are *cognates*; so are English *frigid*, Spanish *frio*, French *froid*, Italian *freddo*, Latin *frigidus*; and English *cold*, German *kalt*, Dutch *koud*, Latin *gelidus*.

agnomen (ag NOH muhn) *n.* An *agnomen* is a nickname. It is from Late Latin, composed of the prefix *ag-*, developed from *ad-* (toward—indicating addition) under the influence of *agnoscere* (to recognize), plus *nomen* (name). In olden days, the Romans formed the custom of tacking an additional name onto the names of famous persons as an indication of a great achievement or special characteristic. Thus, the Roman satirist Gaius Petronius (died A.D. 66) was the official in charge of entertainments and the authority on matters of taste and elegance at the court of Nero (37–68; see **arbiter**), and acquired the title of *arbiter elegantiae*. He gained the *agnomen* "arbiter" and became known as "Petronius Arbiter" (Petronius the Arbiter). Quintus Fabius Maximus Verrucosus, a Roman general of the second century B.C. (see **cunctator**), became famous for his successful delaying strategy against the Carthaginians in the Second Punic War. He acquired the *agnomen* "Cunctator" (Delayer, Postponer), and was popularly known as "Fabius Cunctator" (Fabius the Delayer). There were two Roman generals who distinguished themselves in Africa, Publius Cornelius Scipio Major (Scipio the Elder—Scipio Sr., c. 234–183 B.C.), victorious over Hannibal, and his adopted grandson, Publius Cornelius Scipio Aemilianus Minor (Scipio the Younger—Scipio Jr., c. 185–129 B.C.), who destroyed Carthage. To each, the Romans attached the *agnomen* "Africanus," to commemorate their African exploits, and each was known as "Scipio Africanus" (Scipio of Africa). In more recent times, we have invented sobriquets of the type of "Honest Abe," "Lucky Lindy," and "Tricky Dick," preferring to put our *agnomina* before the familiar form of the given name. From these customs begun in ancient Rome, *agnomen* had gained the force of "nickname" generally. For a fuller list of *agnomina*, see also **antonomasia**. *Cognomen* (kog NO muhn) is related but different. Its principal meaning is "surname," but it, too, has acquired the additional meaning of "nickname." In ancient Rome, the *cognomen* was the third (usually the last) name or surname of an individual. In the name Publius Cornelius Scipio, *Scipio* was the *cognomen*. The full name of the poet Virgil (70 –19 B.C.) was Publius Vergilius Maro; *Maro* was his *cognomen*. His contemporary Horace (65–8 B.C.)—full name Quintus Horatius Flaccus—had the *cognomen Flaccus*. He was, so to speak, Mr. Flaccus; but who would ever think of T. S. Eliot as *Mr.* Eliot, or W. H. Auden as *Mr.* A?

agon (AG on, -ohn) *n. Agon* is a literary term for "conflict," especially between the protagonist (hero) and the antagonist (adversary) in a drama, or novel. The plots of Shakespeare's tragedies center around clear-cut *agones* (uh GO neez), e.g., those between Hamlet and Claudius, Macbeth and Macduff, Othello and Iago, Richard III and Henry Tudor. The same goes for all those cowboys-and-Indians and cops-and-robbers shows. Note the *-agon-* in both *protagonist* and *antagonist*. *Agon* was taken over intact from the Greek, where it means "struggle, conflict" generally, and in ancient Greek was the term for a "contest" in which prizes were given in athletic events and the arts, including poetry, drama and music. Via Late Latin *agonia*, the Greek *agon* is the source of our words *agony, agonize, agonist* (one engaged in a contest or conflict, or beset by inner conflict; also short for *protagonist*); and it figures as well in the adjective *agonistic* (combative). *Agonistes* is Greek for "champion," as in *Samson Agonistes* of the English poet John Milton (1608–1674) and *Sweeney Agonistes* of the British poet T. S. Eliot (American born: 1888–1965). *Agon* has nothing to do with *agonic* (ay GON ik), an adjective meaning "not forming an angle," from the Greek negative prefix *a-* plus *gonia* (angle).

agonic,   see **agon**

agoraphobia   (ag ur uh FOH bee uh) *n. Agoraphobia* is the morbid dread of being in or crossing an open space. One suffering from this pathological fear would hardly feel at Home on the Range, where the buffalo roam. *Agora* is Greek for "marketplace" or "public square"; *phobia* is based on Greek *phobos* (fearing), and has itself become an English word by extraction from words like *agoraphobia, acrophobia, claustrophobia,* etc. There are those who admire the sight of the wide open fields of the countryside, but who are prevented by *agoraphobia* from walking through them. *Claustrophobia* would disqualify a person from becoming an astronaut; *agoraphobia* would certainly disqualify him from indulging in a space walk. See also **agromania**.

agrestic   (uh GRES tik) *adj. Agrestic* means "rustic" or "rural," but is also used in its figurative sense of "uncouth, awkward, unpolished, boorish," in the description of the behavior of a clumsy country lout or oaf. *Agrestic* is derived from Latin *agrestis* (literally, rustic; figuratively, countrified, boorish), based on *ager* (land, field). *Agrestic* is quite distinct from *agrarian* (uh GRAIR ee uhn), which describes things related to land, like laws, tenure, political or social movements, a type of society, and has nothing to do with behavior, loutish or other. *Agrarian* is from Latin *agrarius*, also based on *ager*. One would never talk of "agrarian behavior" or, conversely, "an agrestic society." Both words go back to the basic Latin *ager*, but go off in entirely different directions.

agromania   (ag ruh MAY nee uh, -MAYN yuh) *n. Agromania* is the morbid desire to live in open spaces, or in isolation. *Agromania* is not quite the opposite of *agoraphobia*, the abnormal dread of open places. People suffering from *agoraphobia* dread being in, or crossing open spaces; those with *agromania* not only do not fear open spaces, they actually have to live in them. Can you imagine a Mr. and Mrs. Sprat suffering from these respective psychological disturbances? *Agromania* is based on Greek *agros* (tilled land; *agro-* is found in *agrology, agronomics*, etc.) plus Greek or Latin *mania* (madness; *-mania* is found in words like *megalomania, monomania*, etc.). See **agoraphobia**.

24

ailurophile (eye LOOHR uh file) *n*. There is a group of *ailuro-* words, all of which can be written *ailouro-* as well, based on *ail(o)uros*, the Greek noun for "cat." These words add familiar Greek suffixes. An *ailurophile* is a cat fancier, a lover of cats, as everybody should be (suffix from *-philos*, dear, beloved). *Ailurophilia* is love of cats, an obvious mark of distinction (adding *-philia*, loving). An *ailurophobe* is a cat hater, or one who suffers from a dread of cats, obviously a pathological condition (*-phobos* fearing). *Ailurophobia* is dread of cats, a condition already characterized (*-phobia*, fear, dread, abnormal aversion or hate). It must by now be clear where the author's sympathies lie. After all, in ancient Rome the cat was a symbol of liberty and in ancient Egypt the cat was held so sacred that, according to the Sicilian historian Diodorus (d. c. 21 B.C.), the killing of a cat, even though accidental, was a capital offense. So much for *ailurophobes*!

akimbo (uh KIM boh) *adj.*, *adv.* Hand(s) on hip(s) and elbow(s) extended outwards. *With arms akimbo* is the usual expression. *There he was, standing with arms akimbo*, evokes the image of someone standing there with legs apart, somewhat like Henry VIII later in life, or just anyone looking straight ahead and saying, "Well?" *Arms akimbo* suggests moods ranging from simple contemplation to expectation to defiance. The English novelist John Galsworthy (1867–1933) wrote of people standing "*akimbo*, surveying their little plots of land." The word is said to be derived from Middle English *in kene bowe* (in keen bow), i.e., in the position of a tautly drawn bow; and to be related to the Icelandic word for "crooked," *kengboginn*, which is reflected in the derivation of our word *kink*. In a column entitled "Jostling With Elbows" (*New York Times*, June 22, 1984) William Safire discusses *akimbo*:

> On occasion, the elbows still go a bit too far. In "Caveat," the memoirs of nuance-ridden Alexander Haig, he captions a picture of himself with hands on hips, elbows prominent: "The 'take-charge' image had taken hold . . . My photograph (jaw jutting, arms *akimbo*), had been on the cover of *Time* magazine . . ."

alaudine, see **accipitrine**

albeit (awl BEE it) *conj*. This conjunction is short for *all though it be that*, via the shorter form *all be it (that)*. It means "although,

25

though, even though, even if," and is a pleasant substitute (if not overdone). Not so many years ago, it was considered archaic by some authorities; indeed, it was so labeled in the first edition of Fowler, which now says, "it has since been picked up and dusted . . ." So now we can say, for instance, that Columbus was a great navigator *albeit* without success in his search for a westward passage to Asia, or that virtue is its own reward, *albeit* often a skimpy one. *Albeit* is a useful word, *albeit* somewhat literary. As we have said, don't overdo it.

alci(di)ne,   see **accipitrine**

aleatory   (AY lee uh tor ee) *adj.* An *aleatory* event is one that depends on luck or chance or contingencies, and is therefore unpredictable. *Aleatory* has certain special uses: in law, a contract is *aleatory* if the obligations of the parties depend on a contingent event; in music and the other arts, where the form *aleatoric* (ay lee uh TOR ik) is more common, the adjective indicates that the performance involves random choices of notes or other elements rather than a fixed score or rigid directions. The origin of the word is found in the Latin noun *aleator* (gambler), based on *alea* (dice game; by extension, chance, uncertainty). For a famous use of *alea*, remember "Jacta est alea!" ("The die is cast!"), the cry of Julius Caesar in 49 B.C. when he crossed the Rubicon, invading Italy from his allotted province of Gaul, defying the Roman senate and launching civil war.

alectoridine,   see **accipitrine**

alexia   (uh LEK see uh) *n. Alexia* is a disorder of the brain that deprives the sufferer of the ability to read; also known as word blindness. *Alexia* is derived from the Greek negative prefix *a-* (not) plus *lexis* (speech), based on the Greek verb *legein* (to speak), as a result of confusion with the Latin verb *legere* (to read). The pathologist who concocted the term *alexia* suffered from a confusion of the classical tongues, a condition for which no medical term has as yet been dreamt up. Suggestion for a word to describe confusion of the classical tongues: *dysetymologia*. This is a condition that has to do with a defect in the educational system. *Alexia* is complete word blindness, while the related, and probably more familiar word *dyslexia* (dis LEK see uh) covers only partial inability to read, also resulting from a brain defect. (*Dyslexia* is from the Greek prefix *dys-* [bad, ill], plus *lexis* and the same confusion.) Those affected with *alexia* cannot read at all; *dyslexia* sufferers have great difficulty learning to read or spell. Neither of these conditions has to do with intelligence, and their cause has not been discovered.

alfresco, al fresco   (al FRES koh) *adj.*, *adv.* The Italian source is *al fresco*, meaning "in the open air." *Fresco* is Italian for "cool," but *al fresco* means "out of doors," whatever the temperature. When you eat at a sidewalk café, you are eating *alfresco*. Picnics are *alfresco* outings, complete with ants and rain. The open-air theater is an *alfresco* entertainment. Street musicians perform *alfresco*. Many people prefer old-fashioned *alfresco* football stadia to those newfangled domes and dromes.

algesia   (al JEE zee uh, -see-) *n.* Most people are familiar with *analgesic* (an al JEE zik) as an adjective meaning "pain-relieving" and a noun for "pain-reliever," perhaps less so with the noun *analgesia* (an al JEE zee uh) meaning "relief of pain." The underlying terms *algesia* (al JEE zee uh) for "sensitivity to pain" and *algesis* (al JEE sis) for "sensation of pain" are much less familiar than the ones beginning with the Greek negative prefix *an-*. All these words involve as a source, via Late Latin, the Greek noun *algos* (pain) and verb *algein* (to suffer). Strange as it may seem, it is a common phenomenon in the English language that the negative of a word is in much more common use than the positive from which it is formed; e.g., *impeccable/peccable; unalterable/alterable; irreproachable/reproachable*— and the list is a long one. The measure of one's *algesia* or sensitivity to pain is often referred to as "threshold of pain," i.e., the point at which a person begins to feel pain. This is also known in the trade as one's *limen* (LYE muhn), a word taken over intact from the Latin meaning "threshold." In any event, the higher the *limen* the better, though bad for the procaine— $C_6H_4NH_2COOCH_2CH_2N(C_2H_5)_2$—business. *Limen* shows up in the formation of the adjective *subliminal* (sub LIM uh nuhl, -LYE muh-), describing stimuli that operate below the *threshold* of consciousness, from Latin prefix *sub-* (under) plus *limen*.

algid (AL jid) *adj. Algid* means "cold, chill, chilly," especially to describe the feeling of chill one has in certain illnesses. It is from the Latin *algidus* (cold), related to the verb *algere* (to be cold), and the verb *algescere* (to catch cold). The related noun *algor* designates the kind of chill that hits one at the onset of fever; it was taken over intact from the Latin noun *algor* (cold), and has nothing to do with **algorism** or **algorithm**, or for that matter, **algolagnia**.

algolagnia (al guh LAG nee uh) *n. Algolagnia* is a term used in psychiatry for sadomasochism, the derivation of sexual enjoyment from undergoing or inflicting pain. There are other *algo-* words (see *algor*, discussed under **algid**, and **algorism**). *Algolagnia* is derived from the combination of Greek *algos* (pain) and *lagneia* (lust, coitus), a very different derivation from those of the other *algo-* words.

algorism (AL guh riz um) *n.* This is the name of the Arabic numbering system, using the figures 1 to 9 plus the zero. The derivation is from Middle Latin *algorismus*, from the Arabic *al* (the) plus *Khuwarizmi*, the surname of a ninth-century Arabic mathematician. *Algorithm* is sometimes used as a synonym, but is also used to designate a set of rules for the solution of a mathematical problem in a finite number of steps. These words are entirely unrelated to **algolagnia**, with its very different meaning and derivation.

algorithm, see **algorism**

aliment (AL uh munt) *n. Aliment* is nourishment, nutriment, anything that feeds or sustains. *Alimentum* is Latin for "food," based on the verb *alere* (to nourish). The related adjective is *alimentary* (al uh MENT uh ree), often found in the term *alimentary canal*, the passage from mouth to anus involved in the digestive process. Sherlock Holmes did not say, "*Alimentary*, my dear Watson," but the American humorist and drama critic Robert Benchley (1889–1945) said, in one of his side-splitting short films entitled *Through the Alimentary Canal with Gun and Camera*, "We now come to the stomach [Benchley using a pointer and a diagram on an easel], which we will call 'Prince Charming,' " *Enteron* (EN tuh ron) is another term for *alimentary canal*; it comes, via New Latin, from the Greek, where it means "intestine." A further Latin

28

word for "nourishment" is *alimonia* (also based on *alere*, nourish), from which we get *alimony*, provision for food, and usually lots more.

aliquant,   see **aliquot**

aliquot   (AL i kwut), *adj.*; **aliquant** (AL i kwunt) *adj. Aliquot* is usually found in the term *aliquot part*, and describes a quantity that is contained in a larger quantity an even or integral number of times. Example: 3 and 5 are *aliquot parts* of 15. Less often met with is *aliquant*, also usually coupled with *part*. An *aliquant part* is a quantity contained in a larger quantity an uneven number of times. Example: 3 and 5 are *aliquant parts* of 16. *Aliquot parts* are exact divisors; *aliquant parts* are not. *Aliquot* was taken intact from Latin, where it means "some, several"; *aliquant* is from Latin *aliquantus*, meaning "of some size, more or less great." The English uses seem somewhat arbitrary, considering their ancestry, but there's often many a slip 'twixt the Latin or the Greek and the English.

allochthonous,   see **autochthon**

alpha and omega   (AL fuh and oh MEE guh, -ME-) *n. Alpha* and *omega* are the first and last letters of the Greek alphabet. The phrase the *alpha* and *omega* is used to mean "the beginning and the end" in the Revelation of St. John 1:8. The *New English Bible* version:

> "I am the *Alpha and Omega*," says the Lord God, who is and who was and who is to come, the sovereign Lord of all.

The *King James* version:

> "I am *Alpha and Omega*, the beginning and the ending," saith the Lord, which is, and which was, and which is to come, the Almighty.

In P. D. James's *Innocent Blood* (Charles Scribner's Sons, New York, 1980), the troubled protagonist Philippa, in the Minster at York (England), gazes at the medieval stained glass image of God the Father. "Before him was an open book. *Ego sum alpha et omega*. How simple life must be for those who could both lose and find identity in that magnificent assurance." *Alpha and omega* has another figurative use, to mean "the principal element, the all-important feature." Rice is the *alpha and omega* of the diet of many far eastern people. Planning is the *alpha and omega* of a successful enterprise. The Greek alphabet comes in handy in other ways: *iota*, the ninth Greek letter, is used to mean "a very small amount, a jot." Example: That man is a dunce; he hasn't an *iota* of common sense! Other Greek letters are used as symbols in the sciences: *pi*, for example, is the ratio between the size of the circumference of a circle and its diameter (3.141592+), and then there are all those college fraternities.

amaranthine (am uh RAN thin, -thine), *adj*. It is the figurative use of this lovely word meaning "everlasting, unfading" that we run into in literature. Thus, in *Siegfried's Journey 1916–1920* (Faber and Faber Limited, London, 1945) the English poet and writer Siegfried Sassoon (1886–1967) refers to the *"amaranthine* essays" of the English critic, essayist and caricaturist Max Beerbohm (1872–1956). And the English poet William Cowper (1731–1800), in *The Garden*, wrote:

> The only *amaranthine* flower on earth
> Is virtue . . .

Literally, *amaranthine* means "resembling the *amaranth*" (AM uh ranth), a legendary flower that never dies. In botany, *amaranth* is the name given to plants of the genus *Amaranthus* that bear beautiful blossoms and showy foliage. That name came from the Greek *amaranton*, formed from the neuter form of *amarantos* (unfading), based on the negative prefix *a-* (un-) plus the stem of the verb *marainein* (to fade). The unfading flower has given us an unfading word.

ambagious (am BAY jus) *adj*. An *ambagious* path is a circuitous or roundabout one. *Ambages* (am BAY jeez) *n. pl.*, should you run into it in an ancient tome, is an archaic word for "winding paths." *Ambagious* comes from Latin *ambagiosus*, based on Latin prefix *ambi-* (both—as found, e.g., in *ambidextrous, ambiguous*, etc.) plus *ag-*, stem of the verb *agere* (to move). The expression *to go round Robin Hood's barn* is to reach the correct conclusion by an *ambagious* route. There is also a French expression that describes the taking of an *ambagious* or roundabout way: *prendre le chemin des écoliers*, literally, to take the schoolboys' route, evoking the image of the loitering schoolboy, getting to school by the most circuitous route, to delay the agony of the classroom. Whether it's the schoolboys' route or the one round Robin Hood's barn, it's the *ambagious* way to get there.

ambulatory, see **ademption**

amerce (uh MURS) *vb.* To *amerce* a person convicted of a crime is to impose a fine in an amount fixed by the court in its discretion rather than one set by statute, or to impose any other discretionary penalty. In old Anglo-French, *a merci* meant "at (someone's) mercy," and from that phrase the Middle English verb *amercy* developed and gave us the verb *amerce*. An arbitrary or discretionary fine or jail term or other penalty is called an *amercement* (uh MURS munt). *Amerce* can be used in the general sense of "punish," without reference to a discretionary, as opposed to a fixed, penalty, but the usual implication is that of a fine or other sentence determined by the court in its sole discretion. Shakespeare used the verb in *Romeo and Juliet* (Act III, Scene 1), when the Prince, learning of the death of his kinsman Mercutio, killed by Tybalt, and the killing of Tybalt by Romeo, imposes the sentence of exile on poor Romeo:

> And for that offence
> Immediately we do exile him from hence;
> . . . My blood for your rude brawls doth lie a-bleeding;
> But I'll *amerce* you with so strong a fine
> That you shall all repent the loss of mine.

Exile was the *amercement* imposed by the Prince, acting judicially, in his discretion. What with the disparity of sentences in the criminal courts of the United States nowadays, it would appear that *amercement*, with the implication of arbitrariness, is the order of the day.

amicus curiae (uh MEEK us KYOOR ee ee) *n.* Literally, in New Latin, "a friend of the court," an *amicus curiae* is a disinterested adviser to the court in a litigation, a person or organization not a party to a lawsuit, that nonetheless volunteers, or, on occasion, is invited by the court to advise it in pending litigation. The *amicus curiae*, with no financial interest in the outcome, is nevertheless concerned because of the principle or public policy involved. There can be more than one *amicus curiae* in a given case; the plural of *amicus* is *amici* (uh MEEK ee), and the *curiae* stays unchanged. The *amicus curiae* may submit a brief expressing an opinion, or supply information, or do both.

ampersand   (AM pur sand, am pur SAND) *n*. The symbol for *and*, written &, or, in the italic form *&*. The word *ampersand* is a corruption of *and per se and*, i.e., *and by itself and* (*per se* is Latin for "by itself" or "in and of itself"). A close examination of the italic form of the symbol reveals an *e* and the cross of the *t*, thus spelling *et*, Latin for "and." Well into the 18th century, children were given hornbooks, lightweight boards about nine by five inches serving as a backing to a single sheet of paper containing the alphabet, the Lord's Prayer, a table of Roman numerals and the formula for exorcism. The sheet was covered by a thin piece of transparent horn (the bony substance of which certain animal growths are composed). Shakespeare mentions the hornbook in *Love's Labour's Lost* (Act V, Scene 1), when Armado asks Holofernes, "Monsieur, are you not lettered?" and Moth, the page boy, interjects, "Yes, yes, he teaches boys the hornbook." All this by way of introducing the fact that at the end of the alphabet in the hornbook an *ampersand* was added (. . . x, y, z, &). In this little essay we have learned about *ampersands* & hornbooks & a tiny bit of Shakespeare & an even tinier bit of Latin.

amphibology   (am fuh BOL uh jee) *n*. *Amphiboly* (am FIB uh lee) is a variant. An *amphibology* is a sentence or a phrase that is ambiguous because of its uncertain construction, allowing of two interpretations. *Amphibology*, generally, is ambiguous writing. The problem most often arises because of the misuse of pronouns and the resulting uncertainty about their antecedents. William Safire, in his "On Language" column in *The New York Times Magazine* of November 4, 1984, furnishes an excellent example of *amphibology*: "Joe and Mike took his sister and her friend to the disco, but they didn't want to dance." Safire goes on to ask: "Who (sic) does *his* refer to, Joe or Mike? And who are *they*, the two girls or

32

all four of the confused wallflowers?" Fowler gives an example that has nothing to do with pronouns or antecedents. After the definition "a statement so expressed as to admit of two grammatical constructions each yielding a different sense," we read: "*Stuff a cold and starve a fever* appears to be two sentences containing directions for two maladies, but may also be a conditional sentence meaning if you are fool enough to stuff a cold you will produce and have to starve a fever." *Amphibology* comes from Late Latin *amphibologia; amphiboly* from Latin *amphibolia. Amphibolic* (am fuh BOL ik) is the adjective. All these words go back to the Greek *amphibolos* (ambiguous).

amphigory (AM fuh gohr ee) *n*. Also **amphigouri** (AM fuh goor ee). An *amphigory* is a senseless concoction or rigamarole, usually of meaningless verse; often a parody. From the French *amphigouri*, composed of the familiar Greek prefix *amphi-* (both) plus *gouri*, of unknown derivation. The verses of an *amphigory* may sound well, but on inspection, prove to make no sense whatever. The English poet Swinburne (1837–1909) was known for his sensuous, musical style, as in his verse drama *Atalanta in Calydon*, and his collection *Poems and Ballads*. He wrote a parody of his own style entitled *Nephelidia. Brewer's Phase and Fable* gives the opening lines, an excellent example of an *amphigory*:

> From the depth of the dreamy decline of the dawn
> through a notable nimbus of nebulous noonshine,
> Pallid and pink as the palm of the flag-flower
> that flickers with fear of the flies as they float,
> Are they looks of our lovers that lustrously lean
> from a marvel of mystic miraculous moonshine? *etc.*

Beyond question, the best known *amphigory* in all English literature is *The Jabberwocky*, the poem found on a table by Alice, the heroine of *Through the Looking-Glass* (1872), the sequel of *Alice's Adventures in Wonderland* (1865), by the English writer and mathematician Lewis Carroll (pseudonym of Charles Lutwidge Dodgson, 1832–1898), about which poor Alice remarked: " . . . it's all in some language I don't know." The opening quatrain reads:

> 'Twas brillig, and the slithy toves
> Did gyre and gimble in the wabe:

33

All mimsy were the borogroves,
And the mome raths outgrabe.

Later in the poem, there are the lines:

Come to my arms, my beamish boy!
O frabjous day! Calooh! Callay!

and Alice says: "It seems very pretty, but it's *rather* hard to understand! . . . Somehow it seems to fill my head with ideas—only I don't exactly know what they are . . . !" What a marvelous comment on an *amphigory*!

anabasis (uh NAB uh sis) *n*. In its most general sense, an *anabasis* is a military expedition in the nature of an advance. Its antonym, or opposite, is a *katabasis* (kuh TAB uh sis), a retreat, in military terms. More narrowly, an *anabisis* is a military march from a coast to the interior of a country. One of the most famous *anabases* in classical history is that of Cyrus the Younger (c. 424–401 B.C.), the Persian prince who marched against his brother Artaxerxes II, as related by the Greek historian and essayist Xenophon (c. 434–385 B.C.) in his classical account *The Anabasis*, the schoolboy text in the teaching of classical Greek that is the counterpart of Caesar's *Gallic Wars* in the Latin course. *Anabasis* is a Greek word whose literal meaning is "stepping up," from the prefix *ana-* (up) plus the noun *basis* (stepping). A *katabasis* is a march from the interior to the coast. It is a Greek word with the literal meaning of "stepping down," from the prefix *kata-* (down—a variant of *cata-*; and *katabasis* can be spelt *catabasis*) plus our old friend *basis*. Ten-thousand Greeks, hired as mercenaries by Cyrus the Younger for his *anabasis*, in a famous retreat after the battle of Cunaxa and the death of Cyrus, marched northward *to* the coast in the *katabasis* also reported by Xenophon in his *Anabasis*. The retreat of over 300,000 Allied troops from Dunkirk in 1940 completed their *katabasis* from the coast of France when they were rescued by a catch-as-catch-can fleet of British ships and boats.

anacoluthia (an uh kuh LOO thee uh) *n*. This is a grammatical term denoting the lack of syntactical sequence or want of coherence in a case where the latter part of a sentence is rhetorically out of keeping with the earlier part; in short, the juxtaposition in one sentence of two grammatically incomplete and incompatible constructions. *Anacoluthia* is derived from the Greek *anakolouthia*, based on the negative prefix *an-* plus the adjective *akalouthos* (marching together). An *anacoluthon* (an uh kuh LOO thon) is an instance of this; for example: "If you go on flouting the basic rules of social behavior—well, what do you think will happen?" The "if" clause (see **apodosis** and the discussion of *protasis* in that entry) should grammatically be followed by a "then" clause, a conclusion: "If you go on flouting the basic rules of social behavior, (then) you'll find yourself in lots of trouble (or words to that effect). So you'd better behave; if you don't—well—what more can I say?"

analects (AN uh lekts) *n. pl.* Sometimes *analecta* (an uh LEK tuh). *Analects* or *analecta* are collected fragments or passages from the words of an author (sometimes a number of authors). The *Analects of Confucius*, for example, is a collection of his sayings and discourses from the fourth century B.C. The term is usually applied to literary gleanings from the works of a single author; in that use, *analects* differ from an anthology. Via Latin *analecta*, the word is derived from Greek *analekta* (things gathered). All we have left of the works of certain classical poets and writers, like Sappho, the foremost of the early Greek lyric poets (early sixth century B.C.), and Ennius, the father of Latin poetry (239–c. 169 B.C.), are *analects*.

anamnesis (an am NEE sis) *n.* This pleasant-sounding word serves a number of purposes. In general, *anamnesis* is reminiscence. In the field of medicine, it is a patient's recital of his medical history to his doctor. In psychiatry, an *anamnesis* is a case history. In Proustian terms, it is a remembrance of things past. In Platonic terms, it is the recollection of a previous existence. *Anamnesis* comes intact from the Greek, where it means "remembrance" generally, and is based on the prefix *ana-* (again, back) plus the verb *mimnestein* (to remind, recall to memory). Anything that recalls to mind earlier experiences may be described as *anamnestic* (an am NES tik). A scent, a tune, the timbre of a voice, a bit of landscape can have an *anamnestic* effect. Sometimes, *anamnesis* and nostalgia go hand in hand.

anaptyxis, see **epenthesis**

anastrophe (uh NAS truh fee) *n. Anastrophe* is a rhetorical de-vice—the inversion of the normal order of words—for dramatic effect. *Anastrophe* was taken intact from the Greek, where it means "a turning back," formed from the prefix *ana-* (against) plus *stro-phe* (turning about), based on the verb *strophein* (to turn). It takes a number of forms: subject after verb: "Came the dawn." "Able was I ere I saw Elba." "And damned be him who first cries, 'Hold, enough!' " And from the poem *The Old Vicarage, Grantchester* by the English poet Rupert Brooke (1887–1915):

> Stands the Church clock at ten to three?
> And is there honey still for tea?

and

> Unkempt about those hedges blows
> An English unofficial rose.

Object before subject "Me he condemned, him he acquitted." Preposition after noun: "No trace of him was found the world around." Adjective after noun, as in a play-review by the American writer and critic Dorothy Parker (1893–1967): "*The House Beau-tiful* is the play lousy"—two *anastrophes* at a clip! The same Dor-othy gave us more examples (subject after verb) in her 1927 poem, *Enough Rope*:

> Four be the things I am wiser to know:
> Idleness, sorrow, a friend, and a foe.
> Four be the things I'd been better without:
> Love, curiosity, freckles, and doubt.

Verb after adverbial clause: "When lilacs last in the dooryard bloomed . . . ," from the poem of that title by the American poet Walt Whitman (1819–1892); and *By Love Possessed*, title of the novel by the American novelist James Gould Cozzens (1903–1978). Preposition after noun:

> It was young David, lord of sheep and cattle
> Pursued his fate, the April fields among . . . ,

the first lines of the poem *Five Smooth Stones* by the English novelist and poet Stella Benson (1892–1933).

anatine, see **accipitrine**

anchorite   (ANG kuh rite) *n.* An *anchorite* is a hermit, a recluse, particularly one who has gone to a remote place to enter upon a life of religious retreat. The older form, *anchoret* (ANG kuh rit, ret) is rarely seen. The word is from Greek *anachoretes*, based on the verb *anachoreein* (to retire, withdraw), via Middle Latin *anachorita*. The English poet Lord Byron (1788 –1824) wrote of things *(Childe Harold's Pilgrimage)* that "Might shake the saintship of an *anchorite* . . ." *St. Simeon Stylites* (*stylites* is Greek for "of a pillar") was a famous *anchorite*, a Syrian hermit of the fifth century who lived for more than 35 years on a tiny platform atop a high pillar. Many *anchorites*, dubbed "stylites," imitated his withdrawal into seclusion. An earlier *anchorite* was St. Anthony of Egypt (c. 251– c. 350), who became a recluse at the age of 20 and went into total seclusion when he was 35. He was the *anchorite* who resisted every temptation the devil could devise, and lived alone in the desert for the last years of his life. His life inspired *The Temptation of St. Anthony*, one of the masterpieces of the French novelist Gustave Flaubert (1821–1880). An *anchorite* is the ultimate loner.

androgynous   (an DROJ un us) *adj.* An *androgyn* (AN druh gine) is an organism, human or other, that is of both sexes. *Androgynos* is Greek for "hermaphrodite," based on *andros*, genitive (possessive) form of *aner* (man) plus *gyne* (woman). *Androgynous* is used in botany to describe plants bearing both stamens and pistils in the same cluster. Applied to man and other animals, *androgynous* describes specimens having the characteristics of both sexes. This can refer to sexual organs or other physical characteristics, or to personality or temperament. The English poet and philosopher Samuel Taylor Coleridge (1772–1834) said, "The truth is, a great mind must be *androgynous*." The noun *androgyny* (an DROJ uh nee) is a synonym of *hermaphroditism*, but can also mean "effeminacy" in men; but never confuse *androgyny* with *homosexuality*, an altogether different story. A great male ballet dancer should be

37

androgynous, in the sense of combining in one body and temperament masculine strength and feminine grace.

anguine, see **accipitrine**

anile (AN ile, AY nile) *adj. Anile* applies only to females, meaning "like a doddering old crone," full of confusion, fussy manners, and silly, nervous questions. These all mark *anile* conduct. *Anile* comes from Latin *anilis* (pertaining to or like an old woman) and its noun *anility* (uh NIL ih tee) from Latin *anilitas* (a woman's old age), both based on *anus* (old woman). Note: There are two entirely separate Latin words spelt *a-n-u-s* (most probably pronounced differently—we don't know how classical Latin was pronounced—and declined differently), one meaning "anus," the other "old woman." It is fortunate that we do not pronounce *anile* "AN il" by analogy to one of the permissible pronunciations of *senile* (SEE nil) or to the way we pronounce *futile* in American (FYOO tul—the English say FYOO tile), else there would be confusion between *anile* and *anal* (a word popular from Freud), which comes from the other Latin *a-n-u-s*. *Anile*, restricted to women, is narrower than *senile* (SEE nile, -nil, SEN ile), which applies to both sexes, like its noun *senility* (suh NIL ih tee), indicating loss or serious decline of mental powers. *Senescent* (suh NES unt) means "growing old" and is used of either sex (from Latin *senescens*, present participle of *senescere*, to grow old). Despite the remark in *Tristram Shandy* by the English novelist and clergyman Laurence Sterne (1713–1768) about "the nonsense of the old women (of both sexes)," you can call an old woman *senile* but you can't call an old man *anile*.

animadversion (an uh mad VUR zhun, -shun) *n. Animadversion* is the making of adverse comment or criticism, the casting of aspersions; an *animadversion* is a critical, usually censorious observation or comment. Drama and literary critics seem to find it easier to indulge in *animadversion* than to find occasion for praise. Their *animadversions* can put untimely ends to gallant efforts and, at times, cut short careers that might have flourished. The Scottish author James Boswell (1740–1795), biographer of Samuel Johnson (1709–1784), the great English lexicographer, poet, and critic, spoke of the latter's "*animadversion* upon his old acquaintance." The English poet William Cowper (1731–1800) said of a critic,

38

"[His] *animadversions* hurt me . . . In part they appeared to me unjust, and in part ill-natured." This was a case where the *animadversions* did no lasting harm! This word is from Latin *animadversio* (observation, blame, censure), based on *animus* (mind) plus *advertere* (turn towards). Man is so ready to criticize, blame, and censure that in both Latin and English, a word that originally denoted the simple act of *turning the mind towards* someone or something has taken on the meaning of "blaming" or "censuring."

anodyne (AN uh dine) *n*. In medical circles, an *anodyne* is a painkiller, but in general use, an *anodyne* is anything, material or nonmaterial, that relieves pain or distress, physical or emotional. *Anodyne* is also an adjective, meaning "pain-relieving" or "soothing" generally. It is from Greek *anodynos* (painless), based upon Greek prefix *an-* (not, without) plus *odyne* (pain). The Irish statesman and orator Edmund Burke (1729–1797) spoke of "the *anodyne* draught of oblivion." In medicine, opiates and narcotics are used as *anodynes*. Massages and baths are *anodyne* treatments in osteopathy. When a person is depressed or distressed, a change of scene can have an *anodyne* effect. Music (the food of love—that has charms to soothe a savage breast) can be effective as an *anodyne* to the distress of one in an emotional crisis.

anoesis (an oh EE sis) *n*. *Anoesis* is a feeling or sensation or emotion unaccompanied by an understanding of it; purely passive receptiveness without awareness of what's really being presented, or, as the psychologists express it, without cognitive content. *Anoesia* (an oh EE zhee uh, -zee-) or *anoia*, taken intact from the Greek, based on negative prefix *a-* plus *noos* (mind), means "want of understanding" in Greek and is used in English as a term for extreme mental deficiency or idiocy. *Anoetic* (an oh ET ik), the adjective, might come in handy as a description of the mentality that has led to the proliferation of atomic weaponry.

anomie (AN uh mee) *n*. This is the word for a situation affecting an individual, a group, or a society when the usual standards of social conduct fail to operate, producing social chaos, a breakdown of all social values, a condition often found among displaced persons in this world full of refugees. *Anomie* comes from Greek *an-*

nomos (law). The adjective describing the condition is *anomic* (uh NOM ik). *Anomie* is characterized by a feeling of hopelessness and a loss of a sense of purpose, stemming from the breakdown of the rules of social behavior. *Anomie* was widespread among the inmates of the Nazi concentration camps. The faces and attitudes of people confined in refugee centers in war zones like Lebanon, or after natural disasters like earthquakes, indicate the state of mass *anomie*.

anopheline, see **accipitrine**

anserine, see **accipitrine**

ant(a)ean (an TEE uhn) *adj*. An *antaean* person is one of tremendous strength, immensely robust, sturdy and earthy, whose power is quickly and easily renewed after apparent exhaustion. The adjective comes from *Antaeus*, of Greek mythology, who lived in ancient Libya in North Africa. He was a wrestler of gigantic proportions and superhuman strength, the offspring of Gaea, goddess of the earth, and Poseidon, god of the sea. He was possessed of a unique characteristic, which gave him a tremendous advantage over all other wrestlers: every time he was flung to earth, his strength was renewed—indeed, he became stronger than before. Remember: the earth was his mother. Hercules had to wrestle with him, and overcame the problem of Antaeus's ever-renewable vigor by lifting him into the air and crushing him. Clever Hercules! Antaeus's quality of drawing strength from the earth was celebrated in the poem *The Municipal Gallery Revisited* by the Irish poet William Butler Yeats (1865–1939), containing these lines:

> John Synge, I and Augusta Gregory, thought
> All that we did, all that we said or sang
> Must come from contact with the soil, from that
> Contact everything *Antaeus*-like grew strong.

(Incidentally—and this has nothing whatever to do with *Antaeus* or *antanean*—that same poem has these two beautiful lines:

> Think where man's glory most begins and ends,
> And say my glory was I had such friends.

Yeats was referring to the Irish poet and dramatist John Millington Synge (1871–1909), who wrote *The Playboy of the Western World* and *Riders to the Sea*, and the Irish playwright Lady Augusta Gregory (1859–1932), the author of many plays, including *Spreading the News* and *The Full Moon*. Another incidental: in 1902, Lady Gregory, Yeats, and others founded the Irish National Theater, which became the Abbey Theater, where Synge was an associated dramatist.) To get back to our headword: It would be appropriate to say that Yeats and Synge were *antaean* figures!

antelopine,   see **accipitrine**

antepartum,   see **parturition**

anteprandial,   see **preprandial**

antipodal   (an TIP uh dul) *adj.* As a geographical term, *antipodal* applies to places on the globe that are located diametrically opposite each other, like the United States and Australia. *Antipodal* is taken from the Greek, where it means "(those) with the feet opposite," based on the prefix *anti-* (against, opposite) plus *podes* (feet). Used figuratively, as a general term, *antipodal* means "diametrically opposite." Debating teams argue *antipodal* points of view. It has been said that a man and wife with *antipodal* temperaments supplement each other which makes for a good marriage. *Antipodes* (an TIP uh deez), *n. pl.*, are, literally, places on the globe diametrically opposite each other, or people who dwell in *antipodal* places; figuratively, the term applies to any opposites. The English poet John Keats (1795–1821) wrote:

> The poet and the dreamer are distinct,
> Diverse, sheer opposite, *antipodes*.
> The one pours out a balm upon the world,
> The other vexes it.

The American psychologist Edward Bradford Titchener (1867–1927) said: "Common sense is the very *antipodes* of science." The *Antipodes* are a small island group southeast of and belonging to New Zealand.

antonomasia   (an tuh nuh MAY zhuh) *n.* This word covers two

41

related but distinct rhetorical devices: (1) the identification of an individual by the use of an epithet, designation, or title in place of his real name, or, conversely, (2) the use of the name of a person who is the embodiment of a particular characteristic or type of achievement—a name out of history, that has passed into the language—to designate an individual with the same characteristic or background. Examples of (1): *his lordship* or *grace* or *majesty, the gentleman from Arizona, my learned adversary, the Chief Justice, the Right Honourable Member* (of Parliament); as to particular individuals, especially historical persons, *the Great Engineer* (President Hoover), *Il Duce, Der Führer, The Unready* (Ethelred II, King of England, 978-1016; unready was a corruption of *redeless*, meaning "lacking in wisdom"), *Le Roi Soleil* or *The Sun King* (Louis XIV of France, 1638 -1715),*Le Gros* or *The Fat* (applied to Charles III of France, 839-888, and Louis VI of France, 1081-1137; Alfonso II of Portugal, 1185-1223, was also known as "The Fat"), *The Cunctator* or *Delayer* (General Quintus Fabius Maximus Verrucosus of Rome, second century B.C.—see **cunctator**). Examples of (2): a *Casanova* or *Don Juan* (a libertine), a *Hitler* (a detestable demagogue or dictator), a *Solomon* (a wise man), a *Sherlock* (an able sleuth, anyone who can unravel a mystery), a *Raffles* (a smooth, glamorous crook). For a fine example of *antonomasia*— a word taken intact from Latin, which got it from a Greek noun based on the verb *antonomazein* (to rename)—there is a tale about two eminent pianists who heard the great Polish pianist Paderewski play for the first time. "What do you think?", one of them asked the other after the concert. "Good," was the reply, "but he's no Paderewski."

apatetic (ap uh TET ik) *adj.* This unfamiliar word looks like a misprint; it isn't—no *h* after the first *t*. It is a zoological term, describing animals or insects or creatures of the sea that can change color or form or both for purposes of camouflage, a mighty handy talent in the survival business. *Apatetic* comes from Greek *apatetikos* (deceiving), based on the verb *apateuein* (to deceive). What immediately comes to mind, of course, is the chameleon, known for its ability to change skin color to blend with its surroundings, a trait so well known that the adjective *chameleonic* (kuh mee lee ON ik), applied to persons, means "changeable, inconstant." The chameleon, it so happens, is also noted for its very slow locomo-

42

tion, which makes it look apathetic as well as *apatetic*. There are *apatetic* species of moth that can fold their wings over their bodies, hang onto a branch, and make themselves look like twigs, and there are other *apatetic* insects, animals and fish capable of amazingly effective camouflage. One might be tempted to use the word in describing certain politicians.

aperçu (ah per SEE—*ee* being approximate, somewhere between *ooh* and *ee*, the *u*-sound in French) *n*. An *aperçu* is an intuitive insight, a glimpse, an immediate appreciation, a hasty glance leading to a quick view; also used as a general survey, outline, rough outline, summary. *Aperçu* is a French word, the past participle of the verb *apercevoir* (to perceive) used as a noun; literally, something perceived. Its common use is to denote an insight that inspires one as a result of an intuitive understanding as opposed to a labored study. Striking *aperçus* spring up in old proverbs, the lines of great poets, especially Shakespeare, and the works of the pioneers of psychology and psychiatry, particularly Freud. As to the *u*-sound in French mentioned above, see the quotation from Fowler under **fin de siècle**.

aph(a)eresis (uh FER ih sis) *n*. *Apheresis* is one of three grammatical terms that deal with the omission of one or more letters from a word. The other two, as one moves through the word, are *syncope* (SIN kuh pee) and *apocope* (uh POK uh pee). *Apheresis* is omission at the beginning of a word; examples: *especial* became *special*; *adder* used to be *nadder* (*a nadder* turned into *an adder*); *cute* came from *acute*; *squire* from *esquire*; *count* from *account*. *Syncope* is omission from the middle; examples: *briticism* should logically be *britannicism*; *conservativism* was reduced to *conservatism*; *idololatry* became *idolatry*; *pacificist* was shortened to *pacifist*; *symbolology* to *symbology*. In poetry, an apostrophe is used, as in *e'en* (even), *e'er* (ever), *ne'er* (never). A subdivision of *syncope* is *haplology*, where a syllable, rather than a single letter, is omitted from the middle, as in the case of *briticism*, *conservatism*, and the other examples given under *syncope*. *Haplology* is derived from the Greek adjective *haploos* (single, simple) plus *logos* (word). *Apocope* covers the loss of final letters or syllables; examples: *cinematograph* went to *cinema*; *curiosity* became *curio* (in context); *mine* to *my*, *thine* to *thy*. All these grammatical terms are from the

43

Greek: *apheresis* from *aphairesis* (taking away), based on prefix *ap-* (shortened form of *apo-*, away) plus *hairein* (to snatch); *syncope* from *synkope* (cutting short), based on prefix *syn-* (with, together) plus *koptein* (to cut); *apocope* from *apokope* (cutting off), based on prefix *apo-* (away) plus *koptein* (to cut). The *biz* in *show biz* is a case of double *apocope*, for which there is no single term. We could invent one: *diapocope*. Better not. See also **haplology**.

apocalyptic (uh pok uh LIP tik) *adj. The Apocalypse* (uh POK uh lips) is the last book of the New Testament, the Revelation of St. John the Divine. An *apocalypse* (lower case *a*) is a revelation. The word is derived, via Late Latin, from Greek *apokalypsis* (revelation), based on the verb *apokalyptein* (to reveal). Since so many revelations, beginning with St. John's, have dealt with imminent doom, the adjective *apocalyptic* has come to signify the prediction of disaster around the corner and the end of the world. One reads of the *apocalyptic* vision of the prophets of doom. Those who fear the end of life on earth through atomic warfare are prone to speak in *apocalyptic* terms (and who can blame them?) of the Big Bang that will end everything that began with a Big Bang, if we accept that version rather than *Genesis*.

apocope, see **aph(a)eresis**

apodictic (ap uh DIK tik) *adj.* Also **apodeictic** (ap uh DIKE tik). A statement is *apodictic* if it is necessarily true, without need for demonstration or proof. On the third of July, the statement "Tomorrow will be the Fourth of July" is *apodictic*. An *apodictic* statement is self-evident, axiomatic, unquestionable, incontestable. *Apodictic* comes, via Latin *apodicticus*, from Greek *apodeiktikos*, formed from the prefix *apo-* (away, from, off) plus *deiknynai* (to show, demonstrate). It is true that since Einstein and relativity, "facts" once thought to be *apodictic* ("A straight line is the shortest distance between two points") have turned out to be open to question, or at least, to interpretation under certain circumstances. But the fourth dimension doesn't much enter into the lives of plain folk like you and me.

apodosis (uh POD uh sis) *n.* A conditional sentence has two parts, one that expresses the condition, usually introduced by *if*, the other that states the consequence of the condition's being fulfilled, often introduced by *then*. The *if* clause is the *protasis* (PROT uh sis); the *then* clause is the *apodosis*. If it rains, then we'll postpone the picnic. *If it rains* is the *protasis; then we'll postpone the picnic* is the *apodosis*. Both words are from the Greek: *protasis* (literally, a stretching forth; by extension, a proposition); *apodosis* (literally, a turning; by extension, an answering clause). The next time someone makes you an offer based on an outrageous condition, just tell him to go away and take his *protasis* with him! If he seems puzzled, tell him to buy a copy of this book.

apogee (AP uh jee) *n*. This is a term used in astronomy to designate the point in the orbit of a celestial body at which it is the most distant from the earth. The *perigee* (PER ih jee) is the point in the orbit at which the heavenly body is nearest the earth. *Apogee* comes from the Greek *apogaion* (off-earth), based on prefix *apo-* (from) plus *gaia*, a variant of *ge* (earth). *Perigee* is from the Greek *perigeion* (close to the earth), based on prefix *perì-* (about, around) plus *ge* (earth). Both terms are used chiefly with respect to the movements of the moon and man-made satellites. *Apogee* is used figuratively to mean "apex, highest point, climax" in any situation. Cf. the use of the astronomical terms *zenith* and *nadir*, but *perigee* does not appear to have a figurative use corresponding to that of *apogee*. It can be said that the work of the Italian sculptor, painter, and architect Michelangelo (1475–1564) was the *apogee* of Renaissance art. One might have used *zenith* in place of *apogee* in the last sentence; but in describing the opposite—the low point—use *nadir*, never *perigee*. Incidentally, *apsis* (AP sis) is the inclusive term in astronomy for either of the two points in question: the *higher apsis* is the point in any eccentric orbit farthest from the center of attraction, i.e., the *apogee*; the *lower apsis* the point nearest to that center, i.e., the *perigee*. *Apsis* is from Greek *hapsis* (felloe, i.e., rim of a wheel; arch; vault; and *felloe*—also *felly*—is from Middle English *felwe*).

apolaustic (ap uh LAW stik), *n.*, *adj.* An *apolaustic* person is one whose aim in life is the attainment of enjoyment, who expends his energy in the search for pleasure, a *hedonist* (HEE duh nist) whose doctrine is that pleasure is the highest good; a *sybarite* (SIB uh rite) is devoted to luxury. All these words relate to *la dolce vita* rather than to the lofty concept of the pursuit of happiness mentioned in our Declaration of Independence. The search for pleasure: the Greeks had more than one word for it. *Apolaustic* comes from their adjective *apolaustikos*, related to the verb *apolauein* (to enjoy). *Hedonistic* (and *hedonism, hedonic, hedonics,* and *hedonistics*) come from the Greek noun *hedone* (pleasure). *Sybarite* we get from the ancient Greek city of Sybaris in southern Italy, famous for the luxurious life style of its inhabitants. But what's left of all that?

Appollonian, see **Dionysian**

apopemptic (ap uh PEMP tik) *adj. Apopemptic* describes anything addressed to one departing, whether spoken or sung, a farewell message, a valedictory. It is from Greek *apopemptikos* (pertaining to sending away), based on prefix *apo-* (away) plus *pempein* (to send). The advice of Polonius to his son Laertes in Shakespeare's *Hamlet* (Act I, Scene 3) is one of the most eloquent (if long-winded) *apopemptic* speeches in literature. Good advice, too. *Apopemptic* describes messages to, rather than from those taking leave. Thus, it does not apply to a farewell address, like George Washington's, or to those so eloquently delivered by divas (like the Austrian-American contralto Ernestine Schumann-Heinck, 1861–1936) on their oft-repeated retirements from the operative stage. Today's practically automatic *apopemptic* message is "Have a nice day!" to which the American columnist Russell Baker (born 1925) once thought of replying, "I will, if I can find one."

apophasis (uh POF uh sis) *n.* When you say: "It is quite unnecessary for me to mention his many valorous deeds" or "It goes without saying that . . ." or "We can omit any reference to . . ." or "Why even mention the fact that . . . ," you are indulging in *apophasis*—the art of mentioning something while declaring your intention not to mention it, denying your need to bring up a subject while you proceed to bring it up quite distinctly. This is an effective device to emphasize the subject you're "not going to go into." "I will not speak of his countless misdeeds!" "Why even mention his disloyalty to the flag?" *Apophasis* was taken over from the Greek. It is related to another rhetorical trick, *paralipsis* (par uh LIP sis), the suggestion through brief mention of a topic that there's a lot more being left out. "He's a reckless fellow—not to go into other

46

shortcomings'' or ''There is hardly room in this brief space to set forth the complete record of his wanton violations of decency.'' This word is from Greek *paraleipsis* (omission); omission can be more effective, at times, than enumeration.

apophony, see **ablaut**

aporia (uh POH ree uh, -PAW-) *n. Aporia* is a term in rhetoric, for a doubt real or professed (usually the latter), about how to start, where to begin, what to say, how to go on. In the science of logic, a branch of philosophy, *aporia* is the problem of establishing the truth of a proposition where there is conflicting evidence on both sides of the question. *Aporia* has also been defined in the general sense of a ''difficulty,'' which would embrace its special meanings in both rhetoric and logic. Its commonest use is in rhetoric. For example, ''It's hard to know just where to start . . .,'' says the orator, who has practiced his speech and knows perfectly well where he's going to begin. Or, ''What can one say about the evils of . . . ?'' asks the speaker, whose notes contain exactly what to say about the evils of. . . . *Aporia* is an effective tool to appeal to the emotions of members of an audience, who are thus invited to participate in the speaker's (or writer's) professed dilemma and start thinking more actively about the subject of the discourse. From the Greek negative prefix *a-* plus *poros* (passage).

aposiopesis (ap uh sye uh PEE sis) *n.* When you suddenly break off in the middle of a sentence, leaving it unfinished, as though you are unable or unwilling to continue, you are committing an act of *aposiopesis*. Such an interruption is described as *aposiopetic* (ap uh sye uh PET ik). These words come from the Greek *aposiopaein* (to be completely silent). The breaking off is meant to be significant to the hearer, who is called upon to supply the missing words from his own imagination. An *aposiopesis* is a pregnant silence, a stopping short for rhetorical effect. ''We must go on—if we should stop now—'' is an example of *aposiopesis*. ''If you don't leave this instant—'' bespeaks a warning of a dire result. ''Or else—'' is a common *aposiopesis* with an ominous ring. Perhaps the commonest *aposiopesis* in all conversation (especially in the dialogue of inferior plays and novels) is ''You mean—?'' *Aposiopeses* are nothing new; one of the best known in classical literature is found in

Book I of the *Aeneid* of the Roman epic poet Virgil (70–19 B.C.). The rebellious winds have disobeyed the commands of the sea god Neptune to afford safe passage to Aeneas, and have kicked up a bad storm that threatens the fleet. Neptune summons Eurus, the southeast wind, and Zephyrus, the west wind, and lets them have it: "Has pride of birth made you so insolent?/So, winds, you dare to mingle sky and land,/heave high such masses, without my command,/Whom I—? But no, let me first calm the restless/swell; you shall yet atone—another time . . ." (Translation of Professor Allen Mandelbaum of the City University of New York.) The words "Whom I—" are an *aposiopesis*, leaving unsaid the Latin for ". . . will punish . . . ," as clearly indicated by the ". . . you shall yet atone . . ." on the next line. In the original Latin, the words for "Whom I—" are "Quos ego—" and based on this famous passage, the phrase *Quos ego* (kwohs EG o) has come to signify a threat of punishment for disobedience. Eurus and Zephyrus knew perfectly well what was meant by Neptune's unspoken words. They were going to catch hell. Neptune's *aposiopesis* spoke volumes! Another word for *aposiopesis* is *abruption* (uh BRUP shun), from the Latin *abruptio* (a breaking off), which gave us *abrupt* as well. In Shakespeare's *Troilus and Cressida* (Act III, Scene 2), Cressida invites the lovesick Troilus to enter her bedchamber. "Will you walk in, my lord?" Troilus: "O Cressida, how often have I wished me thus!" "Wished, my lord?—The gods grant—O my lord!" Troilus asks: "What should they grant? What makes this pretty *abruption*?"

apostil(le) (uh POS til); also **postil** (POS til) *n.* An *apostil* or *postil* is a marginal note, annotation, or comment, especially, in context, an explanatory marginal comment in the Bible. Via Middle Latin, Middle French, and Middle English, the term is most likely derived from the Latin phrase *post illa*, probably short for *post illa verba textus* (after those words of the text). The *a* in the form *apostil* or *apostille* is of doubtful origin. Though *apostil* sometimes refers to annotations of the Holy Scriptures, it is not to be bracketed with the noun *apostle* (one of the twelve sent forth by Christ to preach the gospel), which comes from quite another source: the Greek *apostolos* (literally, one who is sent out, from the verb *apostellein*, to send off). It is often amusing to read the *postils* of previous owners of books you have picked up in a secondhand bookshop.

apothegm (AP uh them) *n*. An *apothegm* is an aphorism, a terse, pithy saying, along instructive lines; an adage, a maxim, usually expressing a universal truth. It is from the Greek *apophthegma* (thing uttered), based on *apo-* (forth, from) plus *phthengesthai* (to speak). Some universally known *apothegms*: Man proposes, God disposes. Art is long, life is short. A bird in the hand . . . A stitch in time . . . A penny saved . . . A fool and his money . . . One good turn . . . There are those who prefer the spelling *apophthegm* with the extra *-ph-*, closer to the original Greek. You may add that *-ph-* if you wish, but don't leave out the *g*, or you'll get *apothem*, (which is pronounced the same way but is a horse of quite a different color: a perpendicular line from the center of a regular polygon to one of its sides; from the Greek *apothema*, based on the same *apo-* plus *thema* (something laid down). From such tiny omissions do great consequences flow. As Hugh Kenner so aptly put it in his review of the new "critical and **synpotic**" edition (edited by Hans Walter Gabler et al.—Garland Publishing) of James Joyce's *Ulysses*, punningly entitled "Leopold's bloom restored" (*Times Literary Supplement*, July 1, 1984): "Weighty issues, as Sherlock Holmes said, can hang upon a bootlace; likewise upon one letter of the alphabet."

apothem, see **apothegm**

apotropaic (ap uh truh PAY ik) *adj*. This adjective describes anything that wards off or is intended to ward off evil influence or ill fortune; from Greek *apotropaion* (something that turns aside evil), neuter of *apotropaios* (averting, turning away), based on prefix *apo-* (away) plus *trope* (turning). We have all heard or read about the evil eye, the widespread belief, from olden times down to this very day, that there are people able to injure or even kill with a glance. (This has nothing whatever to do with "if looks could kill," which is concerned with hatred rather than the evil eye.) The ancients used a variety of *apotropaic* charms, amulets, gestures, symbols, and votive offerings to avert the effect of the evil eye. Some of the gestures were designedly obscene. *Apotropaism* (ap uh truh PAY iz uhm) is the science and art of warding off evil, usually by rituals and incantations. Many years ago, the author himself, as an indiscreet youth, snapped a photo of an ancient white-haired crone in the Italian countryside, carrying an incredible load of faggots on

49

her head. She promptly hurled the faggots to the ground and engaged in an obscene ritualistic sort of dance that lasted a few seconds, and then turned her head and spat over her left shoulder three times. Let's hope her *apotropaic* efforts were successful.

appanage   (AP uh nij) *n*. This is the technical term for estates or income granted to a member of a royal family, usually by the sovereign to a younger relative, but since there are so few of that class around any more, the term is rarely met with in its literal sense except in histories or historical novels. More broadly, it is a term covering anything rightfully belonging to one's station, and even more generally, any natural endowment or adjunct. The English poet and essayist Coventry Patmore (1823–1896) used the term figuratively in the expression, ". . . beauty, which is the natural *appanage* of happiness . . ." The origin of this noun is found in Middle Latin *appanagium* (endowment), related to the verb *appanare* (literally, to supply with bread; by extension, to endow with a revenue or maintenance), based on the prefix *ap-*, used before *p* as a variant of *ad-* (to) plus *panis* (bread). The richer enjoyment of life and of the arts in particular is an *appanage* of a classical education. Do not confuse this word with *empannage* (om puh NAHZH), which is a term for the tail of an airplane, including the stabilizer, elevator, vertical fin, and rudder. *Empannage* was taken over intact from the French word for "feathering," and by extension, for those same airplane terms, and the fins or vanes of a bomb as well.

aprosexia   (ay pro SEKS ee uh) *n*. This is the term for a person's inability to keep his mind on the subject, or to keep paying attention generally. This word comes from Greek negative prefix *a-* (un-, in-, non-, etc.) plus *prosexis* (heedfulness), based on the verb *prosechein* (to heed). There are those who simply cannot sustain attention; the mind wanders. They suffer from *aprosexia*. This will interfere radically, for example, with a student's ability to take proper notes. A boring lecturer can add to the problem. *Aprosexia* sufferers don't do well with nagging spouses or long-winded tellers of tales.

apsis,   see **apogee**
50

aquiline, see **accipitrine**

arable (AR uh bul) *adj. Arable* land is capable of cultivation, suitable for farming, able to produce crops; plowable. From Latin *arabilis*, based on the verb *arare* (to plow). The Israelis converted great expanses of desert sand into *arable* soil through proper irrigation and farming. It is useless for governments to distribute land among penniless peasants unless it is *arable*.

arbiter (AR bih tur) *n.* An *arbiter* (not to be confused with *arbitrator*) is one who has the absolute power to pass judgment. He acts *arbitrarily*, and is accountable to no one. An *arbitrator* acts as an appointed judge or referee in a dispute referred to him by the parties. He may not act *arbitrarily*, but must abide by the rules of procedure and act judicially, and he is accountable to the appropriate authorities. *Arbiter* was taken over intact from Latin; *arbitrator* is from Late Latin, derived from *arbitratus*, past participle of the verb *arbitrari* (to judge, decide); and *arbitrary* and its adverb *arbitrarily* come from Latin *arbitrarius* (arbitrary, or uncertain—because dependent on an *arbiter's* decision). The Latin expression *arbiter elegantiae* (or *elegantiarum*) is the title of an *arbiter* of fashion and gracious living, an authority on elegance and matters of taste. The most famous of these was the Roman satirist Gaius Petronius (died c. 66), who, holding that position in the court of the Emperor Nero (37–68), was in charge of the imperial entertainments. He was known as Petronius Arbiter, famous for his own extravagant dinners and lavish entertainments, and for his satirical writings, chiefly the *Satyricon*, especially the story of *Trimalchio's Dinner*, a comic episode of vulgar display by a nouveau riche freed slave. See **agnomen**. The English essayist Sir Richard Steele (1672–1729), in *The Spectator*, wrote of "Fashion, the *arbiter*, and rule of right." The English poet Lord Byron (1788–1824), in his *Ode to Napoleon Bonaparte*, called him (after his exile) "The *Arbiter* of others' fate/A Suppliant for his own!" In *Paradise Lost*, the English poet John Milton (1608–1674) wrote that ". . . high *arbiter*/Chance governs all," and that ". . . overhead the moon/Sits *arbitress*," giving *arbiter* its feminine form *(-ess)*, a practice now decried by ardent feminists who object to poet*ess*, sculptr*ess*, Jew*ess*, etc. (but *actress* seems to some acceptable, and *countess, baroness, mistress* must be, as well as *lioness*?). Today's *arbiters* of fashion, like the American professional hostess (another -*ess*!) Elsa Maxwell (1883–1963), "society" columnists, self-appointed and -anointed social "leaders," and proprietors of the "in" spots like the once super-exclusive Studio 54 on New York's West side, have their brief spans of glory and soon fade away, while Petronius *Arbiter* lives on.

Arcadian (ar KAY dee un) *adj.* *Arcadian* (often with a lower case *a*) means "rustic, pastoral," and by extension "innocent, unspoiled." An *arcadian* life is one of happiness, peace, and simplicity. The name, according to mythology, came from Arcas, a son of the god Zeus. It was adopted by the English poet, soldier, and statesman Sir Philip Sidney (1554–1586) for his unfinished romance *Arcadia*, written in 1578–1580 and circulated only in manuscript while he lived. A simpler and complete original version appeared in print only in 1926. *Arcadian* has become a byword for bucolic bliss. Nonetheless, in a number of early paintings, there appears a tomb inscription reading "Et in Arcadia ego" (Even in Arcadia am I [death]). But away from that gloomy observation: the *arcadian life* is one of serenity and unalloyed joy. Do not confuse *Arcadia* with *Acadia*, scene of the famous poem *Evangeline* ("This is the forest primeval . . .") by the American poet Henry Wadsworth Longfellow (1807–1882), where life for the French settlers turned out to be anything but serene.

archetype (AR kih tipe) *n.* The *archetype* of anything is its original model, its prototype. In Latin, *archetypum* means "original," taken over from Greek *archetypon* (pattern, model), neuter of *archetypos*, based on prefix *arche-* (primitive) plus *typos* (mold). The English historian and statesman Thomas Macaulay (1800–1859) called the British House of Commons "the *archetype* of all representative assemblies." The adjective is *archetypal* (AR kih tye pul) or *archetypical* (ar kih TIP ih kul). The American novelist Sinclair Lewis (1885–1951) created an *archetype* in the novel *Babbitt*, whose protagonist of that name became the *archetype* of the smug American, a devout conformist who subscribes to conventional middle-class ideas of business success and material gains (*babbitt*, with a lower case *b*, has become a common noun denoting such a person), just as Casanova is the *archetypical* rake, Sherlock Holmes the *archetypical* detective (*sherlock*, too, is now a common noun),

52

Shylock the *archetypical* relentless moneylender (a *shylock* is a usurer), Lolita the *archetypical* nymphet, and Emma Bovary, the *archetypical* discontented, conceited self-glamorizing wife, whose name gave rise to the noun *bovarism* (BOH vuh riz um), signifying that type of self-delusion.

arctoid (ARK toyd) *adj.* *Arctoid* means "bearlike, ursine." There is a zoological superfamily known as the *Arctoidea* (ark TOI dee ah) that includes raccoons and weasels as well as bears. *Arctoid* is derived from the Greek noun *arktos* (bear), and an *arctophile* is a bear fancier, a lover of bears. The term has been extended to cover one who loves teddy bears, like Sebastian in *Brideshead Revisited*, by the English novelist Evelyn Waugh (1903–1966). *Teddy bears* were named after Theodore Roosevelt, whose nickname was *Teddy*. Legend has it that he spared the life of a bear cub while hunting. *Arktos* gave rise to the adjective *arktikos*, meaning "northern," literally "of the (Great) Bear," the most promiment northern constellation, whence *arctic*. *Arktos* is also the Greek name for the constellation *Ursa Major*, but in English it includes *Ursa Minor* as well. The bear is a symbol of Russia, especially the Northern Bear or "Russian Bear," beloved of political cartoonists. Trained bears figure prominently in Russian circuses. The Russians, generally speaking, are *arctophiles* (*arktos* plus -*phile*, dear, beloved). *Arktos* is also the basis of the name of the brightest star in the northern hemisphere, *Arcturus*, which you can find by following the curve of the tail of Ursa Major.

arctophile, see **arctoid**

arête (uh RATE) *n.* This is the geological term for a ridge with a very sharp crest, found in rough mountain country, especially the type that has been cut through by glaciers. *Arêtes* are common in the Alps. The word was taken from the French, which derived it from the Latin *arista*, which included among its several meanings "fish-spine." There is another word spelt the same way except for the absence of a circumflex and pronounced differently—a word that has nothing to do with ridges: *arete* (AIR uh tay, -tee), taken from the Greek, and signifying the sum of good qualities that together constitute character—courage, virtue, excellence. This word gave rise to *aretology* (air uh TOL uh jee), a tale of the great feats

53

of gods and heroes. *Arete* is related to the Greek verb *areskein* (to please, satisfy).

aristology (air is TOL uh gee) *n. Aristology* is the art and science of dining; from Greek *aristos* (breakfast, luncheon—the context, or fuller explanation, would determine which) plus *logos* (discourse). It is the gourmet, not the gourmand, who is interested in *aristology* and devotes time and effort to its practice. Petronius (see **arbiter**) and Lucullus (see **Lucullan**) were practitioners of *aristology* in ancient times; more recently, Brillat-Savarin, the French jurist, writer, and epicure (1755–1826), wrote a witty discourse on the art of dining, entitled *La Physiologie du Goût (The Physiology of Taste)*. And more recently than that, there was Auguste Escoffier (c. 1847–1935), who rose to be head chef at the Savoy in London, and invented peach Melba and other sensational dishes. All these people were *aristologists* (air is TOL uh jists); their interests and activities were *aristological* (uh ris tuh LOJ uh kul). Synonyms for *aristologist* more frequently met with are *epicure* and **gastronome**.

arras (AIR us) *n.* An *arras* is a wall hanging, especially a tapestry. The noun comes from the town of Arras, the capital of Pas-de-Calais in northeastern France, once renowned for the manufacture of tapestries. An *arras* is a convenient thing to hide behind; Shakespeare certainly thought so, and found it convenient as a dramatic prop in a number of his plays. In *Hamlet* (Act II, Scene 2), Polonius suggests to the King that, to test Hamlet's sanity, "Be you and I behind the *arras* . . ." to see how Hamlet acts when alone with Ophelia. It was behind the *arras* in Queen Gertrude's bedroom that Polonius hid, and was stabbed for his troubles. "Polonius hides behind the *arras*," reads the stage direction in Act III, Scene 4. Further directions: Gertrude calls for help, Polonius echoes her call and Hamlet "draws" and "makes a pass through the *arras*," then "lifts up the *arras* and discovers Polonius," the "wretched, rash, intruding fool." Falstaff hides behind an *arras* in *Merry Wives of Windsor* (Act III, Scene 3). He is in Ford's house, when Mistress Page approaches. Falstaff cries, "She shall not see me: I will ensconce myself behind the *arras*." In *King John* (Act IV, Scene 1), Hubert tells the two attendants who were to put out young Arthur's eyes, "Heat me these irons hot; and look thou stand/Within the *arras* . . ." And the *arras* figures in several other Shakespeare plays as well. Apparently, the *arras* was sometimes used for purposes other than as a wall hanging. The English poet William Cowper (1731–1800) wrote of "Stateliest couches with rich *arras* spread." Writing of her childhood in Knole, her vast, complex ancestral home in Sevenoaks, Kent, the English poet, novelist, and gardener extraordinary Vita Sackville-West (1892–1962) wrote a poem *To Knole* about her early wanderings around the great house on lonely days:

> My fingers ran along the tassels faded;
> My playmates moved in *arrases* brocaded;
> I slept beside the canopied and shaded;
> Beds of forgotten kings . . .
>
> I contemplated long the tapestries . . .

The *arras* is hardly ever used in interior decoration nowadays, and they don't come from Arras any more, but if you do run across one, you'll know what to call it.

arriviste   (air e VEEST) *n.* An *arriviste* is a very unpleasant character: an upstart, a pushy, aggressive person who manages to achieve his goal of power, money, status, or other type of what he considers success through unscrupulous methods; a self-seeker, a parvenu, always on the make. The word is taken from the French, where it is a general term for an unscrupulous careerist, whether or not he has as yet succeeded in "arriving." The American novelist John Hersey (b. 1914) wrote of "an impoverished family of high breeding and training that sneers self-consolingly at vulgar *arrivistes*." In *The English Companion* (Pavilion Books, London, 1984), the contemporary English novelist, editor and columnist Godfrey Smith (b. 1926) writes of Winston Churchill (1874–1965): "His closest friends—Beaverbrook, Bracken and Birkenhead—were known to his wife as the three terrible Bs. All were self-made men: adventurers and *arrivistes*."

artifact   (AR tuh fakt) *n.* Anything made or worked on by man is an *artifact*. A tree occurs in nature. When it is felled and the trunk is sawn into certain lengths and then one piece is carved by a sculptor and another made into a dugout canoe, both resulting objects are *artifacts*. So is a chair, a table, a rug, a lamp, a pin, a pen, a pan—obviously, the list is endless, because new *artifacts* are always being created. The term is usually applied to something relatively simple or small. One would not classify the *Empire State Building* or the *Queen Elizabeth II* as an artifact; they consist of a very great number of *artifacts*, including nuts and bolts. *Artifact* is derived from the Latin phrase *arte factum* (something made with skill). The dictionaries use terms like "made by man" or "product of human work," but how about a nest made by a bird or a dam made by beavers? They are certainly "made with skill." Should we not broaden the definition to include things made by any animal? Spiders' webs, bees' honeycombs? Make your own list. In any event, do not confuse *artifact* with *artifice*, which is quite a different story.

artifice   (AR tuh fis) *n.* An *artifice* is a trick, a ruse, a stratagem; *artifice*, generally, is cunning, trickery, guile, craftiness. You might think, then, that an *artificer* (AR tif ih sur) is a cunning, sly, tricky fellow, but you would err. An *artificer* (not a common word) is simply an inventor, a craftsman, a person clever in devising ways of making things, and not the least bit tricky or deceitful. *Artifice*, a much commoner word than *artificer*, is nevertheless a back formation from the latter. Strange are the ways of language. We have many *art-* words: *artful, artifice, artifact* (with which *artifice* should never be confused), *artificial, artisan, artless,* etc., all based on *art-*, the stem of Latin *ars*, whose principal meaning is "skill." An *artless* person is not, however, an unskillful one: he is simply straightforward, free from deceit, guileless. An *artful* person is full of guile, cunning and crafty, the opposite of *artless*. Remember the *artful dodger* in *Oliver Twist*? To get back to *artifice*: President Nixon's dirty tricks operators were masters of *artifice*. The *artifice* of the haggling casbah tradesman is a memorable experience for the *artless* Western tourist.

ascesis   (uh SEE sis) *n. Ascesis* is self-discipline, and can be used as a synonym of *asceticism. Ascesis* is one of those cases of an unfamiliar word that underlies a familiar one, here *ascetic* (uh SET ik). An *ascetic* is one who practices *ascesis*, i.e., gives up the normal pleasures of life, preferring the rigors of self-denial to the satisfactions flowing from material gain. As an adjective, *ascetic* describes such a person, one who pledges himself to rigorous abstinence. *Ascesis* is from Greek *askesis* (exercise, training); *ascetic* from Greek *asketikos* (hardworking), and they both go back to the Greek verb *askeein* (to work hard, discipline oneself). *Ascesis* is good for the body, good for the mind, good for society, and all too rare.

ashram (AHSH rum) *n*. This is a Hindi word, which you may run across in any one of today's spate of novels set in India. An *ashram* is a hermitage, a religious retreat for a colony of disciples, a place for religious instruction or exercises. *Ashrams* play an important part in the lives of millions of Hindus. The word comes from the Sanskrit *asrama* (place for religious exercises), based on prefix *a-* (towards) plus *srama* (fatigue, exertion). An *ashram* need not be a temple, but can be any meeting place where people congregate for exercise or religious teaching.

asinine,   see **accipitrine**

aspergillum (as pur JIL um) *n*. This word, not to be confused with *aspergillus* (as pur JIL us), is the name of the short-handed instrument bearing a brush or small perforated globe containing a sponge, used by clerics for sprinkling holy water. It comes from the Latin verb *spergere* (to sprinkle), the past participle of which, *aspersus*, gives us *aspersorium* (as pur SAW ree um), a synonym of *aspergillum*, and also the name for a holy water vessel. *Aspergillus*, on the other hand, is the botanical term for a fungus with a knoblike top bearing bristles that make it resemble an *aspergillum*. It causes certain animal diseases and we certainly don't want any of those in church! On the matter of confusion between words resulting from the change of a single letter, see **formication**, and the last sentence of **apothegm**.

aspine,   see **accipitrine**

asseverate (un SEV uh rate) *vb*. To *asseverate* something is to assert it earnestly, to declare it seriously, emphatically, solemnly, and with confidence. Our language got it from the Latin *adseveratus, asseveratus*, past participle of the verb *adseverare, asseverare* (to asset confidently, strongly), the *d* of the prefix *ad-* often changing to *s* before another *s*. The *-sever-* part is based on the Latin adjective *severus* (serious). In the criminal courts, the accused often *asseverates* his innocence. Elected officials *asseverate* that they will faithfully perform the duties of their office, uphold the Constitution, etc. The author of this book *asseverates* that he has run across these 1,000 words in the course of his reading, and not simply plucked them out of an unabridged dictionary—except for a very small number that stared him in the eye while he was consulting a dictionary in connection with one that had already challenged him!

asthenic   (as THEN ik) *adj. Asthenia* (as THEE nee uh), *n.*, is debility, weakness, loss of strength or vigor. One suffering from *asthenia* is *asthenic*, weak, narrow-chested, slender. *Asthenic*, describing a physical type, denotes slightness of build, as opposed to *athletic*, designating sturdiness and well-built body structure, and to *pyknic* (PIK nik), describing squatness, overweight, a rounded build characterized by a large belly, small hands and feet, short legs and neck and a round face. *Asthenic* comes from Greek *asthenikos* (weak), based on *a-* (not) plus *sthenos* (strength); *athletic* from Greek *athletikos*, based on *athleein* (compete for a prize—*athlos* means "contest"); *pyknic* from Greek *pyknos* (thick), having nothing to do with the picnic celebrated in the play by the American dramatist William Inge (b. 1913) or the painting by the French impressionist Edouard Manet (1832–1883), that type of outing (once described by a friend of the author as "organized discomfort") being derived from German *Picknick*, which came from French *pique-nique*, which appears to have come from nowhere. These derivations are no picnic! *Asthenic* and *pyknic*, standing alone, can be used as nouns designating the respective physical types. *Athletic* is not used as a noun. It is a comon adjective; the other two are not, and should be avoided in giving specifications to Hollywood Central Casting.

astride,   see **bestride**

asyndeton   (uh SIN dih ton, -tun) *n.* This is the grammatical term for the omission of a copulative (connecting: see **copula**) conjunction—usually *and*—a favorite, and rather unattractive rhetorical device in advertising copy. Example: "Smoothikreme will eliminate wrinkles, make you look years younger!" It would be hateful enough *with* the conjunction, but somehow is more so with *asyn-*

58

deton. The term comes from Greek *asyndetos* (not connected), based on negative prefix *a-* and *syndetos*, past participle of the verb *syndeein* (to link). One of the best known and most effective examples of *asyndeton* is Caesar's "Veni, vidi, vici." ("I came, I saw, I conquered.") Another one—a naval message from World War II—and a fine show of alliteration in the bargain: "Sighted sub, sank same." Great stuff, even if apocryphal. Still another: "Have gun, will travel." In these cases, as opposed to its use in advertising, *asyndeton* is most effective; the insertion of *et* in Caesar's message, or *and* in the naval flash, would have destroyed the dramatic impact. The opposite of *asyndeton* is *polysyndeton* (pol ee SIN dih ton), which is the use of a string of identical conjunctions in succession: "She has everything: youth and looks and money and talent!" Quite a girl. *Polysyndeton*, modeled on *asyndeton*, was formed, via Late Latin, from Greek prefix *poly-* (many) plus the same *syndetos*.

ataraxia (at uh RAK see uh), **ataraxy** (at uh RAK see) *n.* An idyllic state, one of complete serenity, free from anxiety, the cares of the world, or any sort of emotional upset. One thinks of the inhabitants of Shangri-la as enjoying *ataraxia* in their hidden paradise. The adjectives *ataractic* (at uh RAK tik) and *ataraxic* (at uh RAKS ik) are sometimes used to denote tranquilizing drugs. All these words come, via Latin, from Greek *ataraxia* (calmness); *ataraktos* means "undisturbed," based on the negative prefix *a-* plus *tarak-*, a variant stem of the verb *tarassein* (to disturb). *Ataraxia* was the state of calm and indifference sought as a goal by the Stoics, members of a philosophical school founded by Zeno about 300 B.C., which taught the rigid suppression of passions, self-indulgence, and unjust thoughts. The teaching of indifference to pleasure or pain led to the definition of *stoical* as "impassive" with the implication of austere courage and submission without complaint to the inevitable hard knocks of life. That's *ataraxia*.

atrabilious (a truh BIL yus) *adj.* We know about *bile*, the name of the liver secretion that helps in the digestion of fats (if your liver is working properly) and its figurative meaning of "ill temper," and the adjective *bilious*, dealing with excessive secretion of the stuff and the consequent suffering, and also figuratively used for both "peevish" and "extremely distasteful." We then come to

59

atrabilious, describing one who is simply dejected, or actively irritable, wrathful, bad-tempered—the context should make it clear which is meant. *Atra* is the feminine form of the Latin adjective *ater* (black—dead black, as opposed to *niger*, glossy black); add *atra* to *bilis* (bile; by extenstion, anger) and you get *atra bilis* (literally, black bile; metaphorically, melancholy, dejection). A variant form is *atrabiliar* (a truh BIL yur) and the condition is *atrabiliousness*. The English novelist and poet Aldous Huxley (1894–1963)—he of *Brave New World*—wrote, in *The Ninth Philosopher's Song*:

> Then brim the bowl with *atrabilious* liquor!
> We'll pledge our Empire vast across the flood:
> For Blood, as all men know, than water's thicker,
> But water's wider, thank the Lord, than Blood!

atticism   (AT ih siz um) *n. Atticism* (often with a lower case *a*) is concise, superior, polished discourse and diction. The adjective *attic* describes elegant, subtle, incisive expression and articulation, with a strong admixture of subtle wit. The English poet John Milton (1608–1674) wrote:

> What neat repast shall feast us, light and choice,
> of *Attic* taste . . .

and the Roman rhetorician Quintilian (c. 35–c. 95) praised the *Attic* style in these terms:

> The distinction between *Attic* and Asiatic orators is of great antiquity, the *Attic* being regarded as compressed and energetic in their style, the Asiatics as inflated and deficient in force.

Attica was the name of a region in the southeasterly part of ancient Greece. It was under the rule and influence of Athens, whose culture reached its height around the middle of the fifth century B.C.—the age of Pericles, the great poets, dramatists, sculptors and architects. The Roman historian Pliny the Elder (23–79) wrote of "sal atticum" (Attic wit—literally, Attic salt; *sal* (salt) was used figuratively by the Romans to mean "wit"). *Attic* wit is dry, delicate, subtle wit. The Romans had a verb *atticisare* ("atticise") to describe the imitation of Athenian diction and expression. *Atticism*, then, is the art of the elegant, well-timed expression, refined simplicity laced with sophistication and wit. In more modern times, the distinction between these two styles has been described in a learned article by Bryan A. Garner in Volume X, No. 3 of *Verbatim, The Language Quarterly*, which includes this passage:

> English inherited two strains of literary expression, both deriving ultimately from Ciceronian Latin. On the one hand is the plain style now in vogue, characterized by unadorned vocabulary, directness, unelaborate syntax, and earthiness. (This style is known to scholars as Atticism.) On the other hand we have the grand style, which exemplifies floridity, allusiveness, formal sometimes abstruse diction, and rhetorical ornament. Proponents of this verbally richer style (called Asiaticism) proudly claim that the nuances available in the "oriental profusion" of English synonyms make the language an ideal putty for the skilled linguistic craftsman to mold and shape precisely in accordance with his conceptions.

Well may you ask, what has this to do with the *attic* of a house, the room or story just under the roof? Here is the answer: In the residences of the rich in old *Attica*, there was often a small row of columns or **pilasters** placed on the roof, as a decorative feature. Neo-Grecian architecture became fashionable in England in the 17th century. In error, the top floor of a building fashioned in the *Attic* style was called the "Attic storey" (*story* meaning "floor of a house," has an *e* before the *y* in British English). Error, because the *Attic* feature was a façade, whereas the English imitation was an enclosed floor. In time, the upper case A became a small *a*, the "storey" was dropped, and we wound up with, simply, *attic*.

Augean, see **herculean**

aulic (AW lik) *adj. Aulic* describes things pertaining to a royal court. It comes from the Greek adjective *aulikos* (courtly), based on *aule* (court, hall). The English poet and writer Walter Savage Landor (1775–1864) wrote of "Eccelesiastical wealth and *aulic* dignities." In 1501, Maximilian I of the Holy Roman Empire established the *Aulic* Council, which acted as a supreme court. There aren't many *aulic* activities these days, because there aren't many courts any more. When Elizabeth II of England receives an ambassador, creates knights, dames, or barons, and distributes other

New Year or Birthday Honours, or gives a state dinner, the goings-on can be described as *aulic* activities.

autarchy; autarky (AW tar kee) *n*. Although some authorities consider these **homophonic** words interchangeable, they mean different things, are differently derived, and should be kept separate. *Autarchy* is absolute sovereignty, and *an autarchy* is an autocratic government. An *autarch* (AW tark) is an absolute ruler or tyrant. *Autarky* means "self-sufficiency," and is a term aplied to a nation that is economically self-sufficient, not dependent on foreign trade or help from any foreign government. Both words are derived from Greek: *autarchy* from *autarchia* (self-rule), based on the noun *archos* (ruler), *autarky* from *autarkeia* (self-sufficiency), based on the verb *arkeein* (suffice). *Autarch* is from *autarchos* (autocratic). In all these words, the prefix *aut-* is a shortened form of *auto-* (self-, a prefix we see in many English words, like *automatic, automobile*, etc.). Although their use is not common, it is well to understand their difference in meaning and derivation on the rare occasion of meeting one or both of them.

autism (AW tiz um) *n*. *Autism* (from Greek *autos*—self) is a morbid mental conditon that causes withdrawal into a private world of fantasy and prevents communication with the real world. The adjective is *autistic* (aw TIS tik), often found in the term *autistic child*, because the condition appears to affect children especially; they lose contact with reality, and seem unable to respond to their environment, or to grasp objective actuality. No determination has been made of the cause of this pathological condition, nor has any cure been discovered.

autochthon (aw TOK thun) *n*. An *autochthon* is an aborigine, one of the original, or at least earliest recorded, inhabitants of a region, like the aboriginal tribes of America. In the field of ecology, the term *autochthon* covers the native flora and fauna of a region. The adjective is *autochthonous* (o TOK thuh nus), meaning "indigenous" or "native." *Autochthon* is Greek for "of the land itself," based on the prefix *auto-* (self, same) plus *chthon* (earth, land). Other *-chthonous* words are *allochthonous* (uh LOK thuh nus), using the Greek prefix *all-*, from *allos* (other), and *heterochthonous* (het uh ROK thuh nus), using the Greek prefix *hetero-*,

62

from *heteros* (other). Both these words mean "foreign, not indigenous." *Allochthonous* is found in geological studies of minerals and rocks originating in one place but found elsewhere as a result of the movement of the earth's crust (see **tectonics**). *Heterochthonous* is often used in the field of biology, in discussions of foreign flora and flauna, not native to the region.

avifauna (ay vuh FAW nuh) *n.* The *avifauna* of an area consists of the birds native to that region. *Avi-* is a Latin prefix, from *avis* (bird), and our word *fauna*, denoting the animal life native to a given area, is from Latin *Fauna*, a goddess, sister of *Faunus*, a mythological deity of the forests. The fauna of a region (*fauna* being the wider term) includes, of course, the *avifauna*. *Piscis* is Latin for "fish," and, logically enough, the *piscifauna* is the fish life of a given region, also included in the general term *fauna*.

avine, see **accipitrine**

bacchanal (BA kuh nal) *n.* Bacchus (BAK us), also known as Dionysus (dye uh NY sus), was the god of wine in classical mythology. He lent his name to the noun *bacchanal*, which usually denotes an orgy or a drunken revel, but the word can also mean "drunken reveler," though it is not commonly used that way. *Bacchanalia* (bak uh NAY lee uh, -NALE yuh) was the name of an ancient triennial festival in honor of Bacchus, but is now used with a lower case *b* to denote any drunken party, not necessarily a sexual orgy, but accidents can happen. The adjective *bacchanalian* (bak uh NAY lee un, -NALE yun) can describe activities all the way from orgiastic or debauched to less serious goings-on, like merely uninhibitedly festive shenanigans, usually involving the consumption of large quantities of intoxicating beverages. A related word, *bacchant* (BAK unt) also means "drunken reveler," and with an -*e* added, a female of that category. The most common of all these words related to the god Bacchus is *bacchanalian*, and it usually applies to what the Sunday supplements used to call "wild parties," a term that covered a multitude of sins.

bacchant(e), see **bacchanal**

bahuvrihi (bah hooh VREE hee) *n.* A *bahuvrihi (nice word!)* is a compound noun or adjective consisting of two parts, an adjective and a noun, the combination describing someone or something characterized by what is denoted by the noun element. Complicated? Not so very; here are some examples: *bluebell* (the flower), *bonehead, hard-hearted, redcoat* (a British soldier in the American revolution), *redhead, yellowlegs* (an American shore bird). *Bahuvrihi* is a Sanskrit (an Indo-European Indic language that goes back to the 13th century B.C. as a literary language of India) word meaning, literally, "with much rice," based on *bahu-* (much) plus *vrihi* (rice), and is itself a model of a *bahuvrihi.* The author apologizes if this discourse seems too *heavy-handed* (another example) an exposition. The English poet Gerard Manley Hopkins (1844–1889) used a *bahuvrihi* in his poem *Felix Randal*:

> Felix Randal the farrier, O is he dead then?
> My duty all ended,
>   Who have watched his mold of man, big-boned
> and hardy-handsome,
>   Pining, pining.

Big-boned is the *bahuvrihi; hardy-handsome* doesn't qualify.

ballyrag (BAL ee rag), **bullyrag** (BOOL ee rag) *vb.* To *ballyrag* or *bullyrag* someone is to harass or abuse him, in the more violent sense of the word, or less dramatically, to tease him. Fowler says that the derivation is unknown, and that *ballyrag* is the far more common and preferable form, but other dictionaries give *bullyrag* as the first choice. To *rag* someone is to tease him, in American usage, but in British usage, to do rather more than that: to persecute him with crude practical jokes, with *rag* also a noun denoting that kind of tormenting behavior. The *bullyrag* form probably has some connection with *bully,* embellished by *rag.* In any case, *bally-* or *bullyragging* is reprehensible abusive horseplay and badgering, the kind employed, for example, in the sort of fraternity hazing that is a practice now mercifully fading from the scene.

basilisk (BAS uh lisk, baz-) *n.* This was the name, in ancient mythology, of a deadly creature, represented from time to time as

64

a dragon or serpent, claimed by the ancients to have been hatched by a serpent from the egg of a cockatrice (of which more later). It could kill by its breath or gaze. Nowadays, the term is applied in zoology to certain tropical lizards who can run upright, even across the surface of water, at dizzying speeds, and to a species of wren, and figuratively, to an "evil eye," especially in the context of a person who can "kill" one's reputation, like a malicious critic or a lethal gossip. In *The Faerie Queene*, the English poet Edmund Spenser (c. 1552–1599) wrote that:

> The Basilisk . . .
> From powerful eyes close venim doth convey
> Into the lookers hart, and killeth farre away.

Basilisk comes, via Late Latin *basiliscus*, from Greek *basiliskos* (princeling), diminutive of *basileus* (king). There are adjectives *basciliscine* (bas uh LIS in, -ine, baz-) and *basiliscan* (bas uh LIS kuhn, baz-). There is a theory that the use of *basilisk* to denote certain animals, like the lizards and wrens (a species called "kinglets") mentioned above, all of whom have crownlike crests, harks back to the crowns of the kings and princelings of ancient times. Kin to the *basilisk* is the *cockatrice*, also a monster of fable, common in heraldic art, a composite beast endowed with wings, a dragon's tail, and the head of cock. Isaiah says (11:6-8): "The wolf shall dwell with the lamb . . . the sucking child shall play on the hole of the asp . . . and the weaned child shall put his hand on the *cockatrice'* den . . ." (i.e., the most dangerous of creatures shall not harm the weakest of God's children). But the misogynous English dramatist John Gay (1685-1732), in *The Beggar's Opera*, warns:

> Man may escape from rope and gun;
> Nay, some have outliv'd the doctor's pill:
> Who takes a woman must be undone,
> That *basilisk* is sure to kill.
> The fly that sips treacle is lost in the sweets,
> So he that tastes woman, woman, woman,
> He that tastes woman, ruin meets.

Thus, *basilisk* and *cockatrice* have been used to designate a treacherous, evil person bent on destruction. Shakespeare was keenly aware of the *cockatrice's* power, like that of the *basilisk*, to kill with a look. In *Twelfth Night* (Act III, Scene 4), Sir Toby Belch has engineered a duel (that will never occur) between the cowardly Sir Andrew Aguecheek and the terrified Viola [see reference to this in **clodpoll**] and describes each to the other as a mortally dangerous adversary. He says, "This will so fright them both that they will kill one another by the look, like *cockatrices*." In *The Rape of Lucrece*, Shakespeare describes the ominous Tarquin as "Here with a *cockatrice'* dead-killing eye . . ."; in *Romeo and Juliet* (Act III, Scene 2), Juliet speaks of " . . . the death-darting eye of *cockatrice* . . ." in Richard III (Act IV, Scene 1), the Duchess of York, King Richard's mother, cries:

> O! my accursed womb, the bed of death,
> A *cockatrice* hath thou hatch'd to the world,
> Whose unavoided eye is murderous.

Gorgons were no fun, either: their glance turned their victims to stone. Someone with a good working knowledge of the ways of *basilisks, cockatrices,* and Gorgons must have invented the expression, "If looks could kill . . . !"

bathysiderodromophobia   (bath ee sid uh roh droh moh PHO bee uh) *n.* This **sesquipedalian** jawbreaker denotes a subdivision of claustrophobia: the dread of subways (undergrounds, in Britain), wholly independent of the terror of the violence that has become characteristic of them. In the same way that **floccinaucinihilipilification** was built of bits and pieces of Latin, this word was put together from a series of Greek elements. This is how it works: *bathys* (deep); *sidero-*, from *sideros* (iron); *dromo-*, from *dromos* (running); *-phobia*, from *phobos* (fearing). That is, *fear of* deep, i.e. *underground*, iron, *i.e. rail*, running, i.e. *way*. Doubtless, in view of what has been happening in the New York subways, this phobia (usually defined as "obsessive or irrational fear or anxiety") doesn't seem all that irrational any more, merely somewhat enhanced.

battology   (buh TOL uh jee) *n.* This is the word for tiresome, excessive, useless, futile repetition in speech or writing. Never, please never, and I mean never—but never!—indulge in *battology*.

The word comes from Greek *battologia* (stuttering). To be guilty of this wearisome exercise is to *battologize* (buh TOL uh jize), which also includes the equally annoying, needless, and tiresome repetition of mannerisms. The perpetrator is known as a *battologist* (buh TOL uh jist) and the adjective describing the offending person or his behavior is *battological* (bat uh LOJ ih kul). The origin of these words is said to be *Battos*, who, according to the Greek historian Herodotus (c. 484–c. 425 B.C.), implored the Delphic Oracle to tell him how to correct his stammer.

bedizened (bih DYE zund) *adj.* This word is a participal adjective, formed from the rarely encountered verb *bedizen*, to dress or adorn (someone) in a gaudy, showy, vulgar manner. To be *bedizened*, then, is to be dressed that way. The American essayist and novelist Kenneth Roberts (1885–1957) used it in that sense in describing a character as "a bold and shameless creature, *bedizened*, painted and overdressed." Although there is no logical reason why *bedizened* should not be applied to both sexes, the word seems always to evoke the image of a meretricious woman. Early movie vamps like Pola Negri, decked out in ropes of pearls and skirts of fringe and heavily made up, were prototypes of the *bedizened* woman, the shameless hussy. The American producer of musicals Florenz Ziegfield (1867–1932) bedecked his ladies of the ensemble in an exaggeratedly *bedizened* manner, utilizing lots of feathers and glittering fake jewelry in their outfits. The word has an interesting origin. We start with the common prefix *be-* used in the formation of verbs like *bedeck, befriend, belittle,* add *dizen*, an archaic verb meaning "adorn with finery," which itself comes from *dis-* (based on Low German *diesse*, meaning "bunch of flax on a distaff"—and thus we see the origin of *distaff* itself) and tack on the suffix *en*, used to form verbs from adjectives (*fasten, shorten, sweeten)* or from nouns (*heighten, lengthen, strengthen)*, and come up with *bedizen*. All that remains is to add the participial ending -*ed*, and voilà!

belated (bih LAY tid) *adj. Belated* is the adjective for anything that comes too late, that happens after the customary or expected time, like the *belated* birthday greetings you remember to send on the 14th to your friend whose 50th occurred on the 12th. You can buy cards with "Better late than never" on the outside and apologetic doggerel on the inside. A *belated* arrival at a dinner party can be very embarrassing. The adverb is *belatedly* (bih LAY tid lee). Mail often arrives *belatedly* nowadays. Shakespeare's great "seven ages" speech by Jaques in *As You Like It* (Act II, Scene 7) speaks of ". . . the whining school-boy . . . creeping like snail/Unwillingly to school," perhaps taking what the French call the "chemin des écoliers" (the roundabout way; literally, the schoolboys' route), and we get a picture of the little chap making a *belated* appearance, quailing before the angry schoolmaster. *Belated* is a combination of the prefix *be-*, used in the formation of verbs (e.g., *become, bedizen, befriend, bewitch*) plus *late* plus the *d* of the participial ending *-ed*. The verb *belate* (to delay) is itself archaic.

beldam   (BEL dum) *n.* A *beldam*, despite the look of the word (*belle dame* is "fair lady" in French) is a hag, an ugly old woman, or a shrew regardless of her age. Shakespeare used *beldam* in the now obsolete sense of "grandmother" in *The Rape of Lucrece:* "Time's glory is . . . /To show the *beldam* daughters of her daughter . . ." He used it in the modern meaning as well, in *Macbeth* (Act III, Scene 5), when the witches ask Hecate why she is angry and she answers: "Have I not reason, *beldams* as you are, /Saucy and overbold?" And in *King John* (Act IV, Scene 2), Hubert de Burgh tells the King about dreadful portents: "My lord, they say five moons were seen tonight . . . /Old men and *beldams* in the streets/Do prophesy upon it dangerously . . ." A man should never address his fair companion as "beldam"; it means the opposite of what it appears to mean.

benighted   (bih NYE tid) *adj.* A *benighted* person is unenlightened, intellectually barren, morally ignorant. The Dark Ages in Europe (from the fall of the Roman Empire to the beginning of the Middle Ages, i.e., from about A.D. 500 to 1,000) were in many respects *benighted* times, replete with crime and superstition. The word is a combination of the prefix *be-* (see **bedizened** for a discussion of *be-*), the noun *night* (in the figurative sense of "darkness") and the common suffix *-ed*, forming participial adjectives as in *crossed swords, belated news,* etc. The English author and poet Rudyard Kipling (1865–1936), in his famous *Fuzzy-Wuzzy* poem, had this to say:

68

So 'ere's *to* you, Fuzzy-Wuzzy, at your 'ome in the Soudan;
You're a pore *benighted* 'eathen but a first-class fightin' man . . .

In the poem *Comus*, the English poet John Milton (1608-1674) wrote:

. . . he that hides a dark soul and foul thoughts
Benighted walks under the midday sun . . .

(like mad dogs and Englishmen?). We would describe as *benighted* those poor teenagers whom the Ayatollah sends to their death in the war with Iraq, wearing the "key to heaven" around their necks.

besom (BEE zum) *n.* A *besom* is a broom, especially the sort one sees in the European countryside, made of dried twigs tied around a stick. Its derivation is from Middle English *besem*; cf. German *Besen* (broom). In Isaiah 14:22-23, we read of the Lord's anger against Babylon and its people: "For I will rise up against them . . . I will make it a possession for the bittern, and pools of water; and I will sweep it with the *besom* of destruction, saith the Lord . . ." *Besoms* are witches' favorite means of transportation. *Besom* sounds like a relic of bygone days, but *besoms* are by no means extinct and can be found in many an English and European home and shop. *Besom*, in the Scottish Lowlands, is slang for "prostitute" or "slut," and *jumping the besom* is the failure to go through with the marriage ceremony after the publication of the banns in the parish church as notice of an intended marriage. To *hang out the besom* is to lead a bachelor's life and sow some **belated** wild oats while one's wife is away on a visit. The French use the idiom *rôtir le balai* (literally, roast the *besom*) to mean "go on a spree, lead a fast life."

bestride (bih STRIDE) *vb.* When one spreads his legs on both sides of something, he is said to be *astride* (uh STRIDE) it. Under the headline SHOCK END TO CHARITY PARA JUMP in the May 16, 1984, edition of the (London) *Daily Telegraph*, we are advised that ". . . out of the 30 novices who descended on Northumberland from 2,000 feet, one woman broke a leg, another her ankle, and one man landed *astride* a bull." *Bestride* is the verb; *astride* a preposition, though it can also be used as an adverb or an adjective, to describe an action or a posture with legs apart, on either side of something—horse, fence, or, under certain circumstances, bull. *Bestride* is used in its literal sense when you mount and *bestride* a horse or a fence. In a figurative sense, to *bestride* is to tower over something, to dominate it. The name of Shakespeare *bestrides* the centuries. He used the word in a dramatic way, combining the literal and figurative senses. In *Julius Caesar* (Act I, Scene 2), Cassius complains to Brutus of Caesar's rise to glory:

> Why, man, he doth *bestride* the narrow world
> Like a Colossus; and we petty men
> Walk under his huge legs . . .

We find *bestride* again (in the alternative past tense *bestrid*; the usual form is *bestrode*) in *Antony and Cleopatra* (Act V, Scene 2). Antony is dead; Cleopatra, mourning him, laments to Dolabella:

> His legs *bestrid* the ocean; his rear'd arm
> Crested the world . . .

Remember the distinction: when you *bestride* something, you are *astride* it. Both words are based on *stride*, which comes from Middle English *striden*.

bête noire (bet nuh WAHR) *n.*, *adj.* This is a French expression (literally, *black beast*) taken into English to describe anything that is a pet aversion, a bugbear, a thorn in one's side. A *bête noire* can be a person, an object, a chore, anyone or anything that one simply can't stand. To a child, spinach can be a *bête noire*. The caption under a Carl Rose cartoon in the December 8, 1928, issue of *The New Yorker* (mother and child) reads:

> "It's broccoli, dear."
> "I say it's spinach, and I say the hell with it."

To some, Wagner may be a *bête noire*; to others, hard rock may qualify. Contemporary painting is a *bête noire* to countless thousands, nay, millions. Choose your own: ballet, corned beef and cabbage, Liberace, politicians, wine connoisseurs; long airplane trips, missiles, New Year's Eve parties, children in TV commercials, all TV commercials, books about words . . .

bibelot (BIB loh) *n.* A *bibelot* is a knick-knack or small curio; the word implies beauty or rarity or both. *Bibelot* is a word taken over from the French, and is not to be confused with *bauble* (BAW bul), which is a cheap, showy trinket or gewgaw (GYOOH gaw, GOOH-). *Bibelot* is the proper term for those mantel ornaments tourists pick up in their travels and like to strew around the house to remind them of their happy days in foreign and exotic places.

bibliobibulus, see **pecksniffian**

biblioclast, see **bibliopole**

bibliognost, see **bibliopole**

bibliogony, see **bibliopole**

biblioklept, see **bibliopole**

bibliomania, see **bibliopole**

bibliopegy, see **bibliopole**

bibliophage, see **bibliopole**

bibliophobe, see **bibliopole**

bibliopole (BIB lee uh pole) *n.* Most of us are familiar with *bibliophile* (lover and collector of books) and *bibliography* (compilation of books on a given subject). There are less familiar *biblio-* words, like *bibliopole*, a bookseller, especially one who deals in secondhand and rare books, derived from Greek *bibliopoles* (bookseller), made from the common Greek prefix *biblio-*, based on *biblion* (book) and suffix *-pol*, based on *polesthai* (to sell). Since books play such an important role in our lives, it is not surprising that our language contains a large number of *biblio-* words, with suffixes based on Greek nouns or verbs. Here is a partial list: *biblioclast* (BIB lee uh klast), a multilator of books; *bibliognost* (BIB lee og nost), an expert on books; *bibliogony* (bib lee OG uh nee), book production and publishing; *biblioklept* (BIB lee uh klept), a book thief; *bibliomania* (bib lee oh MAY nee uh), immoderate zeal in the collection of books; *bibliopegy* (bib lee OP uh jee), book-binding; *bibliophage* (BIB lee uh faje), a bookworm; *bibliophobe* (BIB lee uh fobe), one who fears or hates books; *bibliotaph* (BIB lee uh taf), a book hoarder; *bibliotiks* (bib lee OT iks), handwriting and document analysis to authenticate authorship. The plural of Greek *biblion* is *biblia*. The English essayist Charles Lamb (1775–1834) invented the words *a-biblion*, an "unbook" or "nonbook," based on the Greek negative prefix *a-* plus *biblion*. In "Detached thoughts on Books and Reading" he wrote:

> I can read anything which I call a book. There are things in that shape which I cannot allow for such. In this catalogue of books which are no books—*biblia a-biblia*—I reckon Court Calendars [this is a reference to the Royal Court, not legal courts], Directories . . . the works of Hume, Gibbon, Robertson, Beattie, Soame Jenyns, and, generally, all those volumes which 'no gentleman's library should be without'.

He disagreed with Thomas Jefferson (1743–1826), who wrote to a friend in 1771, providing a list that should be in "a gentleman's library"—a long list, containing books on law, history, religion, and the "fine arts," including Pope, Dryden, Shakespeare, Congreve, Voltaire, Rousseau, and Molière. In any event, if you are a *bibliophile* or suffer from *bibliomania*—but certainly not if you are a *biblioklept* or a *biblioclast* or a *bibliophobe*—seek out a good, reliable *bibliopole*. See also *bibliobibulus* under **pecksniffian**.

bibliotaph, see **bibliopole**

bibliotiks, see **bibliopole**

bicameral (bye KAM ur ul) *adj.* This is a term used in government to describe a legislative system consisting of two houses, an upper and a lower, like the Senate and the House of Representatives, which together constitute the Congress of the United States. The United Kingdom has a *bicameral* system, the House of Commons and the House of Lords, and other countries have two legislative chambers as well, but the powers of the respective houses and the relationships between them vary from nation to nation. *Unicameral* (yooh nuh KAM ur ul) applies to a system consisting of only one branch or chamber. *Bi-* and *uni-* are prefixes taken from Latin, and *camera* is Late Latin for "chamber." (Cf. *bicycle* and *unicycle*.) The *bi-* in *bicameral* is a true *bi-*, unlike the *bi* in bikini, which was mistaken for the prefix meaning "two," so that when daring ladies discarded the bra, the residual scanty nether covering was erroneously touted as the "monokini"!

bifurcate (BYE fur kate) *vb.*, *adj.*; (BYE fur kit) *adj. Bifurcate*, the verb, is both transitive and intransitive: to *bifurcate* a road is to fork it into two branches; a road or stream so divided can be said to *bifurcate*. The adjective *bifurcate* describes any road or stream thus divided, and the process is *bifurcation* (bye fur KAY shun). *Bifurcate* comes from Middle Latin *bifurcatus*, past participle of *bifurcare*, based on prefix *bi-* (twice) plus *furca* (fork). Apart from its principal use in connection with roads, there is a philosophical term, *bifurcation theory*, signifying the division of reality into two parts, the world as it exists in the mind and the external world as it exists in actuality.

billingsgate (BIL ingz gate) *n. Billingsgate* is foul and abusive language, coarse invective. The word comes from Billingsgate, London, for hundreds of years the site and name of a fish market where fish sellers and porters were notorious for their foul, coarse language. The market was near a gate in the old city wall named after a property owner, Billings. To *talk billingsgate* (sometimes capitalized) is to indulge in vituperation and vilification. The women who worked there were particularly offensive; from the Middle English *fisshwyf* we get *fishwife*, a term applied to coarse, vituperative, foul-tongued women who belie the traditional gentility of their sex. These lines appear in *The Plain Dealer*, a play by the English poet and dramatist William Wycherley (c. 1640–1716):

> QUAINT: With sharp invectives—
> WIDOW: Alias, *Billingsgate*.

birrellism, see **obiter dictum**

bisontine, see **accipitrine**

bissextile (bye SEKS til, bih-) *adj.* A *bissextile* year, commonly known as a "leap year," is one of 366 days, containing a February 29. The *bissextus* (bye SEKS tus, bih-) is February 29 itself. The

73

extra day is added to our regular calendar year every fourth year except for centenary years (those ending in -00) not evenly divisible by 400 (e.g., 1700, 1800, 1900—in this connection you might like to refer to the entry **aliquot, aliquant**). The extra day in a *bissextile* year, also known as an "intercalary" day (see **intercalate**), is added to make up for the difference of approximately one-fourth of a day between the 365-day year (also known as a "common year") and the astronomical year of approximately 365.25 (to be exact, 365.2422) days, the time it takes for the earth to travel its elliptical course around our sun. The difference between 365.25 and 365.2422 is made right by the loss of three days in the 400-year period between each pair of consecutive centenary years not evenly divided by 400. The word *bissextile* doesn't have a thing in the world to do with bisexuality. It comes from Late Latin *bissextilis*, based on *bissextus*, based in turn on Latin *bis* (twice—the French still shout "Bis!" at concerts in place of "Encore!") and *sextus* (sixth). But why? Because in the old Julian calendar (reformed by Pope Gregory XIII, 1502–1585, to become the calendar now in use, called "Gregorian" after that innovative Pope), instead of adding a day at the end of February, the Romans had two February 24s; and February 24 was the sixth day before March 1 (the Calends of March), which in their calendar was New Year's Day—which explains why our tenth, eleventh and twelfth months are named after the Latin for *eight* (octo), *nine* (novem), and *ten* (decem). The *annus bissextus* was the year *(annus)* when the sixth *(sextus)* day before March 1 occurred twice *(bis)*. Hence, *bissextus* (twice sixth). If all this astronomical discussion is too complicated, just remember that leap year is the time when it is proper for ladies to propose marriage to gentlemen, and let it go at that.

bivouac   (BIV ooh ak, BIV wak) *n. Bivouac* is a military term for an improvised encampment in the open air, usually consisting of tents, exposed without protection to enemy fire. To *bivouac* is to set up such an arrangement. *Bivouac* was taken over intact from the French, which got it from Swiss German *Beiwacht*, now *Biwak* in modern German. Though *bivouac* is a technical term in military parlance, it has been used jocularly to denote any point of assembly. "Where shall we *bivouac* for tea, darling?" You may want to decline the invitation from one taking such liberties with the language. The American poet Theodore O'Hara (1820–1867) wrote

The Bivouac of the Dead to commemorate the American soldiers fallen at the battle of Buena Vista during the Mexican War of 1847:

> On Fame's eternal camping ground
> Their silent tents are spread,
> And Glory guards, with solemn round,
> The *bivouac* of the dead.

bloviate   (BLOH vee ate) *vb*. To *bloviate* is to declaim or orate longwindedly and bombastically. Doesn't it sound that way? Blowhards *bloviate*, and doubtless the *blo-* of *bloviate* has something to do with *blowing*, as in blowing your own horn or blowing a blast on a wind instrument or blowing off, in the sense of "talking boastfully" and at great length. It was characteristic of Southern senators, old style, to *bloviate*, often to empty Senate chambers. Commencement speakers sometimes have a tendency to *bloviate*; a waggish friend has commented that the ending is preferable to the commencement. Motto for speakers: Don't *bloviate*.

bolt   (bohlt) *vb*. *Bolt* has a great many meanings, as a noun, a verb, both transitive and intransitive, and even as an adverb (e.g., *bolt* upright), but one meaning as a verb may be unfamiliar: to "sift," usually through fine-meshed cloth; and a *bolter*, in this context, is such a sieve. The common use of both verb and noun is in the sifting of flour or meal, where *bolt* has the force of "refine" or "purify" through the sifting process. To *bolt* can also mean to "examine" through sifting, as in a laboratory, in a situation where larger and smaller particles have to be separated. *Bolt* has been used figuratively as well, as it was by the English journalist and pamphleteer Sir Roger L'Estrange (1616–1704), who wrote: "Time and nature will *bolt* out the truth of things." This brings to mind the aphorism of the Roman philosopher and dramatist Seneca (c. 4 B.C.–A.D. 65): "Time discovers truth." The old proverb, "Truth is the daughter of time," inspired the English novelist Josephine Tey (1897–1952) to entitle her novel in defense of Richard III *The Daughter of Time*, a book that will enlighten those misled by the libels of the English chronicler Holinshed (or Hollingshead—take your choice: died c. 1580), Sir Thomas More, the English statesman (1478–1535), later canonized, and William Shakespeare. My, how far we've come from *bolt*!

bombilate (BOM buh late), also **bombinate** (BOM buh nate) *vb.* To *bombinate* or *bombilate* is to hum, buzz, drone, or boom; taken from Middle Latin *bombilare/bombinare* (to buzz), based, via Latin *bombus*, on Greek *bombos* (hum, boom, or deep, hollow sound, especially of trumpets), where we also get *bomb*, which booms rather than hums, except that the buzz-bombs of World War II did both over England. Flies and mosquitoes annoy us by *bombilating* or *bombinating* continually, while the *bombilation* of bees, for some reason, is a rather pleasant sound. After all, the bees are extremely useful, while one wonders why flies and mosquitoes were ever put on earth. If one said that the sound of a loud buzz-saw was an *abombinable* noise, one would undoubltedly and perhaps deservedly be greeted with the groans that customarily accompany **paronomasias**.

bombycine, see **accipitrine**

bonhomie (BON uh mee) *n.* This word, taken from the French (where it is pronounced bo no MEE), means "geniality, straightforward good nature, open-hearted friendliness." The French based *bonhomie* on the noun *bonhomme*, denoting a simple, good-natured fellow, sometimes with an implication that he may be too simple for his own good, overly credulous, something of a schlemiel; but there is no such implication in the English use of *bonhomie*. The related adjective *bonhomous* (BON uh mus) is little used, and rightly so, for it has an unpleasant sound, though it might be helpful in a limerick involving *anonymous*. There is a very nice **clerihew** built around *bonhomie*:

> John Stuart Mill
> By a mighty effort of will
> Overcame his natural *bonhomie*
> And wrote 'Principles of Political Economy'

boniface (BON uh fase) *n.* A *boniface* is an innkeeper. *Boniface* was the name of the jovial innkeeper in *The Beaux' Stratagem*, a comedy by the Irish playwright George Farquhar (1678–1707) which was produced in the last year of his young life. Farquhar wrote in the period of the British Restoration, and was the author of a series of rather licentious comedies notable for their flowing natural dialogue. There had been a hearty innkeeper named *Bonifazio* in the comedy *La Scolastica* by the Italian poet Ludovico Ariosto (1474–1533), and there would appear to have been a connection between that Bonifazio and Farquhar's Boniface. The success of Farquhar's last comedy and masterpiece was so great that the name *Boniface*, at first associated with only hearty, jovial innkeepers, acquired a lower case *b* and was eventually applied to any innkeeper, whatever his disposition.

bonnyclabber   (BON ee klab ur) *n.* Bonnyclabber, sometimes shortened to *clabber*, is thick sour milk, naturally clotted as it turns, a kind of buttermilk, a very refreshing drink, they say. The derivation is from two Irish words: *bainne* (milk) and *claba* (thick), related to *clabair* (clapper, or churn paddle). It wasn't to the taste of the English poet Ben Jonson (c. 1573–1637), who wrote, in his poem *The New Inn*:

> It is against my freehold, my inheritance,
> My Magna Charta, *cor laetificat*,
> To drink such balderdash or *bonny-clabber*!
> Give me good wine!

Magna Charta (or Carta) was the "Great Charter" of rights and liberties forced by the Barons from King John of England in 1215 at Runnymede; it became a symbol of civil liberties, like our Bill of Rights. *Cor laetificat* is Latin for "It gladdens my heart." *Balderdash*, which now means "nonsense, senseless twaddle," once was the name for a worthless mixture of liquors, a meaning now obsolete. To rare Ben Jonson, *bonny(-)clabber* must have been used in the generic sense of any unpalatable potion.

bosky   (BOS kee) *adj.* When you come across a woody bit of country, covered with shrubs, you are in a *bosky* place. *Bosk* is an archaic word for a small thicket of bushes, and comes from Middle English *boske* or *buske*, from which we get *bush*. *Boskage* or *boscage* (BOS kij) means "thicket" or "grove" but is rarely used. The Scottish novelist and poet Sir Walter Scott (1771–1832, famous for *Ivanhoe*, the dreaded reading requirement of high school students), wrote of traveling "through *bosk* and dell," and the American author Henry James (1843–1916) described "long *bosky*

77

shadows" in a country scene. The British use *bosky* in a wholly unrelated colloquial sense for "tipsy." On a hot, sunny day, it is pleasant to find a *bosky* spot and relax in the shade. If you should suggest such a maneuver to a companion who is not familiar with *bosky*, say "Tut-tut!" and refer your uncultured friend to Walter Scott and Henry James. There is a related verb, to *embosk* (em BOSK), which denotes the act of shrouding or hiding something, someone, or oneself with greenery, foliage, or plants, the way some people like to *embosk* a summerhouse with vines, or themselves in a leafy recess or arbor, or a bower intertwined with climbing vines.

boustrophedon (booh struh FEE don, bou-, booh STRAHF eh don) *adj.*, *adv.* Based on the Greek noun *bous* (ox) plus the verb *strephein* (to turn), this word applies to writing, as in early Greek inscriptions, where the lines run alternately in opposite directions, i.e., from right to left and left to right. That is the way an ox turns as it ploughs—in rows that alternate in direction. Nowadays, when a word processor types from a disc, the typing moves that way but in the alternate lines running from right to left, the spelling is in reverse so that it all reads left to right in the end. It works the same way in the Semitic countries where the reading is from right to left. This type of writing is referred to by name in *Justine*, the first novel in *The Alexandria Quartet*, by the English novelist Lawrence Durrell (b. 1912), as the method used by an Egyptian secret society. It is sometimes referred to as "serpentine" writing.

bovarism, see **archetype**

bowdlerize (BOHD luh rize; BOUD-) *vb.* To *bowdlerize* a writing, such as a play, a novel, a history, an essay, a speech, is to expurgate it, particularly in a priggish, prudish, squeamish way. The word, together with the related group—*bowdlerist, bowdlerizer, bowdlerization, bowdlerism,* etc.—comes from the English editor Thomas Bowdler (1754–1825), famous or, better, notorious for his ten-volume expurgated edition of Shakespeare, as well as his "cleaned-up" editions of the Bible and the monumental six-volume *History of the Decline and Fall of the Roman Empire* by the English historian Edward Gibbon (1737–1794), usually referred to as "Gibbon's Decline and Fall." Bowdler described his edition of Shakespeare as one "in which nothing is added to the original

78

text; but those words are omitted which cannot with propriety be read aloud in a family.'' There have been *bowdlerizing* authorities in more recent days, like the Hays Office, which held sway over the censorship of American films, and the Lord Chamberlain's Office which did the same to English stage productions—both authorities now happily consigned to history. Over the years, there have been other censorship bodies in the form of watch and ward societies formed for the purpose of guarding the morals of communities. "Lay on, Macduff, and darned be him . . ." etc. ?

brabble   (BRAB ul) *n.*, *vb.* *Brabble* is loud, acrimonious wrangling. To *brabble* is to engage in quarrelsome arguments, usually stubborn ones, about trifles. We get this word from the Dutch verb *brabbelen* (to wrangle). In Shakespeare's *Titus Andronicus* (Act II, Scene 1), the Moor Aaron, beloved of the evil Tamora, Queen of the Goths, comes upon her sons Demetrius and Chiron, both smitten with Lavinia, Titus's daughter, wrangling and threatening each other. Aaron exclaims:

> Away, I say!
> This petty *brabble* with undo us all . . .
> For shame, be friends . . .

And in *King John* (Act V, Scene 2), the Dauphin, after listening to the Bastard's long plea for peace, says:

> We grant thou canst outscold us: fare thee well;
> We hold our time too precious to be spent
> With such a *brabbler* . . .

Brabble has an almost onomatopoeic sound.

braggadocio   (brag uh DOH shee oh) *n.* *Braggadocio* is boasting, bragging, vainglorious talk; a *braggadocio* is a braggart. *Brag* goes back to the Middle English noun *brag* and verb *braggen*. *Braggadocio* comes from a character named *Braggadocchio* in *The Faerie Queen* of the English poet Edmund Spenser (c. 1552–1599), a braggart who is really a coward at heart. He invents all sorts of glories for himself, but is eventually unmasked and sneaks off amid jeers. Spenser formed the name from *brag*, adding the suffix *-ade*, often used in forming nouns of action, and then the Italian augmentative suffix -*occhio*. Cf. **fanfaronade, gasconade, rodomontade, thrasonical**.

brannigan (BRAN uh guhn) *n*. This word has two distinct meanings. A *brannigan* is a drinking spree. To go on a *brannigan* is to go on a bender, of the lost weekend variety. *Brannigan* is also the name for a row, a squabble, usually over a difference of opinion. Town councils sometimes get into a *brannigan* over the route to be followed by a proposed new road, or the location of the new town hall. *Brannigan* is a not unusual surname, with an Irish sound, and the likelihood is that the common noun stems from the proper one, but let's not get into a *brannigan* about the derivation of the word.

brattice (BRAT is) *n*., *vb*. A *brattice* is a partition of wooden planks or strong tarred cloth, known as *brattice-cloth*, forming an air passage or shaft lining to ventilate a mine, and the verb to *brattice* is to provide a mine with such a system. The wall of separation in a mine shaft or gallery deflects air toward the locations where the miners are working. The word is from Middle Latin *bretescia* or *bratascia*. In olden times, *brattice* was the term applied to a wooden tower used in siege tactics, or a roofed gallery on the wall of a castle that commanded the wall-face below, for nice activities like pouring down boiling oil and that sort of fun.

bravura (bruh VYOOR uh) *n*. In music, *bravura* denotes either the florid style that shows off the technical artistic skill of a virtuoso, or the showy piece or passage itself that demands tremendous spirit and dash in execution. The American novelist Washington Irving (1783–1859) wrote of "listening to a lady amateur skylark it up and down through the finest *bravura* of Rossini or Mozart." The English novelist and essayist Maurice Hewlett (1861–1923) wrote of "that careless fling of the voice, that happy rapture, that *bravura* which makes the listener's heart go near to burst with . . . joy." *Bravura* characterizes brilliant coloratura singing but can apply to brilliance and dexterity in instrumental playing as well, and the music requiring it. *Bravura* can be used as an adjective as well, as in a *a bravura performance*. Apart from its technical use in music, *bravura* can apply to any daringly brilliant or dashing display, as in acting. Anyone who remembers the exploits of Douglas

Fairbanks, Sr. (1883–1939) in the old movies was indeed treated to exhibitions of theatrical *bravura*. Soldiers of fortune lead lives of *bravura*, which is an Italian word meaning "skill, deftness, bravery, spirit"—the kind of performance that elicits shouts of "Bravo!" But never confuse *bravura* with *bravado*, which is an ostentatious, pretentious show of defiance and swagger, and not nearly as nice as *bravura*.

bretelle   (brih TEL) *n.* A *bretelle* is a shoulder strap, one of a pair of ornamental suspender-type attachments to the front and back of a garment. Via the French, it comes all the way from Old High German *brittil* (bridle), and one can easily trace the etymological development. *Bretelles* are sewn to the back of the garment and fastened, usually clipped rather than buttoned, to the front of the waistband. Nowadays, they're called shoulder-straps or suspender-straps; "bretelles" won't get you very far in a children's shop today. They are found principally on little boy's short pants, up to age four, and little girl's skirts, up to age eight, and can be plain or ornamental.

brobdingnagian,   see **lilliputian**

brummagem   (BRUM uh jum) *n., adj.* As an adjective, *brummagem* describes anything showy but shoddy, inferior, worthless; as a noun, it denotes a showy, inferior, worthless object. *Brummagem* is an old local variant of *Birmingham*, the second largest city of England, in the northwestern part of the county of Warwickshire, where inferior trinkets, toys, imitation jewelry and the like were once manaufactured in quantity. The name was first applied to a counterfeit coin made in Birmingham in the 17th century, and was later applied to the miscellaneous output of shoddy articles produced there. The first syllable, *brum-*, resulted from a transposition of the letters of the first syllable of *Birmingham* and the corruption of the rest of the name. *Brum* is occasionally used as a nickname for *Birmingham*, and can also denote the Birmingham dialect, one extremely hard to follow, not only for Americans but also for Britons from other parts of the country. A limerick invented by the late Royal Ballet conductor and composer Constant Lambert (1905–1951) begins:

There was a young lady of Birmingham
Who paraded the streets with a dirmingham.

Those familiar with *Brum* as a slang name for *Birmingham* were meant to recognize the nonsense word *dirmingham* as a back formation (of sorts) from *drum*!

bubaline, see **accipitrine**

buteonine, see **accipitrine**

Byzantine (BIZ uhn teen, -tine; bih ZAN tine) *adj.* Literally, this adjective describes anything having to do with Byzantium, an ancient Greek city on the Bosporus, rebuilt in 330 by the Roman Emperor Constantine I (288–337), who named it Constantinople after himself; it was renamed Istanbul in 1930. Based on the complex and labyrinthine political maneuvering that surrounded old Byzantium, the adjective *Byzantine* has come to apply to any activity of a devious and surreptitious nature, or at least so intricately involved as to give that impression. The operations of the intelligence departments of governments are *Byzantine* in the extreme, so much so that it is often very difficult, if not impossible, to follow the novels about spies and counterspies and double agents which make such compelling, if not always entirely clear, television series. It is also enormously difficult to sort information out of the *Byzantine* complexity of government records. Tourists in eastern countries are familiar with the *Byzantine* tactics of the merchants of the casbah.

caballine, see **accipitrine**

cachinnate (KAK uh nate) *vb.* To *cachinnate* is to laugh raucously, immoderately, convulsively. The word comes from *cachinnatus*, past participle of the Latin verb *cachinnare* (to laugh loudly). The adjective to describe such laughter is *cachinnatory* (kak uh NATE uh ree); the noun is *cachinnation* (kak uh NAY shun). One might guess that *cachinnation* and *cackle* are etymologically related. Not so: *cackle* is of Middle English origin, *cackelen*, cognate with Dutch *kakelen*. The American naturalist and essayist John Burroughs wrote of someone who "*cachinnated* till his sides must have ached." *Cachinnate* is not precisely an onomatopoeic word, but there is something in the sound of it (the identity with the pronunciation of the first syllable of *cackle*?) that suggests laughter.

cacodemon, see **cacoepy**

cacodoxy, see **cacoepy**

cacoepy (kuh KOH ih pee) *n. Cacoepy* means "incorrect pronunciation"; *orthoepy* (or THOH ih pee) means "correct pronunciation." These words are from Greek *kak(o)epeia* and *orth(o)epeia* respectively; *kakos* (bad) gives us the prefix *caco-*, as, e.g., in *cacophony*, while *orthos* (straight) gives us the prefix *ortho-*, as in, e.g., *orthodox*. There is a group of *caco-* words that go back to *kakos*: *cacography* (kuh KOG ruh fee), bad handwriting or spelling, from *kakos* plus *graphein* (to write); *cacology* (kuh KOL uh jee), bad choice of words or incorrect pronunciation, from *kakos* plus *logos* (word). Apart from writing, spelling, and pronunciation, *cacodemon* (ka koh DEE mun) is an evil spirit or a malicious person, from *kakos* plus *daimon* (spirit); *cacodoxy* (KAK oh doks ee), wrong opinion, incorrect doctrine, from *kakos* plus *doxa* (belief); and *cacoethes* (kak oh EE theez), an irresistible urge, from *kakos* plus *ethos* (habit). There are a couple of strange hybrid (Greek-Latin) expressions: *cacoethes loquendi*, the irresistble urge to speak (*loquendi* is a form of the Latin verb *loqui*, to speak); and *cacoethes scribendi*, the irresistible urge to write (*scribendi* is a form of the Latin verb *scribere*, to write), sometimes called the "itch to scribble," an affliction that has undoubtedly played a large part in the production of this book.

cacoethes, see **cacoepy**

cacography, see **cacoepy**

cacology, see **cacoepy**

Cadmean (kad MEE un) *adj.* This adjective means, literally, "pertaining to Cadmus," a figure in Greek mythology, the Phoenician prince who introduced the alphabet to Greece. The adjective is found in the expression *Cadmean victory*, one of disastrous cost to the victor. Cadmus slew the dragon that guarded the Fountain of Dirce, near Thebes in Boeotia, and then planted its teeth, from which the Sparti, fully armed warriors, sprang intending to kill Cadmus, but he threw a precious stone into their midst, and they, fighting among themselves to gain possession of it, killed one another except for five survivors, with whom Cadmus founded Thebes. Hence, a *Cadmean victory* is one gained at tragic cost, like the costly victory won against the Romans by King Pyrrhus of Epirus at Asculum in 279 B.C., in the course of which he lost the flower of his army. "One more such victory and I am lost," cried Pyrrhus, thus originating the phrase *Pyrrhic victory*, a goal attained or a victory gained, like Cadmus's, at too great a cost. *Cadmean* and *Pyrrhic* victories aren't worth winning.

caducity (kuh DOOH sih tee, -DYOOH-) *n. Caducity* is another word for senility, the infirmity of old age, frailty. Another distantly related meaning is "transitoriness." It comes, via French *caducité* (decrepitude), based on French *caduc* (broken-down, frail, perishable—and therefore transitory), from the Latin verb *cadere* (to fall). The etymologically related adjective *caducous* (kuh DOOH kus, -DYOOH-) is a term used in branches of biology. In zoology and botany, it describes parts that tend to fall, like the leaves of deciduous trees, or to shed, like the skin of snakes; in other words, parts that are lost but are renewed in the natural cycle (and are therefore "transitory"), without reference to decrepitude or senility.

caducous, see **caducity**

calligraphy (kuh LIG ruh fee) *n. Calligraphy* is used in a variety of ways that relate to its Greek origin, *kalligraphia*, based on *kallos* (beautiful) and *graphein* (to write): beautiful penmanship, fancy, highly decorative handwriting with flourishes of the sort common in Victorian and earlier times—the kind seen in old deeds and other documents—and the word can denote the art of beautiful penmanship itself. In contemporary usage, however, it has one meaning that ignores the *kallos* part of its Greek origin: simply, "handwriting," as opposed to printing or typing. The *calligraphy* found in

18th-century manuscripts is often a work of art in itself. When this author was very young, one studied *calligraphy* (called "penmanship") in elementary school; the favorite system was the "Palmer method." Somewhere along the line, with a fine disregard for the etymology of *calli-*, *calligraphy* came to be used simply as a learned synonym for *handwriting*, whether beautiful or a scrawl resembling hen tracks.

callipygian (kal uh PIJ ee un), **callipygous** (kal uh PYE gus) *adj*. Both forms of this adjective describe a person (presumably female) endowed with beautiful, shapely buttocks; presumably female, at any rate, because of the fame of the *Callipygian* Venus, a marble statue of a female discovered in the Emperor Nero's Domus Aurea (Golden House) in Rome, now on show at the Museo Nazionale (National Museum) in Naples. The Greek adjective is *kallipygos* (having beautiful buttocks) based on *kallos* (beautiful) plus *pyge* (rump). It is a great asset to a woman to be *callipygian* or *callipygous*, and in this author's mind, there stirs the memory of the use of *callipygian* in some enthusiast's description of Gypsy Rose Lee (Rose Louise Hovick, 1914–1970), the **ecdysiast** who took her work very seriously.

calque (kawk) *vb*. Also **calk**. To *calque* is to make a copy of a drawing plan, etc., by the following ingenious method: You rub the back of what you want to copy with a coloring substance like chalk or pastel crayon, put a piece of paper or other surface beneath it, then pass a blunt needle or stylus over the lines to be copied so as to leave a tracing on the surface you have placed beneath what you want to copy, et voilà! We get *calque*, via French *calquer* (to trace) and Italian *calcare* (to trace, to trample), from the Latin verb *calcare* (to trample). This is a process somewhat similar to the "rubbing" technique described under **frottage**—the one relating to church floors, not the second one, relating to crowded subway cars!

came, see **quarrel**

cameline, see **accipitrine**

campestral (kam PES trul) *adj*. Also **campestrian** (kam PES tree uhn). *Campestral* is descriptive of anything relating to open country and fields, or any crop growing in level fields. The word is derived from the Latin adjective *campester* (flat, of level country), based on *campus* (level space, field, plain). Our word *camp* also comes from *campus* (an army would not ordinarily pitch a camp on other than level ground), and *campus*, the grounds of a university or other school, is simply the adoption of the Latin noun for a specialized use.

canine, see **accipitrine**

Canossa (kuh NOS uh; in Italian, kah NAW sa) *n.* As an entry in this book, the place-name *Canossa* is one of interest only in the phrase *go to Canossa*, which is a picturesque way of saying "humble oneself, undergo humiliation, eat humble pie," or less dramatically, "submit." Canossa, a hamlet in north central Italy in the Apennines, is the scene of a ruined castle once the home of the Canossa family who ruled over most of Tuscany in the 10th and 11th centuries. Pope Gregory VII was a guest at the castle in January 1077. He had excommunicated Holy Roman Emperor Henry IV during a political controversy between church and state. The Emperor humbled himself by going to Canossa and standing three days barefoot in the snow dressed as a penitent before being admitted into the pope's presence. The excommunication was withdrawn but the dispute soon flared up once more. Centuries later, when Chancellor of Germany Otto von Bismarck (1815–1898) was involved in a state-church controversy with Pope Pius IX, he refused to bend the knee and stated in the Reichstag (German parliament) in 1872: "Nach Canossa gehen wir nicht!" ("We shall not go to Canossa!"). Bismarck knew his history. A compromise was reached, and ever since, to *go to Canossa* is to yield, submit, give in, surrender, capitulate, bend the knee, throw in the towel, cry uncle. "Lay on Macduff, and damned be him who first" *goes to Canossa*.

capreoline, see **accipitrine**

caprine, see **accipitrine**

carapace (KAR uh pase) *n.* A *carapace* is the hard covering of all or part of the backs of certain animals, like the upper shell of a

86

turtle or the armor on the dorsal part of an armadillo. It is also known in zoology as a "shield" or "test," a word that has a special use in that field designating the protective shell or other hard covering of some invertebrates like sea urchins and starfishes. *Carapace* comes from the French, which got it from the Spanish *carapacho* (origin unknown—and the usual Spanish for *seashell* is *concha*). An animal equipped with a *carapace* is said to be *carapaced*, and the covering is described as *carapacic* (kar uh PAY sik) or *carapacial* (kar uh PAY shuhl). *Test*, in this context, is from Latin *testa* (shell or tile), and gives us *testaceous* (teh STAY shus), describing any animal bearing a shell or *carapace*.

carnassial (kar NAHS ee ul) *n.*, *adj.* This dental term describes a tooth adapted for the tearing of flesh. It is derived, via the French adjective *carnassier*, from *carn-*, the stem of the Latin noun *caro* (flesh), the same *carn-* as we find in *carnal*, *carnivore*, etc. As a noun, *carnassial* is known as a *scissor-tooth*. It is the largest premolar upper tooth of a carnivore. The term is used with respect to all carnivorous animals except man.

carphology,   see **floccillation**

carpology,   see **floccillation**

carrel (KAR ul) *n.* In olden times, a *carol* was a small enclosure in a cloister that served as a study, built against a window on the inner side. That word, now archaic, became *carole* in Middle English, and is the ancestor of our word *carrel*, which is a cubicle built into a library stack, used for individual study away from the madding, whispering, shuffling, coughing crowd in the general reading-room. It is sometimes spelt *carrell*.

cartography (kar TOG ruh fee) *n.* *Cartography* is the art of map-making, and one engaged in that activity is a *cartographer* (kar TOG ruh fur). *Cartomancy* (kar TOH muhn see) is fortune-telling based on the interpretation of playing-cards, and is as reliable as tea-leaf reading and the examination of palms. A *cartogram* (KAR toh gram) is a map in diagrammatic form showing statistical data. The first syllable of all these words is derived from the Latin *c(h)arta* and Greek *chartes* (sheet of paper); *cartograph* and *car-*

tograher add *-graph* and *-grapher*, respectively, from Greek *graphein* (to write). *Cartomancy* adds *-mancy*, from Greek *manteia* (**divination**). *Cartology* (kar TOL uh jee) is the science of maps, charts, etc., and adds the suffix *-logy*, common in the names of sciences (*geology, philology,* etc.), based on Greek *logos* (word, discourse).

cartomancy, see **cartography**

caryatid   (kar ee AT id) *n.* This is an architectural term for a sculpture of a woman in classical Greek dress, used as a column, as in one of the porches of the Erechtheum, the beautiful temple on the Acropolis at Athens. Greek architects likewise used *atlantes* (plural of *atlas,* in architectural parlance), also known as *telamones* (plural of *telamon*), male sculptures, for the same purpose. *Caryatid* has a sad and interesting derivation. It is from Greek *Karyatides* (columns in the figure of women; literally, women of Karyae, a city of ancient Laconia), so named because Karae sided with the Persian King Xerxes I (c. 519–465 B.C.) and his army at Thermopylae in 480 B.C., and after their defeat, the Greeks sacked Karyae, massacred all the men and took the women into slavery. The Greek sculptor Praxiteles (fl. c. 350 B.C.) symbolized the disgrace by using female figures as columns.

Cassandra   (kuh SAN druh) *n.* Cassandra is a figure from Greek mythology, the daughter of King Priam and Queen Hecuba of Troy, endowed by Apollo with the gift of prophecy. However, she refused his advances, and in revenge, he brought down upon her the curse that, though her prophecies invariably proved true, no one would ever believe them. Her name has become an epithet for a prophet of gloom, especially one whose dire predictions are disregarded. She is a character in Shakespeare's *Troilus and Cressida.* In Act V, Scene 3, she tells her father to hold back his son Hector from the war: "Unarm, sweet Hector," she begs and later, "Lay hold upon him, Priam . . ."

> He is thy crutch; now if thou lose thy stay,
> Thou on him leaning, and all Troy on thee,
> Fall all together."

Priam begs his son to go back: "Cassandra doth foresee . . ." Troilus says of Cassandra:

> This foolish, dreaming, superstitious girl
> Makes all these bodements [predictions].

Cassandra predicts Hector's death and the fall of Troy; she's right; no one believes her. A *Cassandra*, then, is one who prophesies doom, usually to a heedless audience; the very antithesis of a Pollyanna, the irrepressibly optimistic heroine of the 1913 novel of that name by the American writer Eleanor Hodgman Porter (1868–1920). "Don't be a Cassandra, always looking on the dark side of things!" people will exclaim, without realizing that Cassandra's predictions of disaster and doom were right on the money.

catachresis (kat uh KREE sis) *n. Catachresis* covers a group, if not a multitude, of sins: the misuse or wrong application of a word, attempting to give it a meaning that it does not have; stretching or straining the meaning of a term; the use of a word in an erroneous form arising from popular eytmology. Examples of misuse: a *chronic* illness when one means a *severe* one (an illness can be chronic without being severe); a *mutual* friend instead of a *common* friend (if you and someone have a friend in common, there is nothing mutual about it); **restive** when one should say *restless* (*restive* implies impatience with restraint or control, not general unquiet, unease or unsettledness). Stretching the meaning: the use of *alibi* for *excuse* (*alibi* should be confined to a defense in criminal law by way of proving that the accused was somewhere other than the scene of the crime at the time of its commission—its use for *excuse* in general is what Fowler calls "slipshod extension"). Erroneous folk etymology: *crayfish*, and its variant *crawfish*, are not fish at all, but rather, small lobster-like crustaceans, that got the name from Middle English *crevis*; a *demijohn* is not a "half-john," there being no such measure as a "john"; it is a large bottle with a short, narrow neck, named, so they say, after a certain Dame Jeanne who had that unfortunate shape; a *Jerusalem artichoke* has nothing to do with that great city, but acquired its name from the Italian *girasole articiocco*, an edible sun-flower that *turns* (in Italian, *gira*) with the *sun* (in Italian, *sole*, as in *O sole mio!*). This type of *catachresis* is not really a wrong usage but rather a usage based upon a false derivation. *Catachresis* itself is derived from *katachresis*, Greek for "misuse," built from *kata* (against) and *chresis* (use).

catamite   (KAT uh mite) *n.* A *catamite* is a boy kept by an older man for pederastic purposes, or, in language less clinical, as a young lover. Such a companion was known in Latin as a *catamitus*; the word was a corruption of *Ganymede*, the Greek name of the cup-bearer of Zeus. Ganymede, in classical mythology, the successor of Hebe, daughter of Zeus and his wife Hera, was the personification of youthful male beauty. A Trojan youth, he was carried up to Olympus and made immortal. A recent (1983) police raid in England upon the premises of an organization formed for the purpose of rounding up young boys for training as *catamites* netted a large group of middle-aged members. De gustibus . . . The keeper of a *catamite* is known as a *pedophile* (PEE duh file, PED-), the name for an adult having sexual desire for a child, and this condition is labeled *pedophilia* (pee duh FIL ee uh, -FEEL yuh, ped uh-). The first syllable of these words may also be spelt *paed-; pedo-* and *paedo-* words are based on the Greek prefix *paido-*, from *paid-*, the stem of *pais* (child)—except for a few *pedo-* words (e.g., *pedology, pedometer*) based on *ped-*, the stem of Latin *pes* (foot). The novel *Earthly Powers* (Simon & Schuster, New York, 1980) by the English writer Anthony Burgess (b. 1917), opens: "It was the afternoon of my eighty-first birthday, and I was in bed with my *catamite*, when Ali announced that the archbishop had come to see me." Some opening!

catawampus,   see **goluptious**

catechumen   (kat uh KYOOH mun) *n.* In church parlance, a *catechumen* is a neophyte, a person being instructed in the basic principles of Christianity. In the days of the early Christian church, the term applied to a converted heathen or Jew taking instruction preparatory to baptism. Figurately, *catechumen* has been extended to cover anyone being taught the rudiments of any subject. *Catechumen* is derived from Late Latin *catechumenus*, taken from the Greek *katechoumenos* (a person receiving oral instruction), based on the verb *katechein* (to teach by word of mouth). We are more familiar with the word *catechism*, the question and answer book

90

containing a summary of the principles of Christianity, or the body of questions and answers used as a test in that field. The Late Latin name for the question and answers book was the *catechismus*. To *cathechize* (KAT uh kize) is to teach via the catechism, but here, too, the meaning has been extended to cover any close or excessive questioning, especially one invading the privacy of an individual.

cater-cousin (KAY tur kuz un) *n.* A *cater-cousin* is not a relative at all, but rather a close friend, an affectionate, intimate pal. The word is built from *cater* (provide food) and *cousin*, used in the extended sense in which we give that name to persons of like natures, tastes, proximity, etc., in the way we speak of our "Canadian cousins" or Harvard men refer to their "Yale cousins" (when they're not insulting them). The *cater-* part indicates the mutual assistance aspect of close and loving friendship, in which the parties *cater* to each other's needs. In Shakespeare's *Merchant of Venice* (Act II, Scene 2), Launcelot Gobbo, Shylock's servant, beseeches Bassanio to take him into service, complaining of what a hard master Shylock is. Gobbo, Launcelot's father, pleading his son's case, tells Bassanio: "His master and he, saving your worship's reverence, are scarce *cater-cousins* . . ." In other words, Shylock and Launcelot weren't what you'd call loving friends.

caterwaul (KAT ur wol) *n.*, *vb.* To *caterwaul* is to screech or howl, like a rutting cat, or to engage in a brawl the way fighting cats do. *Caterwaul* is also used as a noun to depict any screeching session, but the form *caterwauling* is more common. This onomatopoeic word comes from Middle English *caterwawen*, based on *cater* (tomcat) plus *wawen* (to howl). The rarely seen English verbs *waul* and *wawl*, variants of *wail*, must enter into the etymological picture as well. Shakespeare was fond of the word, using it in almost identical lines in both a comedy and a tragedy. In *Twelfth Night* (Act II, Scene 3), Sir Toby Belch, Sir Andrew Aguecheek, and the Clown are carrying on, talking loudly and singing late at night in a room in Countess Olivia's house, when her maid Maria breaks in, crying: "What a *caterwauling* do you keep here!" In *Titus Andronicus* (Act IV, Scene 2), when the nurse, holding the black baby in her arms, cries to the Moor Aaron: " . . . we are all undone. Now help, or woe betide thee evermore!" he replies: "Why, what a *cauterwauling* dost thou keep!" *Cauterwauling* is a good word to describe the sound of a calliope, or the sound of two bands too near each other in a parade, or the screaming of the young guests at a children's birthday party. There are times when the angry exchanges between nations at the U.N. degenerate into a *caterwauling* of accusation and venom (but better to let off steam than bombs).

cathartine, see **accipitrine**

causerie (koh zuh REE) *n*. A *causerie* is a chat or, more often, a brief, informal, or light-hearted essay or article on a literary subject or another of the arts. It is a word taken into our language from the French, where, too, it is used to mean a "chat" or "gossip," and in its other use, a "chatty essay," often in the nature of a review. *Causerie* goes back to the French verb *causer* (to chat), and that in turn stems from the Latin verb *causari* (to plead in court), based on *causa* in the sense of "lawsuit." The term originated with the "Causeries de Lundi" ("Monday Chats"), a weekly series of newspaper criticisms during the years 1851 to 1862 by Charles Augustin Sainte-Beuve (1804–1869), the French literary critic and historian. In our own day, the weekly series "On Language" by William Safire in *The New York Times Magazine* might well qualify as *causeries* and, though not on literature or the arts generally, so might the "Observer" columns of Russell Baker in the same newspaper. A critic friendly to this author has attached the same label to these brief dissertations on words, but that may be stretching a point or a definition.

cavil (KAV uhl) *n.*, *vb*. To *cavil* is to carp or quibble, to raise picayune, inconsequential, and usually irritating objections, to offer gratuitous criticisms, to find fault for the sake of finding fault. As a noun, a *cavil* is that sort of annoying trivial objection, a bit of pointless carping, that adds nothing but irritation. In Latin, *cavillari* means to "scoff" or "jeer," the nouns *cavilla* and *cavillatio* mean "raillery," and a *cavillator* is a quibbler; *cavilla gratia cavillae* (like *ars gratia artis*, as it were). In Shakespeare's *Henry IV, Part 1* (Act III, Scene 1) there is a furious argument between Hotspur and Owen Glendower about the division of some land, and Hotspur cries:

> I do not care: I'll give thrice so much land
> To any well-deserving friend;
> But in the way of bargain, mark ye me,
> I'll *cavil* on the ninth part of a hair.

Note *cavil on*; nowadays it's *cavil at* or *cavil about*. The Irish statesman and writer Edmund Burke (1729–1797) condemned "*cavilling* pettifoggers and quibbling pleaders." Lawyers are known to *cavil* tirelessly and endlessly at the terms of an agreement.

cenotaph, see **sarcophagus**

cento (SEN toh) *n. Cento*, adopted from the Latin, which took it from the Greek *kentron* (patchwork), is the technical name for a work, usually a poem, composed by piecing together the writings of earlier writers or poets. On occasion, the meaning of *cento* has been extended to include any conglomeration or string of commonplace phrases and quotations. Sometimes the *cento* is built from the writings of one author in a way that creates a new meaning; sometimes passages from a variety of writers are used. This was a frequent practice in ancient Greece and Rome, after the golden age had passed. The Roman poet Ausonius (c. 310–c. 395), author of travel poems and family sketches, composed a marriage poem from selected verses of Virgil (70–19 B.C.), the foremost of Roman poets. Ausonius actually concocted a set of rules for the composition of *centos*. There were *Homerocentos* made up of passages from the Greek epic poet Homer (8th century B.C.), the *Cento Virgilianus* using verses from Virgil, and hymns consisting of lines from the *Odes* of the Roman lyric poet Horace (65–8 B.C.). Nobody worried about plagiarism in those days, apparently. In any event, the exploited poets weren't around to do any complaining.

centripetal (sen TRIP ih tul) *adj. Centripetal* describes anything that is being forced inward toward a center or an axis, as opposed to *centrifugal*, describing anything being forced outward, away from a center or axis. The term *centripetal force* denotes a force moving something toward the center or axis around which it is moving, and *centrifugal force* is one directing something away from the center or axis. A boat or a swimmer unfortunate enough to be caught in an eddy would be forced toward the center and tend to be sucked down, while a penny on a turntable would be whirled off by *centrifugal force*. *Centripetal force* directs the movement of eddies and whirlpools. *Centripetal* is derived from New Latin *centripetus* (seeking the center), based on *centri-*, the combining form of Latin *centrum* (center), plus the Latin verb *petere* (to seek). *Centrifugal* uses the Latin verb *fugere* (to flee).

cerebrate (SER uh brate) *vb*. To *cerebrate* is to use the mind, to think, or, in **transitive** use, to think about. *Cerebration* (ser uh BRAY shuhn) is the working of the brain. *Unconscious cerebration* is the term used in psychology to describe the reaching of mental results without conscious thoughts. The American novelist Henry James (1843–1916), in *The American*, wrote of "the deep well of *unconscious cerebration*." Both verb and noun are derived from Latin *cerebrum* (brain), which has been taken into English (SER uh brum; suh REE bruhm), to denote the front part of the brain, which controls voluntary movements and coordinates mental activity. In *The Human Comedy*, the American historian James Harvey Robinson (1863–1936) wrote: "Political campaigns are designedly made into emotional orgies which endeavor to distract attention from the real issues involved, and they actually paralyze what slight powers of *cerebration* man can normally muster." Note Robinson's date of death—many years before television served to exacerbate the situation. How timely his words are in this year of our Lord 1988!

cerulean (suh ROOH lee uhn) *adj*. *Cerulean* is the color deep blue or azure, derived from Latin *caeruleus* (blue), based on *caelum* (sky). The name "bluestocking" was given, in the mid-18th century, to intellectual, literary women with scholarly interests and ability. According to the Scottish biographer James Boswell (1740–1795) in his *Life of Dr. Johnson*, there were "bluestocking clubs" which met for intellectual and literary enlightenment with leading figures of the London literary scene and were always attended by a Mr. Stillfleet, a leading conversationalist who always wore blue stockings. Some of the women affected them in place of the conventional black silk, thus giving rise to the colloquialism *bluestocking*, later often shortened to *blue*. Jocularly, *blue*, in this sense, came to be referred to as "cerulean," heaping jocularity upon jocularity—good, clean fun among the **literati**—if you can bear it.

94

Nowadays, the term is applied merely as a color, and not too commonly at that.

cervine, see **accipitrine**

cetacean (sih TAY shun) *n.*, *adj.* A *cetacean* is a member of the Cetacea, an order of marine mammals that includes whales, dolphins, and porpoises; and *cetacean* is the adjective for any of those creatures. *Cetus* or *cetos*, from Greek *ketos*, is Latin for any large creature of the sea, such as whale, dolphin, seal, etc., and is the basis for the zoological order and our noun and adjective. *Cetacean* has been used in a figurative sense to describe mammoth objects, like a huge hill or mountain looming in the distant haze. A hangar of immense proportions will house one of these *cetacean* 747s whose shape suggests the humpbacked whale.

chaffer (CHAF ur) *n.*, *vb. Chaffer* is haggling, dickering, hard bargaining, and to *chaffer* is to engage in those activities. Anyone who ventures into a shop in a North African casbah will soon be deeply involved in *chaffer. Chaffer* is used as well for "chatter" or "bandying words," quite apart from the element of trading or haggling. It comes from Middle English *chaffare*, derived from *chapfare* (trading journey), based on Old English *ceap* (trade, bargain—from which we get *cheap*) plus *faru* or *faran* (journey—from which we get *fare*). According to the author's *British English, A to Zed* (Facts On File, 1987), the British used to use the noun *chapman* for "peddler" (which they spell *pedlar*) and still use *cheapjack* for "hawker" at a fair, and as an adjective for "shoddy" (the kind of goods hawkers at fairs usually offer). The *chap-* in *chapman* and the *cheap-* in *cheapjack* both come from the Old English *ceap* mentioned above.

charadrine, see **accipitrine**

charivari, see **shivaree**

chiaroscuro (kyah ruh SKYOOR oh) *n. Chiaroscuro* is the use and effect of gradations of light and shade in a picture, especially when there is a pronounced contrast. *Chiaroscuro* can produce dramatic and emotional effects in the hands of a master like the Dutch painter Rembrandt (1606–1669), whose use of *chiaroscuro* produced a sublime effect. In his masterpiece *The Night Watch*, his genius for the production of space and form through the use of *chiaroscuro* reaches the heights of this technique. *Chiaroscuro* is an Italian word, made up of *chiaro* (light—from Latin *clarus*) and *oscuro* (dark—from Latin *obscurus*). We get *clear* and *obscure* from these Latin words as well. One can speak of the *chiaroscuro* of a scene in nature, like a forest that admits a mottled light, or mountains lit here and there through breaks in the clouds. *Chiaroscuro* has been used figuratively in discussions of literary works, as a term descriptive of the juxtaposition of contrasting moods. In another figurative use, *chiaroscuro* can be employed attributively, meaning "half-hidden, half-revealed," as in a *chiaroscuro explanation* or *report*, full of half-truths, with gradations of revelation and concealment.

chiliast, see **millenarian**

ch(e)irognomy (kih ROG nuh mee) *n.* Without stopping to discuss old familiars based on the Greek noun *cheir* (hand), like *chiropody (-ist)* or *chiropractic (-tor)*, there is a group of less common *chiro-* words (the *e* is normally omitted in America, as opposed to the practice in Britain) to which we may direct our attention. *Chirognomy*, adding Greek *gnome* (understanding) is palmistry. *Chirography* (kih ROG ruh fee), drawing on the Greek verb *graphein* (to write), is handwriting or penmanship, and a *chirographist* is a handwriting expert, the type important in authenticating documents and revealing forgeries. *Chiromancy* (KIH ruh man see), using the Greek noun *manteia* (**divination**), is another word for palmistry, foretelling the future by studying the hand, often practiced in a tent by a lady in multicolored garments.

chirography, see **ch(e)irognomy**

chiromancy, see **ch(e)irognomy**

choler (KOL ur) *n.* *Choler* is anger, irascibility, hotheadedness, irritability, and a person exhibiting these unhappy traits is said to be *choleric* (KOL ur ik, kuh LER ik). In Middle English and Middle Latin, *choler* was *colera*, and that, via Latin *cholera*, came from Greek *cholera*, which was the name of various intestinal diseases endemic in the Far East and all too often epidemic in other parts of the world. In Shakespeare's *King Richard II* (Act I, Scene 1), Bolingbroke and Mowbray are having a furious row in the presence of the monarch, and Richard says:

> Wrath-kindled gentlemen, be rul'd by me,
> Let's purge the *choler* without letting blood.

The English essayist Joseph Addison (1672–1719), writing in *The Spectator*, has this to say: "A reader seldom peruses a book with pleasure until he knows whether the writer of it be a black man or a fair man, of a mild or *choleric* disposition, married or a bachelor." (A strange observation; it certainly doesn't hold true today!) The Swiss poet and theologian Johann Kaspar Lavater (1741–1801), in his *Aphorisms on Man*, wrote: "Venerate four characters: the sanguine who has checked volatility and the rage for pleasure; the *choleric* who has subdued passion and pride; the phlegmatic emerged from indolence; and the melancholy who has dismissed avarice, suspicion and asperity."

chrestomathy   (kres TOM uh thee) *n*. A *chrestomathy* is a book containing a collection of selected passages, usually from the works of a single author, especially in a foreign language, for use in teaching and learning that language. They are in common use in high school and college foreign language courses. The word comes from Greek *krestomatheia*, based on *krestos* (useful) plus *math-*, a variant stem of *manthanein* (to learn). *Chrestomathies* based on the works of the French poet and fabulist La Fontaine (1621–1695) and the German poet, novelist, and dramatist Goethe (1749–1832) were used during this author's schooldays.

chthonic, chthonian,   see gnome

cicerone   (sis uh RONE ee, chee chuh-) *n*. A *cicerone* is a guide, especially the type that points out and explains to visitors the antiquities and history of a site. These guides are named after the Roman orator, statesman, and writer Cicero (106–43 B.C.) on the theory that a good, knowledgeable guide should have the information, education, and eloquence of a Cicero. One can hardly visit certain famous spots (the Pyramids, the Roman Forum, Fontaine-bleau, Pompeii) without being importuned by a host of *cicerones* (or *ciceroni*) who would be delighted, for a consideration, to show you around and tell you rather more than you wanted to know about the lore and curiosities of the place. But there are very good *cicerones* too, who do know their stuff and can really enlighten the visitor. Who can ever forget the *cicerone* of Italian origin at Versailles, an ardent admirer of Louis XIV, who pointed to the fourteen busts of Louis in the Hall of Mirrors and explained that they served the purpose of supporting the king's wigs. "Dat-a Looie, he's-a change-a da wig-a fourteen-a times a day; dat-a Looie, he was-a some-a boy!" That was more dramatic than anything else this author had ever heard about Looie.

ciconi(i)ne,   see **accipitrine**

Cimmerian   (sih MEER ee uhn) *adj. Cimmerian* is a poetic word for "dark and gloomy." In *The Odyssey* (XI, 14), Homer tells of the *cimmerians*, a people that lived in everlasting night in a land "beyond the ocean stream" where the sun never shines. In *L'Allegro*, the English poet John Milton (1608–1674) writes of the "dark *Cimmerian* desert" where he bids loath'd Melancholy to "ever dwell." Before Milton was born, the poet Edmund Spenser (c. 1552–1599) mentioned the "Cimmerian shades" in *Virgil's Gnat*. Because of the classial myth about a *Cimmerian* people dwelling in perpetual night, their name became a symbol of darkness and gloom, and the adjective has been used in the sense of "gloomy," intensely dark, cavernous" by later writers. There was an actual Cimmerian people, who dwelt on the shores of the Black Sea in southern Russia and gave their name to Crimea. They were driven out by invaders in the eighth century and scattered, but have left us the legacy of their name, evocative of deep, eternal, cavernous gloom and darkness.

cisalpine   (sis AL pine, -pin) *adj.* This adjective, like the others discussed below, was derived from one concocted by the ancient Romans from their point of view, which was exceedingly self-centered at the height of their imperial power. *Cis* is a Latin preposition meaning "on this side of," so that *cisalpinus* described anything on "this" (the Roman, naturally) side of the Alps, i.e., the southern side, and that gave us *cisalpine*. (*Cis Tiberim* means "on this side of the Tiber," *cis Rhenum* "on this side of the Rhine," the adjective *cisrhenanus* means that as well, and so on, always from the viewer's, speaker's, or writer's point of view.) *Cisatlanticus*, which gave us *cisatlantic*, applies to anything on "this" side of that ocean, depending on which way you're looking, and *cismontanus* gave us *cismontane*, describing what's on "this" side of whatever mountains are being referred to, and in Roman times, that almost always had to do with the Alps. Likewise, the Romans used their preposition *trans* (across, to the other side of) in the formation of *transalpinus* (beyond the Alps), *transmarinus* (beyond the ocean, overseas), and *transalpine*, *transmarine* and *transmontane*, the last of these existing also in the variant form *tramontane* (the Romans didn't like three-consonant combinations). *Tra(ns)montanus* (on the other side of the mountains) eventually acquired the meaning "foreign," and not surprisingly, that came to have the effect of "barbarous" as well. *Tra(ns)montanus* was used as a noun meaning "alien," and, where xenophobia exists (and where doesn't it?), that means "barbarian." For centuries, white people were known as "white devils" in China. *Ultra* is another Latin preposition meaning "beyond, on the far side of," and that combined to form the Middle Latin adjectives *ultramarinus* (beyond the sea), which gave us *ultramarine*, and *ultramontanus* (beyond the mountains), which gave us *ultramontane*. *Ultramarine* happens also to be used as a noun for a pigment originally made of powdered lapis lazuli and later certain other substances, and is also used as an adjective for "deep blue," probably using Latin *ultra* in the sense of "more than," i.e., deeper even than the blue of the sea. (This is only a guess.) Summarizing: *cisalpine* (this side of the Alps); *transalpine* (the other side of the Alps); *cisatlantic* (this side of the Atlantic); *cismontane* (this side of the mountains); *transmontane* and *ultramontane* (the other side of the mountains—what the bear saw when he went over the mountain?); *transmarine* and *ultramarine* (the other side of the ocean). *Transatlantic*, a familiar word, has come to describe anything not only on the other side of the Atlantic, but anything crossing or reaching across that body of water, like fame, success, an idiom, custom, or other cross-cultural aspect of life.

cisatlantic,   see **cisalpine**

cismontane, see **cisalpine**

clabber, see **bonnyclabber**

clamant (KLAY munt) *adj.* This adjective, derived from Latin *clamans*, the present participle of the verb *clamare* (to cry out), is synonymous with *clamorous* (KLAM ur uhs) in the sense of "noisy," but has the additional meanings of "urgent, pressing, insistent." Noisy, vociferous people can be described as *clamant*, but one may speak also of the *clamant* needs of the people, like those millions suffering in many parts of Africa today (1988). *Clamant* is a literary word, as is its noun *clamancy* (KLAY mun see), meaning "urgency."

clerihew (KLER ih hyooh) *n.* E. Clerihew Bentley (1875–1956), an English writer, invented a verse form consisting of a comic, usually nonsensical jingle composed of two rhyming couplets, with lines of unequal length and a complete disregard for meter. The first line is or contains the name of a notable person; the rest of the jingle tells a ludicrous tale about him, purporting, in a fanciful and often satirical way, to present the essence of his life and character. The first of these appeared in Clerihew's *Biography for Beginners*, published in 1905, and they came to be known as *clerihews*, with a lower case *c*. Two of his own favorites were:

> It was a weakness of Voltaire's
> To forget to say his prayers,
> And one which, to his shame,
> He never overcame.

> Sir Christopher Wren
> Said "I'm going to dine with some men.
> If anyone calls,
> Say I'm designing St. Paul's."

Here are some more:

> Henry Ford
> Has a secret hoard
> To which he adds a dime
> From time to time.

> It only irritated Brahms
> To be tickled under the arms.

What really helped him to compose
Was to be stroked on the nose.

George the Third
Ought never to have occurred.
One can only wonder
At so grotesque a blunder.

Others have attempted the form. A friend of the author, a specialist
in difficult rhymes, came up with:

Gilbert Keith Chesterton
Weighs, it must be confessed, a ton.
Too much grub,
That's the rub.
—Stephen Barr, Woodstock, N.Y.

And here is an anonymous one:

Johann Sebastian Bach
Was fond of sighing "Ach!"
Instead of saying "Guten Morgen"
He'd play his Toccata and Fugue on the organ.

cleromancy, see **divination**

cloaca (kloh AY kuh) *n.* A *cloaca* is a sewer; the use of the word,
taken over intact from the Latin, implies that an ancient sewer is
involved. Another meaning, though rare, is "privy," and in zoology, *cloaca* is the name of the common chamber or cavity into
which the intestinal, urinary, and generative canals discharge in
birds, reptiles, some fish and other animals. The adjective is *clo-
acal* (kloh AY kul). In ancient Rome, the main sewer was known
as the *Cloaca Maxima*, constructed to drain marshland at the foot
of the Capitoline and Palatine hills. *Cloacina* (kloh uh SYE nuh)
was the Roman goddess of sewers (sewers had gods too!). The
English dramatist and poet John Gay (1685–1732), remembered
today chiefly for *The Beggar's Opera*, wrote satirical mock pastor-
als, including *Trivia* (1716) making fun of London life. In *Trivia*
we find these lines:

Then Cloacina, goddess of the tide,
Whose sable streams beneath the city glide,

101

Indulged the modish flame: the town she roved,
A mortal scavenger she saw, she loved.

Sable streams is pretty romantic descriptive poetry for what's involved!

clodpoll (KLOD pole), also **clodpole** and **clodpate**, *n.* All these variants mean the same thing: "blockhead, oaf, lout." A *clodhopper* is a peasant, boor, or bumpkin, though the usual meaning of the plural, *clodhoppers*, is a "pair of stout, sturdy, heavy shoes," the type you expect a *clodhopper* to wear. The first syllable, *clod-*, is itself a word: a *clod* is a lump, usually of earth or clay, and pejoratively, *clod* on its own can mean "blockhead." Its derivation is from Middle English *clodde*, and the word is related to *clot*, familiar from medical usage, but also with the primary meaning of "lump." In Britain, *clot* is a strong slang pejorative for "fool" or "jerk." ("She's suffering from marital thrombosis," quipped the English doctor, "having a *clot* for a husband." Mild British humor.) Shakespeare used *clodpole* in *Twelfth Night* (Act III, Scene 4), when Sir Toby Belch refuses to deliver Sir Andrew Aguecheek's letter challenging the supposed page to a duel, saying that the letter, "being so excellently ignorant, will breed no terror in the youth; he will find it comes from a *clodpole*." In *King Lear* (Act I, Scene 4), we find the form *clotpoll* (the Elizabethans were fairly relaxed about spelling) when Lear wants to hear from the exciting Oswald and says to one of his knights: "Call the *clotpoll* back." *Clodpoll* is a word that somehow, though not onomatopoeic, sounds like what it means, and is applicable, alas, to a fair number of people in the world—some of them in high places. (But please, no political discussion.)

cloistered (KLOY sturd) *adj.* A *cloistered* life is a sheltered, secluded one, far from the madding crowd. This adjective comes from the noun *cloister* (KLOY stur), the name for a place of religious seclusion, like a convent or a monastery, and in extreme cases, an **eremite's** cave, although the term has on occasion been used figuratively to include any secluded, out-of-the-way place of refuge. *Cloister* was *cloistre* in Middle English, derived from the Latin *claustrum* (barrier), which came to mean "enclosed place" in Middle Latin. Another Latin word for "enclosed place" is *clausum*, the neuter form of *clausus*, past participle of *claudere* (to shut, close). Though *cloistered* is based upon *cloister*, one does not have to dwell in a *cloister* (in its literal sense) to lead a *cloistered* life. Those fortunate enough to enjoy the serenity of the countryside, away from the hurly-burly of the crowded city, can claim the joys of a *cloistered* existence. Other participants in a *cloistered* life are ivory-tower academics and poor little rich girls, and we may as well include lighthousekeepers and oil-rig workers.

clowder   (KLOU dur) *n.* A *clowder* is a group of cats. In the case of collective nouns generally (a *pride* of lions, an *exaltation* of skylarks, a *pod* of whales), the word for *group* or *collection* is followed by the name of the creature—fish, flesh, fowl, or insect. *Clowder* is an exception, in that the word by itself designates the animal in question. *Clowder* is thought to be a variant of *clutter*, utilized for this special purpose. It somehow sounds pejorative— an aspersion on that most noble of creatures (other than man?)— the cat. Perhaps on the streets of Venice, or in the Coliseum of Rome, where the cats roam about scrounging for food, a mass of them appear as a clutter, but that's not their fault. In a home, where they're cherished, they don't make a clutter, but a graceful and decorative group. *Clowder*, indeed!

clyster   (KLIS tur) *n.* A *clyster* is an enema, a liquid injected into the intestines for flushing them out. *Clyster* comes from the Greek noun *klyster*, based on the verb *klyzein* (to rinse out). A related noun is *clysis* (KLEYE sis), a general medical term for the washing out of any bodily cavity. A *clyster-pipe* is a nozzle for introducing the enema into the body—not a particularly attractive bit of apparatus. In Shakespeare's *Othello* (Act II, Scene 1), the evil Iago, jealous of Cassio because Othello promoted him to be lieutenant rather than Iago, plans revenge by planting into Othello's head the belief that Cassio and Desdemona, Othello's wife, are lovers. When Cassio innocently takes Desdemona's hand during a conversation, Iago mutters, in an aside: "He takes her by the palm . . . it had been better you had not kissed your three fingers so oft . . . Yet again, your fingers to your lips? Would they were *clyster-pipes* for your sake!" Shakespeare could hardly have chosen a nastier image to portray Iago's detestable character!

cockatrice, see **basilisk**

coetaneous, see **coeval**

coeval (koh EE vul) *n.*, *adj.* As an adjective, *coeval* means "of the same age or duration" or "contemporary"; as a noun, a *coeval* is a contemporary. Another adjective, *coetaneous* (koh ih TAY nee us), is synonymous with *coeval*. Both stem from Latin; the prefix *co-* is a shortened form of *com-* (with, together) used before vowels. *Coeval* comes from Late Latin *coaevus*, based on *co-* plus Latin *aevum* (age). *Coetaneous* is from Latin *coaetaneus*, based on *co-* plus *aetas* (age). The American Civil War began on April 12, 1861, and ended on April 9, 1865; Abraham Lincoln died on April 15, 1965. Thus it can be said that the Civil War was practically *coeval* with the last four years of Lincoln's life. In the substantive sense, *coevals* can apply to two persons of unequal age, but who were alive at the same time—i.e., contemporaries. The Italian artists Michelangelo (1475–1564) and Da Vinci (1452–1519) can therefore be designated *coevals*, despite the difference in their actual ages. This is not a common use; they would more likely be described as "contemporaries." And it might be best to avoid the danger that *coevals* be misunderstood as "co-villains" (perish the thought!).

cognate, see **agnate**

cognomen, see **agnomen**

cognoscenti (kon yuh SHEN tee, kog nuh-) *n. pl.* The *cognoscenti* are those having special knowledge, the connoisseurs of the arts. The singular, rarely used, is *cognoscente* (same pronunciation as the plural). *Conoscente* (without the *g*) is the present participle of the Italian verb *conoscere* (to know), but the Italians went back to the original Latin *cognoscere*, inserting the *g* and producing the -yuh- sound. Bach fugues appeal principally to the *cognoscenti*. Abstract painting and contemporary music are the special province of the *cognoscenti*. At the **vernissages** of art exhibitions, you will meet the *cognoscenti* en masse. The term would not be applied to those well versed in the history and statistics of the various sports but unfamiliar with what's going on in twelve-tone music or retrospectives of Kandinsky, Arp & Co.

collective noun; noun of multitude; noun of assembly. These three mean the same thing: a noun, singular in form, but denoting a collection of persons, animals, or things, for example: an army, a crew, a herd, a family, a jury, a committee, a series. Such a noun can take a singular verb or a plural, depending on whether it implies a single entity or its individual components, thus: my family *is* my inspiration; my family *are* all tall. Some such nouns are quite familiar: a *pride* of lions; some rather exotic: an *exaltation* of skylarks. There is a legend about four dons who met at a pub once a month to report on any new specimens that might have come their way, like a *cloud* of WASPS (an *Aristophanes* of WASPS, perhaps, or even an *Aristophanes* of *Clouds*—or are we going too far?), a *plague* of Frogs (on a day's trip to Channel ports from Calais), a *Fauré* of warlike 19th century French composers? Well, while the dons were downing their first beers, three ladies of the evening happened to stroll in. "What about them?" asked one of the boys. "A trey (tray) of tarts?" ventured one of them. "A volume of Trollope's?" suggested the second. "Or a flourish of strumpets?" proffered the third. But "an anthology of pro's" put an end to the contest. See also **paronomasia**.

collocutor (KOL uh kyooh tur) *n.* A *collocutor* is a person who participates in a conversation. Thus, the expression *my collocutor* means "the person talking to me." Fowler, in the section on PRONUNCIATION under the heading "French Words," tells us not to try to pronounce a French word in the middle of an English sentence as a Frenchman would in a French sentence. He says: "It is a feat that should not be attempted. The greater its success as a *tour de force*, the greater its failure as a step in the conversational progress; for your *collocutor*, aware that he could not have done it himself, has his attention distracted whether he admires or is humiliated." We are more familiar with the noun *colloquy* (KOL uh kwee), meaning "conversation, conversational exchange, dialogue," which can also be used in the sense of "conference." There is also the noun *colloquium* (kuh LOH kwee um) for an informal group discussion. The adjective colloquial (kuh LOH kwee ul) is used of informal speech or writing, and the noun *colloquialism* (kuh LOH kwee ul iz um) applies to a word or phrase used *colloquially*. *Collocutor* is less frequently met with. All these words go back to the Latin verb *loqui* (to talk), its past participle *locutus* (cf.

105

elocution, circumlocution, etc.), and the prefix *con-* (together, with), which built *colloqui* (to converse) and its past participle *collocutus.*

colophon   (KOL uh fon, -fun) *n.* A *colophon* is a publisher's logo or house device or imprint, like the double-B symbol on the cover of the Ballantine edition of this book. Originally, the *colophon* was a notation appearing not at the front, but at the end of a book or manuscript, setting forth the title or subject, the name of the author, the printer's name and the date and place of printing and publication, sometimes with a bit of sales talk in praise of the work. *Colophon* was taken from the Greek noun *kolophon* (summit, finishing touch). In addition, there is a legend about the horsemen of *Kolophon,* an ancient city in Asia Minor, one of the 12 in Ionia. It was famed for its cavalry, according to this version, who had the reputation for turning the tide of battle and gaining victory in war by their last charge; hence the word *kolophon* for what used to appear at the very end of the book—the finishing touch. The old idiom *add a colophon* meant "give a final stroke" and *from title-page to colophon* is a British expression for "from cover to cover."

colubrine,   see **accipitrine**

columbarium   (kol um BAR ee um) *n.* A *columbarium* is a burial vault with niches for the placing of cinerary urns, i.e., vessels containing the ashes of the dead. Another wholly distinct and rather more cheerful meaning is "columbary" (KOL um ber ee), which is a synonym for "dovecote." Both *columbarium* and *columbary* come from Latin *columba* (dove), and the rather strange coupling of these quite distinct structures under one label has to do with the similarity of cellular construction typical of both, with all those pigeonholes, as it were, or should they be called "doveholes"?

columbine,   see **accipitrine**

comestible   (kuh MES tuh bul) *adj. Comestible* means "edible," and in the plural it is used as a noun meaning "food" generally. Late Latin produced the adjective *comestibilis,* based on Latin *comestus,* past participle of *comedere* or *comesse* (to consume, eat up—the Latin infinitive had both forms). *Esculent* is another adjec-

106

tive for "edible," and as a noun, embraces anything edible, but appears to apply especially to vegetables. *Esculent* is derived from Latin *esculentus* (edible), based on *esca* (food), related to the verb *edere* or *esse* (to eat—again, both forms were used), the verb that gave rise to *comedere/comesse*, from which we got *comestible*. Thus, we see the etymological relationship between *comestible* and what at first seems to be a wholly different word, *esculent*, a synonym. It is more likely that you will meet up with *comestible* than run across *esculent*, but as far as your health is concerned, you needn't worry; you can eat (subject to your particular diet restriction) anything *comestible* or *esculent*.

comity (KOM ih tee) *n*. *Comity* is mutual civility, friendliness, and consideration. *Comity* between labor and management is essential for the success of a commercial enterprise. Our country could not have prospered or even continued to exist without *comity* among the colonies and then the states. This word is derived from the Latin noun *comitas* (courtesy, friendliness), based on the adjective *comis* (kind, courteous). In international law, the term *comity of nations* (*comitas gentium*, in New Latin) signifies international courtesy, more specifically a nonmandatory, informal code to which the courts of a country defer in determining questions involving the interests of another country, and effect is given to the laws of one country within the territory of another.

commensal (kuh MEN sul) *n*., *adj*. Literally, this adjective describes people eating together at the same table. *Mensa* is *table* in Latin, and one of the meanings of our adjective **mensal** (different from the one discussed under **hedomadal**) is "relating to the table" or "used at table." The Middle Latin adjective *commensalis* led to our *commensal*. When it is used of animals or plants, *commensal* describes types living together, or a type living on or in another, without harm to either. In sociology, *commensal* describes any individual or social group living in the same area as another person or group of a different social order and having different customs, without opposition or territorial or other competition with each other. Used as a noun, *commensal* is a synonym for *messmate*. In the plant and animal world, *commensals* live without parasitism, in a type of partnership not quite so intimate as symbiosis, a mutually beneficial relationship.

commination (kom uh NAY shun) *n. Commination* is the denunciation and threat of punishment, especially of sinners, through divine vengeance ("Vengeance is mine, etc."), and any such threat is described as *comminatory* (kuh MIN uh tor ee; KOM uh-). In ecclesiastical parlance, *commination* is the recital of God's threats against sinners, read in the Anglican liturgy on the first day of Lent, Ash Wednesday, which got its name from the Roman Catholic ritual of sprinkling on penitents' heads the ashes of burnt palms from Palm Sunday, the Sunday before Easter. The Latin source is *comminatio*, from *comminatus*, past participle of *comminari*, based on the intensive prefix *com-* plus *minari* (to threaten). To *comminate* (KOM in ate) is to threaten; a verb not to be confused with **comminute**, an entirely different affair.

comminute (KOM uh nooht, -nyooht) *vb.* To *comminute* is to crush, pulverize, reduce to *minute* particles; from Latin *comminutus*, past participle of *comminuere* (to break into pieces), based on intensive prefix *com-* plus *minuere* (to lessen), related to our words *minus* and *diminish*, and to Latin *minor* (less). A synonym of *comminute* is *triturate* (TRIT uh rate), from Late Latin *trituratus*, past participle of *triturare* (to thresh). The worst kind of bone break is a *comminuted fracture*, in which the separated parts are broken into small fragments. *Comminute* has nothing in common with *comminate*, a wholly different kettle of fish, both as to meaning and derivation.

compendious (kom PEND ee us) *adj.* A *compendious* treatment of a subject is a concise one. The noun *compendium* (com PEND ee um) denotes a brief survey, a concise treatment, an abridgement or summary, usually of a broad subject, as in a *compendium of astronomy*, or a *compendious treatise on modern physics*. For some reason, *compedium* and *compendious* seem to evoke, erroneously, the image of a fully detailed extensive treatment. On the contrary, they stress the concept of conciseness and abridgement. *Compendious* comes from the Latin *compendiosus* (brief). *Compendium* was taken as is from the Latin, where it means "shortening" or "abbreviation," and was based on the familiar prefix *con-* (together, with) plus *pend-*, the stem of the verb *pendere* (to weigh, consider). "Weighing together," by transference, came to mean "shortening." Language development never ceases to surprise.

108

compotation   (kom puh TAY shun) *n. Potation* (poh TAY shun) is the act of drinking, or the drink itself, particularly an intoxicating quaff. It is from Latin *potatio* (a drinking), based on *potatus*, the past participle of *potare* (to drink). *Compotation* is the act of drinking in company with another or others, and here, too, the implication is that of imbibing intoxicating beverages, or group tippling. The Latin prefix *com-* (with, together—as in *combine, commingle,* etc.) plus *potatio* gave us *compotation*. In classical Greece it was customary among the upper classes to have an after-dinner party for drinking and conversation, known as a *symposion,* a word formed of the Greek prefix *syn-* (with, together—as in *syndrome, synergy,* etc.) plus *posis* (a drinking). *Compotation,* then, was a direct Latin translation of the Greek *symposion,* which became *symposium* in Latin, and later, by extension, acquired its modern meaning.

conation   (koh NAY shun) *n. Conation* is the area of one's active mentality that has to do with desire, volition, and striving. The related word *conatus* (koh NAY tus) is the resulting effort or striving itself, or the natural tendency or force in one's mental makeup that produces an effort. *Conative* (KOHN uh tiv) is the term in psychology that describes anything relating to *conation.* All these words come from Latin *conatus,* past participle of the verb *conari* (to try). The Scottish philosopher Sir William Hamilton (1788– 1856) considered *conation* to be one of the three divisions of the mind, the one that included desire and volition, the other two being cognition (perception, awareness) and feeling. The English theologian and philosopher William Paley (1743–1805) asked: "What *conatus* could give prickles to the porcupine or hedgehog, or to the sheep its fleece?" *Conation* differs from **velleity** (the wish without the effort).

concatenation   (kon kat uh NAY shun) *n.* A *concatenation* of events is a chain or series of happenings leading, usually, to a denouement or outcome. The implication from the use of *concatenation* is that the outcome or result was interesting or dramatic or in some way significant, and that the events in the *concatenation* were in themselves fortuitous and connected chronologically rather than logically. The alarm clock failed to go off, he missed his usual train, he took a later one, he took the only seat which happened to be next to the only girl in the world, and they lived happily ever after. "In the beginning, God created the heaven and the earth . . . So God created man in his own image." No *concatenation* there; it just happened that way. There are those who differ, and ascribe the existence of the universe and the development of man to an extremely long and complicated *concatenation*. There is a verb *concatenate* (kon KAT uh nate), to link together in a series, but it is rarely met with. It comes from Latin, *concatenatus*, past participle of *concatenare*, based on Latin prefix *con-* (together) plus *catena* (chain). *Concatenation* is from Latin *concatenatio*. It was a *concatenation* of errors and bellicose aims that led to both the First and Second World Wars. Go back over your own biography and you will discover that it is a *concatenation* of events from beginning to today. Did your grandparents (and how did they meet?) arrange your parents' marriage, or did your mummy and daddy meet in a singles bar? Etc.

concinnity (kun SIN i tee) *n.* To *concinnate* (KON suh nate) is to fit or blend elements together so skillfully and appropriately that they form a harmonious and elegant whole. The verb is derived from Latin *concinnatus*, past participle of *concinnare* (to arrange or put together with care), based on prefix *con-* (together) plus *cinnare*, related to the adjective *concinnus* (well put together, pleasing because of harmony and proportion) and the noun *concinnitas* (elegance, harmony of style). Latin *cinnus* is a mixed drink (cocktail?). *Concinnity* is a term used in rhetoric to denote close harmony of tone, and, in context, of logic in discourse. *Concinnous* (kun SIN us) means "elegant, harmonious as to style." In his *Diaries 1920–1922* (Faber, London, 1981), the English poet and novelist Siegfried Sassoon (1886–1967) discusses the clavichord:

> The diminutive remoteness of the clavichord makes one realise [British spelling] how crude one's auditory palate is. The problem is how to be exquisite without lapsing into preciosity. *Concinnity* is a quality which can be acquired by collocution with a clavichord . . . The clavichord belongs to the Ultima Thule of acoustics. The notes evoke hyperphysical sweetness and sensitivity . . . Orpheus might have made such music at a special recital for glow-worms [British spelling again] and tiny moonlight-coloured [more British spelling] moths.

110

Phew! This passage is followed by a Sassoon poem entitled *Clavichord Recital* that starts:

> Mute were the neighboring nightingales
> When Orpheus touched his clavichord . . .

Concinnity showed up a year earlier in *"Shakespeare" Identified* (Duell, Sloan & Pearce, New York, 1920) by J. Thomas Looney (pronounced LONEY), who "identified" Shakespeare with Edward de Vere, 17th Earl of Oxford (1550–1604), a courtier at the court of Queen Elizabeth I and a lyric poet known as Lord Bulbeck—pronounced BOOL bek—until 1562) believed by the so-called Oxfordian school to have written Shakespeare's dramas. This belief was based on an appreciation of the style of de Vere's lyric poetry:

> If to these qualities we add an intense sensibility to all kinds of external impressions, and a faculty of passionate response, brought to the service of clear, intellectual perceptions, we shall have seized hold of the outstanding features of de Vere's mentality. The result is the production of poems which impress the mind with a sense of their unity. The ideas cohere, following one another in a natural sequence, and leave in the reader's mind a sense of completeness and artistic finish. That this *concinnity* is characteristic of Shakespeare's mind and work needs no insisting on at the present day.

(All of the foregoing to the contrary notwithstanding, this author agrees with the American scholar and biographer Marchette Chute [b. 1909; *Shakespeare of London*, E.F. Dutton, New York, 1957] that Shakespeare's plays were written by Mr. Shakespeare.)

concupiscence (kon KYOOH pih suns) *n. Concupiscence* is ardent sexual desire, in any degree from sensuous longing to raw lust. The adjective is *concupiscent* (kon KYOOH pih sunt). These words stem from Late Latin *concupiscentia*, formed from the Latin verb *concupiscere* (to desire ardently, covet), based in turn on the prefix *con-* (used as an intensive with the force of "completely"), plus *cupere* (to desire). A related adjective, *concupiscible* (kon KYOOH pih suh bul), from Late Latin *concupiscibilis*, formerly meant "desirable," but Shakespeare used it in the sense of "lecherous"—active rather than passive in the lust department—in *Measure for Measure* (Act V, Scene 1), when Isabella tells Duke Vincentio the truth about his faithless deputy Angelo:

> . . . the vile conclusion
> I now begin with grief and shame to utter:
> He would not, but by gift of my chaste body
> To his *concupiscible* intemperate lust
> Release my brother . . .

condign (kon DINE) *adj.* This adjective is used chiefly in the expression *condign punishment*, where it means "fitting, proper, adequate, well-deserved." It comes from Latin *condignus* (very worthy). Originally, *condign* could apply to many situations, including those involving praise as well as punishment. Shakespeare used it that way in *Loves Labour's Lost* (Act I, Scene 2), in an amusing colloquy between the "fantastical" Spaniard Armado and his page, Moth, whom he praised as "pretty, and apt." Moth asks, "Speak you this in my praise, master?" and Armado answers, "In thy *condign* praise." Its application is now virtually confined to *punishment*, or, in the proper context, *fate, suffering,* and the like. *Condign* punishment is deservedly severe; it must be severe as well as deservedly so. This, of course, is just what the English poet and dramatist W. S. Gilbert (1836–1919, the "Gilbert" of Gilbert and Sullivan) had in mind when he wrote, in *The Mikado*:

> My object all sublime
> I shall achieve in time—
> To let the punishment fit the crime—
> The punishment fit the crime . . .

and what was earlier intended in Exodus 21, 23–25:

> . . . life for life,
> Eye for eye, tooth for tooth, hand for hand, foot for foot,
> Burning for burning, wound for wound, stripe for stripe . . .

In Roman times, this primitive penal system was known as *Lex Talionis*, the Law of Retaliation (note the *-tal-*), or in simpler terms, *tit for tat. Talio* is Latin for "retaliation" and is the basis for the rarely met word *talion*. Getting back to "life for life": capital punishment has much gone out of style, at least in many parts of the civilized world, though in some parts it's rearing its ugly *caput* again. And the Ayatollah Khomeini's interpretation of *condign*, whatever the word is in Iranian, is something else again, what with

112

stoning, the cutting off of hands, and other delectable arrangements. Incidentally, stay off the booze in Saudi Arabia.

condottiere, see **grisaille**

congener (KON juh nur) *n.* A person, animal, or thing of the same kind or nature as another is a *congener* of that other. In the world of flora and fauna, a *congener* is a member of the same genus as another. The goldfinch is a *congener* of the canary. The American elk is a *congener* of the European red deer. In both cases, one might add "and vice versa," of course. The adjectives are *congenerous* (kon JEN ur us) and *congeneric* (kon juh NER ik); also *congenetic* (kon juh NET ik), meaning "having a common origin." All these words are derived from the Latin prefix *con-* (with) plus *genus* (kind). Persons alike in nature, character, conduct, or action may be described as *congeners.* Napoleon Bonaparte (1769–1821) and Alexander the Great (356–323 B.C.), in their generalship and insatiable thirst for conquest, were *congeners.*

congeries (kon JEER eez, kun JIR eez) *n.* Fowler says most dictionaries favor the pronunciation "kon JER ih eez"—four syllables—but later on, makes the following comment about words ending in *ies*:

> **-ies, -ein.** Until recently the dictionaries prescribed a disyllabic pronunciation of *-ies* for words of Latin origin such as *series, species, rabies, caries, scabies.* But in fact few doctors pronounce the second syllable of *rabies* and *caries* differently from that of *herpes,* and almost everyone takes the same liberty with *series* and *species.* It is better to bow to the inevitable than to persist in a vain attempt to preserve what we suppose to have been the way the Romans pronounced these words, and the dictionaries now recognize *eez* for most of them, if only as alternatives.
>
> Words ending *ein(e) (protein, caffeine, codeine)* are rebelling in the same way, even though they are less commonly used; *een* is likely to establish itself; modern life is too hurried for these niceties.

113

A *congeries* is a disordered heap of things, a collection or aggregation piled together any old way. There can be a *congeries* of concrete objects, like documents, boxes, objets d'art, or a *congeries* of nonmaterial things, like ideas, concepts, thoughts, theories. As we walk along a beach, looking down, we see a *congeries* of pebbles and shells of all sizes. From a great height, a settlement or a parking lot looks like a *congeries* of little packages or boxes. A visit to a children's playroom usually confronts one with a *congeries* of playthings. An accused person often splutters a *congeries* of unconvincing explanations and excuses. The word was taken over intact from Latin, where it means "heap, mass, pile, accumulation," and is related to the verb *congerere* (to collect, bring together), from whose past participle, *congestus*, we get our noun *congestion* and adjective *congested*. *Congeries* doesn't change in the plural, so that an erroneous singular, *congerie* or *congery* (usually pronounced KON juh ree), has been concocted and must be avoided. This is as good a place as any to remember that *kudos*, from Greek *kydos* (praise, honor, glory), is singular, and there is no such thing as one kudo, or for that matter, one mump or one measle.

conglobate (kon GLOH bate, KONG-) *adj.*, *vb. Conglobate*, as an adjective, describes anything formed into a ball, like a lump of clay or a pat of butter. As a verb, transitive or intransitive, to *conglobate* is to form into a ball or sphere. A variant of the verb is *conglobe* (kon GLOBE), which comes from the Latin prefix *con-* (together) plus *globus* (ball, sphere—from which we get our noun *globe*). *Conglobate* is from Latin *conglobatus*, past participle of *conglobare* (form into a ball or sphere). The Latin noun *conglobatio* has a more abstract meaning: "crowding together." We are more familiar with our word *conglomerate* (*n.*, *adj.*—kon GLOM ur it; *vb.*—kon GLOM uh rate), derived from Latin *con-* plus *glomus* (ball of yarn). The English novelist Virignia Woolf (1882–1941), in Volume V of her *Diary*, says that she keeps it for a "run of her pen," a "scribble." It is her "running ground," her "fidget ground." "I wish," she writes, "I could *conglobulate* thoughts like Gide [the French novelist and essayist (1869–1951)]." Mrs. Woolf either slipped into *conglobulate* as an echo of *conglomerate*, or casually invented it—and made a better-sounding word.

connubial (kuh NYOOH bee ul, -NOOH) *adj. Connubial* love or discord is that between spouses; *connubial* means "matrimonial" or "conjugal," describing anything relating to matrimony. It comes from Latin *conubialis*, based on *conubium* (marriage, wedlock). The English poet Lord Byron (1788–1824) wrote, in *Don Juan*:

> Romances paint at full length people's wooings,
>   But only give a bust of marriages;
> For no one cares for matrimonial cooings,
>   There's nothing wrong in a *connubial* kiss:
> Think you, If Laura had been Petrarch's wife,
> He would have written sonnets all his life?

In *Paradise Lost*, the English poet John Milton (1608–1674) wrote of Adam and Eve:

> Into their inmost bower
> Handed they went; and eas'd the putting off
> These troublesome disguises which we wear,
> Strait side by side were laid, nor turned I ween
> Adam from his fair spouse, nor Eve the rites
> Mysterious of *connubial* love refused . . .

The English novelist Charles Dickens (1812–1870), in *Pickwick Papers*, put these words into Mr. Sam Weller's mouth:

> The wictim o' *connubiality*, as Blue Beard's domestic chaplain said, with a tear of pity, ven he buried him.

consanguinity (kon sang GWIN ih tee) *n. Consanguinity* is blood relationship resulting from the sharing of ancestors; from Latin *consanguinitas*, based on prefix *con-* (with) plus *sanguis* (blood). People related by blood are said to be *consanguineous* (kon sang GWIN ee us). In Shakespeare's *Twelfth Night* (Act II, Scene 3), Sir Toby Belch and Sir Andrew Aguecheek are singing drunkenly late at night in a room in the house of the rich Countess Olivia. Her woman Maria breaks in: "What a *caterwauling* do you keep here!" Says Sir Toby: "My lady's a Cataian [Cathayan, i.e., Chinese]; we are politicians . . . Am I not *consanguineous*? Am I not of her blood? Tillyvally [a term of contempt], lady!" Malvolio, Olivia's steward, shows up and chastises the revelers: "My lady bade me tell you, that, though she harbours you as kinsman [there really is *consanguinity* between Sir Toby and the Countess] . . . she is very willing to bid you farewell.'' In other words, *consanguinity* goes only so far, and mustn't be abused. Degrees of *consanguinity* form the basis of statutory formulas for the distribution of the estates of persons dying intestate (i.e., without a will) as well as defining permissible and incestuous marriages. These formulas vary from state to state, country to country, church to church. In parts of the United States, marriages between first cousins are prohibited as involving too close a degree of *consanguinity*. The Roman Catholic Church has very strict rules on *consanguinity* as an impediment to marriage. In some cases, relatives of a deceased spouse are counted as having the same degree of *consanguinity* as the bereaved spouse's own family. Henry VIII of England married his brother Arthur's widow, Katharine of Aragon, but only pursuant to a papal dispensation. After an unsuccessful struggle with the papacy to have the dispensation declared invalid, Henry obtained a divorce when Archbishop Cranmer proclaimed the marriage invalid because it violated the law respecting *consanguinity*. Henry was excommunicated—the rest is history. (See also **sanguinary**.)

contemn (kun TEM) *vb.* To *contemn* is to despise, regard with scorn and disdain. The person or thing so regarded may be described as *contemnible* (kun TEM nuh bul). The noun *contempt* and the adjective *contemptible* are much more common and familiar than the verb *contemn* and its adjective *contemnible*, nor has *contemn* any related active adjective like *contemptuous*. The coexistence of the *contemn* and *contempt* groups results from the inflection of the Latin verb *contemnere*, whose past participle is *contemptus*; and it is well known that we have taken our English words rather arbitrarily and often quite at random from this or that form of Latin and Greek verbs. Ecclesiasticus 19:1 tells us: "He that *contemneth* small things shall fall by little and little," modernized by the *New English Bible* as "Carelessness in small things leads little by little to ruin." (It was the *King James Version* that warned P. T. Barnum not to disdain Tom Thumb, no doubt.)

contumacy (KON tooh muh see, -tyooh-) *n.* *Contumacy* is obstinate disobedience, stubborn and unreasonable resistance or perverseness, rebelliousness. The adjective, *contumacious* (kon tooh MAY shus, -tyooh-), describes all these disagreeable qualities. A

116

contumacious person is intractable, pigheaded, or, as the British say, "bloody-minded." *Contumax* means "insolent, defiant" in Latin, based on the intensive prefix *con-* plus the verb *tumere* (to swell, to puff up), or possibly *temmere* (to despise), from which we get **contemn**, *contempt*, *contemptuous*, etc. *Contumacy* and *contumacious* often imply contemptuous opposition to lawful authority, like the attitude of some trade unions toward court decisions, as in the miners' strike in Great Britain in 1984 under the leadership of its president Arthur Scargill. Do not confuse *contumacy* with **contumely**, though both may have derivations involving the Latin verb *tumere* (to swell).

contumely   (KON toohm lee, -tyoom-; kon TOOH muh lee, -TYOOH-; KON tum lee) *n.* As to this profusion of pronunciations, Fowler points out that the famous line from the "To be, or not to be" soliloquy in Shakespeare's *Hamlet* (Act III, Scene 3): "The oppressor's wrong, the proud man's *contumely*," favors something close to the first one given above, which he describes as *KO ntoom li. Contumely* is contemptuous language or treatment; humiliation, insult, by word or deed. It is from Latin *contumelia* (insult). The English philosopher Francis Bacon (1561-1626) wrote: "It were better to have no opinion of God at all than such an opinion as is unworthy of him; for the one is unbelief, the other is *contumely*." The adjective is *contumelious* (kon too MEE lee us, -tyoo-). Shakespeare was fond of it. In *Henry VI, Part 1* (Act I, Scene 4), Lord Talbot tells the Earl of Salisbury of his treatment as a prisoner of the French in these terms:

> With scoffs and scorns and *contumelious* taunts,
> In open market-place produced they me,
> To be a public spectacle to all . . .

The adverb had already shown up in Scene 3, when the Mayor of London, coming upon the brawling forces of Gloucester and Beaufort, cries:

> Fie, lords! that you, being supreme magistrates,
> Thus *contumeliously* should break the peace!

In *Henry VI, Part 2* (Act III, Scene 2), Queen Margaret describes the Earl of Warwick in these words:

He does not calm his *contumelious* spirit . . .

And in *Timon of Athens* (Act V, Scene 1), Timon describes war as ". . . *contumelious*, beastly, mad-brained . . .," anticipating General William Tecumseh Sherman (1820–1891) by a good many years: "War is cruelty . . . War is . . . barbarism . . . War is hell."

copacetic   (koh puh SET ik) *adj.* This is a bit of slang, the origin of which is unknown according to all the dictionaries consulted. It appears in a number of forms.: *copasetic, copassetic, copesetic,* as well as the spelling in the headword above. It means "fine and dandy, completely satisfactory, just great, in good order, excellent, in fine shape," and would be found in sentences like, "If only Harry were here, everything would be *copacetic*," or, "The weather was great, they all showed up on time, it was *copacetic*." As an interjection, *copacetic* means "All clear!" Despite the dictionaries' disclaimer of any knowledge of the origin of this word, it would appear to emit echoes of words like *sympathetic* and *empathetic* with a hint of *compassion* thrown in for good measure, all of which express feelings of emotional kinship, understanding, and in a sense, satisfaction. Any suggestions?

coprologic(al),   see **scatalogy**

copula   (KOP yuh luh) *n.* A *copula* is a link or tie, something that serves to join things together. In grammar, it is a word or phrase that links the subject and predicate in a sentence. In *John is a trustworthy friend* or *Mary is a marvelous woman* the verb *is* is the *copula*. In *Fred, poor chap, has been quite ill, but he seems a lot better now,* the *copulas* (or *copulae,* if you prefer) are *has been* and *seems.* In these examples, all the *couplas* are verbs, known as *copulative* (KOP yuh lay tiv, -luh-) verbs. *And* is a *copulative* conjunction. Conjunctions that do not link, but offer a choice or a contrast, are *disjunctive* (dis JUNGK tiv). In *poor but proud, but* is *disjunctive*; the same goes for *or* in *this or that.* The distinction between *copulative* and *disjunctive* conjunctions becomes important in determining the verb number after a compound subject. Sam *and* John *are* here. Sam *or* John *is* here. *Copula,* taken intact from Latin, is the basis of the Latin words *copulare* (to join together) and *copulatio* (union), and the source of our *couple* (noun and verb),

118

and *copulate* and *copulation*, a specialized type of union. *Copula*, in the original Latin, appears in one of the odes of the Roman poet Horace (65–8 B.C.), Book I, Ode 13 (Wickham translation):

> Thrice happy they, and more than thrice
> whom an unbroken bond *(copula)* holds fast,
> and whom love, never torn asunder by foolish
> quarrelings, will not loose till life's last
> day!

And the great English poet William Butler Yeats (1865–1939), in his *News for the Delphic Oracle*, wrote of a lovely scene where

> . . . *nymphs and satyrs*
> *Copulate* in the foam . . .

In *Sweeney Agonistes*, the American-born English poet T. S. Eliot (1888–1965) wrote:

> Birth, and *copulation*, and death.
> That's all the facts when you come to brass tacks.

In Shakespeare's *King Lear* (Act IV, Scene 6), Lear rants:

> The wren goes to 't, and the small gilded fly
> Does lecher in my sight.
> Let *copulation* thrive . . .

(Does this not bring to mind the Cole Porter song *Let's Do It?*) In any case, we see that the little word *copula* and its derivatives have played a great part in literature, to say nothing of life itself!

coracle (KOR uh kul) *n.* A *coracle* is a small oval-shaped row-boat, constructed of wickerwork or interwoven laths, covered with watertight material like tarred or oiled canvas, animal skins, etc. These are used on the inland waterways of Ireland and Wales, and here and there in the west of England. The making of *coracles* is an old and fast-becoming extinct local craft, and one rarely sees a *coracle* afloat any longer. As might be expected, the derivation is not from classical Greek or Latin, but rather from Welsh *corwgl*, related to Gaelic *curach* (boat), and has nothing whatever to do

119

with oracles or miracles, though it seems a miracle that *coracles* remain afloat.

corban   (KOR bun) *n.* A *corban* is any gift offered to God in fulfillment of a vow. In Hebrew the word is *qorban* (offering, sacrifice); its literal meaning is "drawing near." We read in Genesis 22 how God put Abraham to the test by telling him to offer his son Isaac as a sacrifice. When Isaac asked Abraham, "Where is the young beast for the sacrifice?" the father answered that God would provide it, but as Abraham took the knife to kill his son, the Angel of God stopped him and a ram was substituted. The ram, not Isaac, became the *corban*. The next time you swear to God: "If You would only . . . , I'll . . . ," and describe your *corban*, be sure you can provide it!

corvine,   see **accipitrine**

cosmical,   see **acronical**

cosmogony   (koz MOG uh nee) *n. Cosmogony* is a theory of the origin of the universe, not to be confused with *cosmology*, the science of the universe, its structure and evolution. Both words are based on the Greek noun *kosmos* (cosmos, universe): *cosmogony* uses the suffix *-goneia*, based on *gonos* (seed, creation), which gives us the suffix *-gony*, appearing in words denoting origination, like *monogony, theogony,* etc.; whereas *cosmology* uses the suffix *-logia*, based on *logos* (word, discourse), a suffix which gives us the suffix *-logy*, appearing in names of sciences, like *philology, theology,* etc.

cosmology,   see **cosmogony**

costive   (KOS tiv) *adj.* A *costive* person is one in the unfortunate state of being constipated—a member of the great TV audience watching the display of the countless remedies that leave the unhappy sufferer beaming and brimming over with health, happiness, and indomitable energy after one dose. *Costive* is never heard on the air, but "regular" regularly is. Via Middle English and Middle French, *costive* is derived from Latin *constipatus*, past participle of *constipare* (to press together). There is something about a tight anal sphincter that somehow led to the figurative use of *costive* in the sense of "niggardly." The British statesman and author Lord Chesterfield (1694–1773) used it that way in giving his Polonius-to-Laertes type of guidance (see *Hamlet*, Act I, Scene 3) to his son, advising him: "You must be . . . close, but without being *costive*."

coulisse (kooh LEES) *n. Coulisse* has a number of meanings. Basically, a *coulisse* is a piece of wood having a groove along which a panel can slide. The side-flats of a theater run along *coulisses*, and from that use *coulisses*, the plural, is used for the wings themselves, or the space between two wing-flats. The British use *coulisse* in the sense of "corridor" as well, and from that it came to mean a place for any informal discussion or negotiation. *Coulisse* means "groove" in French, where it also has the sense of something that slides in a groove. A *portcullis* is a heavy grating, usually in a medieval castle, that can be let down to close a gateway and prevent access. It slides along grooves in the sides of the gateway. *Portcullis* (port KUL is) is from Old French *porte coleice* (sliding door). The *-cullis* in *portcullis* is related to *coulisse*, which is based on the French verb *couler* (to flow or glide).

coup de grâce (kooh duh GRAS; the *s* is sounded). This expression, taken over from the French *coup de grâce*, means, literally, "blow of mercy"—the death blow mercifully given to end suffering, as in the case of a horse with a broken leg, or a still squirming victim of a firing-squad with a poor aim. But *coup de grâce* is used figuratively to denote any decisive finishing stroke that once and for all settles a matter and has nothing to do with mercy—often, quite the contrary. The resignation of a leading member of a political party might be a *coup de grâce* ensuring defeat in the middle of an election campaign. The revelations on Nixon's tapes delivered the *coup de grâce* that put an end to his presidency. Thus, a term originally based on the concept of compassion has taken quite a different turn, and now signifies a final, convulsive, destructive blow. Caution: sadly, all too often, the *grace* in this expression is mispronounced as *grah*, like the *gras* in *pâté de foi gras*, which has a lovely taste but a silent *s*. And remember, the *p* in *coup* is silent, and not to be confused with the *p* in *coupe*, as in *coupe Hélène* (a stewed pear with chocolate sauce), which also has a lovely taste but a sounded *p*. To come out with *coup de* *gras* or *coupe de grâce*, or, heaven forbid, *coupe de gras* (which would mean "cup of fat") would deliver a *coup de grâce* to one's hope to be taken for a man of the world.

cozen (KUZ un) *vb.* To *cozen* someone is to cheat, trick, defraud, swindle, or beguile him, and *cozenage* (KUZ uh nij) is the practice of these unseemly acts: trickery and swindling. The origin of *cozen* is in question. It is believed by some authorities to be derived from the French verb *cousiner* (to claim kinship; by extension, to deceive through a false claim of kinship). The British statesman Oliver Cromwell (1599–1658), in a 1654 speech to Parliament, said: "Feigned necessities, imaginary necessities, . . . are the greatest *cozenage* that man can put upon the Providence of God, and make pretences to break down rules by." In Shakespeare's *Othello* (Act IV, Scene 2), Iago's wife Emilia, bewildered by Othello's accusations against Desdemona, exclaims:

> I will be hang'd, if some eternal villain,
> Some busy and insinuating rogue,
> Some cogging [i.e., tricking], *cozening* slave, to get some office,
> Have not devised this slander.

The English poet John Dryden (1631–1700) wrote these pessimistic lines:

> When I consider life, 'tis all a cheat;
> Yet, fool'd with hope, men favour the deceit;
> Trust on, and think tomorrow will repay:
> Tomorrow's falser than the former day;
> Lies worse, and, while it says we shall be blest
> With some new joys, cuts off what we possest.
> Strange *cozenage*! None would live past years again,
> Yet all hope pleasure in what yet remain;
> And, from the dregs of life, think to receive,
> What the first sprightly running could not give.

The English historian and statesman Macaulay (1800–1859) thundered against a political opponent: "He had *cozened* the world by fine phrases!" One who indulges regularly in the unwholesome practice of *cozenage* is a *cozener*.

crambo (KRAM boh) *n.* This is the name of a rhyming game, between individuals or teams. One side concocts a line of verse to which the opposing side must find a rhyme, but no word occurring in the first line must appear in the answering line. In the variation *dumb crambo*, rhymes of the given word are pantomimed or acted out in charades until guessed. In *Love for Love*, by the English dramatist Congreve (1670-1729), we hear: "Get the maids to *crambo* of an evening and learn the knack of rhyming." The word *crambo* was taken over from Latin *crambe*, based on Greek *krambe* (cabbage) and is thought to be short for *crambe repetita*, literally, *cabbage reclaimed*—cold cabbage warmed up and served again— figuratively, stale repetition, the same old story, as used by the Roman satirist Juvenal (c. 60-140), who wrote (translation of Lewis Evans): "Cabbage cooked twice wears out the master's life."

crapulent (KRAP yoo lunt, -yuh-) *adj.* The unfortunate who can properly be described as *crapulent* is one suffering the effects of imbibing too freely or eating to excess. If such overindulgence is chronic, he can be called *crapulous* (KRAP yoo lus, -yuh-), but, in the confusing ways of our language, that term is also sometimes used as a synonym of *crapulent*. *Crapulent* comes from Late Latin *crapulentus*, based on Latin *crapula* (drunkenness), which was an import from Greece, where *kraipale* meant "hangover"; and the condition is *crapulence*. *Crapulous* is from Late Latin *crapulosus*. None of these words has anything to do with the vulgar word that forms the first syllable of each and has an altogether distinct etymology: Middle English *crappe*, from Dutch *krappe* (chaff—the husks thrown away in threshing—whence the word came to mean "worthless stuff, refuse").

crapulous, see **crapulent**

credenza (krih DEN zuh) *n.* This word, taken intact from the Italian, means "sideboard" or "buffet." In ecclesiastical parlance, a *credenza* is a "credence table," a side table or a shelf for holding the bread and wine used in the Eucharist, the Holy Communion. In olden times, credence tables were used for a different purpose: to hold food to be tasted by the host or one of his staff before being served to guests, to convince them that it wasn't poisoned (comforting thought). *Credence* comes from Middle Latin *credentia* (literally, belief, credit; later, it came to mean "sideboard, buffet"),

123

based on the Latin verb *credere* (to believe). One had to *believe* in one's hosts in those days, especially at places like the Borgias'. *Credenzas*, nowadays, are innocent enough articles of furniture, far removed from anything so naughty as poisoning one's guests.

crepuscular (krih PUS kyuh lur) *adj.* From the Latin noun *crepusculum* (twilight), based on *crespus*, a variant of *cresper* (dark) plus the suffix *-culus*, attached to diminutives, we get *crepuscule* (krih PUS kyoohl, KREP uh skyoohl), meaning "twilight, dusk." The adjective *crepuscular*, in its literal sense, is applied to anything resembling twilight, and as a zoological term, to animals and insects that come out at dusk. Figuratively, *crepuscular* can be used to describe things dim or indistinct. The Russian novelist Turgenev (1818–1883), in the Harry Stevens translation of *Fathers and Sons*, made dramatic and moving use of the term in the sense of "indistinct":

> That vague, *crepuscular* time, the time of regrets that resemble hopes, of hopes that resemble regrets, when youth has passed, but old age has not yet arrived.

crescive (KRES iv) *adj.* *Crescive* describes anything that is increasing, growing. The Latin verb *crescere* means "to grow," and the form *increscere* gave us *increase*. A rare meaning of *crescent*, based on *crescens*, present participle of *crescere*, is "increasing, growing." The *crescent moon* is one in its first quarter and gains its name because it is bound to *increase*. The *croissants* we eat are not going to grow; quite the contrary—but the literal meaning of *croissant* is "growing," that word being the present participle of the French verb *croître* (to grow). As a noun in French *croissant* means "new moon" and many other things, including the delectable *crescent*-shaped roll.

cresset (KRES it) *n.* A *cresset* is a metal basket mounted on a pole for use as a torch, or hung on a chain and used as a lantern, containing oil, pitch-soaked wood, or any slow-burning combustible whose fire will serve as an illuminant or beacon. *Cressets* were placed in courtyards, on wharves and lighthouses and the like. There is doubt about its derivation: it is either from Old French *craisset*, which gave rise to French *graisse* (grease), or from Old French

124

creuset or *crasset*, from which modern French *creuset* (crucible) was derived. The English poet John Milton (1608–1674) wrote of

> . . . Blazing *cressets* fed
> With naphtha and asphaltus . . .,

and later, his countryman, the poet Shelley (1792–1822), used *cresset* in the figurative sense of any illumination in writing of

> A *cresset* shaken from the constellations . . .

In Shakespeare's *Henry IV, Part I* (Act III, Scene 1), in an angry exchange between Hotspur and Owen Glendower, the latter, boasting of his powers, says:

> . . . at my nativity
> The front of heaven was full of fiery shapes,
> Of burning *cressets*, and at my birth
> The frame and huge foundation of the earth
> Shak'd like a coward.

And Hotspur answers:

> Why, so it would have done
> At the same season, if your mother's cat
> Had but kitten'd, though yourself had ne'er been born.

cricetine, see **accipitrine**

criticaster, see **poetaster**

crocket (KROK it) *n.* This is an architectural term, denoting a decorative feature of certain structures of the Middle Ages. A *crocket* is an ornament, usually in the form of curled leaves, buds, or flower petals, on the inclined sides of a pediment, spire or pinnacle of a building, or on capitals or the coping of gables. They curve up and away from the surface to which they are attached and turn down part of the way upon themselves, with a knob at the end. One would find *crockets* on medieval cathedrals, palaces, and other public buildings. *Crocket* comes from Middle English *croket* (hook), and is not to be confused with **crotchet**, which is quite a different matter.

crocodiline,　see **accipitrine**

cromlech,　see **dolmen**

crotaline,　see **accipitrine**

crotchet　(KROCH it) *n*. This word has a number of distinct meanings: a small hook; any hooked tool or instrument; in British English, a quarter note (in music); and, strange to say, an eccentricity, whim, peculiarity, quirk. It is from this last meaning that we get the adjective *crotchety* (KROCH ih tee): grouchy, crabbed, cranky, irascible, eccentric, capricious, whimsical, erratic. Obviously, its meaning of "hook" or "hooked instrument" is related to *crochet* (kro SHAY) and *crocheting* (kro SHAY ing, the pronunciation having taken over from the French), needlework done with a hooked needle, and to the shepherd's staff or bishop's crozier, both known as "crooks." There is, of course, the informal use of the word *crook* to mean "dishonest person"—someone not entirely straight, as it were. (Remember "Your President is not a *crook*," the proud statement made on the air by Richard M. Nixon?) It takes some imagination, however, to make the jump from *small hook* to *eccentricity* or *quirk*, except that there is something "out of line" about both hooks and eccentricities. "Faith, thou has some *crotchets* in thy head now," says Mistress Ford to her husband in Shakespeare's *Merry Wives of Windsor* (Act II, Scene 1), signifying that he is acting oddly. The adjective *crotchety* is commoner than the noun, especially in phrases like *crotchety old man*, descriptive of a curmudgeon. *Crotchet* and *crotchety* come from Middle English *crochet* (hook). Speaking of quirks and whims, see also **maggot**.

cryptesthesia　(kript es THEE zhee uh, -zhuh) *n*. This is another word for "clairvoyance," perception that is acute beyond normal limits. The word derives from the Greek prefix *krypto-* (hidden, secret), based on *kryptein* (to hide), plus *aisthesis* (perception). We find *crypto-* in such words as *cryptogenic*, describing a disease of unknown origin, *cryptogram*, something written in code, etc. People endowed with *cryptesthesia* are said to be *cryptesthetic* (kript es THET ik); they have the supranormal power of "seeing" things not visible to the generality of mankind, together with special intuitive understanding of people and things.

cuculine,   see **accipitrine**

cucullate   (KYOOH kuh late) *adj. Cucullate* means "hooded" or "cowled," i.e., having or wearing a hood or a cowl, like that worn by monks and members of the Ku Klux Klan. The word comes from Late Latin *cucullatus* (hooded), based on Latin *cucullus* (covering, hood). *Cucullate* sometimes adds a *d* to form *cucullated*, with the same meaning. There is a medieval proverb that goes "Cucullus not facit monachum." ("The cowl does not make a monk.") The Albanians say (in Albanian, naturally): "It takes more than a hood and sad eyes to make a monk." (Didn't somebody say: "Clothes make the man"?) The English poet Richard Lovelace (1618–1656), in *To Althea: From Prison*, wrote: "Stone walls do not a prison make,/Nor iron bars a cage," while his countryman William Wordsworth (1770–1850) disagreed to a degree, in *Humanity*: "Stone walls a prisoner make . . ." The Greek philosopher Aristotle (384–322 B.C.) said: "One swallow does not make a summer," but the American poet Robert Lowell (1917–1977) differed, writing in his poem "Fall": "One swallow makes a summer." We have come a long way from *cucullate*, but a couple of detours do not a journey make—or do they?

cucumiform   (kyooh KYOOH muh form) *adj.* This adjective describes anything shaped like a cucumber, which is *cucumis* in Latin. The great English lexicographer and writer Dr. Samuel Johnson (1709–1784) had this to say about that misunderstood vegetable: "A cucumber should be well sliced, and dressed in pepper and vinegar, and then thrown out, as good for nothing." There is no record that he had anything against *cucumiform* objects. Zucchini, a variety of summer squash, are *cucumiform*: likewise most bananas. Or should we say, echoing Johnson's prejudice, that cucumbers are zucchiniform or bananiform—except that there are no such words in the dictionary. There must be lots of things shaped like a cucumber, else *cucumiform* never would have been invented. Make your own list.

culicine,   see **accipitrine**

cumbrous (KUM brus) *adj. Cumbrous* is a synonym of *cumbersome* (KUM bur sum); they both mean "burdensome, unwieldly, impeding, getting in the way of," and come, respectively, from Middle English *cumberous* and *cummyrsum*. The verb *cumber* (KUM bur), to hamper, burden, or trouble, is from Middle English *cumbren* (to harass). We are more familiar with *encumber* (en KUM bur), and *encumbrance* (en KUM bruns), a burden and, in law, a lien on property, like a mortgage. All these Middle English sources go back to Late Latin *cumbrus* (heap), from Latin *cumulus* (heap), which came into English intact meaning "heap" and gave its name to a certain type of cloud formation as well. We read in Luke 10:44 that "Martha was *cumbered* about with much serving . . ." (According to the New English Bible, she was ". . . distracted by her many tasks . . ." but *burdened* seems closer to the situation; and in the parable about the barren fig-tree, Jesus tells of the man who says to his vineyard-keeper, "Cut it down; why *cumbreth* it the ground?" The New English Bible puts it: "Why should it go on using the soil?") The word *cumber-ground*, for "useless thing," comes from this story. The general idea behind all these *cumber* words is, in a nutshell, that of *burdening*.

cunctator (kungk TAY tur) *n.* A *cunctator* is a procrastinator, a dilatory character, one who postpones, delays, lingers, hesitates, put things off. This word was taken over intact from the Latin, where it was based on *cunctatus*, the past participle of the verb *cunctari* (to delay, to linger). "Never put off to tomorrow," says a friend of the author, "what you can postpone indefinitely." *Cunctator* became a nickname or **agnomen** of Quintus Fabius Maximus Verrucosus, a Roman general in the second century B.C., who acquired the epithet for his cautious tactics against Hannibal and the Carthaginians in the Second Punic War (218–201 B.C.), by avoiding pitched battle while harassing the enemy along the way. He has gone down in history as *Fabius Cunctator* (Fabius the Delayer). The title was at first meant to be derogatory, but later acquired a laudatory aspect in view of the eventual effectiveness of the delaying tactics. The Roman statesman and orator Cicero (106–43 B.C.), in *On Old Age*, quoted the poet Ennius (239–169 B.C.) thus: "One man, by delaying [*cunctando*, in the original], saved the state for us." Nowadays, ancient history forgotten, a *cunctator* is simply a procrastinator, a postponer, a wavering, indecisive individual afraid

128

to take decisive action, rather than a cautious wait-and-see type who finally exhausts the adversary.

cuneal (KYOOH nee ul), **cuneate** (KYOOH nee it, -ate) *adj.* These are alternative forms of the adjective meaning "wedge-shaped," and apply to anything in that configuration; in botany, to leaves that are triangular and taper to a point. *Cuneiform* (kyooh NEE uh form, KYOOH-) also means "wedge-shaped," and is almost always applied to the written characters found in ancient Assyrian, Babylonian, Persian, Hittite, etc., clay inscriptions. The term *cuneiform* was the brain child of the English orientalist Prof. Thomas Hyde (1636–1703) of Oxford. This form of script dates back to about 3800 B.C. and was still in use for a brief period after the birth of Christ. It was deciphered in 1802 by the German archaeologist and philologist Georg Friedrich Grotefend (1775–1853). That was some decoding job! All these *cune-* terms are based on Latin *cuneus* (wedge).

cusp (kusp) *n.* A *cusp* is a point; our word is simply the stem of the Latin noun *cuspis*. *Cusp* has a number of technical meanings in various branches of science, the most familiar denoting the points or horns of a new moon. *Cusp* plays a part in the formation of the familiar names of certain teeth: *cuspid* and *bicuspid*. *Cuspidate* (KUS pih date) is the adjective describing anything ending in a point, like *cuspidated* leaves or teeth. There are no points or *cusps* on *cuspidors*, however; that word is from the Portuguese, where it means "one who spits," based on *cuspir* (to spit), and that, in turn, goes back to the Latin verb *conspuere* (to spit upon), formed of prefix *con-* (as an intensive) plus *spuere* (to spit), whose past participle gave us *sputum*. It's a long way from new moons to sputum, but, to misquote the Greek geometrician Euclid (fl. 300 B.C.) even further (What he said to Ptolemy I, King of Egypt, c. 367–283 B.C., was: "There is no royal road to geometry," usually misquoted as "There is no royal road to learning."), there is no short road between *cusps* and *cuspidors*.

cybernetics (sye bur NET iks) *n. Cybernetics* is the comparative study of control functions and systems in human bodies and mechanical or electric systems (e.g., computers) designed to replace them. The word, like *economics, politics,* etc., is treated as a singular. *Cybernation* (sye bur NAY shun) is control by machines, and is related to automation, which replaces human thought and manual labor in many phases of manufacturing. The American mathematician Norbet Wiener (1874–1964) is considered the father of *cybernetics*. He had many interesting things to say about the new science. It was in 1948 that he said:

> We have decided to call the entire field of control and communication theory, whether in the machine or in the animal, by the name of *Cybernetics*, which we form from the Greek for steersman. [The Greek noun is *kybernetes*.] . . . This new development [automation] has unbounded possibilities for good and for evil.

In the year of his death, 1964, he wrote *(God and Golem, Inc.)*:

> The future offers very little hope for those who expect that our new mechanical slaves will offer us a world in which we may rest from thinking. Help us they may, but at the cost of supreme demand upon our honesty and intelligence. The world of the future will be an ever more demanding struggle against the limitations of our intelligence, not a comfortable hammock in which we can lie down to be waited upon by our robot slaves.

Automate . . . and vegetate?

cyclopean, -ian   (sye kluh PEE un, -KLOH pee-) *adj*. A Cyclops was a member of a fabled race of giants living mainly in Sicily, who had only one round eye in the center of the forehead. They forged iron for Vulcan. Their name in Greek was *Kyklops* ("Round-Eye"), based on *kyklos* (circle) plus *ops* (eye). From the name *Cyclops* we get the adjective *cyclopean* (or *-ian*; upper or lower case *c*) meaning "gigantic, vast." In his poem *King's Cross Station* (one of London's railroad terminals), the English essayist, novelist, critic, and occasional poet G. K. Chesterton (1874–1936) wrote:

> Or must Fate act the same grey farce again,
> And wait, till one, amid Time's wrecks and scars,
> Speak to a ruin here, 'What poet-race
> Shot such *Cyclopean* arches at the stars?'

(Note that the poet used the *-ean* spelling, but the *-ian* stress, as required by the meter.) The arches in King's Cross Station are quite vast. Shakespeare was familiar with the Cyclops. In *Titus Andronicus* (Act IV, Scene 3), Titus exclaims:

> Marcus, we are but shrubs, no cedars we;
> No big-bon'd men fram'd of the Cyclops' size;
> But metal, Marcus, steel to the very back . . .

And in *Hamlet* (Act II, Scene 2), the First Player recites:

> And never did the Cyclops' hammer fall
> On Mars's armour, forged for proof eterne,
> With less remorse than Pyrrhus' bleeding sword
> Now falls on Priam.

Cyclopean is a fine adjective to use in indicating vastness, but make sure it is not applied in any ambiguous situation where it may be mistaken to mean ''one-eyed.''

cygnine, see **accipitrine**

cymotrichous (sye MOT rih kus) *adj.* If you are *cymotrichous*, you have wavy hair, and that pleasant condition is known as *cymotrichy* (sye MOT rih kee). These terms are formed from two Greek words, *kyma* (wave) and *thrix* (hair), whose stem is *thrich-*. If you are *leiotrichous*, you have straight, smooth hair, and that state of affairs is designated *leiotrichy*. Those words are from Greek *leios* (smooth) plus, once again, *thrix*. Should you have crisp and woolly hair, you can be described as *ulotrichous*, and said to enjoy—or suffer from—*ulotrichy*, which covers that situation. These last two words are derived from Greek *ulos* (woolly, curly) and our old friend *thrix*. Suggested sign for a beauty parlor out to win over the lexicographical set, especially etymologists with an anthropological bent: TIRED OF YOUR LEIOTRICHOUS OR ULOTRICHOUS CONDITION? COME IN AND LET US MAKE YOU CYMOTRICHOUS! If the sign doesn't appeal to lexicographers or anthropologists, it might pull in the hypochondriacs.

cyprine, see **accipitrine**

dacelonine, see **accipitrine**

daedal(ian), see **icarian**

daltonism (DAHL tun iz um) *n. Daltonism* is color blindness, especially the congenital inability to distinguish between red and green, so named after the English physicist and chemist John Dalton (1766–1844), who suffered from it and first described it in 1794. The label *daltonism* was introduced by the Scottish physicist Sir David Brewster (1781–1868), the inventor of improved lighthouse illumination and the kaleidoscope. Dalton formulated a law in physics known as "Dalton's Law": The total pressure exerted by a mixture of gases is equal to the sum of the partial pressures of the individual component gases. There are various degrees of *daltonism*, all the way from total (inability to distinguish any colors) to complete partial (confusion of certain bright colors) to incomplete partial (nonrecognition of composite and neutral shades). Sufferers from total color blindness can be guided by traffic lights because the red light is on top, the yellow in the middle, and the green at the bottom, and the position of the brightest itself tells the tale. Gentlemen suffering from *daltonism* don't always prefer blondes.

dap (dap) *n., vb.* To *dap* is to fish by letting the bait bob up and down on the surface of the water. As a noun, *dap* is the name for bait used in that fashion. *Dap* has another meaning: When a ball *daps*, it bounces on the ground, and a *dap*, in this context, is a bounce. The origin of *dap* is obscure, but it is thought to be related to *dab* in the sense of "strike lightly" or "hit feebly" or just "tap." *Dab* is from Middle English, and is considered to be an imitative, if not an onomatopoeic, word.

debouch (dih BOOSH, -BOUCH) *n*. As a military term, *debouching* or *debouchment* is used of troops marching out of a narrow passage, like a defile, into open country. In geography, a river or stream is said to *debouch* when it flows out of its confining banks to open country, or out of a narrow valley into a broader one. The general idea behind *debouch* is to emerge, whether referring to troops, a stream, a river, or a road, from a narrow space into an open area. A river can *debouch* into a sea, a street into a square. *Bouche*, derived from Latin *bocca* (cheek, mouth), is French for "mouth," and the French verb *déboucher* gave us *debouch*.

debridement (dih BREED munt) *n*. In surgery, *debridement* is the removal of dead, torn, or contaminated tissue or of any foreign matter from a wound. The word was taken over intact from the French noun *débridement* (literally, unbridling), based on the verb *débrider* (to unbridle a horse—but in surgery, to relieve a constriction by incision). In the imagination of the French, the stripping away of contaminated tissue from the body, often involving the removal of constricting matter, evoked the image of taking the *bridle* off a horse, which, in a sense, is the removal of a constriction; hence *débridement*; thence *debridement*.

decussate (dih KUS ate, DEK uh sate) *vb*.; (dih KUS ate, -it) *adj*. To *decussate* is to cross or intersect in the form of an *X*. As an adjective, *decussate* applies to anything so divided. In botany, *decussate* leaves are pairs running along the stem at right angles to the adjoining pair. *Decussate* road intersections are not common, or safe. The derivation is from Latin *decussatus*, past participle of *decussare* (to divide in the form of an *X*), based on *decussis*, a Roman coin of *decem* (ten) *asses* (an *as* being an ancient monetary unit weighing twelve ounces); the *decussis* was marked with the Roman numeral *X*. Seems a long way from an ancient Roman coin to an uncommon intersection.

defalcation (dee fal KAY shun, -fol-) *n*. *Defalcation* is missappropriation of money or property by a person holding it in a fiduciary capacity, like a trustee, guardian, public official, or corporate officer. It comes from Middle Latin *defalcatio* (taking away), based on Latin *defalcatus*, past participle of *defalcare* (to cut off). *Falx* is

133

Latin for "scythe" and its stem, *falc-*, is the source of our word *falcate*, meaning "curved," like a scythe or sickle. Scythes cut things off; so do *defalcators*, in their evil way. It's bad enough to steal a stranger's money; *defalcation* from a trusting soul is worse. A guardian found guilty of *defalcation* would surely be removed and should go to jail. The noun *peculation* (pek yuh LAY shun) covers a wider area, being applicable to any case of embezzlement, though, like *defalcation*, it can be applied to misappropriation of public funds, or, more narrowly, to money or property entrusted to one's care. A mayor's *peculation* of public funds would drive him out of office. Both *defalcation* and *peculation* amount to dipping into the till. *Peculation* and its verb *peculate* (PEK yuh late) are from the Latin noun *peculatus*, based on the past participle of the verb *peculari* (to embezzle), literally to "make public funds private," i.e., make them one's own—a case of illegal "privatisation," as it were, to borrow a British term much in vogue in the Thatcher government, which wants to end state ownership of industries and sell them back into private hands, i.e., to "privatise" them. This is another case of British usage in which *public* and *private* confuse Americans. In Britain, a *public* school is a *private* school, and what Americans call a "public school" is a *state* school. In the matter of the state's selling state-owned industries to the public, the British Government calls it "privatisation," while Americans would call it "going public." Incidentally, many words ending in *-ize* in American spelling end in *-ise*, sometimes either *ise* or *ize* (why?) in British usage. Hence the *s* in the English *privatisation* mentioned above. Getting back to *peculation* and *peculate*, they are etymologically related to *peculiar*, from Latin *peculiaris* (as one's own), in the sense of "distinctly characteristic of" or "belonging exclusively to" someone or something, as in the *peculiar* (i.e., characteristic) sounds of the music of a certain composer, or the *peculiar* properties or effects of a certain drug. When a person *peculates*, he makes someone else's property *peculiar*, as it were and so to speak, to himself (temporarily, we hope, until the law catches up with the miscreant).

defenestration   (dee fen ih STRAY shun) *n. Defenestration* is the act of throwing someone (yes, someone!) or something out of a window. To *defenestrate* (dee FEN ih strate) a person or a thing is to engage in that activity—a strange one indeed, since these words are more commonly applied to situations where what is thrown out of the window is a person, rather than a thing. It is surprising, in view of what must be the infrequency of this type of activity, that there exists a word for it, but then, there exists a word for just about everything. There is a famous incident in history when an act of *defenestration* of people was committed: the *Defenestration* of Prague. It seems that, just before the outbreak of the Thirty Years War in 1618, the two principal Roman Catholic members of the Bohemian National Council were thrown out of a window of the castle at Prague by the Protestant members—one way to settle an argument. They weren't killed. The castle had a moat in which the *defenestrated* twain were lucky enough to land, with only minor injuries. Strangely enough, it is once more to Prague that we have to travel to find a more recent (and this time fatal) instance of what might have been *defenestration*. Jan Masaryk (1886–1948, son of Tomas Garrigue Masaryk, first president of Czechoslovakia) was foreign minister of the Czech government-in-exile in London during World War II. He returned to Prague, retaining that post, when that war ended. A short time after the communist coup in 1948, he fell to his death from a window. Despite the official explanation of suicide, the circumstances have never eliminated the possibility of dastardly *defenestration*. In *A Time of Gifts* (John Murray, London, 1977), the English writer Patrick Leigh Fermor (b. 1915) tells us of the martyrdom of St. Johannes Nepomuk in 1393 by the henchmen of King Wenceslas IV. They hurled Johannes into the River Vltava (also known as the Moldau) from a bridge in Prague. Mr. Fermor adds in a footnote: "There are several instances of *defenestration* in Czech history, and it has continued into modern times [referring, no doubt, to poor Masaryk]. The martyrdom of St. Johannes is the only case of depontication, but it must be part of the same Tarpeian tendency." Mr. Fermor is referring to the Tarpeian Rock—the Mons Tarpeius—on the Capitoline Hill in ancient Rome, from which criminals and traitors were hurled to their death.

dehisce (dih HIS) *vb.* To *dehisce* is to gape, open up, crack, or split. The noun for this activity is *dehiscence* (dih HIS uns), which has a special meaning in biology, denoting the bursting of plant capsules for the scattering of seeds. The derivation is from Latin *dehiscere* (to gape, part) and its noun *dehiscentia* (gaping, splitting open). Writers have used *dehisce* quite outside the field of biology, in describing the splitting of the material in an article of clothing, like the thin silk or voile of a woman's blouse. In such cases, however, we are happy to report that nothing like seeds, or anything else, was scattered.

deicide, see **aborticide**

deictic, dictic, see **elenchus**

deipnosophist (dipe NOS uh fist) *n.* This label is applied to a "table-philosopher," a person who converses eruditely at the dinner table. This noun is derived from two Greek words: *deipnon* (dinner) and *sophos* (wise). It was taken from a work entitled *The Deipnosophistae* (Banquet of the Sophists) by Athenaeus, a Greek writer who flourished about the beginning of the third century A.D. The terms *sophist* and *sophistry* have acquired the pejorative implication of speciousness and fallacious reasoning and rhetoric, but in Athenaeus's time, the sophists of ancient Greece were a class of respected itinerant teachers and lecturers. The eminent English lexicographer, poet, critic, and conversationalist Dr. Samuel Johnson (1709–1784) is the foremost example of a *deipnosophist* that leaps to mind. He made of conversation a fine art. More recent *deipnosophists* were H. L. Mencken, the American writer and critic (1880–1956), the American social and literary critic and writer Edmund Wilson (1895–1972), and several members of the Bloomsbury group—the English cultural set that made Bloomsbury Square in London the center of its activities, starting around 1904 and continuing for over three decades. The most famous members were Lytton Strachey, E. M. Forster, Roger Fry, Vita Sackville-West, Virginia Woolf and her husband Leonard, John Maynard Keynes, and Clive Bell. They assembled on Thursday nights for conversations of high literary quality. Any one of these *deipnosophists* would have been an ornament at your dinner table.

delphi(ni)ne, see **accipitrine**

deltiology (del tee OL uh jee) *n.* This term denotes the collection and study of picture postcards, an activity that engages the attention of a surprisingly large number of persons, and constitutes the business of a number of companies. The subject matter of the postcards is of incredible variety: anything from family groups to ancient bathing beauties to public ceremonies to landscapes to Hollywood stills to salacious Coney Island (New York) and Brighton Beach (England) caricatures to sentimental doggerel. People collect just about everything these days: "Early plastic," like objects made of celluloid, is the vogue at the moment; a short time ago it was old bourbon bottles. *Deltiology* comes from Greek *deltion* (small writing-tablet) plus suffix *-logia*, denoting "study."

démarche   (day MARSH) *n*. This is a French loan word meaning "gait," and by extension, "measure, step, course," as in *resort to a* (certain) *measure*, or *take a step*, or *follow a course*. A *démarche* is a plan of action, or a change in a course of action. It is a term often used in the field of diplomacy and denotes a political step or course of action, usually one initiating a fresh policy. At this moment of history (note that we avoided "point in time"), when our foreign policy seems to shift from day to day, *démarche* is a very handy word that one is likely to run across in the columns of the pundits.

demit   (dih MIT) *vb*. This verb is used both transitively and intransitively (see **transitive**), and is found most commonly in Scotland, but used elsewhere as well. To *demit* a position is to resign it, to give it up or relinquish it, and it often refers to public office. **Intransitively**, to *demit* is simply to resign. It comes from Latin *demittere* (to send down), based on the prefix *di-*, a variant of *dis-* (away, apart) plus *mittere* (to send). Because of his need for "the woman I love," Edward VIII of England (1894–1972) *demitted* his throne in 1936—i.e., he abdicated.

demiurge   (DEM ee urj) *n. Demiurge* is the name given by the Greek philosopher Plato (B.C. 327–447) to the Creator, the artificer of the world. Gnosticism, a belief of early Christian times, taught that creation was a process of emanation from the original essence or Godhead, and that the *Demiurge*, creator of the material world, was not God, but the Archon, chief of the lowest order of spirits or powers emanating from the supreme Deity. The *Demiurge* endowed mankind with the psyche, the sensuous aspect of the soul, while God himself added the pneuma, the rational aspect. *Demiurge* comes from the Greek *demiourgos* (worker for the people), based on *demos* (people; cf. *democracy*) plus *ergos* (worker; cf. *erg*, unit of work or energy). The *demi-* of *demiurge* has nothing to do with the *demi-* that we took from the French, as in *demigod* or *demitasse*, and they took from the Latin *dimidius* (half).

demography (dih MOG ruh fee) *n.* This is the study of population, a term derived from two Greek words: *demos* (the people) and *graphein* (to write—the suffix *-graphy* is familiar from *geography, stenography*, etc.). *Demography* includes the study of vital and social statistics, such as the birth, marriage, and death rates, migration patterns and population distribution, and, on the basis of the ascertainment of trends, makes predictions as to probable future social changes. *Demographics* (dih muh GRAF iks), treated as a singular noun, is a term for the statistical data of a population, especially those concerning income, education, average age, etc., and as a plural noun, denotes the facts derived from the data. The adjective is *demographic* (dih muh GRAF ik). The *demographic* data of New York City indicate a trend toward the building of high-rental apartment units. A *demographer* (dih MOG ruh fur) is one engaged in *demography*. With the use of polls and computers, *demography* is tending to become an exact science, and is a very useful tool for those advising candidates for public office.

demotic (dih MOT ik) *adj. Demotic* pertains to anything relating to the common people. In that sense, it can be used as synonymous with "popular." *Demotic* has a narrow, specialized sense as a designation of a simplified form of ancient Egyptian writing in which the priests kept their records. The adjective comes from the Greek *demotikos* (popular, plebeian), based on *demotes* (a plebeian) and *demos* (the common people, the populace). *King Demos* is a facetious term for the electorate, the common people who select the ruler and in that way are "sovereign," as though political machines and chicanery didn't exist. *Demo-*, the Greek prefix from *demos*, is found in words like *democracy* and *demography*. *Demotics*, treated as a singular noun, is sometimes used as a synonym of *sociology*, the study of people, their care and culture.

dendrochronology (den droh kruh NOL uh jee) *n.* Formed of three Greek nouns, *dendron* (tree), *chronos* (time), and *logos* (word,

138

discourse), *dendrochronology* is the dating of past events through the study of the annual growth rate of tree rings. *Dating*, in a number of sciences, is the determination of the age of objects or events, based on various techniques, including the natural radioactivity of certain minerals, identification of fossils, the carbon-14 method, pollen analysis, and cross-checking with *dendrochronology*, where the age of ancient wood is determined by the ring pattern in its cross section. The pattern of ring widths reflects local climatic phenomena which occurred when the section of wood was part of a living tree. Through the use of overlapping patterns in various samples, *dendrochronological* dating has been carried back over 8,000 years.

depontication, see **defenestration**

derisory (dih RYE suh ree) *adj*. One must be careful about the meaning of this word, especially to avoid identifying or confusing it with *derisive* (dih RY siv). At one time, the dictionaries, both American and English, made no distinction, but those days are— or should be—over: whereas *derisive* means "showing or express- ing derision, ridiculing," *derisory* means "inviting or worthy of derision," or, as Fowler puts it, "too insignificant or futile for serious consideration; it is applied to offers, plans, suggestions . . . the word is no longer needed in the sense [i.e., "showing deri- sion"] now nearly monopolised by *derisive* . . ." Both *derisory* and *derisive* stem from the Latin *derisus*, past participle of the verb *deridere* (to mock—from which we get *deride, derision*, etc.), formed of the prefix *de-*, used as an intensive, plus *ridere* (to laugh— from whose past participle, *risus*, we get words like *risible* and *risibility*). Remember the distinction: If a silly proposition is of- fered, one's attitude would be *derisive*; the proposition itself would be *derisory*.

descant (DES kant) *n*.; (des KANT) *vb*. A *descant* in music is an accompaniment above the theme, harmonizing with it or serving as a counterpoint. At times, it is simply the alto voice raised an octave. It is also used as a term in part music for the soprano voice or, in a wider sense, any melody. As a general term outside the music field, a *descant* can be a comment on any subject. As a verb, to *descant* (note different stress) is to sing or, used as a general term outside the field of music, to comment at length on any subject, and there is the variant *discant* (dis KANT). The derivation is from Middle Latin *discanthus*, which goes back to the Latin verb *cantare* (to sing). In *Paradise Lost*, the English poet John Milton (1608–1674) wrote of the "wakeful nightingale":

> She all night long her amorous *descant* sung . . .

Shakespeare liked the word. He used it twice in *Richard III*: once as a verb, Act I, Scene 1, by Richard, as Duke of Gloucester, in the soliloquy that opens the play:

> Now is the winter of our discontent
> Made glorious summer by this sun of York . . .
> Have no delight to pass away the time,
> Unless to spy my shadow in the sun
> And *descant* [comment] on mine own deformity . . .

and again as a noun, in Act III, Scene 7, when Buckingham advises Richard to look coy and pious but then to accept the crown:

> Look you get a prayer-book in your hand
> And stand between two churchmen, good my lord;
> For on that ground I'll build a holy *descant* [song, melody] . . .

In his poem *The Passionate Pilgrim*, Shakespeare uses *descant* once more as verb:

> Good night, good rest. Ah! neither be my share:
> She bade good night, that kept my rest away;
> But daff'd me [turned me away] to a cabin hang'd with care,
> To *descant* on the doubts of my decay.

[Two notes: 1. Shakespeare stressed the first syllable in both noun and verb uses of *descant*. 2. Shakespeare innocently libeled Richard, who was neither a rascal nor a hunchback. He gave credence to Henry VII's public relations people—and had to court the Tudor Queen Elizabeth's favor as well. The best authorities prove that Richard was a good guy.]

desiderative   (dih SID uh ray tiv) *n.*, *adj.* This is a grammatical term for a verb derived from another verb, that expresses the desire to do that which is denoted by the underlying or primitive verb.

Examples: The Latin verb *micturare* (to desire to urinate; see **micturate**) is the *desiderative* or *desiderative verb* derived from the verb *mingere* (to urinate), whose past participle is *mictus*; the verb *esurire* mentioned under **esurient** means to "hunger," and is the desiderative of *edere* (to eat), whose past participle is *esus*. This grammatical phenomenon is found in Greek as well as Latin.

desideratum (dih sid uh RAY tum) *n.* A *desideratum* is something desired or needed, the lack of which is a matter of wide concern. It is the neuter form of *desideratus*, the past participle of the Latin verb *desiderare* (to desire). Hamlet (Act III, Scene 1), in his "To be . . ." soliloquy, calls death and the end of all the ills "the flesh is heir to" a "consummation devoutly to be wished," which in itself is a good definition of a *desideratum*. Peace on earth is a *desideratum*; a cancer cure is a *desideratum*; racial harmony is a *desideratum*. The related verb, to *desiderate* (something) is to feel (it) to be lacking, to regret (its) absence. Fowler gives us a warning about this word. He describes it as ". . . a useful word in its place, but . . . so often misplaced that we might be better without it. Readers . . . do not know the meaning of it, taking it for [a] pedantic or facetious form of *desire* . . . Writers . . . are ill-advised in using the word unless they are writing for readers as learned as themselves . . ." What one *desiderates* is a *desideratum*.

desinence (DES uh nuns) *n. Desinence* is an ending, a termination; *desinent* (DES uh nunt), the adjective, means "terminal, final," describing anything that puts an end to, or constitutes the end of something. Thus, in a sonnet, the 14th line is the *desinence*; in *La Divina Commedia (The Divine Comedy)* of the Italian poet Dante Alighieri (1265–1321), the 33rd canto of *Paradiso (Paradise)* is the *desinent* one. In a sequential novel like *Strangers and Brothers* (Faber & Faber, London, 1940–1949; Macmillan, London, 1951–1970), the 11-volume series by the English writer C. P. Snow (Baron Snow of Leicester, 1905–1980), the eleventh volume (*Last Things*) is the *desinence*, or the *desinent* installment. *Desinent* and *desinence* can also be applied to a word ending or suffix, like the *-logy* in *geology, theology*, etc. *Desinence* is, via the French and Middle Latin *desinentia*, from Latin *desinens*, the present participle of the verb *desinere* (to put down, leave), based on the prefix *de-* (down) plus the verb *sinere* (to allow).

desipient   (dih SIP ee unt) *adj*. This word means "foolish, silly," and its related noun *desipience* denotes that state, with the implication of "folly" or "frivolousness" rather than downright foolishness. The American humorist Artemus Ward (Charles Farrar Browne, 1834–1867) spoke of "occasional *desipience*," echoing the lovely line in Ode 12 of Book IV of the Odes of the Roman poet Horace (65-8 B.C.): "It is pleasant to be frivolous on occasion." (*Dulce est desipere in loco*.) It follows the line: *"Misce stultitiam consiliis brevem"*; in the Wickham translation, the couplet goes: "Mix with your sage counsels some brief folly. In due place to forget one's wisdom is sweet." The English author Samuel Butler (1835–1902, the *Erewhon* man, not the *Hudibras* man, 1612–1680) in his *Further Extracts from the Note-Books*, concocted a jocular conflation of Horace's famous *Dulce et decorum est pro patria mori (It is a sweet and becoming thing to die for the fatherland—Ode 2 of Book III) and the line quoted above from Ode 12 of Book IV, coming up with the hybrid Dulce et decorum est desipere in loco*, to the effect that it is not only sweet, but becoming as well, to play the fool at the right time and place. Horace would have agreed. The English poet Charles Stuart Calverley (1831–1884) in a poem entitled *Beer*, wrote:

> When 'Dulce est desipere in loco'
> Was written, real Falernian winged the pen.

(Falernian wine, made from grapes in Falernus, in the district of Campania in southwest Italy, was Horace's favorite, celebrated by his contemporary Virgil, 70–19 B.C., as well.) *Desipient* and *desipience* are derived from the Latin verb *desipere* (to be silly) and its present participle *desipiens*. *Desipere*, in turn, is formed of the Latin prefix *de-* (away from) and *sapere* (to be wise or sensible), whose present participle *sapiens* gave us our word *sapient*.

deus ex machina   (dee us eks MAK uh nuh, day-). This term is a Latin translation of the Greek *theos ek mekhanes*, meaning, literally, "a god from the machine." What machine? The one that was operated in the classical Greek theater, a platform on which

142

the gods rested, from which one or more of them could be let down to the stage, to intervene supernaturally in settling the affairs of mortals. (If the deity in question happened to be female, the *deus* would be a *dea*.) From this theatrical convention of ancient times, the expression has taken on the significance of any contrived providential device to unravel plot difficulties. The *deus ex machina* that solves the problem so abruptly can be a person or an event. It is a favorite device of dramatists and novelists who build up complicated situations that would be almost, if not quite, impossible to resolve without such contrived and often inartistic intervention. The United States Marines were the *deus ex machina* that saved the day in many an old movie. Authors shamelessly resort to the long arm of coincidence as the *deus ex machina* that suddenly makes everything come out just right.

dianoetic   (dye uh noh ET ik) *adj*. This adjective applies to anything pertaining to reasoning, especially that of the digressive or discursive type, or to the intellect in general. It is formed from the Greek prefix *dia-* (through—as found in words like *diagnosis, diameter*) plus the verb *noeein* (to think), so that its literal meaning is "through thought." Conclusions reached *dianoetically* are reasoned, as opposed to those achieved intuitively. *Dianoia* (dye uh NOY uh) is a Greek word for "knowledge through intellect"; formed of *dia-* plus *nous* (mind, intellect), it is a term used by the Greek philosopher Plato (427–347 B.C.). It applies to knowledge of the real world as it exists, which can—according to Plato—only be approximate, as opposed to the ideal world, which exists only in the imagination. *Dianoia* is usually translated, therefore, as "opinion," as distinguished from certainty.

diaphoretic,   see sudorific

diaskeuast   (dye uh SKOOH ast) *n*. Literally, a reviser or interpolater, from the Greek verb *diaskeuazein* (to make ready), based on prefix *dia-* (through, across, by) plus the noun *skeuos* (tool). A *diaskeuast* is an editor, and it is to be hoped that the *diaskeuast* editing this work will not have to do too much revising or interpolating! The next time this author has a serious disagreement with his editor, it will be pleasant to accuse him or her of being a *dia-*

skeuast (it does sound like a term of abuse) and silently await the reaction.

diaspora　(dye AS pur uh) *n*. This term, taken over intact from the Greek where it means "dispersion" (based on prefix *dia-*, meaning inter alia, "through" and "thoroughly," plus the verb *speirein*, to scatter), means "scattering, dispersion." With a capital *D*, the *Diaspora* is the name given to the scattering of the Jews after the Babylonian captivity, and is also used collectively for the dispersed Jews. In the age of the Apostles *Diaspora* was the label of the Jews living outside Palestine, and the term is now used to describe those living outside Israel. The General Letter of James (1:1) is addressed "to the twelve tribes which are scattered abroad." As a general term, with a lower case *d*, *diaspora* describes the situation of any group bound by common national origin or creed that is dispersed outside the boundaries of its country. The *diaspora* of the African black peoples as slaves has resulted in minority problems in many parts of the world.

diatribe　(DYE uh tribe) *n*. A *diatribe* is a bitter denunciation, a vilifying invective. Cf. **philippic**. It has an unusual derivation, from Greek *diatribe* (spending of time, pastime, discourse—words hardly related to the present meaning of *diatribe*), related to the verb *diatribein* (to rub away, erode), based on prefix *dia-* (through) plus *tribein* (to rub—a verb that helps to explain **tribadism** as well). Apparently, the effect of a *diatribe* is to wear away or wear down the person at whom it is directed, the way the Roman politician and conspirator Catiline (c. 108–62 B.C.) was worn down by the "Catilinian Orations" aimed at him by the Roman statesman and orator Cicero (106–43 B.C.) which brought about the conspirator's downfall.

didelphine,　see **accipitrine**

didine,　see **accipitrine**

digitigrade,　see **plantigrade**

diglot　(DYE glot) *n.*, *adj. Diglot*, as an adjective, means "bilingual"; as a noun, a "bilingual book or edition." It is from the Greek *padjective diglottos*, based on the prefix *di-* (two, double) plus *glotta*

144

(tongue). There is a great deal of controversy in the United States on the subject of bilingual, or *diglot*, teaching in our public schools to accommodate the large number of Spanish-speaking Puerto Ricans now living in urban centers. A book in a foreign tongue with the English translation interlined, or on facing pages, like certain "trots" or "ponies," especially in the classics (usually forbidden by the school authorities), is a *diglot*. There are perfectly legitimate *diglots* of some of the classics, like the edition of *La Divina Commedia (The Divine Comedy)* of the great Italian Poet Dante Alighieri (1265–1321) with translation on facing pages by Professor Harry Morgan Ayres (1881–1948), with whom the author attended some classes at the University of Rome in 1926/7 while the professor was on sabbatical from Columbia University—a marvelous translation.

digraph (DYE graf) *n.* A *digraph* is a combination of two letters representing a single sound, like the *ai* in *main*, the *ea* in *meat* or *great*, the *sh* in mush, the *ch* in *much*, the *th* in *this* or *thin*, the *ph* in *digraph*. There are *trigraphs* as well: the *tch* in *match*, the *eau* in *beau*, the *ght* in *tight*. Digraph comes from the Greek prefix *di-* (two) plus *graphe* (mark), related to the verb *graphein; trigraph* from the Greek or Latin prefix *tri* (three) plus *graphe*. The *digraph* differs from a diphthong in that the latter produces a gliding sound, like the *oi* in *boil* or *toil* or the *oy* in *joy* or *toy*, though some authorities equate the two or at least say that they are "loosely" one and the same. The Greek alphabet uses diphthongs, but single letters where we use consonantal *digraphs*: θ for *th* as in *thin*; Φ for *ph*; X for *ch* as in German *ach*; Ψ for *ps* as in *psalm*. The Cyrillic alphabets (Russian, Bulgarian, Serbian, etc.) do the same.

dingle (DING gul) *n.* A *dingle* is a narrow, shady dell or dale, or a small, deep ravine or valley, depending on the context. It is also known in England as a *dimble*, a word now obsolete in the United States, except in some dialects, and where so used, it imples that a stream runs through a little valley. *Dingle* has some wholly unrelated further uses: as a storm door or shed, in some parts of the northern United States, and in others, as the tinkle of a little bell. As a verb, it can mean to "tinkle" or "jingle" like a bell, or

145

to "tingle" in the cold. As a synonym of *dell*, *dingle* is from Middle English *dingle* meaning "deep dell" or "hollow," and is related to Old English *dung* (dungeon) and Old High German *tunc* (cellar).

Dionysian (dye uh NISH un, -NIS ee un) *adj.* In Greek mythology, *Dionysus* (dye uh NYE sus) was the god of wine, fertility, and drama; Bacchus was his Roman counterpart, with the emphasis on the wine. He was worshipped in drunken, orgiastic festivals called "Dionysia," involving performances from which Greek tragedy and comedy evolved. The adjective *Dionysian* referred to the god, but because of the nature of his worship, it acquired, with a lower case *d*, the sense of "wildly uninhibited, frenzied, orgiastic." Its diametrical opposite was *Apollonian* (ap uh LOH nee un), an adjective applied literally to the cult of Apollo, the classical god of beauty, music, poetry, healing, and prophecy, and with a lower case *a*, as in the case of the extension of *dionysian*, it was broadened to mean "serene, composed, placid, poised." Nowadays, much of rock music and the concomitant dancing it inspires have a *dionysian* atmosphere and beat, often inexplicable and distressing to the folks who were brought up on *apollonian* love songs.

discrete (dih SKREET) *adj.* This adjective, too often confused with another that is pronounced the same way and is actually an anagram of it—the familiar word *discreet*—means something quite different: "separate, detached, distinct," and in context, "discontinuous," or "abstract," the opposite of *concrete* in the realm of concepts and thinking. They have a common origin, in the Latin *discretus*, the past participle of the verb *discernere* (literally, to separate, set apart; figuratively, to distinguish, discern). Somehow, the Latin participle separated into both *discreet* (circumspect, careful in one's actions, wise in keeping information to oneself) and *discrete*, with the meanings listed above. The noun related to *discrete* is *discreteness*; the noun from *discreet* is *discretion*. *Discretion*, not *discreteness*, is the better part of valor. Fowler says that *discrete* should be accented *DIH skreet*, like *concrete* (*KONG kreet*) in some of its meanings, with the incidental effect of distinguishing it from *discreet*. Our form of government consists of three *discrete* parts: the executive, the legislative, and the judicial. They don't always act discreetly.

146

disembogue (dis em BOHG) *vb*. When something is said to *disembogue*, it is pouring forth and discharging its contents, whatever they may be. This term is used especially of rivers and streams discharging their waters into a lake or ocean. *Disembogue* can also be used transitively in the general sense of "cast out" or "discharge": a stream can *disembogue* its waters into a lake. *Disembogue* is derived from the Spanish verb *desembocar*, based on Spanish prefix *des-*, from Latin *dis* (away) plus *embocar* (to enter the mouth, from Latin prefix *in-*, into, plus Latin *bucca*, cheek or mouth). Used of flowing waters discharging into open waters, as a term in geography, *disembogue* is synonymous with **debouche**.

disjunctive, see **copula**

dithyrambic (dith uh RAM bik) *adj*. This adjective is based on the noun *dithyramb* (DITH uh ram), from the Greek *dithyrambos*, which was the name given to a wild, vehement ancient Greek choral chant, hymn, or song, and later to any impassioned, sublime prose or poetry, usually irregular in form. *Dithyramb* applies, literally, to that type of composition, but by extension, to any literary form that is rapturous and expressive of wild enthusiasms. *Dithyrambic* poetry was originally a wild, rapturous chant to Dionysus (Bacchus, in Roman mythology) and its invention is ascribed to the Greek poet Arion of the seventh century B.C., who must have been a pretty good musician as well as poet, for, according to the Greek historian Herodotus (c. 484–425 .B.C.), it was good enough to charm at least one savage beast: Thrown into the sea by pirates, Arion was saved by a dolphin charmed by his song. To carry on *dithyrambically* about something, like a work of art, a performance, an exhibition, a landscape, or the object of one's ardor ("This time it's different!") is to be wildly enthusiastic, nay rapturous on the subject, sometimes stretching the patience of the listener to the breaking point.

diurnal (dye UR nuhl) *adj*. *Dirunal* means "daily," as in *the milkman's diurnal route*, or "daytime" in its attributive use, "active by day," as in *the diurnal* (as opposed to the nocturnal) *activities* of certain animals and insects. The English poet Swinburne

(1837–1909), in *The Garden of Proserpine* (Proserpine was Pluto's wife, and queen of the underworld), used *diurnal* in the second sense:

> Then star nor sun shall waken
>   Nor any change of light:
> Nor sound of waters shaken,
>   Nor any sound or sight.
> Nor wintry leaves nor vernal,
> Nor days nor things *diurnal*;
> Only the sleep eternal
>   In an eternal night.

Earlier, his countryman Wordsworth (1770–1850), in *A Slumber Did My Spirit Seal*, used it in the first sense:

> A slumber did my spirit seal;
>   I had no human fears:
> She seemed a thing that could not feel
>   The touch of earthly years.
>
> No motion has she now, no force;
>   She neither hears nor sees;
> Rolled round, in earth's *diurnal* course
>   With rocks, and stones, and trees.

and again, in *Influence of Natural Objects*:

> Yet still the solitary cliffs
> Wheeled by me—even as if the earth had rolled
> With visible motion her *diurnal* round!

Shakespeare used it in the same sense, in *All's Well That Ends Well* (Act II, Scene 1), when Helena tells the King of France that she will cure him of his fistula

> Ere twice the horses of the sun shall bring
> Their fiery torcher [torch-bearer] his *diurnal* ring . . .

Diurnal is from Latin *diurnus* (daily—based on *dies*, day). Cf. **quotidian,** which also means "daily," but only in the first sense, and **hebdomadal.**

divagate   (DYE vuh gate, DIH-) *vb.* To *divagate* is to stray, wander, ramble; the word is used in the realm of speech and the realm

148

of the physical world. As to speech, to *divagate* is to digress, to ramble, to be discursive. In the physical world, one reads of a stream *divagating*, and the *divigation* (dye vuh GAY shun) of a country brook is one of the prettiest features of the landscape. *Divagate* comes from the Latin *divagatus*, past participle of the verb *divagari* (to stray, wander off), based on the prefix *di-*, a variant of *dis-* (away, apart) plus *vagari* (to wander), which gave us the noun *vagary* (vuh GAR ee, VAY guh ree), an unpredictable, erratic happening, and the adjective *vagarious* (vuh GAR ee us), erratic, capricious, though it can mean "wandering" or "roving" as well. When a speaker succumbs to excessive *divagation*, his audience often succumbs to sleep. To dispense with *divagation*, at a conference, for example, is to get down to business. Do not confuse *divagate* with *divaricate* (dye VAR uh kate, dih-), which means to "diverge, spread apart, branch off," from Latin *divaricatus*, past participle of *divaricare* (to spread asunder, stretch apart), based on prefix *di-*, a variant of *dis-* (apart, asunder) plus *varicare* (to straddle), and the related adjective *varicus* (with feet apart, straddling).

divaricate, see **divagate**

divination (div uh NAY shun) *n. Divination* is prophecy, augury, the foretelling of the future. There are all kinds of methods described in history, from the inspired Delphic oracle priestess to the spiritualistic medium in a trance, the fortune-teller gazing into a crystal ball, the use of playing or tarot cards, the reading of palms, and the casting of lots, also known as *cleromancy* (KLER uh man see), from Greek *kleros* (lot) plus *manteia* (divination). *Divination* is from Latin *divinatio*, based on *divinatus*, past participle of *divinare* (to soothsay), from which we get our verb to *divine*, meaning to "prophesy." The Latin is related to *divus* (god), a noun connected with *deus* (god), since the art of foretelling was a *divine* or superhuman attribute. The meaning of *divination*, as a literary word, has been extended to include "intuition." And remember that it is through the use of *divining* or dowsing rods, usually forked hazel sticks, that we locate unseen underground things, like water or metal deposits, an occupation that combines augury and intuition and perhaps a bit of godliness? or quackery?

docent (DOH sent) *n.* A *docent* is a university lecturer. The letterhead on the office stationery of the Austrian neurologist (and founder of psychoanalysis) Sigmund Freud (1856–1939) read:

> Dr. Sigm. Freud
> *Docent* für Nervenkrankheiten
> a. d. Universität

meaning "Lecturer on Neurosis at the University." Sometimes the word is used as a shortened form of *privatdocent, -zent* (pree VAT doh tsent), a private lecturer paid by his students, especially in Germany. *Docent* was taken, via German *Dozent*, from *docens*, present participle of *docere* (to teach). *Doctor*, in Latin means "teacher," and is related to *doctus*, the past participle of *docere*. Thus, it is the title of certain university degrees, as well as the common name for "physician" and in shortened form—*doc*—a common form of address from cabbies to passengers. To get back to *docent*: The American poet David McCord (b. 1897), in a 1945 poem *What Cheer*, wrote:

> The decent *docent* doesn't doze;
> He teaches standing on his toes.
> His student dassn't doze and does.
> And that's what teaching is and was.

dolmen (DOL mun) *n.* This is the name of a type of prehistoric structure, generally considered to be a tomb, formed of a large flat stone laid across two or more large vertical stones. We got the word from the French, who took it over from *tolmen*—hole of stone, in Cornish, a Celtic language that became extinct c. 1800. (One Dorothy Pentreath of Mousehole, in Cornwall, England [pronounced *Mowzl*, meaning "place in the sun," and having nothing to do with either mice or holes], is said to be the last person who could converse in Cornish.) *Cromlech* (KROM lek), from Welsh *crom*, the feminine form of *crwm* (bent, crooked) plus *llech* (flat stone), is the Welsh equivalent of a Cornish *dolmen*, though *cromlech* applies equally to any circular group of large erect stones lacking a capstone. Welsh is still spoken in Wales; indeed, there is an active and growing movement to enlarge its use in both speech and on radio and television. The Constantine *Dolmen* in Cornwall is one of the largest, 33 feet long, 14 ½ feet high, and 18 ½ feet across; it consists

150

of a huge capstone supported by two natural rocks. Another famous large *dolmen* in Cornwall is known as the "Trethevy Quoit." The best-known cromlechs are Wayland Smith's Cave in Berkshire, Kit's Coty House in Kent, both in England, and the Killing-Stone in Louth, Ireland. There are many *dolmens* or *cromlechs* all over Britain. Now, after all this archaeology, do not confuse *dolmen* with *dolman*, a woman's cloak with capelike arm pieces.

doran   (dor AN) *n.* This is an acronym for *D*oppler *ran*ge, and is the name given to an electronic device used in navigation for computing range. It is based on the principle of the "Doppler effect," named after the Austrian physicist C. J. Doppler (1803–1853) who was the first to note the change in the frequency of sound and light waves that occurred when the distance between source and receiver varied. We have all noted the change in the pitch of a locomotive bell or horn as the train leaves or approaches us: When a train engine rushes by ringing its bell (that doesn't happen much any more) or blowing its horn, the pitch decreases and the sound fades as the train zooms off. The *doran* was developed to measure distance based on the variation of pitch resulting from the Doppler effect, through a correlation best left to physicists.

doxology   (dok SOL uh jee) *n.* A *doxology* is a hymn in praise of God. The *Greater Doxology* is the hymn *Gloria in Excelsis Deo* (Praise to God in the Highest) said or sung as part of the Mass or Eucharist. The *Lesser Doxology* is the *Gloria Patri* (Glory be to the Father, etc.) said or sung at the end of each psalm in the liturgy. The hymn by Bishop Thomas Ken (1637–1711):

> Praise God, from whom all blessings flow,
> Praise Him, all creatures here below,
> Praise Him above, ye heavenly host,
> Praise Father, Son, and Holy Ghost

is also known as the *Doxology*. In using the term, one must specify which *Doxology* is meant. It is derived from Greek *doxologia*, based on *doxa* (honor) plus the suffix *-logia*.

dragoman   (DRAG uh mun) *n.* A *dragoman* is an interpreter, sometimes also a guide. The term is usually applied to persons who professionally interpret Near Eastern languages, particularly Arabic, Turkish, and Persian, for government offices, tour companies, and the like. The word has traveled all the way from Arabic *targuman* to Medieval Greek *dragomenos* to Old Italian *dragomanno* to Middle French *dragoman*, whence we adopted it: quite a trip! The plural should be *dragomans*, because the final syllable hasn't a thing in the world to do with our word *man*, but English-speaking people, assuming that it did, formed the originally erroneous plural *dragomen*, which has now become a permissible alternative. "Insistence on *-mans*," says Fowler, "is didacticism." *Didacticism*, according to Schur in *1000 Most Important Words* (Ballantine, New York, 1982; Facts On File, New York, 1984), ". . . often covers the situation where communication is overburdened with instructions and explanations."

dragoon (druh GOOHN) *n.*, *vb.* To *dragoon* is to coerce by vigorous, oppressive measures. *Dragoon* was originally the name of a member of certain cavalry regiments or a mounted infantryman armed with a carbine or short musket; modern land tactics have made it an obsolete military term. As a verb, it was used at first to describe the setting of *dragoons*, later, soldiers generally, against opposing forces; then to denote any persecution by armed forces. In current usage, it has come to signify the forcing of any action through oppressive measures, and generally means to "coerce." In recent times, Cambodian town-dwellers were *dragooned* by communist authorities into leaving their urban quarters for the inhospitable open country, where many perished. The term comes from *dragon*, a word at first used by the French for "pistol hammer" because of its resemblance to that legendary creature, and later to the musket and finally to the soldiers so equipped. Other authorities propose a different derivation, directly from the fabulous beast because of the fire-spouting action of the carbine. Except in history books and historical novels, you will not ordinarily run into *dragoon* except as a verb meaning "coerce." The ending *-oon* originates from French words ending in stressed *-on*, especially those whose Italian equivalents end in *-one*, as in *balloon* from French *ballon*, Italian *ballone*, buffoon from french *buffon*, Italian *buffone*, *dragoon* from French *dragon*, Italian *dragone*.

driad, see **oread**

152

dubiety (dooh BYE ih tee, dyooh-) *n. Dubiety* is doubtfulness. A *dubiety* is a matter of doubt, and is also known as a *dubiosity* (dooh bee OS ih tee, dyooh-). These words, as well as *dubious, dubitable, indubitable*, etc., are of course related to *doubt*, derived from the Latin verb *dubitare* (to waver). *Dubiety* is directly from the related Latin noun *dubietas* (doubt). All the "doubt" words go back via the Latin adjective *dubius* (doubtful) to *duo* (two) *viae* (ways), i.e., fluctuating. An extreme form of *dubiety* is *Pyrrhonism* (PIR uh niz um), a term based on the name of the fourth century Greek philosopher Pyrrho, who founded a school of sceptical philosophy holding that nothing was capable of proof and nothing was real but sensations. Who knows?

dubiosity, see **dubiety**

dyslexia, see **alexia**

dysteleology, see **teleology**

eburnean (ee BUR nee un) *adj*. Anything of ivory or like ivory may be described as *eburnean*; less often, *eburneous* (ee BUR nee us). *Eburnation* (ee bur NAY shun, eb ur-) is a medical term for a pathological condition in which bone or cartilage becomes dense and hard like ivory and is said to be *eburnated* (uh BUR nate ud). All these words stem from the Latin adjective *eburneus* or *eburnus* (made of ivory), based on the noun *ebur* (ivory).

ecdysiast (ek DIZ ee ast), *n*. This word was ingeniously and humorously coined by the American writer, critic, and philologist H. L. Mencken (1880–1956) as a "dignified" synonym for *stripper* or *stripteaser*. Mencken's invention was based on the noun *ecdysis* (EK dih sis), a biological term for the casting off of an outer coat, like the shedding of skins by snakes or of shells by crustaceans, a word taken over from the Greek *ekdysis* (getting out). Apparently, Mr. Mencken felt that Gypsy Rose Lee (Rose Louise Hovick, 1917–1970) contributed enough to our culture to warrant a title superior to "stripper." After all, undertakers are now morticians, hairdress-

153

ers beauticians, and garbagemen are sanitation engineers. What with the bikini, the monokini (erroneously derived: the *bi-* in *bikini* has nothing to do with the prefix of duality, as *bicycle, bisexual,* etc., but rather with the atoll Bikini), and finally the spread of the cult of nudism, *ecdysiasm* (invented by the author: cf. *enthusiasm,* or should it be *ecdysiastics:* cf. *gymnastics?*) has become commonplace.

ecliptic, see **solstice**

ecumenical (ek yooh MEN ih kul) *adj.* We are accustomed to meeting this word in connection with movements fostering worldwide Christian unity and the merging of religions in general. The basic thrust of *ecumenicalism* (ek yooh MEN ih kuh liz um), however, is wider: It can pertain to any movement, or for that matter, anything that can be described as "general" or "universal," like an *ecumenical* protest against atomic warfare. *Ecumenical* comes, via Latin *oecumenicus* (belonging to the entire inhabited world), from Greek *oikoumenikos*, based on the verb *oikein* (to inhabit), and sometimes drops the final *-al,* or spells the first syllable *oe,* staying closer to the Greek. *Ecumenicalism* is sometimes shortened to *ecumenism* (ek yooh MEN ih zum) or *ecumenicism* (ek yooh MEN ih siz um). They all denote the beliefs and program of the *ecumenical movement,* whose goal is the unification of all Protestant sects to begin with, and eventually of all Christian doctrines and churches. The World Council of Churches, established in 1948, is the chief instrument of *ecumenicalism*. The Roman Catholic Church has urged *ecumenical* contact with other faiths, especially since the Second Vatican Council in the early 60s. The visit of Pope John Paul II to Canterbury Cathedral in 1984, where he prayed alongside the Archbishop of Canterbury, was a high point. There are international interdenominational organizations all over the world that aim at worldwide religious unity. One God? Why not one Church? God surely is a polyglot.

edacious (ih DAY shus) *adj. Edacious* means "voracious, devouring, gluttonous" and *edacity* (ih DAS ih tee) means "voraciousness, gluttony." *Edacious* is from Latin *edaci-,* the stem of the adjective *edax* (gluttonous, greedy), and *edacity* from latin *edacitas* (greediness, gluttony). They all go back to the Latin verb

154

edere (to eat), which is also the basis of *edible*. The Roman poet Ovid (43 B.C. – C. A.D. 18), in his *Metamorphoses* (15.234) wrote of *tempus edax rerum* (time the devourer of [all] things). Though the use of *edacious* is now felt to be on the humorous side—a sort of fancy word for "greedy" or "insatiable"—it has been used by a number of writers in the phrase *edacious time*, referring back to old Ovid, in situations where erosion and destruction resulting from the passage of time is involved, and applied to the crumbling of monuments as well as the fading of fame. In *The Bigelow Papers* (Series II), the American poet and essayist James Russell Lowell (1819–1891), referring to the site of the battle where the minutemen repelled the British on April 19, 1775, wrote: "The Concord bridge has long since yielded to the *edacious* tooth of Time."

effluvium   (ih FLOOH vee um) *n.* An *effluvium* is an unpleasant or downright noxious exhalation, slight, sometimes invisible, and therefore doubly dangerous, of minute particles; foul and disagreeable vapors from decaying matter, often affecting the lungs, eyes, etc., adversely. *Effluvium* is a Latin word, meaning a "flowing out," related to the verb *effluere* (to flow out). There are other words that come from the same Latin source: *effluence* (EF looh uns), *effluent* (EF looh unt), *efflux* (EF luks), all denoting something that flows out. These are not to be confused with *effluvium*, which involves unpleasant odors or emanations like those coming from garbage dumps or decaying corpses, foul and often harmful. In Bhopal, India, on December 4, 1984, the accidental release of a toxic cloud from a Union Carbide chemical plant killed some 2,500 people and injured—maimed or blinded or both—about 200,000 more, in the worst industrial accident in history. Some *effluvium*!

effuse   (ih FYOOHZ) *vb.* **Transitively**, to *effuse* is to disseminate, pour forth; **intransitively,** to flow out. Pronounced differently (ih FYOOS), as an adjective, *effuse* means "spread out loosely" and is used chiefly as a botanical term. We are familiar with the adjective *effusive* in the sense of "excessively demonstrative," as a description, e.g., of a gushing young fan meeting a celebrity, but the verb *to effuse* is rarely encountered and easily mistaken as equivalent to "be *effusive*" or "act *effusively*." This may be an echo of the use of *enthuse* meaning "to show enthusiasm" or "be enthusiastic" a use, incidentally, to be decried as substandard despite its acceptance by many who should know better. (Fowler calls *enthuse* a "back-formation . . . of U.S. origin which in neither country [i.e., Britain or America] has emerged from the stage of slang, or at best colloquial.") *Effuse*, on the other hand, is perfectly legitimate, when used correctly. It is from the Latin *effusus*, past participle of *effundere* (to pour out).

eidetic (eye DET ik) *adj*. This adjective describes persons endowed with the faculty of retaining a vivid and clear image of something previously seen. An *eidetic* person can readily reproduce in his mind, with great accuracy and detail, what he has seen recently or long since. *Eidetic* imagery has been found to be one of the most important elements of chess mastery. *Eidetic* comes from the Greek adjective *eidetikos*, based on *eidos* (something seen, a form; cf. **eidolon**).

eidolon (eye DOH lun) *n*. An *eidolon* is an apparition, image, specter, or an idealized figure, an idol. This is a word taken intact from the Greek, where it means "phantom," based on the Greek noun *eidos* (form—related to the verb *idein*, to see). *Eidos*, too, has been taken over intact, to mean "idea, essence, ideal," and was derived via Late Latin *idealis*. The American poet, essayist, and diplomat James Russell Lowell (1819–1891), in *Among My Papers* (Series II), used the phrase 'No real giant, but an *eidolon* of the mind," and another American poet, Edgar Allen Poe (1809–1849), in *Dreamland* wrote this scary couplet:

> An *Eidolon* named Night
> On a black throne reigns upright.

Ah, those Bostonians, who knew their Greek and so enriched their language!

eldritch (EL drich) *adj*. Anyone or anything described as *eldritch* is weird, eerie, uncanny, spooky, even frightful. There is disagreement about the origin of this word. Some say it is based on Anglo-Saxon *aelf* (elf) and *rice* (powerful, or realm). Elves are mythological creatures in the nature of sprites who can be mischievous and even malicious. Others trace *eldritch* to Old English *el* (strange, uncanny) and *ric* (creature). Still others say that it comes from Old English *elfrice* (fairy realm). Alternative spellings are *eldrich* and *elritch*. However it is spelt or derived, *eldritch* is certainly connected with *elf* and *elfish*. It is not a common word, and more likely to be met with in Scotland than elsewhere. But you don't have to travel to the Highlands of Scotland to meet an *eldritch* creature; the streets of any town are full of them.

eleemosynary (el ih MOS uh ner ee, -MOZ-, el ee uh-) *adj.* An *eleemosynary* institution is one supported by and dispensing charity, like the United Way, the March of Dimes, the American Red Cross and the Salvation Army. The word comes from Middle Latin *eleemosynarius*, based on Latin *eleemosyna* (alms) taken from Greek *eleemosyne* (mercy, compassion), which gave us the much shorter word *alms* as well. A favorite response of a lawyer friend of the author to a client expressing dismay at the size of a bill is "Sir [or Madame], I do not pretend to be an *eleemosynary* institution!" This does not always serve to calm the client.

elenchus (ih LENG kus) *n.* An *elenchus* is a logical refutation, any argument that refutes another argument. *Elenctic* (ih LENG tik) is the adjective, and applies to indirect methods of proof, like cross-examination, as opposed to *deictic* (DIKE tik) or *dictic* (DIK tik) which pertains to direct methods of proof, like syllogism. *Elenchus* is, via Latin *elenchus*, from Greek *elenchos* or *elegkhos* (refutation), based on *elenchein* (to refute). *Deictic* is from Greek *deiktikos* (serving to show), based on *deiknynai* (to show). The philosophical term *Socratic elenchus* describes a method of eliciting the truth by short questions and answers, and was one phase of the Socratic method, based on question-and-answer procedure, introduced by Socrates, the great Athenian philosopher (c. 470–399 B.C.). The next time your opponent in an argument goes into irrelevancies, hurl at him the lovely phase: "Ignoratio elenchi!" Those Latin words mean "ignoring the argument," and amount to the fallacy of ignoring the point in question and arguing to the wrong point, refuting a proposition different from what you have set forth. An *ignoratio elenchi* is a ponderous (and, it is hoped, crushing) way of saying, "Irrelevant!"

elenctic,   see **elenchus**

elephantine   see **accipitrine**

ellipsis   (ih LIP sis) *n. Ellipsis* is a term in grammar for the omission from a sentence of a word or words needed to complete the construction or the sense. Intentional *ellipsis* in printing is indicated by a variety of symbols, including a series of periods (. . .) or of asterisks (***). *Ellipsis* in grammar is demonstrated in the following examples, the omission indicated by a series of plus signs (+ + +): It is a question whether the evils of narcotics is greater than + + + alcohol (+ + + indicates the omission of *those of*); John Gielgud is as good an actor + + +, if not + + + better + + + than Laurence Olivier (omissions: *as, a* and *one*); No other writer has + + + or can hope to attain the heights of Shakespeare (omission: *attained*). This last is a common type of *ellipsis*, where the construction of different parts of the sentence varies because of the difference of the auxiliary verbs required: in this case, *has*, requiring a past participle, and *to*, requiring an infinitive— *has attained, to attain*. Examples of permissible (intentional) ellipses: The torrential rains were unexpected and the workmen + + + forced to quit work. (A second *were* before *forced* can be omitted and makes the sentence smoother.) He is fortunate, and I + + + unfortunate. (An *am* before *unfortunate* would be grammatically correct, but the sentence is more effective without it.) Fowler has an exhaustive article on *ellipsis*. The adjective related to *ellipsis* is *elliptical* (ih LIP tih kul). When it is used as a description of speech or writing, it is pejorative, indicating that the language is excessively economical, tending to be ambiguous, or even cryptic. *Elliptical* happens also to serve a second purpose, in geometry, as descriptive of an object or a figure having the shape of an ellipse, but the uses are so far apart that the context must eliminate any possibility of confusion. Cf. **aposiopesis**, another sort of omission.

embonpoint   (awn bawn PWAN—all *n*'s pronounced nasally as in French) *n., adj.* This is a term taken from the French, and pronounced in the French manner—but see **fin de siècle** as to the limitations when it comes to the pronunciation of French words in an English sentence. *Embonpoint*, as a noun, means "plumpness," and as an adjective, indicates a well-fed appearance. It was formed from the phrase *en bon point*, meaning, literally, "in good form, in good condition." To describe a person in this way is usually

158

meant as a compliment, but sometimes it has a humorously pejorative twist, suggesting that the subject has fed not wisely but too well. Photographs (especially in profile) of such well known "figures" as President William Howard Taft (1857–1930), "Diamond Jim" Brady (1856–1917) and Edward VII of England (1841–1910) display good examples of *embonpoint*.

embosk, see **bosky**

embrangle (em BRANG gul) *vb*. To *embrangle* is to entangle, enmesh, confuse, muddle, perplex. An employee given contradictory instructions by different superiors becomes *embrangled* in general, and particularly as to what he's supposed to do. Executives who can't delegate are often *embrangled* about conflicting priorities. *Embrangle* is from prefix *em-* (a variant of *en-* before *b* or *p*, as in *embed, embody, empathy*) plus *brangle*, an obsolete word meaning "brawl" as a noun and "wrangle" as a verb; *brangle* is a fusion of the two.

emolument (ih MOL yuh munt) *n*. An *emolument* is compensation for services rendered, in the form of a salary or a fee, as opposed to an *honorarium* (on uh RARE ee um), a voluntary payment for services when the situation is such that there is no legal obligation to pay. *Honorarium* is sometimes a more or less euphemistic substitute for *fee*, and is a term derived from the neuter form of the Latin adjective *honorarius* (done or given as an honor). When you see your doctor, you get a bill and pay him an *emolument*. When the Queen of England is visited by hers, if he receives anything, it's an *honorarium*. The author once bought a used Bentley from an English lawyer who had received it from the Queen's obstetrician as an *honorarium*; the latter had received it from Her Majesty as an *honorarium*; the author paid the lawyer cold cash. *Emolument* is from Latin *emolumentum* (gain, profit—originally a miller's fee, based on prefix *e-*, from, plus *molu-*, a variant of *moli-*, combining form of *molere*, to grind). Do not confuse *emolument* with *emollient* (ih MOL yunt), a softening agent used on skin or tissue; derived from Latin *emolliens*, present participle of *emollire* (to soften), based on the adjective *mollis* (soft).

empennage, see **appanage**

empyrean (em puh REE un, -pye-; em PIR ee un) *n.*, *adj.* This is the name of the highest of the five heavens in the system codified by the Alexandrian mathematician and astronomer Ptolemy (fl. 127–151). This heaven, in that system, consisted of pure fire, and, in the Christian doctrine, was considered the seat of deity and the angels. The adjective is *empyreal* (em PIR ee ul; em puh REE ul, -pye-), but *empyrean* serves as an adjective as well. Apart from their use in the Ptolemaic system, *empyrean* enjoys the general meaning of "sky, heaven," and the adjective means "heavenly, celestial." Both words come from the Greek *empyrios* (fiery). In *Paradise Lost*, the English poet John Milton (1608–1674) penned these lines:

> Now had the Almighty Father from above,
> From the pure *Empyrean* where he sits
> High-thron'd above all height, bent down his eye.

enate, see **agnate**

encephalon (en SEF uh lon) *n.* This is a medical term for "brain," taken from the Greek noun *enkephalos*, based on the prefix *en-* (in) plus *kephale* (head). Some of us may be familiar with the terms *encephalogram* (en SEF uh luh gram) and *encephalograph* (en SEF uh luh graf) for an X-ray of the brain, and *encephalitis* (en sef uh LYE tis) for inflammation of the brain, without realizing that the basis of these and other related medical terms is *encephalon*. Some of these other terms are *encephalomalacia* (en sef uh loh muh LAY shuh), degeneration of the brain, *encephalomyelitis* (en sef uh loh mye uh LYE tis), inflammation of the brain and spinal cord, *encephalotomy* (en sef uh LOT uh mee), dissection of the brain, and *encephalitis lethargica* (en sef uh LYE tis luh THAR juh kah), i.e., sleepy-sickness, not to be confused with sleeping-sickness, commonly associated with Africa and the dreaded tse-tse fly. Remember that all these (and other) terms starting with *encephal(o)* come from the Greek word for "brain."

ench(e)iridion (en kye RID ee un) *n.* An *ench(e)iridion* is a handbook, a manual, a reference book, possibly a short treatise serving as a ready reference source, any of those types of thing small enough to be carried around "in the hand," i.e., handy, conveniently available. It is synonymous with a *vade mecum* (VAY

160

dee MEE kum, vah-). *Encheiridion* is a Greek word, based on the prefix *en-* (in) plus *cheir* (hand), plus the suffix *-idion*, which has a diminutive effect. *Vade mecum* is a Latin phrase for "Go with me," that acquired the status of a noun applicable generally to something for frequent or regular use that one would carry around with him, like a memorandum book or pocket encyclopedia, a ready reference manual, an instruction booklet with directions for the use of portable tools and that sort of thing. The two rather quaint terms are quite useful, and their synonymity gives the writer his choice between the two classical tongues.

enchorial (en KOR ee ul) *adj.* *Enchorial* describes something used by the people of a particular country; something domestic. Its common use appears to be as a description of **demotic** writing. It is derived, via Late Latin *enchorius*, from Greek *enchorios*, based on prefix *en-* (in) plus *chora* (place, country). Though *enchorial* is a rare word, there is no reason why one cannot characterize as *enchorial* reggae, the Jamaican music of the people that developed in the 1960s among the poor blacks, especially the Rastafarian religious sect; or raga, the popular Hindu melodic form; or ragtime, the American musical invention that flourished from the 1890s through the 1910s, and produced Scott Joplin (1868–1917) and the immortal *Maple Leaf Rag*. (Reggae, raga, ragtime: Why all these *r*s and *g*s? Sheer coincidence). *Enchorial* need not be confined to writing or musical forms; it can pertain to dress, diet, marriage, or other customs—anything native to a particular place.

enfilade (EN fuh lade, en fuh LADE) *n.* In French, this word means "suite" (of rooms) or "string" (of words or phrases), and is also a military term for a raking fire from the enemy. We use it to denote an open vista, particularly a suite of rooms in a straight line which, with the doors open, expose to view a straight-ahead vista of a continuous passage. The British use *enfilade* as a term for any series of things arranged as though threaded on a string. They and we also use it to denote a raking fire that covers an enemy position from end to end. As a verb, to *enfilade* is to subject a body of troops, a road, a fortification, etc., to raking firepower. The French noun *enfilade* is derived from their verb *enfiler* (to thread, string), based on *fil* (thread).

161

ennead (EN ee ad) *n.* An *ennead* is a group of nine—persons or things. Whether they know it or not, a baseball team is an *ennead*, a word that comes from the Greek number *ennea* (nine). The combining form of *ennead*, *ennea-*, is found, e.g., in *enneagon*, a polygon with nine angles and nine sides, synonymous with *nonagon* (NON uh gon), formed with the Latin *nonus* (ninth), based on *novem* (nine), from which we got *November*, from Latin *novembris*, which was the ninth month of the early Roman calendar. An *enneahedron* (en ee uh HEE dron) is a solid figure with nine surfaces. Without going into an entire series, we have *monad* (MO nad, MOH-), meaning, inter alia, "single unit," from Greek *monos* (alone); *dyad* (DYE ad), a group of two, from Greek *dyas* (pair); *triad* (TRYE ad), a group of three, from Greek *tria* or *treis* (three), and so on. We are more familiar with the Latin series, *solo, duet, trio, quartet*, etc. In any event, when you follow the next World Series (it used to be known as the "World Serious" among the Brooklyn fans in the golden age of Dem Bums—the Brooklyn Dodgers of blessed memory), remember that it is one *ennead* against another, and may the best *ennead* win!

enormity (ih NOR mih tee) *n.* An *enormity* is an atrocity, something monstrous, outrageous, unforgivably offensive. The Hitler "final solution," with its ensuing genocidal holocaust, was an *enormity* of immeasurable proportions. *Enormities* have been committed throughout history by bloodthirsty conquerors such as Genghis Khan (1162–1227). *Enormity* is derived from the Latin noun *enormitas*, which had the harmless meaning of "irregular shape," and was formed from the prefix *e-* (short form of *ex-* before certain consonants, meaning "away from") plus *norma* (literally, a carpenter's square, and by extension, any rule or standard, from which we get *normal*). *E-* plus *norma* formed the Latin adjective *enormis* (away from the standard, irregular; by extension, enormous). Originally, then, *enormity* meant the same thing as *enormousness* or *immensity*, but over the years it came to be applied only to crimes of *enormous* proportions, i.e., *atrocities*. Its use now to indicate vast size is incorrect. (Fowler is less emphatic; he is content with the warning "inadvisable.") One should not speak of the *enormity* of the Pacific Ocean or the Pyramids or space. There is nothing atrocious about them. One might speak of both the *enormousness* and the *enormity* of the birth rate in India. The Chinese Government considered the *enormousness* of the birth rate there to be such an *enormity* that it formulated a policy of one child to a family. (Incidentally, Fowler says: "*Enormousness* is not a pretty word; the writer [can find] a way out by writing *vastness* or *enormous extent*."

entasis   (EN tuh sis) *n.* This is an architectural term for the slight swelling or convexity given to a shaft or column in order to create the optical illusion that the upright is perfectly straight, and neutralize what would otherwise be the illusion that a column of equal diameter throughout has a slightly concave outline. In the classical Doric column, the swelling begins at the base of the shaft and is at its greatest dimension a bit below its middle point. In the Parthenon (the temple of Athena Parthenos, the virgin Athena, on the Acropolis in Athens), the *entasis* reaches an extent of about ⅜ of an inch from the perpendicular on each side. *Entasis* was taken intact from the Greek, based on the prefix *en-* (in) plus *tasis* (stretch), related to the verb *enteinein* (to stretch tight).

entelechy   (en TEL uh kee) *n.* *Entelechy* is actuality, realized existence, as opposed to mere potentiality. In the vitalist school of philosophy advocated by the German biologist and philosopher Hans Driesch (1867–1941), which holds that phenomena are to a certain extent self-determining and only partly controlled by mechanical forces, *entelechy* is the principle that directs processes in an organism toward realization of a certain end. In *Out of My Depths* (Doubleday, Garden City, N.Y., 1983), Paul West defines *entelechy* as "not only something's is-ness, but how its is-ness had evolved and was evolving." The Irish mathematician and astronomer Sir William Rowan Hamilton (1805–1865) tells us: "Aristotle [the Greek philosopher, 384–322 B.C.] defines the soul, the form or *entelechy* of an organized body." The German philosopher Leibnitz (1646–1716) wrote: "Give the name of *entelechies* to all simple substances or created monads [in the Leibnitz school, a *monad* is an indivisible entity, the ultimate constituent of the universe] for they have in them a certain perfection." *Entelechy* is from Greek *entelecheia*, based on prefix *en-* (in) plus *telos* (goal) plus *echein* (to have). If all this seems somewhat complicated, suffice it to go back to the first sentence, and then talk it over with the first philosopher you happen to run into.

enteron, see **aliment**

entomology (en tuh MOL uh jee) *n. Entomology* is the branch of zoology that deals with the study of insects. The word comes from the Greek prefix *entomo-*, based on *entoma* (insects, from *entoma zoa*, literally "notched animals") plus *logos* (discourse), the source of so many English words ending in *-logy (biology, geology, philology,* etc.) To *entomologize* (en tuh MOL uh jize) is to engage in the study of insects. *Entomophagous* (en tuh MOF uh gus) is a synonym of *insectivorous*, describing any organism that feeds on insects; formed from *entomo-* plus the Greek suffix *-phagous* (eating, feeding on, based on the verb *phagein*, to eat, devour). *Entomology* is a very broad field, since there are over 675,000 (!) known species of insect. Be careful not to confuse *entomology* with a like-sounding word: *etymology* (et uh MOL uh jee), the study of word derivations, from the Greek noun *etymologia* (studying words). Here's a simple mnemonic: *Etymology* is about woids; *entomology* is about ents.

entrepôt (AWN truh poh—*n* pronounced nasally, as in French) *n.* An *entrepôt* is a storehouse or bonded warehouse for the transshipment or distribution of merchandise; a commercial center for export-import transactions. This is a French word, based on the verb *entreposer* (to store), which in turn goes back to the Latin preposition *inter* (between) plus *positum*, past participle of *ponere* (to put or place). *Entrepôt* was modeled on the French noun *dépôt* (depot), but in English the circumflex may be dropped as it has been in *depot*.

eoan (ee O un) *adj. Eoan* describes things pertaining to dawn or sunrise. It is derived, via Latin, from the Greek noun *eos* (dawn), which, with an upper case *E*, was the name, in Greek mythology, for the goddess of dawn, the mother of the winds and the sister of Helios, the sun god. *Aurora* and *Sol* (later Apollo) were the respective Roman names for these sibling gods, whose parents were the Titans Hyperion and Theia. Eos gave us the lovely adjective *eoan*, and Helios the prefix *helio-*, as in *heliolatry* (hee lee OL uh tree), meaning "sun worship," *heliotrope* (HEE lee uh trope), for any plant that turns towards the sun, etc. An *eoan* sky is the sky at dawn. *Eoan* drowsiness is the sleepy feeling on waking at sunrise.

164

The Russian-born American poet and novelist Vladimir Nabokov (1897–1977) used *eoan* in the sense of "early," as in *the eoan stage* [i.e., onset] *of an attack,* in *Look at the Harlequins!* (McGraw-Hill, New York, 1974). Because the sun rises in the east, *eoan* is sometimes used of things pertaining to the east.

epenthesis (eh PEN thih sis) *n. Epenthesis* is the erroneous insertion of an extra sound in the pronunciation (and sometimes, eventually, the spelling) of a word. The intruding insertion can be a consonant (as in prost*r*ate gland) or a vowel (as in burg*u*lar). *Epenthesis* is generic for both; the insertion of a vowel has a name all to itself: *anaptyxis* (an up TIK sis). *Epenthesis* is intact from the Greek, based on the prefix *ep-*, a variant form of *epi-* before a vowel (on) plus prefix *en-* (into) plus *thesis* (something set down). *Anaptyxis* is also intact from Greek, based on the prefix *ana-* (back) plus the verb *ptyssein* (to unfold). Some examples involving consonants: *condrum* (for *condom*); *reastauranteur; scrapegoat; asparagrass. Involving vowels: mischievious* and *grievious; arthuritis, athaletic, fillum* (for *film*). Involving both: *poison ivory*. For another form of messing about with words, see **metathesis.**

epicedium (ep ih SEE dee um, -sih DYE um), **epicede** (EP ih seed) *n.* An *epicedium* or *epicede* is a dirge, an elegy, a funeral song or ode. *Epicedium* was taken intact from the Latin, which took it from the Greek *epikedeion*, a noun formed from the neuter of the adjective *epikedeios* (pertaining to a funeral), based on the prefix *epi-* (upon) plus *kedos* (sorrow). The adjectives *epicedial* (ep ih SEE dee ul) and *epicedian* (ep ih SEE dee un) mean "elegiac." *Epicedia* were the stock in trade of paid mourners, trained to produce the atmosphere appropriate to the sad occasion. Funeral parlors nowadays, especially the fancy ones, have piped-in lugubrious electric organ music to keep the tears flowing—a particularly oppressive type of canned art. "Here they come," says a member of the staff, and somebody behind the scenes presses a button. In the old days, they paid their respects with *epicedia*, and the live music seems a more fitting tribute to the dear departed and the grieving survivors. (See also **threnody.**)

epicene (EP ih seen) *n., adj. Epicene* can be used in a variety of senses. An *epicene*, or *epicene* person, is one having characteristics of both sexes, or one of indeterminate sexual characteristics. *Epicene* can also apply to things; today's fashions in clothes and hair are becoming so *epicene* that it is often difficult to determine the sex of a person even at close range. Another meaning is "effete, weak, ineffectual, feeble." An *epicene* presentation of an advertising campaign, for example, will hardly impress the prospective client. These meanings may seem quite unrelated, but on closer examination, one can imagine a progression from "sharing male and female traits" to "neither one thing nor the other" to "feeble, unimpressive." The word is sometimes applied, in this male-chauvinistic world, to a person who is not adequately macho to the observer, in the sense of "effeminate" as a pejorative. A real he-man ballet dancer who moves with the required grace and delicacy may quite wrongly be labeled *epicene* in the sense of "effeminate" rather than quite correctly in the sense first mentioned above. For those interested in the classical languages, there is a special grammatical use of *epicene*: an *epicene* noun in Latin or Greek is either (1) one that is always of the same gender regardless of the sex of the animal in question (Latin *vulpes* is always feminine, i.e., takes a feminine adjective, whether it means "fox" or "vixen") or (2) one that has a common gender (Latin *bos*, Greek *bous*—bull or cow—will take a masculine or feminine adjective depending on the sex of the animal referred to). Fowler points out that *epicene* "having no real function in English grammar . . . is kept alive chiefly in contemptuous use, implying physical as well as moral sexlessness. . . ."

epicrisis (ih PIK rih sis) *n.* As one can see from the stress on the second syllable, this is not a kind of *crisis*, though both words have a common Greek source. An *epicrisis* is an evaluation, a critical study or estimate, usually of a literary work, supplemented by some discussion of the subject matter. *Crisis* (from Greek *krisis*, decision, related to *krinein*, to judge or decide) is a familiar word. The adjective *critical* relates to *criticism*, but goes off in other directions as well, involving uncertainty and danger (a patient in a *critical* condition, a *critical* wound); and *critical* can also mean "decisive" (a *critical* point in an argument). *Epicrisis* is derived from Greek *epikrisis* (determination), related to *epikrinein* (to judge), based upon prefix *epi-* (upon) plus *krinein* (to judge)—this is the common source referred to above. The adjective *epicritic* (ep uh KRIT ik);

166

sometimes *epicritical*, from Greek *epikritikos* (determinative), is a physiological term describing high sensitivity to variations in pain or temperature ("low threshold") as opposed to *protopathic* (pro tuh PATH ik), describing low sensitivity to such stimuli ("high threshold"). A very versatile source, that little Greek *krisis*.

epideictic (ep ih DIK tik), **epideictical** (ep ih DIK tuh kul), *adj.* These adjectives apply to anything done for show. *Epideictic* is from Greek *epideiktikos*, based on the prefix *epi-* (upon) plus the verb *deiknynai* (to show, display). Show-offs engage in one *epideictic* act after another. The ladies' hats at Royal Ascot are a good example of *epideictic* behavior. The nouveaux riches tend to live in an *epideictic* world, indulging in vulgar display of extravagant apparel, jewelry, objets d'art, cars, and other paraphernalia. Attendance by tone-deaf spectators at the opening night of the opera season, in the old days, was an *epideictic* procedure. So, alack, is often the case with attendance at church. It is likewise to be feared, or at least suspected, that presence at **vernissages** may well be *epideictic* in nature. Can it be that all the French used in the foregoing comment may be an *epideictic* excess?

epigon(e) (EP uh gohn) *n.* An *epigone* is a second-rate imitator of a distinguished predecessor in the arts, philosophy, history, etc., usually one of a previous generation. *Epigonic* (ep uh GON ik) is the adjective, *epigonism* (ih PIG uh niz um) the noun for this sorry practice. These words come, via Latin *epigonus*, from Greek *epigonos* (a person born after—based on the verb *epigignesthai*, to be born after, from prefix *epi-* in the sense of "after" plus *gignesthai*, to be born). The American foreign correspondent and writer Vincent Sheean (1899–1975) wrote of "the obsequious literature of the *epigones*," and the American poet William Rose Benét (1886–1950) said of a minor poet: "Your verse . . . supports a primitive traditionalism and *epigonism*." The American linguists Alexander and Nicholas Humez, in *Alpha to Omega* (David R. Godine, Publisher, Inc., Boston, 1981), quote the definition by the Roman rhetorician Quintilian (c. 35–c. 95) of the Greco-Roman type of humor known as "urbanitas" ("language with a smack of the city in its words, accent and idiom . . ." and insert in brackets their own comment "at which the fledgling *New Yorker* succeeded so well and at which many of its *epigones* so utterly failed"). *Epigonic* poetry, painting,

167

music, and philosophical or historical writing are imitative of the products of an earlier generation. The American use of *epigone* appears to be a special application of the term to inferior imitators in the arts. The British use it in the singular in the general sense of "one of a later generation," without reference to the arts or imitation, and in the plural to denote "undistinguished descendants of the great," like (meaning no offense) the children of Franklin D. Roosevelt and Winston Churchill. In this use, they are alluding to the classical Greek legend of the *Epigoni*, the seven sons of the original seven heroes known as the "Seven against Thebes." The general idea behind the British use of the word, at least in the plural, is expressed in the oft-repeated opinion of just about every generation surveying its own leaders in politics and the arts, and sometimes in sports, that "they don't make them that way any more," referring nostalgically to the heroes of days gone by.

epinosic (ep ih NOS ik) *adj.* This is a word you won't run into very often. It means both "unhealthy" and "unhealthful." Yes, there is a distinction, as we shall see. *Epinosic* is derived from the Greek prefix *epi-* (upon, over, near, at, after—depending on the context) plus *nosos* (disease). The distinction between *unhealthy* and *unhealthful* is recognized to a certain degree in both American and British dictionaries, in that the first meaning attributed to *healthy* is "in a state of good health," while the first definition of *healthful* is "conducive to good health," i.e., "salutary." However, and in this author's opinion sadly, the two words are also given as mutually synonymous. That really is unfortunate: the nice distinction between *healthy* (in good health) and *healthful* (promoting health) ought to be preserved. The Second Edition of *Webster's Unabridged* condones the blurring, in effect, but has at least the decency to observe that the two words are ". . . interchangeable [only] within certain limits. *Healthy* more frequently applies to that which is in a state of health or vigor; *healthful*, to that which conduces to health . . . a *healthy* (not *healthful*) man; *healthful* (not *healthy*) food . . ." Good old *Webster's Second*! The distinction should not be ignored, in the less than humble opinion of this disinterested but far from uninterested writer. But to get back to our *epinosic*: It appears to cover both *unhealthy* and *unhealthful*, and if you want to preserve the nice distinction recommended above, your definition will have to depend on the context.

epiphany (ih PIF uh nee) *n.* An *epiphany* is the appearance or manifestation of a god to a mortal, or any moment of divine revelation, like the appearance of God in the burning bush to Moses in Exodus 3:2. The word *epiphany* comes from the Greek noun *epiphaneia* (appearance), based on the prefix *epi-* (near, at, before) plus *phainein* (to show) and the related adjective *epiphanes* (manifest). With an upper case *E, Epiphany* is a Christian festival observed on January 6 celebrating the appearance of the Christ-child to the gentiles, the Magi, the three Wise Men from the East. January 6 is the twelfth day after December 25, Christ's birthday, so that Twelfth Night, the eve of the Twelfth Day, used to be a time of feasting and much merrymaking. Shakespeare named his play *Twelfth Night* because it was written to be acted during the Twelfth Night revels.

epiplexis (ep uh PLEK sis) *n.* This is a rhetorical contrivance whereby a speaker, haranguing a crowd, upbraids them in order to incite them. One of the best known uses of *epiplexis* in all drama is the famous speech of the Tribune Marullus to the crowd at the outset of Shakespeare's *Julius Caesar* (Act I, Scene 1). The commoners have come to ". . . make holiday to see Caesar, and to rejoice in his triumph . . ." Marullus cries:

> You blocks, you stones, you worse than senseless things!
> O you hard hearts, you cruel men of Rome,
> Knew you not Pompey? . . .
> And do you now put on your best attire?
> And do you now cull out a holiday?
> And do you now strew flowers in his way,
> That comes in triumph over Pompey's blood?
> Be gone!

That was some *epiplexis*! This word, in Late Latin, meant "reproof," from the Greek, based on the prefix *epi-* (upon) plus the verb *plessein* (to strike at, reprove).

epistemology (ih pis tuh MOL uh jee) *n.* This is an area of philosophy dealing with human knowledge—its origins, characteristics, methods, and limits. The word is formed of the Greek noun *episteme* (knowledge) plus the suffix *-logy*, used in the names of studies and sciences (e.g., *philology, theology*) from *logos* (discourse). *Epistemology* is a science or discipline distinct from logic, treating the operations of the mind in the knowing process. As to the origins of knowledge, empiricism bases all knowledge on the perceptions of the senses, while rationalism asserts that the mind enlarges knowledge with ideas not derived from empirical experience. Realism and idealism differ in that the former teaches that the object of knowledge is real in itself, while the latter makes the object dependent on the activity of the mind. The foregoing is, obviously, the merest sketch of the various departments of *epistemology*. A full treatment would hardly fit within the confines of this book.

epithalamion, epithalamium, see **hymeneal**

epizeuxis (ep ih ZOOHK sis) *n. Epizeuxis* is the immediate repetition of a word for the sake of emphasis, taken, via Late Latin, from the Greek, where it means "fastening together, repetition," based on the Greek prefix *epi-* (upon) plus *zeugnynai* (to join). "Hear, hear!" is certainly a more effective comment than "Hear!" "Well, well!" is many times more expressive than "Well!" and "Again and again and again," a favorite expression of Franklin Roosevelt, made a deep impression on his listeners. "Finally, finally!" is a much more powerful demonstration of satisfaction than one "Finally!" All these are examples of *epizeuxis*. And remember those lines from *The Bells* by the American poet Edgar Allan Poe (1809–1849):

> Keeping time, time, time,
>   In a sort of Runic rhyme,
> To the tintinnabulation that so musically wells
>   From the bells, bells, bells, bells,
> Bells, bells, bells.

and those from the *Elegy to the Memory of an Unfortunate Lady* by the English poet Alexander Pope (1688–1744):

> By foreign hands thy dying eyes were closed,
> By foreign hands thy decent limbs composed,
> By foreign hands thy humble grave adorned,
> By strangers honoured, and by strangers mourned!

eponym (EP uh nim) *n.* An *eponym* is a person from whose
170

name something actually or supposedly takes its name, and words derived from *eponyms* are called "eponymous" (eh PON uh mus). Examples: Amelia Bloomer (1818–1894), associated with the women's rights movement of the last century, gave us *bloomers*. Thomas Bowdler (1754–1825) in 1818 published expurgated editions of Shakespeare and Gibbon's *Decline and Fall*; hence, **bowdlerize**. The French inventor Louis Braille (1809–1852) gave us *braille*. E. Clerihew Bentley (1875–1956), the English writer, invented the **clerihew**. J. T. Brudnell, seventh earl of Cardigan, a British cavalryman of Crimean War fame (1797–1868), gave us the *cardigan*. The French doctor Joseph Ignace Guillotine (1738–1814) designed the *guillotine*. Sir Henry Havelock (1795–1857), an English general in India, created the *havelock*, a cap cover with a back flap to protect the neck from rain and sun. The Austrian physician Friedrich Anton Mesmer (1734–1815) was the father of *mesmerism*. The term *Rachmanism*, unfamiliar to American ears but well known in Britain, denotes, according to the definition given in this author's compilation of Briticisms, *British English, A to Zed* (Facts On File), "the despicable practice of taking over lower-class residential property and deliberately creating intolerable living conditions in order to force the poor tenants to get out, so that the landlord can then turn the property to more profitable commercial uses. The term is derived from a man named Rachman, who in the 1960s pioneered in this type of manipulation." The British Field Marshall Lord Raglan (1788–1855), commander in the Crimean War, was responsible for the *raglan* sleeve. The Marquis de Sade (1740–1814) gave us *sadism*. The fourth earl of Sandwich (1718–1792) created the *sandwich*. The English General Henry Shrapnel (1761–1842) invented the *shrapnel shell*. The French finance minister Étienne de Silhouette (1709–1767) first concocted the *silhouette*. The English Reverend W. A. Spooner (1844–1930) was responsible for *spoonerism*. And, lest you conclude that *eponyms* are practically the exclusive province of long-departed British generals and miscellaneous Europeans of mostly ancient vintage, how about our very own Shirley Temple and the *Shirley Temple hairdo* and the *Shirley Temple cocktail* (for children—no alcohol)? Finally, there are all those dread diseases named after the doctors who first identified and described them: *Alzheimer's, Hodgkin's, Parkinson's*, among—sadly enough—many others. Be all that as it may, do not confuse *eponym* with **toponym**. *Eponym* is derived from the Greek prefix *epi-* (upon) plus *onoma* (name).

equine,   see **accipitrine**

eristic   (eh RIS tik) *n*. Also, as an adjective, *eristical* (eh RIS tuh kul). *Eristic(al)* means "pertaining to controversy." An *eristic* is a quarrelsome, disputatious person, a controversialist, one who enjoys contention and argument for their own sake and loves to "take the other side" to start an argument or keep one going. Such people, often without deep convictions of their own, simply go at it for the enjoyment of the fray. The word is from the Greek *eristikos*, related to the verb *erizein* (to wrangle), based on *eris* (strife, discord). Eris, in Greek mythology, was the goddess of discord, identified in Roman mythology as the goddess Discordia, whose name speaks for itself. What a troublemaker! She and Ate, another Greek goddess, the one who personified recklessness and mischief and vengeance, were responsible for a lot of woe. In Shakespeare's *King John* (Act II, Scene 1) Chatillon, the French ambassador to England, tells King Philip of France of King John's invasion, accompanied by ". . . the mother-queen/An Ate, stirring him to blood and strife . . ." and Antony, in *Julius Caesar* (Act III, Scene 1) soliloquizes:

> And Caesar's spirit ranging for revenge,
> With Ate by his side come hot from hell
> Shall . . .
> Cry 'Havoc,' and let slip the dogs of war . . .

Eris and Ate—quite a pair!

eschatology   (es kuh TOL uh jee) *n*. *Eschatology* is a term in theology, covering any doctrine concerned with final things: death and resurrection, immortality, the second coming of Christ, the last judgment, the future condition of things thereafter. *Eschatology* also denotes the branch of theology that deals with those matters. The word is formed from the Greek adjective for "last," *eschatos*, plus the familiar *-logy* suffix used in the naming of sciences, fields of study, and bodies of knowledge. The adjective is *eschatological* (es kuh tuh LOJ ih kul), and an *eschatologist* (es kuh TOL uh jist) is one devoted to the study of the doctrines defined above.

172

escheat (es CHEET) *n.*, *vb.* This is a legal term in the field of estate inheritance law. Each of the 50 states has a statute specifying how the property of a deceased person is distributed among his heirs or next of kin if he leaves no will. If there is no will and there are no next of kin, the property reverts to the state, and in that case the estate is said to *escheat.* The author has been involved in one peculiar case where the decedent, who had no heirs whatever, did sign a will dividing what he thought was his entire estate among a number of friends, but the percentages bequeathed, as the result of an arithmetical error on the part of the draftsman, totaled only 95 percent. Result: five percent *escheated* to the state in which the deceased had resided. *Escheat* goes back to English Common Law. The word was derived, via Middle English *eschete* and Late Latin *excadere,* from Latin prefix *ex-* (from) plus the verb *cadere* (to fall).

esculent, see **comestible**

estivate (ES tuh vate) *vb.* Most of us are familiar with the verb *hibernate* (HYE bur nate), which applies to the habit of certain animals, like bears, of spending the winter, usually huddled in close quarters, in a dormant state; also of people, in the sense of "withdraw, remain in seclusion, retire," generally regardless of season. It is from *hibernatus,* past participle of Latin *hibernare* (to spend the winter), based on *hiems* (winter). To *estivate* is the corresponding term applied to the summer season: to spend the summer, and it comes from *aestivatus,* past participle of Latin *aestivare* (to spend the summer), based on *aestas* (summer). Such symmetry, for once, in language which so often is arbitrary! Applied to animals, to *estivate* is to spend the summer in a dormant, or at least torpid state, like crabs *estivating* in the sand. The leisured classes often *hibernate* in southern climes and *estivate* at country lodges, in the mountains or by the sea. The English, when India was part of the Empire, *estivated* in their hill stations.

estrus (ES trus) *n.* The *estrus* or *estrum* or *oestrus* is the period when a female animal is in heat or rut, her period of maximum sexual receptivity; via Latin *oestrus,* from Greek *oistros* (gadfly, sting, and by extension, frenzy, as though produced by the sting; and any owner of an unspayed cat will attest to the frenzied sounds emitted by the pet in heat). The *estrone cycle* is the series of physiological changes in the organs of female mammals occurring between rutting periods. *Estrone* (ES trone) is a hormone found in urine during pregnancy and a commercial form of it, also known as *estrin, oestrin, oestrone* or *theelin* is used to remedy *estrogen* deficiency, *estrogen* being a female hormone capable of producing *estrus*. More details can be provided by your friendly neighborhood gynecologist.

esurient (ih SOOR ee unt) *adj.* To be *esurient* is to be hungry (in the literal sense, for food) or greedy (for gain or loot), rapacious. *Esurient* is derived from Latin *esuriens*, present participle of *esurire* (to be hungry; by extension, to long for). The noun is *esurience* (ih SOOR ee uns); the Latin noun is *esuritio*, but we have no such noun as *esurition*. One can never be sure about which part of speech, in the Latin, is going to give us our word. One's *esurience* may be simple gluttony or inordinate rapacity; either way, it is an unlovely quality.

ethnology, see **genethlialogy**

ethology, see **genethlialogy**

ethos (EE thos, ETH os) *n.* The *ethos* of a culture is its basic spirit or character, the fundamental sentiment that pervades its beliefs and practices; the characteristic spirit permeating a nation, an age, or the arts, especially the literature of a social group, whether nation, community, party, or institution. As applied to a nation, according to Fowler, ". . . it is the sum of the intellectual and moral tendencies manifested in what the Germans called the nation's Kultur; like Kultur, it is not in itself a word of praise or blame, any more than *quality*." Applied to drama, *ethos* is the moral constituent that establishes a character's action rather than his thinking or his emotion. *Ethos* was taken intact from the Greek, where it means "custom" or "character."

etiolate, see **etiology**

etiology (ee tee OL uh jee) *n.* In its widest application, *etiology* is the study or the philosophy of causation; more narrowly, the

174

assignment of a cause to a situation. Thus, one might speak of the *etiology* of a custom or ritual. The word comes, via Late Latin, from Greek *aitilogia* (determination of the cause of something), based on the noun *aitia* (cause) plus the suffix *logia* (science, study, body of knowledge). Even more narrowly, in medical science, *etiology* is the study of the cause of diseases, or, more specifically, the actual cause of a disease, e.g., the *etiology* of Legionnaire's Disease. One might be forgiven for the belief that to *etiolate* was to act in the field of *etiology*, but the belief would be quite wrong. To *etiolate* (EE tee uh late) is to bleach or blanch (a plant) by excluding light as done in the cultivation of celery. *Etiolate* is from an entirely different source, the French verb *étioler* (to make or become pale; more specifically, to become stubble, *éteule* being French for *stubble*, from the Latin *stipula*, stalk, straw). *Etiolate*, used **intransitively**, means to "become pale." The process of making something pale, or becoming pale, is known as *etiolation* (ee tee uh LAY shun). Jumping to derivations is as dangerous as jumping to conclusions.

etymon (ET uh mon) *n.* The *etymon* of a word is its original root or true origin, the form from which the ultimate word is derived. For example: the Greek word *eune* (bed, bedroom, sleeping place) is the *etymon* of *eunuch*. So we see that *eunuch* starts out from the *etymon eune*, to which was added the Greek suffix *-ouchos* (keeping), based on the verb *echein* (to keep, hold). In the same kind of development, *cor* (Latin for "heart") is the *etymon* of our adjective *cordial* (friendly, warm and *hearty*), and *kerd*, a noun in the Indo-European family of languages, is thought to be the *etymon* of *cor* and of Greek *kardia*, from which we get *cardiac* and related words and, indeed, the word *heart* itself. *Etymon* may not be a familiar word, but from it we got the familar term *etymology* (et uh MOL uh jee), the study of the derivation of words. *Etymon* was taken intact from the Greek; it is the neuter form of the adjective *etymos* (true, real).

eudemonism (yooh DEE muh niz um) *n.* This is the doctrine or system of ethics that happiness is the test of rectitude or moral virtue; that the basis of moral obligations is found in the likeliness that correct actions will produce happiness. Thus, the related adjective *eudemonic* (yooh dih MON ik) means "conducive to happiness." A *eudemon* (yooh DEE mon) is a good spirit, and *eudemonia* (yooh dih MOH nee uh) is happiness itself. All these words are based on the Greek prefix *eu-* (good: found in words like *euphoria, euphemism,* etc.) plus *daimon* (spirit). *Eudemonism* in the system of the English philosopher Thomas Hobbes (1588–1679) is egoistic; in that of the later English philosopher James Mills (1773–1836), the *eudemonism* is altruistic.

euhemerism   (yooh HEE muh riz um, -HEM uh-) *n.* This word, sometimes capitalized in honor of Euhemeris (see below), is the doctrine or theory that explains mythology as legend based upon actual history, and the gods as originating out of the magnification of exceptional human beings; the interpretation of myths by attribution of their origin to real people or historical events. One who subscribes to that theory is a *euhemerist* and to attribute myths to real persons and events is to *euhemerize* (yooh HEE muh rize, -HEM-). This doctrine was originated by Euhemerus, a fourth century B.C. Greek philosopher and mythographer. He was a courtier of King Cassander of Macedonia. In his *Sacred History*, he expounded the theory that the gods were once great kings and exceptional heroes who were revered after death and eventually deified. Euhemerus appears to have been a male chauvinist; apparently, in his system, the goddesses were merely the mates or lady friends of the gods. But how about Aphrodite, Artemis, Athena, Demeter, Diana, Eos, Eris, and all those other girls who seem to have got to Mt. Olympus on their own?

euphuism   (YOOH fyooh iz um) *n. Euphuism* (not to be confused with a look-alike word, *euphemism,* with which it has absolutely no connection) is a flowery, affected, precious, high-flown style of language, written or spoken, in imitation of that of the English writer John Lyly (c. 1554–1606), best known for his two-part didactic romance *Euphues, or the Anatomy of Wit* and *Euphues and his England*, a work that advocated a reform of education and manners. Lyly wrote in an affected style, fashionable and much imitated at the end of the 16th century, full of preciosity, strings of alliteration, and antitheses. Lyly named his protagonist *Euphues* after the Greek adjective *euphues* (well-grown—descriptive of a man of parts), based on the Greek prefix *eu-* (well) plus *phue* (growth), related to the verb *phuein* (to grow).

176

ex post facto (eks post FAK toh). This Latin phrase is the equivalent of "retroactive" or "retroactively" depending on whether the term is used adjectivally or adverbially. Literally, *ex post facto* means "from something done later"; in legal parlance, "on the basis of legislation enacted later." A statute that affects previously completed transactions or previously committed crimes is *ex post facto* legislation, i.e., it seeks to have retroactive effect and thus to change the legal status of an act committed before its enactment. Such legislation, including tax statutes, is occasionally enacted and takes retroactive effect in civil law, but is not effective in criminal law to make illegal what was previously legal, or make punishment more severe than what was on the books when the crime was committed. As to the spelling of the phrase, Fowler says that "the person who knows the Latin words is worse off with it in this disguise than one who does not; it should be *ex postfacto* (*ex* on the footing of, *postfacto* later enactment)." One can only agree (admittedly, it is dangerous not to, with Fowler). As he says, ". . . what is referred to in *facto* is not the 'doing' of the action but the [later] 'enacting' of the law." If in doubt, consult your lawyer.

exanimate (ig ZAN uh mit, -mate) *adj.* The literal meaning is "lifeless"; *inanimate* is a synonym. But figuratively, *exanimate* is not marked by such fatality: it is used to describe one who is disheartened, depressed, dispirited. It is from Latin *exanimatus*, past participle of *exanimare* (to deprive of breath), based on prefix *ex-* (from) plus (or in this case, minus?) *anima* (breath). The condition is *exanimation*. (Mind your *m*'s and *n*'s!)

exegesis (-getics),   see **hermeneutics**

exiguous (ig ZIG yooh us, ik SIG-) *adj. Exiguous* describes things that are meager, in small amount, scanty, sparse, piddling, paltry, skimpy. It comes from Latin *exiguus*, based on prefix *ex-* used as an intensive plus the verb *egere* (to be needy, poor, in want). Despite her great influence on the work of the Roman poets Catullus (c. 84–c. 54 B.C.) and Ovid (43 B.C.–A.D. 18) and the English poet Swinburne (1837–1909), all that is left of the writings of the Greek poet Sappho (c.620–565 B.C.) is an *exiguous* collection of fragments, the longest one consisting of only seven stanzas. Those lean, underweight models who grace our advertisements subsist on an *exiguous* diet. For the noun, one can choose between *exiguity* (eks uh GYOOH ih tee) and *exiguousness* (ig ZIG yooh us nus).

exoteric   (ek su TER ik) *adj. Exoteric* is the opposite of *esoteric*, a more familiar word. Anything *exoteric* is suitable for communication to the common people, the multitude, *hoi polloi*; not for the inner circle, the select few. *Exoteric* things are popular, commonplace, marked by simplicity. *Esoteric* matters are the province of the **cognoscenti**. When, in Shakespeare's *Hamlet* (Act II, Scene 2), the protagonist says to the First Player: "I heard thee speak me a speech once, but it was never acted, or if it was, not above once; for the play, I remember, pleas'd not the million; 'twas caviare to the general [over the heads of the general public; too refined for their palate] . . . ," he was characterizing the play as *esoteric*. Grade B movies and TV sitcoms are *exoteric*. Does this sound snobbish? It is. *Exoteric* is from Greek *exoterikos*, related to *exoteros* (inclined outward); *esoteric* is from Greek *esoterikos*, related to *esoteros* (inner).

factious,   see **factitious**

factitious   (fak TISH us) *adj.* Anything described as *factitious* is contrived and artificial, like the prearranged cheering and waving of crowds awaiting a dictator's harangue. It is insincere, produced artificially, not spontaneous, genuine, or natural, and made to order, as it were. *Factitious* is derived from Latin *factitius*, a variant of *facticius* (artificial), based on *factus*, past participle of the verb *facere* (to make). The "hype" surrounding the appearance of rock superstars or spectacular sporting events is a good example of *factitious* enthusiasm. There are several adjectives that one must be careful not to confuse with *factitious: factious, factitive*, and *fictitious*. *Factious* (FAK shus) describes partisan activities and emotions. Fowler says that "*factious* rancour is the rancour that lets party spirit prevail over patriotism." Political logrolling is a good example of this. *Factitive* (FAK tih tiv) is a grammatical term, describing verbs containing a sense of making, calling, or thinking that take a direct object and an objective complement. Here are

178

some examples: The people *elected* him president. (*Him* is the direct object; *president* is the objective complement.) The group *made* him their leader. An unbiased observer would *call* it a swindle. Sensible people *think* the arms race insanity. In these sentences, the verbs are *factitive*. That adjective is from New Latin *factitivus*, based on the verb *factitare* (to do frequently, to declare [something] to be.) *Fictitious* is a familiar word, synonymous with *false* or *imaginary*, and is derived from Latin *ficticius* (artificial); it needs no discussion here.

factitive,   see **factitious**

faience   (fye ANS, fay-) *n.* This is the name given to any type of glazed earthenware, porcelain, or pottery with brightly colored designs, including majolica (also spelt *maiolica*), which is earthenware covered with a tin oxide glaze and very highly decorated. *Faience* is a fine variety of this type of pottery. Its name is derived from the northern Italian city of Faenza, a ceramic center. Majolica is said to be named after the Island of Majorca, where the finest quality of this type of pottery was originally made. Much of it was shipped to Italy. Majolica from Faenza has a deep blue background, and is produced in the form of tiles, jars, bowls, and panels. The clay object is fired, coated with tin enamel, fired again, painted in flashing colors, and finally fired for a third time.

fainéant   (FAY nee unt) *n.*, *adj.* The acute accent may be omitted. As both noun and adjective, *fainéant* means "do-nothing." A *fainéant* person, or a *fainéant*, is an idler, and his trait is known as *faineancy* (FAY nee un see), *faineance* (FAY nee uns) or *faineantise* (fay nee un TEEZ). *Fainéant* was taken intact from the French, where it was based on the verb *faire* (to do) plus *néant* (nothing). The term *Roi Fainéant* (Do-Nothing King), meaning "puppet king," was applied to the late Merovingian kings of France, the dynasty founded in the fifth century by Merovius, ruler of the Franks (the Germanic tribe that conquered Gaul after the fall of the Roman Empire, and gave us the name *France*). The Merovingians ruled until their power was usurped by the "Mayors of the Palace" (Royal Stewards), and in 751 Pippin III became King of the Franks and did away with their office. *Fainéant* is a fashionable word for "sluggard." In the next edition of the *New English Bible*, shall we be told: "Go to the ant, you fainéant . . ." (Proverbs 6:6)?

falconine, see **accipitrine**

fanfaronade (fan fuh ruh NADE) *n.* This is a lovely word for arrogant bluster, boastful, ostentatious talk or behavior, bragging, bravado. A *fanfaron* (FAN fuh ron) is a braggart, but the word can mean, simply, "fanfare." *Fanfaronade* is from French *fanfaronnade*, taken from Spanish *fanfarronada*. *Fanfaron* was likewise taken from the French, which got it from Spanish *fanfarron* (braggart), and that went all the way back to Arabic *farfar* (garrulous). In Shakespeare's *Merchant of Venice* (Act I, Scene 1), Gratiano describes the kind of man who strives to give an impression of ". . . wisdom, gravity, profound conceit/As who would say 'I am Sir Oracle,/And when I ope my lips let no dog bark!' " This is a classic example of *fanfaronade.* Cf. **braggadocio, gasconade, rodomontade, thrasonical.**

farouche (fuh ROOHSH) *adj. Farouche* was taken over intact from the French, where it has two quite different meanings: "wild, fierce" or "sullen, shy unsociable." When the French describe a woman as "bien *farouche*," they are characterizing her not as *fierce*, but as *very shy*. British dictionaries define *farouche* as "shy, ill at ease, sullen and unsociable, socially inexperienced, unused to company and lacking polish," and although some of them refer to "French: wild," others mention the French origin but refer to Middle Latin *forasticus*, derived from Latin *foras* (out of doors), while American dictionaries refer to "French: 1. fierce; 2. sullenly shy." Fowler says of *farouche*: "The meaning, simply sullen-mannered from shyness (*cheval farouche*, cheval qui craint la présence de l'homme) [*farouche horse, a horse that fears the presence of a man*] . . . is obscured by association with ferocious; according to the OED [*Oxford English Dictionary*] 'the connexion is untenable'; see TRUE AND FALSE ETYMOLOGY." And when we go to that heading, we find in the long list FAROUCHE, not L[atin] *ferox* fierce. So we see that it is Latin *foras* (out of doors; i.e., *wild* in the sense of "untamed," bringing with it the sense of "socially inept," therefore shy and ill at ease, and therefore sullen), rather

180

than Latin *ferox* (fierce) or Latin *ferus* (wild, fierce), that has given us *farouche*.

fascine (fa SEEN, fuh-) *n.* A *fascine* is a bundle of sticks bound together, used to strengthen ramparts in building up military defenses, or to fill in ditches that impede attack, a use that was revived in World War II. *Fascine* was taken from the French, who got it from Latin *fascina* (bundle of sticks). In ancient Rome, the *fasces* (construed as a singular noun; plural of *fascis*, bundle) was a bundle of rods bound with red thongs, with an axe blade protruding, assigned to the high court judges as a symbol of authority. The *fasces* became the symbol of fascism, introduced by Benito Mussolini in 1919. His charming friend Hitler preferred the swastika.

felicitous (fih LIS ih tus) *adj.* *Felicitous* means "befitting, appropriate, strikingly apt, pleasantly ingenious." A *felicitous* expression or act is one exactly suited to the occasion; a *felicitous* comment is one extremely well put, the *mot juste.* A *felicitous* person is one with a particular aptitude for correct or suitable conduct or expression. *Felicitous* is derived from Latin *felicitas* (happiness, good fortune, success), based on the adjective *felix* (favorable, auspicious). The related noun *felicity* (fih LIS ih tee) means "happiness," and to *felicitate* (fih LIS ih tate) is to congratulate; but the special significance of *felicitous* is *appropriateness. Infelicitous* (in fuh LIS ih tus), as one might expect, means "inappropriate" and *infelicitous* remarks are inapt, unsuitable, ill-chosen, gauche, out of place, malapropos, the sort that can cause a bit of squirming by those within earshot. The Irish writer Oscar Wilde (1854–1900) was a master of the *felicitous.* The pompous Mrs. Malaprop, a character in *The Rivals*, a comedy by the Irish dramatist Richard Sheridan (1751–1816), came close to monopolizing the *infelicitous.*

feline, see accipitrine

felloe, see apogee

feracious (fih RAY shus) *adj.* *Feracious* means "fruitful, productive," and comes from Latin *ferax* (fruitful, fertile, prolific), related to the verb *ferre* (to bear, bring forth, produce). We get *fertile* from the related Latin adjective *fertilis. Feracious* can apply

181

to things both tangible and intangible. Thus, it may be said that the spirit of the Renaissance created a *feracious* atmosphere for the development of new approaches to the arts. It is easy to confuse *feracious* with *ferocious*, especially since our rich language includes the adjective *feral* (FEE rul, or FER ul), meaning "wild," and by extension, "ferocious." *Feracious* is far removed from both *feral* and *ferocious*.

feretory　(FER ih toh ree) *n*. A *feretory* is an ornate portable bier or shrine for the deposit of saints' relics after they have been carried in a religious procession, or a chapel in which the shrine is deposited. After the procession, the irreplaceable relics are carefully stowed in a *feretory*. The word is from the Latin noun *feretrum* (bier for carrying a body to the grave), which was derived from the Greek *pheretron* (bier), based on the verb *pherein* (to carry). There are relics of all types, all or part of a saint's body, clothing, almost anything connected with the saint. Alas, many are spurious—the tip of Lucifer's tail, for instance, pieces of the cross, vials of Christ's blood. A reliquary is likewise a receptacle for relics, but it is not portable.

feticide,　see **aborticide**

fin de siècle　(fan duh SYEH kluh—*n* pronounced nasally, second uh almost silent). This French expression means, literally, "end of century"; the century implied is the 19th. The phrase really signifies "toward the end of the 1800s." It refers to the concepts of society, especially the art, characteristic of that period, and broadly means "decadent." That meaning can be understood only as contrasted with the prudery and stuffiness of the greater part of the Victorian age. The expression itself was taken from the title of an 1888 French novel. As to pronunciation, Fowler warns us that "to say a French word in the middle of an English sentence exactly as it would be said by a Frenchman in a French sentence is a feat demanding an acrobatic mouth . . . that should not be attempted. . . . All that is necessary is a polite acknowledgement of indebtedness to the French language."

finjan, fingan,　see **zarf**

fizgig (FIZ gig), **fisgig** (FIS gig) *n.* This peculiar word is the name for an astonishing assortment of things: a gadabout, giddy, flighty, frivolous, flirtatious, fretful, flustered female (how's that for alliteration?); a damp firework that goes off with a loud hiss; a gimcrack or flimsy knickknack; a **crotchet**, whine, or quirk; a harpoon (in this meaning, usually spelt *fish gig* and comes from Spanish *fisga*, harpoon); a spinning or whirling toy that makes a loud, whizzing sound as it rotates. A versatile word, with a versatile derivation: *fizz* (hissing or fluttering sound) or late Middle English *fise* (a term of abuse) or Icelandic *fisa* (to fart) plus Middle English *gigge* (girl). God help lexicographers and etymologists!

flagitious (fluh JISH us) *adj.* A *flagitious* person is a villain, capable of the most shameful wickedness. A *flagitious* crime is an unspeakable heinous offense. A *flagitium*, in Latin, is a disgraceful act, a shameful crime; the related adjective is *flagitiosus* (shameful, infamous, disgraceful). *Flagitious* is a strong word; it makes up in force what it lacks in frequency of use. Its synonyms are *nefarious, heinous, atrocious, iniquitous, villainous, vicious, depraved*—not that "synonyms" are exact equivalents, those nuances always creep in—but *flagitious* is pretty terrible no matter how thin you slice it. The Roman poet Horace (65–8 B.C.) in one of his odes (IV.9.45) wrote (Wickham translation):

> The name of the happy man is
> claimed by him who . . .
> dreads disgrace: [flagitium] as
> something worse than death.

floccillation (flok suh LAY shun) *n.* This is one of two words denoting the delirious picking at bedclothes by feverish patients. The other is *carphology* (kar FOL uh jee), sometimes defined as delirious *fumbling* with bedclothes, but there cannot be any real distinction between delirious picking and delirious fumbling, so the words may, for practical purposes, be treated as synonymous. *Floccillation* is derived from Late Latin *floccillus*, a diminutive of Latin *floccus* (flock of wool), a word that has been taken into English as is. *Carphology* comes from New Latin and Late Latin *carphologia* (fumbling with or picking at blankets), derived in turn from Greek *karphologia*, indicating that this picking and fumbling

183

has been going on for a long time. Since the medical profession seems to need two words to describe this pathological activity, more of this fumbling and picking must happen than meets the layman's eye. But be careful not to confuse *carphology* with *carpology* (kar POL uh jee), a branch of botany concerned with fruits, a word based on Greek *karpos* (fruit). The omission or addition of a single little *h* can make a world of difference—the gulf between delirious fumbling and rational study. See also the last sentence of **apothegm**.

floccinaucinihilipilification (floks ee nos ee nih hil ee pil ih fih KAY shun) *n.* Yes, Virginia, there is a *flocci* . . . etc., albeit it is unlikely that you will run into it or it into you. It exists, a solemn entry in British English dictionaries, a jocular concoction of Latin nouns in the genitive (possessive) case to form a jawbreaker denoting the act of belittling someone or something, expressing the opinion that he, she, or it is of little or no value. The four genitives all mean "trifle" or "nothing" and are: *flocci*, from *floccus* (literally, tuft of wool—from which we get *flock*—but figuratively, trifle); *nauci*, from *naucum* (trifle); *nihili*, from *nihilum* (nothing—from which we get *nihilism, annihilate*, etc.); and *pili*, from *pilus* (literally, a single hair—from which we get *pilose, pilous, pilosity*, etc.—but figuratively, trifle); plus *-fication*, a suffix of action nouns from Latin *-ficatio*, normally related to verbs ending in *-fy*, e.g., *deify/deification, intensify/intensification*, etc. *Floccinaucinihilipilification* is said to have been invented by a group of boys at Eton College in Berkshire, England, founded in 1440 by Henry VI, who would never have anticipated this development. But the Scottish novelist Sir Walter Scott (1771–1852) differs, attributing the invention to the English poet William Shenstone (1714–1763), who, in a 1777 letter, wrote: "I love him for nothing so much as his *f-p-n-p-fication* of money." (See **pelf**.) Shenstone's use of only the initials of the constituent Latin genitives, and the use of *p* instead of *n* as the second one, would seem to indicate that the word was known to him, rather than invented by him, supporting the Eton College attribution.

floccus (FLOK us) *n. Floccus*, which is Latin for "tuft of wool," is English for "tuft of woolly hairs." See **floccillation** and **floccinaucinihilipilification**. *Floccus* gives us lots of words besides those

184

two: *floccose* (FLOK ose, flok OSE), *floccular* (FLOK yuh lur), and *flocculent* (FLOK yuh lunt), all meaning "woolly"; flocculate (FLOK yuh late), to form into wooly tufts; *floccule* (FLOK yoohl) and *flocculus* (FLOK yuh luhs), a small tuft of wool or anything resembling one; *flocculence* (FLOK yuh luns), the state of being woolly. There are others, but by now you've got the general idea. Sheep are woolly, but *flock*, the collective noun for *sheep* (and other animals, including parishioners), has nothing to do with *floccus*; we get that kind of *flock* from Old English *flocce* (*flock*, in the sense of "company," "group," or "gathering"). Under the **rubric** COLLECTIVES, Fowler tells us that *flock*, or its plural, *flocks*, can be used to mean "woollen waste"; thus, we are told, "a mattress of *flock* or *flocks*; the *flock* has, the *flocks* have, not been disinfected." In any event, *floccus* (the Latin one) has certainly supplied us with a flock of words!

floruit (FLOR ooh it) *vb.* In reference books, usually abbreviated to *fl.*, less often *flor.* This is a Latin word, meaning "he (or she) flourished"; the third person singular perfect of *florere* (to bloom, flower; by extension, to be in one's prime, to flourish). In abbreviated form, it is put after the name of a person to indicate when he or she "flourished," i.e., was active, in cases where the dates of birth and death are unknown. If an approximate or questionable date is known, it can be preceded or followed by the letter *c* or *c.*, an abbreviation of the Latin preposition *circa* (about): thus, Archimedes (c. 287–212 B.C.); or a question mark: thus Canalizo [a Mexican general] (1797?–?1847). But if even the approximate dates are unknown, the name is usually followed by *fl.* and a date or an era: thus, Euclid (*fl.* 300 B.C.); Galen (*fl.* 2nd century A.D.); St. Thomas Malory (*fl.* 1470). As time goes on, with more and more data being stored in computers, the famous of our age— Einstein, Marilyn Monroe, et al.—will need no *fl.*s, *flor.*s, *c.*s, or ?s after their names.

flummery (FLUM uh ree) *n.* Used in its literal sense, the name *flummery* covers any one of a number of concoctions made of flour, milk, eggs, and sugar or honey and miscellaneous added ingredients. The term can also cover blancmange, or what the Scots call "sowens" or "sowans," a dish made from the mealy powder remaining with the husks of oats. But if you come across *flummery*,

185

you will find that it will more likely have been used in its figurative, and quite different sense: anything insipid, or false and empty compliments, the kind emanating from sycophants. The literal and figurative senses may be quite distinct, yet there may be a logical connection, for the various drinks listed above seem rather insipid. In any event, *flummery* is from Welsh *llyru*, based on the adjectives *llymrig* (harsh, raw) and *llym* (sharp, severe). So say the dictionaries, but it all seems rather mysterious and flummoxing (no etymological connection) and it would appear more hospitable and kinder to offer someone the literal dish than to dish out the figurative stuff.

foofaraw (FOOH fuh raw) *n.* This bit of informal American, as well as its variant *fofarraw* (FOH fuh raw), has two distinct meanings: a big fuss about very little, i.e., much ado about nothing; or flashy finery, too many frills. Literary policeman's question: "What's going on here? What's all this *foofaraw* about?" Or, in the second sense, from a lady wearing a lorgnette (if you can find one): "She could certainly dispense with all that *foofaraw*!" A lovely-sounding word and, say the authorities, origin unknown; but in the first sense, could it be a corruption of *free-for-all* (in babytalk)? The British appear not to use this word, but, in the *to-do* sense, have a nice equivalent: *gefuffle*, also spelt *kerfuffle* and *cufuffle*, all loosely used as synonyms for their word *shemozzle*, which is also spelt *shemozzl*, *chimozzle*, and at least half-a-dozen other ways—you takes your choice.

formication (for muh KAY shun) *n. Formication* is a tingling sensation, the feeling that ants or other insects are crawling all over you. One might experience *formication* at the sight of something horrifying or terribly frightening. Horror movies are especially aimed at producing *formication* in the audience. *Formica* is Latin for *ant*, and gives us the adjective *formic* (pertaining to ants), the noun *formicary* (ant nest), and *formic acid* (a substance exuded by ants). One must be careful in the pronunciation of this word, the *m* being so close to *n* in the alphabet. See also the last sentence of **apothegm.**

formicine, see **accipitrine**
186

fortis (FOR tis) *n.*, *adj.* The plural of the noun is *fortes* (FOR teez). *Fortis* is a term in phonetics that applies to the sound of letters (or combinations of letters) of the alphabet pronounced strongly, with relatively great muscular force and breath pressure, producing a strong, rather explosive sound. These are *f*, *k*, *p*, *t*, *s*, sometimes *h* and the combinations *sh* and *th* as in *thin*. The term *fortis* was taken over intact from Latin, where it means "strong, powerful." *Lenis* (LEE nis, LAY-), *n.* and *adj.* (plural of the noun is *lenes*, LEE neez, LAY-), is the term in phonetics that applies to letters (or combinations of letters) of the alphabet pronounced with relatively weak muscular force and breath pressure, producing a mild, weak sound. These are *b*, *d*, *g*, *j*, *v*, *z* and the combinations *th* as in *this* and *zh*. *Lenis* was taken as is from Latin where it means "smooth, soft, gentle." [Incidentally, *phonetics* (fuh NET iks, foh-), treated as a singular noun despite its plural form (cf. *economics*, *physics*, etc.), is the science of speech sounds.]

foudroyant (fooh DROY unt) *adj.* *Foudroyant* describes things that are striking, stunning, sudden and overwhelming, dazzling. *Foudroyant* is taken from the French, where it is the present participle of *foudroyer* (strike with lightning), based on *foudre* (lightning), derived from Latin *fulgur* (lightning). There is a special use of *foudroyant* in medicine, where it describes a disease that begins suddenly and in a severe form, like a serious heart attack suffered by a patient who has had no previous history of the illness—an affliction out of the blue. Getting back to the word's general use: One turns a corner and gets one's first sight of the Taj Mahal—the effect is *foudroyant*. The same goes for the immense statuary at Abu Simbel, rescued, in a stupendous engineering feat, from the rising waters of the Nile. But it's not all architecture: Love at first sight is *foudroyant* in the extreme, complete with a rush of blood and palpitations.

freebooter (FREE booh tur) *n.* A *freebooter* is a pirate or buccaneer, one who roves about *freely* in search of *booty*; an anglicization of the Dutch noun *vrijbuiter*, based on *vrij* (free) plus *buit* (booty). *Vrijbuiter* gave rise to another word, *filibuster*, first applied to the pirates of the West Indies in the 17th century, and later to the unlawful groups organized from the United States to invade and foment revolution in some Spanish-American regions, e.g., those of Cuba in 1850–1851, Sonora in 1853–1854, and Lower California in 1855. Shades of Nicaragua in 1986? *Filibuster* was metamorphosed into a term for obstructive tactics in legislative proceedings through endless speeches.

frequentative   (frih KWEN tuh tiv) *n.*, *adj.* A verb, as everyone knows, expresses an action. A *frequentative* verb, or a *frequentative* (used as a noun) serves to express the frequent repetition of that action. This is common in Latin. See, for example, **mussitation**; another case in Latin is *haerere* (to stick)/*haesitare* (to keep sticking), from whose past participle, *haesitatus*, we get *hesitate*—to "keep sticking" without making a decision. *Frequentatives* occur in English as well. Examples: *chat/chatter, twink/twinkle, spark/sparkle, drip/dribble*. In each case, the *frequentative* expresses the continual repetition of the action of the original verb. If you keep *dripping*, you *dribble*; if you keep *twinking*, you *twinkle*; if you go on *sparking*, you *sparkle*, and if this author keeps on *chatting*, he'll be accused of *chattering*.

friable   (FRYE uh bul) *adj.* One might be forgiven for thinking that something *friable* was something that could be fried, i.e., fryable, like a fryer, a young chicken; but like *ply* and *pliable*, *fry* and *friable* are unrelated. *Friable* describes anything easily crumbled or broken, like *friable* rock, or a *friable* growth or tumor that breaks and bleeds. *Fry* and *friable* come from different roots: *fry* is from Latin *frigere* (to roast, parch) while *friable* is from Latin *friabilis*, based on *friare* (to crumble). Sandstone is easy to work because it is *friable*. Blood in the urine is sometimes the result of the breaking of a *friable* polyp on the inner wall of the bladder. Col. Sanders should not come to mind when you see the word *friable*.

fribble   (FRIB ul) *n.*, *vb.*, *adj.* To *fribble* is to trifle, to act in a silly, frivolous way. To *fribble* or *fribble away* one's time is to fritter it away. A *fribbler* is a trifler, but *fribble*, as a noun, can also denote anything trifling or frivolous. As an adjective, *fribble* describes anything that is trifling or frivolous, trivial, inane, vacuous. *Fribble* is thought to be a variation of the rarely seen colloquial verb *frivol*, a back formation from *frivolous*. To *frivol* is to act frivolously, to trifle, and to *frivol away* one's time is to waste it. *Frivolous* itself is from the Latin *frivolus* (inane, trifling, worthless) which can thus be considered the ancestor of *fribble*. There may be an echo of *dribble* here, for *dribble* means, inter alia, to "drivel," and that, in turn, can mean to "prattle childishly" or even idiotically and, in that sense, to behave in a *fribbling* manner. Whether you *fribble*, *frivol*, *dribble*, or *drivel*, you are frittering away your precious time and ought to stop it and get down to business.

fringilline,   see **accipitrine**

frottage   (fraw TAHZH) *n. Frottage* is a word taken over intact from the French, where, based on the verb *frotter* (to rub), it means "rubbing" or "polishing." *Frottage* in English, however, has two very distinct meanings. In the field of arts and crafts, *frottage* is the technique of taking a "rubbing" from an uneven surface, by rubbing graphite over paper laid on top of the rough texture. A common practice in England is to lay a piece of paper on top of a plaque containing an inlaid brass figure embedded in a church floor over a tomb, and to rub a crayon or pencil over the paper in order to obtain a representation of the figure of the entombed personage. In a quite different field, *frottage* is the practice of obtaining sexual gratification by rubbing against someone, both parties usually being clothed. This happens occasionally in crowded subway cars and other confined spaces without the consent of the passive party, who often responds by slapping the naughty one in the face. The active participant is known as a "frotteur" (fraw TUR).

fructiferous   (fruk TIF uh rus, frook-) *adj.* Whereas *fruitful* (meaning literally "bearing fruit abundantly") is used in the main in its figurative sense of "profitable, productive," *fructiferous* is used only in the literal sense of "fruit-producing," referring to the kind of fruit we eat, not the "fruit" of one's labors. *Fructiferous* is from Latin *fructiferus*, based on *fructus* (fruit) plus the suffix *-fer* (producing), from the verb *ferre* (to bear). To *fructify* (FRUK tuh fye, FROOK-) is to bear fruit or to cause to bear fruit, i.e., to fertilize, while *fructuous* (FRUK chooh us) means "productive." A *fruct-* word rarely seen nowadays is *Fructidor*, the name of the twelfth month in the French revolutionary calendar (August 18 to September 16), that being the month when most fruit (*fructus*) is given (*doron* is Greek for "gift"). *Fructidor* is an example of a hybrid word, one composed of parts taken from different languages

(Latin *fructus* and Greek *doron*), like *television*, composed of Greek prefix *tele-* (far) plus *vision*, from Latin *visio* (view).

fructify,   see **fructiferous**

fructuous,   see **fructiferous**

fugacious   (fyooh GAY shus) *adj*. Anything described as *fugacious* is fleeting, short-lived, ephemeral, soon over and done with, the opposite of persistent or lasting. We are familiar with the Latin expression *Tempus fugit* (often inscribed on clocks and sundials). *Fugit* is a form of the Latin verb *fugere* (to flee), but the common translation is *Time flies*, probably because of the alliterative vowel sounds. A related Latin adjective is *fugax* (fleeing, fleeting), the stem of which is *fugac-*. There is another related Latin adjective, *fugitivus*, which gave us *fugitive*. The Roman poet Horace (65-8 B.C.) wrote of "fleeting years (that) slip by" in his lament to his friend Postumus:

> Eheu *fugaces*, Postume, Postume
> Labantur anni.

Infatuations tend to be *fugacious*, as is human physical beauty, all too soon. A politician's strength is based on that most *fugacious* of emotions, public favor. There are two nouns related to *fugacious:* *fugacity* (fyooh GAS ih tee), and *fugaciousness*. *Fugacity* is much easier to pronounce than *fugaciousness*. (Incidentally, *eheu* in Horace's ode means "alas, ah me, woe is me" and that sort of thing, and is pronounced *eh HYOOH*.)

fugle   (FYOOH gul) *vb*. To *fugle* is to act as a model or guide, a semantic change from its basic meaning of to "signal." It is a colloquial word, a back formation from *fugleman*, a political party leader or more generally, the manager, organizer, or spokesman of any type of group. *Fugleman* came to us as a variation of the German noun *Flügelmann* (literally, flank man) based on *Flügel* (wing) plus *Mann* (man), originally a soldier who used to be placed in front of a regiment or company being drilled, to demonstrate the routine, the way airline stewardesses go through the motions while passengers are being instructed in how to behave if . . . The American novelist Jack Kerouac (1922–1969)—whose work was charac-

190

terized by the American writer Truman Capote (1924–1984) in these unkind words: "It really isn't writing, is it? It's . . . er . . . typing."—*fugled* for the entire Beat Generation, those who grew up after World War II and in the late 1950s, defied the conventions, advocated detachment from society, promoted relaxation of the inhibitions it imposed, and supported the ideals of the flower children.

fulciline, see **accipitrine**

fuliginous (fyooh LIJ uh nus) *adj. Fuliginous* describes things that are smoky, sooty, of the color of soot, dusky, dark, dingy, dark gray, dull brown, or black. *Fuliginous* is from Latin *fuliginosus*, based on the noun *fuligo* (soot). Apart from its literal use as a color, *fuliginous* has been used metaphorically, as in the description of an ironical sense of humor, and in such a use, it means "darkly mysterious." Fowler criticizes the use of *fuliginous* in his article on "polysyllabic humor," in which he writes of the "impulse that suggests long . . . words as a means of entertaining the reader or hearer," and gives *terminological inexactitude* for *lie* or *falsehood* as an example "much less amusing at the hundredth than at the first time of hearing." He gives examples other than *fuliginous*, some of which can be found in this very book: **esurient, fugacious, matutinal, minacious,** and in his article on "pedantic humour," he says that "the incongruity between simple things to be said and out-of-the-way words to write them . . . [may have charm] for the reader who never outgrows **hobbledehoy**hood; but for the rest of us it is dreary indeed." (Yet note Fowler's use of **hobbledehoy**hood, based on yet another "challenging word" found in this book.) Under his headword *fuliginous*, he says "Chiefly in POLYSYLLABIC HUMOUR," and then goes on to give as an example: "At present it is a *fuliginous*, not to say mysterious matter." Be all the above as it may, remember that this book is a glossary of "challenging words" explained—not necessarily recommended!

fuliguline, see **accipitrine**

fulvous (FUL vus) *adj. Fulvous* covers a broad range of the spectrum in the tawny department: dull to medium brilliant yellowish brown, gray, or red. It comes from Latin *fulvus* (deep yellow, red-dish yellow, tawny), where the poets used it to describe anything from lions and wolves to sand and gold. There is a species of tropical long-legged duck, the *dendrocygna bicolor*, known as the *"fulvous* tree duck" to those interested in ornithology. *Tawny*, incidentally, comes from Middle French *tané*, past participle of *taner* (to tan).

funambulist   (fyooh NAM byuh list) *n.* A *funambulist* is a tight-rope artist; *funambulism* (fyooh NAM byuh liz um) is the art. To *funambulate* (fyooh NAM byuh late) is to practice the art; *funambulation* (fyooh nam byuh LAY shun) is the act of tightrope walking or dancing; *funambulator* (fyooh NAM byuh lay tur) is synonymous with *funambulist*; and *funambulatory* (fyooh NAM byuh luh tor ee) describes the art or activity. In each case, the first syllable is pronounced like our word *few*. All these words stem from the Latin *funambulus* (ropedancer), based on *funis* (rope) and *ambulare* (to walk).

fundament   (FUN duh munt) *n.* We are familiar with the adjective *fundamental*, a synonym of *basic, underlying*, which describes anything that goes to the root of the matter and is an essential part of whatever may be involved. We speak of *fundamental* rules, *fundamental* principles, a *fundamental* change or revision, a *fundamental* concept or idea. And *fundamentalism* denotes strict observance of traditional orthodox religious beliefs, the infallibility of the Bible as history and the literal acceptance of the creeds as the basic principles of Protestant Christianity. A far cry from *fundament* itself, meaning "buttocks," a.k.a. the *arse, behind, derrière,* and *nates*, with the additional meaning, according to some dictionaries, of "anus," a.k.a. the *ass-hole, bung-hole*, and lots of other disagreeble nicknames. The *fundament*, then, refers to the lower part of the torso in general. (*Fundament* is also used occasionally to denote the physical features of a given geographical area: climate, soil, drainage, etc.) It is derived, via Middle English and Old French *fondemont*, from Latin *fundamentum* (foundation), related to the verb *fondare* (to found, lay the foundation of).

fungible   (FUN juh bul) *n., adj.* A *fungible* article is one that is interchangeable, i.e., it can be exchanged for or replaced by another of similar nature. It is thus differentiated from something that is one-of-a-kind, a unique individual specimen. As a noun, a *fungible* is anything that fits that description, like money, grain, a standard **artifact** like an automobile, umbrella, pen, or article of furniture—things off the assembly line—as opposed to an original work of art. The term *fungible*, in legal parlance, applies to things that are generally classified by number, weight, or measure. *Fungible* is derived from Middle Latin *fungibilis*, based on the Latin verb *fungi* (to serve as or in place of). A pound of mushrooms is *fungible*, but that is because they are replaceable, not because they are *fungi*. To pun is human, to forgive superhuman.

fustian (FUS chun) *n.*, *adj.* A strange word, *fustian*, in the diversity and apparent dissociation of its several meanings. First of all, *fustian* is the name of a thick twilled cotton fabric, or a blend of cotton and flax or low grade wool with a short nap, usually dyed a dark color; and as an adjective, *fustian* describes cloth so made. But *fustian* is now used chiefly in a wholly different sense, miles from cloth or fabric: It means "bombast," written or spoken, "turgid, inflated language, purple prose," and finally, "claptrap, rant, hogwash, palaver, prattle, drivel"; and as an adjective, "pompous, bombastic, nonsensical, worthless." *Fustian* is a Middle English word, from Old French *fustaigne*, derived from Middle Latin *fustaneus*, referring to cloth made in El-Fustat, a suburb of Cairo. This peculiar dichotomy of meanings suggests that the material from El-Fustat was of pretty poor value. Shall we complicate matters further? *Fustian* is also the name of a drink made of white wine, egg yolk, lemon, spices, and other miscellaneous ingredients—a concoction with possibilities. To *fustianize* (FUS chun ize) is to write in a bombastic manner, and a writer who descends to that level is a *fustianist* (FUS chun ist). From the pen of the English poet Alexander Pope (1688–1744), in the *Epistle to Dr. Arbuthnot*, out of his *Prologue to Imitations of Horace*, flow these words:

> Means not, but blunders round about a meaning;
> And he whose *fustian*'s so sublimely bad,
> It is not poetry, but prose run mad.

Shakespeare used *fustian* in *Othello* (Act II, Scene 3), when Cassio, in despair after Othello cashiers him, cries: "I will rather sue to be despised than to deceive so good a commander . . . Drunk! . . . and squabble, swagger, swear, and discourse *fustian* with one's own shadow!'' In *Henry IV, Part 2* (Act II, Scene 4), Doll Tearsheet tells Bardolph: ''For God's sake, thrust him [Pistol] down stairs! I cannot endure such a *fustian* rascal.'' And in *Twelfth Night* (Act II, Scene 5), after hearing Malvolio's doggerel:

> I may command where I adore;
>> But silence, like a Lucrece knife,
> With bloodless stroke my heart doth gore:
>> M, O, A, I, doth sway my life.

Fabian exclaims: ''A *fustian* riddle!'' All these uses refer to bombast, prattle, and drivel. But Shakespeare used *fustian* also in its material sense. In *Taming of the Shrew* (Act IV, Scene 1), Curtis asks Grumio: ''Where's the cook? is supper ready, the house trimmed, rushes strewed, cobwebs swept, the serving men in their new *fustian* . . . ?'' The English dramatist John Heywood (c. 1497- c. 1580), in his play *Faire Maide of the Exchange* (Act II, Scene 2), used *fustian* in the figurative sense: ''. . . Some scurvy quaint collection of *fustian* phrases and uplandish words.'' A strange and versatile word, *fustian*.

gabion (GAY bee un) *n.* A *gabion* is a wickerwork cylinder or bottomless basket filled with earth, formerly used in fortification as a military defense. The same type of wicker container filled with stones and sunk in water was used in laying foundations of dams or jetties. A defense wall formed of *gabions* was known as a *gabionade* (GAY bee un ade); *gabionage* (gay bee un AJE) is the name given to a series of *gabions*; a fortification using *gabions* is said to be *gabioned* (GAY bee und). *Gabion* is a French word, taken from the Italian *gabbione* (large cage), based on *gabbia* (cage; the ending *-one* is an augmentative), derived from Latin *cavea* (cavity, cage). With the availability of poured cement, the *gabion* became outmoded.

galimatias (gal uh MAY shee us, -MAT ee us) *n.* The word, taken intact from the French (who pronounce it: gahl ih MAH tee

194

ah) means "nonsensical talk, gibberish, twaddle, confused and meaningless babble, unintelligible jargon and mishmash," sometimes with the implication that the balderdash is not only senseless but somewhat pompous. The English writer Horace Walpole (1717–1797) used this curious word in describing a certain lady in these terms: "Her talk is a *galamatias* of several countries." It seems likely that *galamatias* is somehow etymylogically related to **gallimaufry,** but where the *-atias* came from is a matter of doubt. One possibility is that it was suggested by the Greek noun *amathia* (ignorance), resulting in a "galamatian" word for "ignorant twaddle."

gallimaufry   (gal uh MAW free) *n.* A *gallimaufry* is a jumble, a hodge-podge, a mishmash, a farrago, a **salmagundi**, a miscellany, a potpourri, an olio, a confused medley. This word has a very *gallimaufry* of synonyms, perhaps because life presents such a *gallimaufry* of *gallimaufries*. It comes from Middle French *galimafrée*, meaning "ragout," and that seems to have come out of the blue. In cooking, a *gallimaufry*, as one might have guessed, is a stew or ragout or hash. The *Times Literary Supplement* spoke of a work "written in a remarkable *gallimaufry* of languages": and *Time* characterized a play as "a *gallimaufry* of didactic speeches, romantic flourishes and characters for several unrelated kinds of plays." The languages of India are a *gallimaufry* of tongues. The English poet Edmund Spenser (c. 1552–1599) called ". . . our English tongue a *gallimaufry* or hodgepodge of all other speeches." Where there is unplanned municipal building, the result is often an unpleasant *gallimaufry* of styles.

gallinaceous   (gal uh NAY shus) *adj.* This adjective is applied to anything having to do with domestic fowls. It is from Latin *gallinaceous* (pertaining to poultry), based on *gallus* (cock), *gallina* (hen). Most people like to eat chicken, but never give a thought to the fact that, at one time, chickens were not domestic, but wild. Darius I (the Great, c. 549–c. 485 B.C.) king of Persia from 521 B.C. to 486 B.C., accomplished many things: put down revolts, set up a vast administrative system, succeeded in lengthy military campaigns (though he lost at Marathon in 490 B.C.). But one of his greatest accomplishments was the domestication of the chicken, a *gallinaceous* feat, and from there it was a straight line to Col. Sanders.

galline, see **accipitrine.**

gambado (gam BAY doh) *n.* This word has several meanings. A *gambado* is one of a pair of large boots or leather gaiters attached to a saddle in place of stirrups, but the term can apply more generally to any long legging or gaiter. In this meaning, *gambado* is based upon the Italian noun *gamba* (leg), which gave us as well the slang for girls' legs, *gams*. *Gambado* (sometimes *gambade*—gahm BADE or gam BAHD) is also used of a leap, bound, or spring of a horse, and more generally, of any fantastic movement, antic, caper, or escapade. In this use, *gambado* is a modification of the French *gambade* (antic, skip, romp, gambol), and we got *gambol* as well from Middle French *gambade*. The context will make it clear which *gambado* one is dealing with, and in any event, boots and gaiters are hardly attached to saddles these days.

gargantuan (gar GAN choo un) *adj.* Anyone or anything described as *gargantuan* is huge, gigantic, vast, of enormous proportions. The adjective, often capitalized, is derived from *Gargantua,* the amiable giant king whose exploits are recorded in the novel of that name, one of the two great satirical works by François Rabelais (1494–1553). His books, full of coarse, broad, boisterous wit and humor, are characterized by the type of licentious language associated with the adjective **Rabelaisian.** Gargantua was noted for his incredibly voracious appetite (*garganta* is Spanish for "gullet"; cf. French *gargouille*, throat, and English derivatives *gargle* and *gargoyle*), so great that on one occasion the insatiable guzzler swallowed whole five pilgrims—with their staves!—mixed in a salad. In Shakespeare's *As You Like It* (Act III, Scene 2), Rosalind asks Celia a torrent of questions about Orlando and winds up: "Answer me in one word." Celia replies: "You must borrow me Gargantua's mouth first: 'tis a word too great for any mouth of this age's size . . ." One can speak of the *gargantuan* appetite of a **trencherman,** the *gargantuan* length of one of those endless historical novels, or the *gargantuan* task of cleaning up after a hurricane. Gargantua fathered the giant Pantagruel, the hero of the other great novel by

196

Rabelais. The giant son lent his name to the adjective **pantagrue-lian.** For a synonym of *gargantuan* derived from another famous satirical novel, see **brobdingnagian.**

garruline,   see **accipitrine**

gasconade   (gas kuh NADE) *n., vb. Gasconade* is inordinate boasting, extravagant bragging. To *gasconade* is to indulge in *gasconade*. The word comes from *Gascony* (in French, *Gascogne*), once a province in southwestern France, whose natives, the *Gascons*, were famous for their boastful ways. A *gascon* (lower case *g*) is a braggart. There are legends about Gascons. "What's your opinion of the Louvre?" someone asks a Gascon, who replies: "Not so bad; it reminds me of the rear of my father's stables." This was extreme **braggadocio** since the Gascons were proverbially poor. Cf. **braggadocio, fanfaronade, rodomontade, thrasonical.**

gastronome   (GAS truh nome) *n.* A *gastronome* is an epicure or gourmet. (Please, despite those permissive dictionaries, do your best to preserve the proper distinction between *gourmet* and *gourmand.*) *Gastronome* is a back formation from *gastronomy* (ga STRON uh mee), the art, lore and science of the true gourmet. Cf. **aristology** and **Lucullan.** *Gastronomy* is derived from the Greek prefix *gastro-* (*gastr-* before a vowel), the combining forms of *gaster* (stomach), as in *gastric, gastritis, gastrointestinal*, etc., plus the Greek suffix *-nomia*, based on *nomos* (law) from which we get *-nomy*, as in *astronomy, economy, bionomy, etc. Gastr-* and *gastro-* words have nothing to do with *gas*, the kind that hurts your tummy and gives us, in addition, the pain of all those television commercials. That word *gas* was coined by the Flemish chemist J. B. van Helmont (1577–1644), suggested by the Greek noun *chaos* (atmosphere; the vast, unfathomable space out of which the universe arose). (In Flemish, the letter *g* is pronounced like the Greek *chi*, or the Yiddish *ch* as in *chutzpa*, so that to van Helmont, *gas*, with *a* as in *art*, wasn't very far from properly pronounced *chaos* in Greek).

gazelline,   see **accipitrine**

genethlialogy   (jih neth lee AL uh jee) *n.* This is a term in the ''science'' of astrology denoting the art of making astrological calculations, also known as ''casting nativities,'' based on the plotting of heavenly bodies at the time of the subject's (victim's?) birth. The Greek noun *genethlialogia* is based on *genethlia* (births) plus the Greek suffix *-logia*, from which we get our familiar *-logy*, as in *astrology, geology, theology,* and some less familiar *-logies*, like *ethnology* (the study of cultures), *ethology* (animal behavior, habitat), *limnology* (lakes and ponds), *malacology* (mollusks), *pedology* (children), *soteriology* (salvation), *storiology* (folklore), *thremmatology* (propagation under domestication), *threpsology* (nutrition), *uranology* (astronomy); and there are many more. But getting back to *genethlialogy*, the related adjective *genethliac* (jih NETH lee ak) is used to describe anything pertaining to birthdays, especially the position of the stars at one's birth, said to be a basic consideration in astrology. *Genethlialogy* is not only an alleged science; it is big business, as evidenced by book and periodical sales, syndicated newspaper columns, correspondence courses and heaven (?) knows what else. There are those who won't make a move without a *genethlialogical* consultation. Heaven (what again?) help them.

gerontology   (jer un TOL u jee) *n. Geront-* is the stem of the Greek noun *geron* (old man), and gives us the prefix *geronto-*. Add the Greek suffix *-logia* to get our *-logy*, used in the names of studies, sciences, or bodies of knowledge, and we wind up with *gerontology*, the scientific study of old age, the process of aging, and the problems of the elderly. There are government bodies and committees, local, state, and federal, that deal with the special problems and needs of the aging. Ah me . . . !

> Gaudeamus igitur
> Juvenes dum sumus.
> Post jucundam juventutem,
> Post molestam senectutem,
> Nos habebit humus.
>
> Let us live then and be glad
> While young life's before us.
> After youthful pastime had,
> After old age hard and sad,
> Earth will slumber o'er us.

This is a medieval student's song, traced back to 1626. So much, then, for *gerontology*!

gerrymander (JER ih man dur, GER-) *n.*, *vb*. A *gerrymander* is the redrawing of the boundaries of electoral districts within a certain area in such a way as to give a political party an undue advantage in election results. The favored party acquires a majority in a large number of districts, the opposing party in fewer districts than before the *gerrymandering*. As a verb, to *gerrymander* is to engage in such shenanigans. The peculiar word came about in an amusing way, from the name of a Massachusetts governor, Elbridge Gerry (1744–1814), whose party so redistricted that state in 1812. (One might have supposed that they had their hands full with the War of 1812, but there's always a little time left over for political skulduggery.) The artist Gilbert Stuart (1775–1828), seeing the map of the redistricting, noted the resemblance of one of the new districts to the outline of a salamander and did a bit of converting of the map to that shape, by adding wings, a head, and a tail. He showed the result to a Boston newspaperman named Russell who coined the word *gerrymander*. Gerry pronounced his name with a hard *g*, but the erroneous *j*-pronunciation so caught on that the word is still occasionally spelt with an initial *j*, possibly (according to Fowler) by association with *jerrybuilt*.

gibbous (GIB us, JIB-) *adj*. This is the description used in astronomy for the moon (or any heavenly body that waxes and wanes like the moon—to our view) when it is more than half "full," so that it appears convex at both edges. *Gibbous* comes from the Latin adjective *gibbosus* (humped), based on *gibba* or *gibbus* (hump), and is also spelt *gibbose* (GIB ose, JIB-). *Gibbosity* (gih BOS ih tee, jih-) is the noun for the quality of being *gibbous*, but in its more general sense applies to any swelling, bump, or protuberance. The monstrosity on the face of Cyrano de Bergerac, or Pinocchio when he lied, was an extreme case of *gibbosity* of the proboscis.

giraffine, see **accipitrine**

glabrous (GLAY brus) *adj*. *Glabrous*, a term used in anatomy, zoology, and botany, describes the condition of any organism that is smooth-skinned, without hair or down, i.e., bald. The Latin

199

adjective *glaber* (hairless) is the source of this adjective. It was because of the *glabrous* condition of Aeschylus's pate (Aeschylus, the father of classical Greek drama, 525–456 B.C.) that an eagle dropped a tortoise on it, in order to break the shell, in the mistaken belief that the *glabrous* dome was a stone. Thus died Aeschylus, or so says the legend. If you have a *glabrous* skull, stay away from places where eagles abound, or wear a wig.

glacis (GLAY sis, GLAS is) *n.* In days of yore, soldiers would build a bank sloping down from their fort, so that an attacking foe would be an easier target for the defenders' missiles. This word is from the French, who got it, via the Old French verb *glacier* (to slide, slip) from Latin *glacies* (ice). Nowadays *glacis* denotes any gentle slope. Forts are obsolete as defenses, and a *glacis* in the old sense wouldn't be much help anyway in the face of rockets and similar contrivances.

glaucous (GLAW kus) *adj.* *Glaucous* describes anything pale bluish green or greenish blue, and in botany, things like plums covered with a fine, powdery whitish, greenish, or bluish bloom. *Glaucescence* (glaw SES uns) is the noun for this quality, and *glaucescent* (glaw SES unt) is the description of anything in nature that is somewhat *glaucous*. *Glaucous* is from the Latin adjective *glaucus* (the *-us* ending of the masculine form of Latin adjectives usually becomes *-ous* in English) meaning "bluish or greenish gray."

gloss (glos) *n., vb.* This word has two entirely distinct meanings, each with its own derivation. We need not dwell on the noun *gloss* meaning "luster" or "shine," sometimes with the implication of a superficial, deceptive appearance, or the verb *gloss* (usually *gloss over*) meaning to "make [something] look good" when it isn't, as when one *glosses over* the flaws in something—whether tangible, like a paint job, or intangible, like a brief or an argument—giving it a specious appearance of soundness. This *gloss* is of Scandinavian origin, from Danish *gloos* (glowing) via Middle High German *glozen* (to shine), and is akin to our word *glow*, from Middle English *glowen*. The other *gloss* is the less familiar one and an entirely different and often confusing matter: *gloss*, meaning "explanation" or "interpretation," usually by means of a note, marginal or interlinear, of a difficult term or obscure expression in a text. The

200

related verb to *gloss* means to "annotate" by the insertion of *glosses*. But—caution here—through confusion with the other gloss, this *gloss* has acquired the meaning of "give a false or specious interpretation of [something]"; and here, too, we see *gloss over*, as in *glossing over* a difficult situation with a past solution that doesn't solve the problem. This *gloss* is via Middle English *gloze* and Late Latin *glos(s)a* (difficult word, and by extension, a word needing explanation, annotation, comment) from Ionic Greek *glossa* (tongue, language). To *gloze* is a derived verb, also with two different meanings: "*gloss* over, explain away," and to "shine or brighten." Fowler has something to say about the confusion between the two *glosses*: "The development of a word meaning explanation into one meaning misrepresentation . . . has meant that in popular as opposed to learned speech . . . *gloss* [meaning "comment"] is seldom without the suggestion of something sophistical. The two verbs, *gloss* (or *gloze*), to comment, and *gloss*, to put a luster on, have been even more closely assimilated into the meaning of extenuate in a specious way, especially the phrasal verb *gloss* or *gloze over*." As stated earlier—caution!

gloze,   see gloss

glyptic,   see glyptography

glyptography   (glip TOG ru fee) *n. Glyptography* is the art of engraving stones and gems. The related word *glyptic* (GLIP tik) describes anything pertaining to carving on gems or stones. *Glyptics* (treated as a singular noun) is the art of gem engraving. *Glyptikos* is the Greek adjective describing that type of engraving or stone carving; *glyptos* means "carved," from *glyphein* (to engrave). *Glyptography* is built of *glyptos* plus *graphein* (to write, draw, engrave).

gnathonic   (na THON ik) *adj.* A *gnathonic* person is a parasite, a fawning toady, a sycophant. *Gnatho* is the name of such a character in *Eunuchus (The Eunuch)*, a comedy by the Roman playwright Terence (c. 190–c. 159 B.C.), and *gnatho* means "parasite" generally in Latin. *Gnathonic* is from Latin *gnathonicus*, an adjective based on the character of *Gnatho* in the play. For another adjective based on another character in the same play, see **thrasonical**.

Gnathos is a Greek noun meaning "jaw," from which we get *gnathic* (NATH ik) and *gnathous* (NATH us), both meaning "pertaining to the jaw," as well as the suffix *-gnathous*, referring to the jaw, as in *prognathous* (PROG nu thus, prog NA-), describing a person having protruding jaws. It is difficult to see the connection between *Gnatho*, the character in *Eunuchus*, and *gnathos* (jaw), unless the parasitic sycophant happened to be acted by a *prognathous* actor.

gnome   (nome, NOH mee) *n.* There are two kinds of *gnomes*: (1) the legendary shriveled old men who live in the interior of the earth and are also known as *trolls* (these are *chthonic* or *chthonian* characters, that adjective meaning "relating to beings dwelling under the earth" in classical mythology, and based on the Greek noun *chthon, earth*) and (2) terse expressions of general truth, also known as *aphorisms*. The first type is quite familiar from childhood literature and cartoons, the second kind less so. The two come from different sources: the little old men from New Latin *gnomus*, the pithy sayings from Greek *gnome* (opinion, judgment). *Gnome*, in the second sense, has a related adjective, gnomic (NOHM ik, NOM ik, take your choice), describing writing full of *gnomes* or maxims or pithy statements of general truth, and a *gnomist* (NOH mist) is a writer of aphorisms, while a *gnomology* (noh MOL uh jee) is an anthology of aphorisms. Fowler points out that there is a *gnomic* past tense, to state a fact true of all times, including the present, thus: "Men were deceivers ever." Certain Greek poets of the seventh and sixth centuries B.C. are known as the *gnomic* poets, because their poetry is *gnomic*, packed with aphoristic statements. There is a series of *gno-* words, all taken from the Greek and related to the verb *gignoskein* (to know): *gnosis* (NOH sis, knowledge of spiritual mysteries); *gnostic* (NOS tik, knowing, especially with respect to mystical and esoteric matters); and the more familiar *agnostic* (ag NOS tik, from the Greek *agnostos*, describing one who asserts that the essential nature of all things, including God, is unknown and unknowable, and that one can know only what one experiences and can believe only in material phenomena). *Gnostic* means "knowing"; *agnostic* is simply *gnostic* with the Greek prefix *a-*, the so-called alpha privative, meaning "not," stuck in front: "not knowing." Another *gno-* word, having nothing whatever to do with trolls, aphorisms, or theology, is *gnomon* (NOH mon), which is the name of the upright part of a sundial that casts the shadow that tells the time. *Gnomon* was taken as is from the Greek, where it means "one that knows" or "indicator," in this case the indicator of the time of day (if the sun is out). Incidentally, why the *k-* in know? Via Middle English, Old English, and Latin, it simply goes back to the second *g-* (via Latin *gnovi,* I know), in *gignoskein.*

gnomon,   see **gnome.** It's a long entry and you'll have to read all the way through.

gnosis, gnostic,   see **gnome**

goliard   (GOLE yurd) *n. Goliards* were itinerant scholars and poets of the 12th and 13th centuries who wrote ribald and satirical Latin verse. They were erudite buffoons and jesters, given to drunken riotous behavior. The word is Middle English, and comes from Old French *goliart* or *goliard* (drunkard or glutton), which was derived, via French *gueule* (throat), from Latin *gula* (throat; by extension, gluttony). The *goliards* begged their way as they wandered about the country, and eventually increased their numbers until they developed into a horde of riotous vagabonds who came to be known as *ordo vagorum* (order of vagabonds; *vagorum* is the genitive plural of the Latin adjective *vagus,* wandering, here used as a noun). Their legendary leader, named Bishop Golias (Goliath), is now thought to be a literary figment, invented **ex post facto** from the name *Goliard.* They were a scandalous bunch, but their Latin verse and songs, modeled after medieval hymns, had literary merit. They were in praise of wine, women, and the open road, often in satirical attack on the immoral side of official church life and its practitioners. Their songs are known as *carmina burana,* after the collection found in the Abbey of Benediktbeuren. A number of them were set to music in 1937 by the German composer Carl Orff (1895–1982) and are often performed as a secular cantata under the title *Carmina Burana.*

goluptious   (gol UP shus) *adj.* This is slang for "delicious, delightful, splendid." The *Dictionary of Slang and Unconventional English* of the British lexicographer Eric Partridge (1894–1979) lists a great many spellings of this scrumptious word: *galoptious, galuptious, goloptious,* plus all of those with the ending *-shus* instead of *-tious*, but states: "The best form is *goluptious*, for the term is a 'facetious perversion . . . of *voluptuous* . . .' according to the English etymologist and lexicographer Ernest Weekley (1865–1954)." Partridge calls it "a fanciful adjective of the *catawampus*, *scrumptious* type . . ." *Catawampus* (also *-pous*, *-ptious*) is slang for "avid, fierce, eager," suggested by *catamount*, a synonym of *cougar*. *Scrumptious is* colloquial for "delectable," suggested by *sumptuous*.

grammalogue   (GRAM uh log) *n.* A *grammalogue* is a word represented by a symbol or letter. *And* is a *grammalogue* represented by the **ampersand** &; *dollar* by $; *cent* by ¢; *pound sterling* by £; *plus* by +; *minus* by −; *divided* by ÷; *times* by ×; in etymology, *derived from* by <; *and so forth* by &c.(as well as by *etc.*). Conversely, a *logogram* or *logograph* (LAWG uh gram, LOG-; LAWG uh graph, LOG-) is a symbol representing a word or phrase. & is the *logogram* of *and*; $ of *dollar*, etc. Both words are constructed, in inverse order, of the Greek nouns *gramma* (letter) and *logos* (word).

grammaticaster,   see **poetaster**

graphology   (gra FOL uh jee) *n.* *Graphology* is the study of handwriting, especially as an indication of the personality, character, disposition, and aptitudes of the writer; the art of inferring those aspects from one's handwriting. A practitioner of this study or art is a *graphologist* (gra FOL uh jist). These words are derived from the Greek noun *graphe* (writing) plus the suffix *logia*, from which we get our suffix *-logy*, indicating a science or study or body of knowledge pertaining to a particular subject, as in *biology, theology, zoology,* etc. *Graphologists* are not "handwriting experts." That is another field entirely: the identification and authentication of signatures or other writings as those of a particular person by close examination of the peculiarities of the script.

grisaille   (grih ZYE, -ALE) *n.* This word was taken over intact from the French, where *gris*, pronounced *gree*, is the word for "gray" and a *grisaille* is the name for any sketch or painting executed wholly in tones of gray. A *grisaille*, then, is a monochromatic work of art in shades of gray, and the term applies to stained glass windows as well as paintings and sketches. There is a related word in French, *camaïeu* (pronounced kah MAH yoo) meaning "cameo" but also applied to a monochrome painting in any shade as well as gray. *Grisaille* was a Renaissance technique of painting that simulated sculpture. One of the foremost examples is the 1436 equestrian portrait in the Cathedral of Florence by the Florentine painter Paolo Uccello (c. 1396–1475) of Sir John de Hawkwood (d. 1394), an English soldier who went to Italy in 1362 and became a *condottiere* (kon duh TYAIR ay), a word taken from the Italian designating a leader of a private army or band of mercenaries in Italy, a type active in the 14th and 15th centuries. *Condottiere* is also applied to any soldier of fortune or mercenary. The Italian word is derived from Latin *conductus* (mercenary soldier; literally, one led), from the past participle of *conducere* (to bring together).

groin, groyne   (groyn) *n.* A *groin* or *groyne* is a small jetty or breakwater extending from a shore to check beach erosion and sand-drifting. The origin of this word is uncertain; it is probably from Old French *groign* (snout) or Latin *grunnire* (to grunt).

groomsman, see **paranymph**

grumous   (GROOH mus) *adj. Grume* is a viscous fluid, especially clotted blood, and from it we get *grumous*, which means "clotted" and applies to things that resemble a clot of blood. Both noun and adjective are from Latin *grumus* (hillock or small heap), which figures as well in the derivation of our word *crumb. Grumous* sounds like an adjective invented by Lewis Carroll for Alice, but no, it's a real word.

gulosity   (gyooh LOS ih tee) *n. Gulosity* is gluttony or greediness. It is a literary word, stemming from Late Latin *gulositas*, derived from Latin *gulosus* (gluttonous), based on *gula* and *gulo* (glutton). One of the most famous practitioners of *gulosity* in literature is Gargantua, a legendary giant renowned for his incredible appetite. His name is based on the Spanish noun *garganta* (gullet). The French satirist François Rabelais (c. 1490–1553) made Gargantua the hero of his novel of that name. He was the father of Pantagruel, whose name is the title of Rabelais's other great novel. Gargantua's great exploits in *gulosity* included that in which he swallowed, in a salad, five pilgrims together with their staves. Our Victorian forebears, with their ten-course meals and vast bellies, were obviously addicted to *gulosity*.

gyre   (jire) *n.* A *gyre* is a ring, a circle, or a circular or spiral turn or movement. *Gyre* is, via Latin *gyrus*, from Greek *gyros* (ring, circle), which gave us the prefix *gyro-* as in *gyrocompass, gyroscope*, etc., and is related to our *gyrate* (whirl, move in a circle), from Latin *gyratus*, past participle of *gyrare* (to wheel around). The English mathematician and writer Lewis Carroll (Charles Lutwidge Dodgson, 1832–1892), in *Through the Looking Glass*, used *gyre* as a verb (with a hard *g* as in *go*) meaning "spin around" or "gyrate" when

> . . . the slithy tove
> Did *gyre* and gimble in the wabe . . .

Gyring, whether with a soft or a hard *g*, and whether in or out of the wabe, makes a person dizzy.

gyve   (jive) *n.*, *vb.* The noun is usually in the plural: *gyves*, which are shackles or fetters, mostly, but not always to bind the legs. To *gyve* is to shackle, bind. It is from Middle English *give* (jive). In Shakespeare's *Romeo and Juliet* (Act II, Scene 2), Juliet says to Romeo:

> 'Tis almost morning; I would have thee gone;
> And yet no further than a wanton's bird,
> Who lets it hop a little from her hand,
> Like a poor prisoner in his twisted *gyves*,
> And with a silk thread plucks it back again . . .

The English poet Thomas Hood (1799–1845) wrote of *gyves*, but for wrists rather than legs, in *The Dream of Eugene Aram*:

> Two stern-faced men set out from Lynn,
>   Through the cold and heavy mist;
> And Eugene Aram walked between,
>   With *gyves* upon his wrists.

So much for *gyves*; *stern-faced* is a **bahuvrihi.**

■■■■

haecceity, see **quiddity**

hagiology (hag ee OL uh jee) *n. Hagiology* is the field of literature treating the lives and legends of the saints. *Hagiography* (hag ee OG ruh fee) is writing in that field. A *hagiographer* or *hagiographist* or *hagiologist* is one who writes about saints. A *hagioscope* (HAG ee uh skope) has nothing to do with writing or saints, but is rather a *squint*, i.e., a small, oblique opening in a church wall affording a view of the high altar. In all these words, an alternative pronunciation of the first two syllables is *hay jee*. Incidentally, a saint, in the technical sense, is a person who is canonized, i.e., officially recognized by the Christian Church as having won a high place in heaven as a result of exceptional holiness, and entitled to veneration on earth. Sainthood, in effect, is a sort of celestial knighthood, bestowed by ecclesiastical authorities; recorded miracles help a lot. The prefix *hagio-* in all the words mentioned above is derived from Greek *hagios* (holy). The following is the opening paragraph of a review by Clare Stancliffe of two books on the subject in the August 14, 1984, issue of the (London) *Times Literary Review* headed "*Hagiographical* Deductions: *Saints and their Cults*, by Stephen Wilson, Editor (Cambridge University Press, 1984) and *Saints and Society*, by Donald Weinstein and Rudolph M. Bell (University of Chicago Press, 1984)":

> Saints, their cults and their lives, are a Cinderella subject. After years of relative neglect, historians and sociologists are now blowing the dust off those innumerable volumes of saints' lives and miracle stories and discovering ways of tapping their contents. Instead of sticking on the question of who St. Nicholas was and what he did, scholars are now asking, what function did he perform in society, and what can we learn from the practice of his cult? As Stephen Wilson succinctly puts it, "saints belong to and reflect the societies which produce and honour

207

them''. A perceptive study of saints' cults therefore yields insights into those societies—insights which are all the more valuable, in relation to societies with restricted literacy, for being based on what people do, not what they say.

hagioscope, see **hagiology**

haha (HAH hah) *n.* A *haha* is a sunk fence, consisting of a ditch that is not visible until one is close upon it; a hidden obstacle, acting as the boundary of a garden or a park. If one is standing on a lawn, for instance, gazing at a bordering field where cattle graze, one might see a herd staring back, but politely stopped at the invisible boundary. The whole landscape seems level and unbroken, with no separation between field and garden, and one wonders at the tact, restraint, and good manners of the animals, but on closer inspection, as one approaches the boundary, a fairly deep ditch with its wall on the lawn side consisting of brick or stone will be discovered and the riddle solved: The cattle simply can't get across the ditch and onto the lawn. *Haha* is taken from the French, and, pronounced *ah-ah,* is believed to owe its origin to the supposed cry of surprise at the discovery of the ingeniously hidden obstacle to the animals' progress, with no hedge or fence to mar the unbroken landscape. The *haha* is no laughing matter. This was the experience of the author very late one moonlit night on his first visit to Glyndebourne, the lovely opera center in the middle of the Sussex (England) countryside, where he was being shown around by a friend connected with that establishment, long after the performance was ended and the audience had departed. As he looked across the beautiful lawn, his gaze was returned by a line of cattle silently and mysteriously standing at attention a short distance away. Only on closer inspection, with the discovery of a *haha*, was the mystery of the respectful herd cleared up. "Aha!" rather than "Haha!" was the visitor's reaction.

halidom (HAL ih dum) *n.* A *halidom* is any holy or sacred place, like a church, a shrine, or a sanctuary. The word comes from Old English *haligdom,* based on *halig* (holy) plus *-dom,* a suffix denoting dominion, state, or power, as in *kingdom, Christendom,* etc., from Old English *dom* (judgment). *Halidom,* with variant spellings, was used in oaths, particularly in Shakespeare. In *Two Gentlemen of Verona* (Act IV, Scene 2), when Julia asks Host a question,

208

he answers: "By my *halidom*, I was fast asleep." In *The Taming of the Shrew* (Act V, Scene 2) when Katharina, after refusing to come to Petruchio, finally does show up, Baptista exclaims: "Now, by my *holidam*, here comes Katharina!" and Nurse uses the same oath in *Romeo and Juliet* (Act I, Scene 3). Another variant occurs in *Henry VIII* (Act V, Scene 1), when the king asks Cranmer. "Now, by my *holidame*,/ What manner of man are you?" These oaths are roughly the equivalent of today's somewhat weaker sounding "For heaven's sake!"

halieutic   (hal ee OOH tik) *adj.*; in the plural, *n. Halieutic* applies to things having to do with fishing. *Halieutics*, plural in form but treated as a singular noun (like *economics, physics*, etc.), is the art and science of fishing, or a treatise on fishing. *Halieutic* comes from the Greek adjective *halieutikos*, based on *halieus* (fisherman), in turn based on *hals* (the sea). The best known treatise on *halieutics* is, of course, *The Compleat Angler; or, The Contemplative Man's Recreation*, of the English writer Izaak Walton (1593–1683), which is not confined to the technique of fishing, but dwells as well on peace and virtue.

hamadryad,   see **oread**

hamartia   (hah mar TEE uh) *n.* The Greeks, who had a word for just about everything (except H-bomb and that sort of thing), concocted *hamartia*, a term for the tragic flaw or defect in the protagonist of a drama that causes an error in judgment and precipitates his downfall. Its general meaning is "fault, failure, error of judgment, sin," and it is related to the verb *hamartanein* (to err). The term was applied originally to Greek tragedy, and the concept was developed in the *Poetics* of the Greek philosopher Aristotle (384–322 B.C.), who wrote that tragedy was an "imitation of a painful action" (usually resulting in death) which by pity and fear purged the soul of those emotions. *Hamartiology* (hah mar tee OL uh jee) is the area of theology that deals with sin—a pretty wide area. It might be said that the *hamartia* of President Nixon and his associates was the failure to recognize the enormity and consequences of the obstruction of justice that led to their downfall. Other examples of *hamartia* are the "pride [that] goeth before destruction and an haughty spirit before a fall" (Proverbs 16:18). The Greek

209

playwright Sophocles (c. 495–406 B.C.), in *Oedipus Rex*, gave examples of *hamartia* in these lines:

> The tyrant is a child of Pride
> Who drinks from his great sickening cup
> Recklessness and vanity,
> Until from his high crest headlong
> He plummets to the dust of hope.

Il Duce and Der Führer should have studied their Sophocles, who further said, in his *Trachiniae:* "A prudent mind can see room for misgivings, lest he who prospers should one day suffer reverse." Reverse indeed: Il Duce was hanged upside down. There is an anonymous Greek proverb, written in the temple at Delphi: "Gnothi seauton" ("Know thyself"), quoted by the Roman poet Juvenal (c. 60–140) in his *Satires:* "From the gods comes the saying 'Know thyself,' " and centuries later by the English poet Alexander Pope (1688–1744) in *An Essay on Man:* "Know thyself . . ." It is only by knowing thyself that thou wilt rid thyself of thy *hamartia*.

haplology   (hap LOL uh jee) *n. Haplology* is the **syncope** of a syllable (see **syncope** under **aph(a)eresis**: the omission of one or more letters from the middle of a word). Some examples of *haplology: conservatism* reduced from *conservativism; idolatry* from *idololatry; syllabication* from *syllabification;* Englishmen say "lit'ry" for *literary* (a double *haplology*: two syllables missing) and children say "lib'ry" for *library. Haplology* is formed from the Greek prefix *haplo-*, combining form of *haploos* (single) plus *logos* (word). **Syncope** involves the loss of a medial letter in poetry: *ever* become *e'er, never ne'er,* while *haplology* involves the loss of a whole syllable. (See also **aph(a)eresis**.)

haptic   (HAP tik) *adj. Haptic* applies to things pertaining to the sense of touch. *Haptics* (treated as a singular) is the science of interpreting data obtained through touch. *Haptotropic* (hap tuh TROP ik) describes things like plant tendrils (leaves or shoots) that curve in response to touch. *Haptotropism* (hap tuh TROP iz um) is the same as *thigmatropism* (thig MAT ruh piz um) or *stereotropism* (ster ee OH truh piz um, steer-), response to the stimulus of touch. The prefix *hapto-* or *hapt-* is based on the Greek verb *haptein* (to touch, fasten); the suffixes *-tropic* and *-tropism* are from the verb *tropein* (to turn); the prefix *thigma-* is from the noun *thigma* (touch)

210

and the prefix *stereo-* is from the adjective *stereos* (solid). These Greek-derived words aren't used about people, but it isn't only tendrils and such that respond to touch. How about lovers, and erogenous zones?

haptotropism,   see **haptic**

hardscrabble   (HARD skrab ul) *adj.* A *hardscrabble* job is one that pays a paltry reward for hard work, a niggardly return for the effort involved, like the *hardscrabble* life of farmers on the dry and stony land of southern Italy. To *scrabble* is to scratch at something, to scramble and grab for something in a disorganized way; a *scrabble* is a disorderly struggle to get hold of something. *Scrabble* is from Dutch *schrabellen* (to scratch), a variant of *schrafen* (to scrape). The *hard-* part is self-explanatory. The concept of *hardscrabble* enters into the frequent jocular (?) response to "How are you?"—"Overworked and underpaid"—sometimes uttered by advertising executives earning not a penny over $250,000 a year.

haruspex   (huh RUS peks, HAIR uh speks) *n.* This was the title, in ancient Rome, of a lower order of priests who prophesied by examining the entrails of animals killed in sacrifice. The custom was handed down by the Etruscans. The practice is known as *haruspication* (hair us puh KAY shun) or *haruspicy* (huh RUS puh see). The verb is *haruspicate* (huh RUS puh kate). *Haruspex* is a Latin word, based on Etruscan *haru*, Latin *hira* (entrail) plus *specere* (to look at: *spexi* means "I have inspected"). The Roman Censor (a government official) Cato (234–149 B.C.) was not impressed by this type of divination. He said: "I wonder how one *haruspex* can keep from laughing when he sees another." This made him very unpopular with *haruspices*.

hebdomadal   (heb DOM uh dul) *adj.* An alternative form is *hebdomadary* (heb DOM uh der ee). In either form, this adjective means "weekly." A *hebdomadal* newspaper comes out once a week. *Hebdomadal* is from Late Latin *hebdomadalis*, *hebdomadary* from Church Latin *hebdomadarius*. Cf. **diurnal** and **quotidian**, both meaning "daily," and *mensal* (monthly). In *The Wrecker*, by the Scottish novelist Robert Louis Stevenson (1850–1894) and his stepson, Lloyd Osbourne, Pinkerton conceives an idea for a new business: "PINKERTON'S HEBDOMADARY PICNICS!

(That's a good, catching phrase, *'hebdomadary,'* though it's hard to say. I made a note of it when I was looking in the dictionary how to spell *hectagonal*. 'Well, you're a boss word,' I said. 'Before you're very much older, I'll have you in type as long as yourself.' . . .) . . . Pinkerton's *Hebdomadary* Picnics was soon shortened, by popular consent, to the Dromedary.''

hebephrenia, see **hebetic**

hebetate (HEB ih tate) *vb.* To *hebetate* is to dull or blunt. The term is applied usually where the *hebetation* (heb ih TAY shun) acts upon a person's sensitivity or a faculty. The political life often tends to *hebetate* one's ethical sensibilities, alas. The verb is derived from Latin *hebetatus*, past participle of *hebetare* (to make dull, to deaden), based on the adjective *hebes* (dull, blunt, sluggish). The expression *sensus hebes* (literally, dull sense; figuratively, dullness of the senses, i.e., insensitivity) appears in the Prologue to the *Polycraticus*, a treatise on government by the English scholar and prelate John of Salisbury (c. 1115–1180). The related noun *hebetude* (HEB ih toohd, -tyoohd) denotes listlessness, lethargy, and the adjective is *hebetudinous* (heb ih TOOHD ih nus, -TYOOHD-). Both words are from Late Latin *hebetudo* (dullness). These *hebe-* words are in no way related to **hebetic** and **hebephrenia**, which involve entirely different derivations.

hebetic (hih BET ik) *adj. Hebetic* applies to anything pertaining to puberty, or happening during puberty. It is derived from Greek *hebetikos* (youthful), based on the noun *hebe* (youth), and it is to be remembered that *Hebe* was the Greek goddess of youth, born of Zeus and Hera (a legitimate birth on Olympus, for a change!) and cup-bearer to the gods, with the power of restoring youth and strength to both gods and mortals. Hebe was succeeded by the god Ganymede, Zeus's cup-bearer, in a bit of political manipulation. On a sadder note: *hebephrenia* is a form of insanity that occurs in late childhood, involving incoherence and delusions, and ending in complete dementia. This term is based on *hebe* (youth) plus the Greek noun *phren* (mind). The *hebe-* in these words has naught to do with the *hebe-* based on Latin *hebes* (dull, blunt) in **hebetate** and **hebetude**.

hebetude, see **hebetate**
212

helot (HEL ut, HEE lut) *n.* A *helot* is a serf, or more generally, a slave. With an upper case *H*, *Helot* was the label given to a member of a class of society owned by the state in ancient Sparta, *helotes* in Latin, *heilotes* in Greek. *Helots* were bound to the land, farmed it, and paid part of the produce to the ruling class, the Spartiates. They could not be sold, and remained for their lives tied to the land, without civil rights of any sort. The story goes that the Spartiates would on occasion make a *Helot* drunk and exhibit him to the youth to demonstrate the evils of drink. The Scottish biographer James Boswell (1740–1795) quotes the English lexicographer and writer Dr. Samuel Johnson (1709–1784) as having said of an acquaintance: "He is a man of good principles; and there would be no danger that a young gentleman should catch his manner; for it is so very bad, that it must be avoided. In that respect, he would be like the drunken *Helot*." *Helot* is used as a biological term applied to a plant or animal living symbiotically with another to which it is subject—a special usage. *Helotism* (HEL uh tiz um, HEE luh-) or *helotry* (HEL uh tree, HEE luh-) is serfdom.

hendiadys (hen DYE uh dis) *n.* The *hendiadys* principle or construction, chiefly a convention of classical Greek and Latin, is one in which two nouns connected by *and*, as though they were independent components, are used to express an idea that would normally be covered by a noun and an adjective. Example: to eat from *dishes and silver* for eat from *silver dishes*; her eyes were like *pools and crystal*, for *crystal pools*. This construction is poetic and infrequently found in English; when used, it is in expressions like *nice and warm* for *nicely warm; try and convince him* for *try to convince him; grace and favour* for *gracious favor*. These illustrations in English are combinations of two adjectives, or two verbs, or two nouns; it is in the classical languages that the construction is normally composed of two nouns, where the second noun serves as an adjective modifying the first. There are expressions mistakenly considered to be *hendiadys*, where the two components connected by *and* are independent, rather than the second noun's being in the subordinate position. Examples: *assault and battery; might and main; toil and moil (moil* means "drudgery"); *hue and cry; leaps and bounds*. These are merely bits of tautology used for emphasis, usually a fruitful source of clichés. *Hendiadys* is, via Middle Latin, from Greek *hen dia dyoin* (one by two).

213

henotheism, see **henotic**

henotic (hen OT ik) *adj. Heno-* is a Greek prefix meaning "one," from *hen*, the neuter form of *heis* (one), and from *heno-* came the Greek adjective *henotikos*, and our word *henotic*, describing anything that tends to unify or reconcile. The blitzkrieg had a *henotic* effect upon the people of London, bringing them together in a way that transcended class distinctions. The *henotic* efforts of Abraham Lincoln helped heal the wounds of the Civil War (though some folks down there seem still to be fighting it, at least verbally). *Heno-* also appears in the noun *henotheism* (HEN uh thee iz um), the worship of one god in particular, one believed supreme or worthy of special veneration, without denying the existence of other gods, representing a stage between polytheism and monotheism. You pays your money and you takes your choice. *Heno-*, plus English *theism*, from the Greek noun *theos* (god), akin to Latin *deus*, gave us *henotheism*.

herculean (hur kyooh LEE un) *adj.* A *herculean* task is one extremely difficult to perform. A *herculean* person is one of the greatest strength and courage, or one of enormous size. Hercules, a great hero of classical mythology, a figure of superhuman strength and valor, was a son of Zeus himself. As penance for killing his wife and children in a fit of madness, Hercules had to perform 12 almost impossible tasks—the 12 labors of Hercules, listed in most unabridged dictionaries—whose accomplishment gained him immortality. (One of the 12 was to cleanse the Augean stables, which housed the herd of 3,000 oxen belonging to King Augeas of Elis in Greece and had not been cleaned for 30 years. Hercules got through that one by diverting the course of a river through the stables. To *cleanse the Augean stables* means, figuratively, to "clear away an accumulation of corruption," and the word *Augean* itself has come to mean, in the figurative sense, "wearisome and distasteful, laborious and unpleasant," as applied to a task or an assignment.) Getting back to old Hercules: Any exceedingly difficult, backbreaking task may be described as *herculean*—one, so to speak, requiring the strength and patience of a Hercules. The English poet John Milton (1608–1674) used *Herculean* (with the alternative pronunciation hur KYOOH lee un; not much heard any more) in the sense of "extremely strong, powerful," when he wrote:

214

So rose the Danite strong
Herculean Samson, from the harlot lap
Of Philistean Dalilah.

But the common use of *herculean* is to describe a particularly on-
erous task. D-Day has often been described as a "*herculean* effort."

hermeneutics (hur muh NOOH tiks, -NYOOH-) *n. Hermeneutics*, treated as a singular noun (like *economics, politics*, etc.), is
the science of interpretation, especially of the Bible. The adjective
hermeneutic or *hermeneutical* means "explanatory," i.e., concerned with interpretation. The word comes from Greek *herme-
neutikos* (skilled in interpretation), related to the verb *hermeneuein*
(to explain, make clear, interpret), all based on the god Hermes,
the herald and messenger of the Greek gods, patron of the arts and
eloquence (and, incidentally, of herdsmen, roads, commerce, invention, cunning, and thievery—he covered a lot of ground! After
all, he did have wings on his ankles, like his Roman counterpart,
Mercury, a mercurial sort of chap.) Any commentary or series of
annotations to a text can be described as *hermeneutic. Hermeneu-
tic(s)* is to be distinguished from an *exegesis* (ek sih JEE sis), which
is the concrete interpretation (also primarily of the Bible) itself; but
the adjective *exegetic* (ek sih JET ik) and the noun *exegetics* are
synonymous with *hermeneutic* and *hermeneutics* respectively. *Exegesis* and its related words are from Greek *exegesis* (interpretation), based on prefix *ex-* (out of) plus the verb *hegeesthai* (to guide).
Irrelevant Note: In a characteristically hilarious piece entitled *The
UFO Menace*, in *Side Effects* (Random House, New York, 1981),
the American humorist, actor, film director, and producer Woody
Allen (b. 1935) narrates an encounter by "two Louisiana factory
workers" that starts: "Roy and I was catfishing in the bog" and
goes on about several creatures who emerge from a bright-yellow
sphere, speaking in a strange tongue. After a while ". . . they had
mastered my own language, but they still made simple mistakes
like using '*hermeneutics*' when they meant 'heuristics.' " It happens that in *1000 Most Important Words* by this author (Ballantine
Books, New York, 1982; Facts on File, New York, 1985), *heuristic*
is defined as a term applied to teaching methods, meaning "helping
to learn, encouraging students to find out for themselves . . . akin
to the Socratic method," and the derivation is given as "from New

215

Latin *heuristicus*, based on Greek *heuriskein* (to find out)." There isn't the slightest connection between the two words, as every extraterrestrial person should know, and those creatures should be ashamed of theirselves.

herpestine,   see **accipitrine**

herpetology   (hur pih TOL uh jee) *n*. *Herpetology* is the branch of zoology that deals with reptiles and amphibians. It comes from the Greek noun *herpeton* (creeping thing, reptile) based on the verb *herpein* (to creep) plus the familiar suffix *-logia*, used in the names of sciences and fields of knowledge, from which we get our common suffix *-logy*. (The all-too-familiar disease *herpes* is a Greek word meaning "creeping," also related to the verb *herpein*.) A *herpetologist* (hur pih TOL uh jist) is a specialist in *herpetology*. *Ophiology* (of ee OL uh jee, ohf-) derived from Greek *ophis* (snake) and *-logia*, is the branch of *herpetology* that deals with snakes, and *ophidian* (oh FID ee un) is both an adjective describing anything pertaining to snakes and a noun meaning "snake," derived from Greek *ophidion*, diminutive of *ophis* (serpent). *Ophiolatry* (of ee OL uh tree, ohf-) is snake worship, formed from same *ophis* plus the suffix *-latry*, based on *latria* (worship), found in words like *idolatry*.

heterochthonous,   see **autochthon**

heteroclite   (HET uh ruh klite) *n*., *adj*. *Heteroclite* means "abnormal, anomalous, off the beaten path," and as a noun, anyone or anything that fits that description—in man, a maverick, someone who doesn't fit the usual pattern, the conventions. Most great men and women were heteroclites—Caesar, Churchill, Shakespeare, Mme. Curie, Einstein. The word is from Greek *heteroklitos*, built on the prefix *hetero-* (other, different; as in *heterogeneous, heterodox*, etc.) plus *klitos* (past participle of *klinein* (to bend)—in other words, "bent the other way." *Klinein* also means to "inflect," and that gives *heteroclite* a special usage in grammar, both as noun and adjective. To *inflect* is simply to vary the ending of a word, depending on its function in a sentence: The *boy* is here; the *boys* are here; the *boy's* eyes are blue; the *boys'* eyes are of different colors. (Inflection applies to adjectives and verbs as well and isn't all that

216

simple, but let's leave it at that.) In Latin, nouns are classified into five "declensions" depending on the way in which they are inflected. If a noun has endings in more than one declension, it is *heteroclite*, or *a heteroclite*. For those who are interested, look up the declensions of *domus* (home) and *pecus* (cattle, or a single head of cattle). That will do for the moment, except for the very *heteroclite heteroclites* who want to keep delving.

heterodox (HET ur uh doks) *adj.* A *heterodox* belief is one not in accord with orthodox doctrines. We are familiar with *orthodox*, from Greek *orthodoxos* (correct in opinion), based on the prefix *ortho-*, from the adjective *orthos* (straight, correct) plus *doxa* (opinion), related to the verb *dokein* (to think); but less so with *heterodox*, from Greek *heterodoxos* (holding another opinion), based on the Greek prefix *hetero-*, from the adjective *heteros* (other, different) plus the same *doxa*. *Heterodoxy* (HET ur uh doks ee) is the word for a *heterodox* view. Orthodox and *heterodox* depend on the individual's point of view. According to the *Memoirs* of the English chemist, writer, and clergyman Joseph Priestly (1733–1804), Bishop William Warburton (1698–1779) remarked to Lord Sandwich (1718–1792; the fourth earl of Sandwich, the eponym of the sandwich, which he invented by ordering a waiter to bring him a slice of ham between two slices of bread so that he could continue gambling all day, as was his wont, without having to stop to use a knife and fork): "Orthodoxy is my doxy; *heterodoxy* is another man's doxy." The English historian Thomas Carlyle (1795–1881), in his *History of the French Revolution*, created the sardonic phrase: "the difference between Orthodoxy or My-doxy and *Heterodoxy* or Thy-doxy." *Doxy* is an archaic jocular word meaning "opinion, doctrine, religious views," back-formed from *orthodoxy* and *heterodoxy*. The other meanings of *doxy* ("paramour" or "prostitute") have nothing to do with the case.

hexaëmeron (hek suh EM uh ron) *n.* The *hexaëmeron* is the six-day period of the creation of the world, or a written report of them, especially *Genesis*. *Hexaëmeron* is formed of the Greek prefix *hexa-*, from *hex* (six) plus *hemera* (day). "And on the seventh day God ended his work which he had made; and he rested on the seventh day from all his work which he had made." (Genesis 2:2.) One might be surprised to read, in the *New English Bible* (2:2):

217

"On the *sixth* day God completed all the work he had been doing . . ." Choose your Bible: It took six days; hence *hexaëmeron*. The word is sometimes written without the *ë*: *hexameron*, and in this form is easy to confuse with the *Heptameron (hepta*, Greek for *seven*), quite a different bit of literature—a collection of medieval stories written by or ascribed to Marguerite of Angoulême, queen of Navarre (1492–1549), supposed to have been told in seven days—or even with the *Decameron (deka*, Greek for *ten*) of the Italian poet and writer Boccaccio (1313–1375), a series of 100 tales to be related among a group of friends within a period of ten days, and much naughtier than the *hexaëmeron*.

hibernal, see **hiemal**

hidrosis, see **sudorific**

hiemal (HYE uh mul) *adj*. Hiemal means "wintry," and is descriptive of anything pertaining to winter. *Hiemal* comes from Latin *hiemalis* (wintry), based on the noun *hiems* (winter). *Hibernal* (hye BUR nul) is synonymous with *hiemal*, and is derived from Latin *hibernalis* or *hibernus*, related to the verb *hibernare* (to pass the winter), whose past participle, *hibernatus*, gave us the verb *hibernate*. What is cozier than to sit by the blazing fire on a raw *hiemal* (or *hibernal*) night?

hieratic (hye uh RAT ik, hye RAT-) *adj*. *Hieratic* and *hieratical* describe things pertaining to the priesthood. In a narrower use, *hieratic* applies to a special form of ancient Egyptian writing based on a simplified, abridged form of hieroglyphs used by priests in record keeping. *Hieratic* is derived, via Latin *hieraticus*, from Greek *hieratikos* (priestly), based on the prefix *hiero-*, from *hieros* (sacred), from which we got such words as *hierarchy, hieroglyphic*, etc. The *-glyph* part comes from Greek *glyphe* (carving), based on the verb *glyphein* (to hollow out). We must remember that the "writing" was originally engraved on clay or stone.

hinny (HIN ee) *n*., *vb*. A *hinny* is the progeny of a female donkey (or she-ass) and a stallion, the converse of a *mule*, which is the result of a union between a male donkey (or he-ass) and a mare, although *mule* is used generically as well to denote any offspring of a donkey and a horse, regardless of the sexes of the cooperating couple. *Mule* is used even more widely in biology to designate any hybrid, and strangely enough, particularly that between canaries and other types of finch. The mule is also a symbol of stubbornness, but the *hinny* has escaped that calumny. *Hinny* is from Latin *hinnus*, derived from Greek *ginnos* or *hinnos* (mule). *Hinny* is also used as a verb meaning to "whinny" or "neigh," coming, via the French verb *hinnir*, from Latin *hinnire*.

hippopotamine,   see **accipitrine**

hippotigrine,   see **accipitrine**

hirudine,   see **accipitrine**

hirundine,   see **accipitrine**

historicism,   see **historicity**

historicity   (his tuh RIS ih tee) *n.* "This ugly word," says Fowler, "has . . . a real use as a single word for the phrase *historical existence*, i.e., the having really existed or taken place in history as opposed to mere legend or literature." In other words, *historicity* is historical authenticity. Did the Red Sea really open at Moses's command? Did the walls of Jericho actually crumble at Joshua's blast? Did the miracle at Cana really occur? There are schools of thought that question the authenticity of these events. This has nothing to do with *historicism* (his TOR ih siz um), which has several distinct meanings: the belief that history is the result of unvarying principles rather than the work of man; excessive respect for historical institutions, such as traditions and laws; a search for principles of historical evolution that explain, and would help to foretell historical happenings or phenomena. (As to *historicity*, see also *mythicize*, discussed under **mythopoeia**.)

hobbledehoy   (HOB ul dee hoy) *n.* A *hobbledehoy* is a clumsy, awkward stripling in the age between boyhood and manhood. (Fowler uses the term *hobbledehoyhood* to denote the condition; see the Fowler quotation in the discussion under **fuliginous**). *Hobbledehoyish* is the adjective. Most dictionaries give up on the derivation: "origin unknown" or "uncertain." The *Random House*

College Dictionary theorizes: "[var. of *hoberdyhoy*, alliterative compound = *hoberd* (var. of *Roberd* Robert) + -Y² + *hoy* for BOY (*b* whence *h* for alliteration's sake)]." (The -Y² referred to is a **hypocoristic** suffix.) This etymological exercise sounds somewhat labored. To quote poor Mercutio in Shakespeare's *Romeo and Juliet* (Act III, Scene 1): "not so deep as a well, nor so wide as a church door . . . 'tis enough, 'twill serve."

hologram, see **holograph**

holograph (HOHL uh graf, hol-) *n.*, *adj.* As an adjective, *holograph*, also *holographic* (hohl uh GRAF ik, hol-), *holographical* (hohl uh GRAF ih kul, hol-), describes a document entirely in the handwriting of its author. As a noun, a *holograph* is the document itself. The word is derived, via Late Latin *holographus*, from Greek *holographos*, based on the Greek prefix *holo-*, the combining form of *holos* (whole, entire) plus *graphos* (written). An authenticated *holograph* letter signed by a famous literary or historical character can become very valuable in the autograph market. *Autograph* can mean anything from a mere signature to anything handwritten, and speaking of autographs brings to mind the caustic comment of the English essayist Charles Lamb (1775–1834) in his "Popular Fallacy XI, That We Must Not Look a Gift Horse in the Mouth";

> A presentation copy . . . is a copy of a book which does not sell, sent you by the author, with his foolish autograph at the beginning of it; for which, if a stranger, he only demands your friendship; if a brother author, he expects from you a book of yours, which does not sell, in return.

(How true, from mine own experience, dear Charles!) Do not confuse *holograph* with *hologram* (HOH luh gram; HOL uh-), formed of the same *holo-* plus *-gram*, from the Greek suffix *-gramma*, combining form of *gramma* (a writing or drawing). A *hologram* is a 3-D image (three-dimensional photograph) made by a process involving lasers.

holus bolus (HOH lus BOH lus) *adverbial phrase*. This colloquial expression means "all in a lump, all at one gulp, all at once, altogether." It is a bit of sham Latin based either on *whole bolus* (a *bolus* being a *lump*, in veterinary medicine a *round mass* larger than the usual size of a pill; more generally, any soft lump, usually of chewed food), or on two Greek words, *holos* (whole) and *bolos* (lump). It can be used where one might have said *in* or *at* or *with one fell swoop* (*fell* meaning "fierce, dire, deadly," and *swoop* meaning "sudden onslaught"), i.e., by one terrible blow, by one decisive act, suddenly. In Shakespeare's *Macbeth* (Act IV, Scene 3), Macduff, on learning from Ross that his "wife and babes" had been "savagely slaughtered," cries, "At one fell swoop?" This terrible "fell swoop" has sometimes been thoughtlessly and jocularly distorted, by those ignorant of its origin, into "swell foop." Blasphemy! Another bit of joke-Latin, *omnium gatherum* (motley collection) formed of Latin *omnium* (of all) and *gatherum* (sham Latin for "gathering") is amusing, and without blame.

homarine,   see **accipitrine**

Homeric   (hoh MER ik) *adj*. Literally, *Homeric* describes anything pertaining to Homer, or resembling him or his works, or worthy of him—Homer, the great Greek poet (c. 850 B.C.) to whom the authorship of *The Iliad* and *The Odyssey* is attributed. In the 19th century, the "Homeric question" was that of the verifiability of that attribution: the question whether the two great epic poems were simply collections of old narrative poems. That dispute of scholars has been ended, and there is general agreement that Homer wrote the poems, based on old legends. *Homeric laughter* is loud and hearty, like the laughter of the gods when they saw the lame Hephaestus (Vulcan, in the Roman Olympian hierarchy) hobble. He took Juno's side in her struggle with Jupiter, who threw him out of heaven. He took nine days to fall and broke a leg when he finally crashed to earth—hence the lameness. Apart from all references to Homer himself, *Homeric* is used figuratively for *heroic, titanic, epic*, as in the *Homeric* conflict of our World Wars. *Homeric* is from the Greek *Homerikos*, based on *Homeros*, the Greek name for *Homer*. The American poet and writer Walt Whitman (1819–1892) wrote: ". . . really great poetry is always (like the *Homeric* and Biblical canticles) the result of a national spirit, and not the privilege of a polished and select few . . ."

hominine,   see **accipitrine**

homonym (HOM uh nim) *n.*, **homophone** (HOM uh fone, HOH muh-) *n.* These words are too often used interchangeably. Strictly speaking (the right way to speak), *homophone* is the more inclusive term: a word pronounced the same as another but differing in meaning, whether spelled the same way or not; whereas a *homonym* is a word pronounced *and* spelled the same way as another, but differing in meaning. Examples of *homophones* that are spelled differently: *heir, air, ere, e'er; two, too, to; straight, strait; stake, steak; freeze, frieze; guilt, gilt; sign, sine.* Examples of *homophones* that are spelled the same way and are therefore *homonyms* as defined above: *till* (until), *till* (cash box), *till* (work the soil); *chase* (pursue), *chase* (work metal); *rock* (sway to and fro), *rock* (stone), *rock* (slang: diamond), *rock* (type of music). *Homophone* is a back formation from *homophonous*, meaning "pronounced the same," from the Greek *homophonos*, based on *homo-* (same) and *phone* (sound). *Homonym* is from the Greek *homonymon*, neuter form of *homonymos*, based on *homo-* (same) and *-onymos*, from *onoma* (name, word). Because of the peculiarities of both spelling and pronunciation in English, there are many sets of *homophones* in our language. It must be hell for foreigners.

homophone,   see **homonym**

honeyfuggle,   see **sockdol(l)ager**

hornbook,   see **ampersand**

horripilation (ho rip uh LAY shun) *n. Horripilation* is gooseflesh, the bristling of one's skin produced by fright or horror, or just extreme cold. This dramatic word comes from Late Latin *horripilatio*, based on Latin *horripilatus*, past participle of *horripilare* (to bristle), which is based in turn on *horrere* (to bristle) fortified by *pilus* (hair). To *horripilate* (ho RIP uh late) someone is to produce *horripilation* in him, i.e., to cause him to suffer gooseflesh, to make his hair stand on end. *Bristling* is what happens when one gets the *feeling* that his or her hairs are standing on end—a phenomenon that is clearly visible when it happens to cats, dogs, and certain other animals, but not to man, for whom it is just a sensation. See **formication** for a somewhat related experience. The English film director Alfred Hitchcock (1899–1980) was a master at directing spine-chilling films that *horripilated* his audience. Ghost stories around a campfire are a good source of *horripilation*, to say nothing of strange sounds downstairs in the middle of the night.

hortatory (HOR tuh tor ee) *adj.* Also **hortative** (HOR tuh tiv). A *hortatory* or *hortative* message or speech is one that urges or encourages a certain course of action. *Hortative* is from Latin *hortativus* (encouraging), based on *hortatus* (encouragement). *Hortatory* is from Late Latin *hortatorius* (encouraging). All these words go back to *hortatus*, past participle of the Latin verb *hortari* (to urge or encourage). We are familiar with our verb to *exhort*, from Latin *exhortari* (to exhort, encourage), which has a somewhat more cogent tone than the adjectives, in that it contains a note of urgency rather than mere encouragement.

houghmagandy (hok muh GAN dee) *n. Houghmagandy* is fornication, a word found mostly in Scotland, denoting a practice that knows no boundaries. And that's the long and short of it.

Hudibrastic, see **ratiocinate**

hugger-mugger (HUG ur MUG ur) *n., vb., adj., adv.* Through all its uses as these various parts of speech, *hugger-mugger* involves two basic concepts, secrecy and disorder. True, these are distinct concepts—except that acts committed clandestinely are apt to be done in haste, and consequently in disorder. In any case, as a noun, *hugger-mugger* means "secrecy, concealment" or "confusion, muddle"; as a **transitive** verb, "to conceal, hush up"; as an **intransitive** verb, "to act secretly," sometimes "to seek secret counsel"; as an adjective, "secret" or "confused"; as an adverb, "secretly" or "in confusion." It was spelt *hucker-mucker* in the 16th century; there was a Middle English verb *mokere* (to conceal, hoard) and a Middle English verb *hoder* (to muddle). Lots of possible derivations; something of a muddle in itself. In Shakespeare's *Hamlet* (Act IV, Scene 5), King Claudius, concerned about "the people muddled" as to the killing of Polonius, tells Queen Gertrude:

> . . . and we have done but greenly [foolishly]
> In *hugger-mugger* to intern him . . .

Here, Shakespeare uses *hugger-mugger* to mean "in secrecy and haste," in a manner that would arouse suspicion of dirty work at the crossroads. *Hugger-muggery* means "secret doings," suggesting haste, concealment and confusion—a word almost onomatopoeic, especially if pronounced in a stage whisper. The American writer Elliot Paul (1891–1958) wrote a detective thriller and dubbed it *Hugger-mugger in the Louvre* (Random House, New York, 1940).

humanist (HYOOH muh nist, YOOH-) *n.* Although the term *humanist* can be applied literally to a student of human nature, the main use of this word is to denote one having deep concern for the welfare of the human race—a matter of no little regard since the invention of the delightful H-bomb. There is also a specialized use of *Humanist* (note upper case *H*) as a label for a member of a contemporary cult substituting faith in man for faith in God; faith in the supreme value and self-perfectibility of the human character. Wrote the American journalist and writer Walter Lippmann (1889–1974), explaining the central doctrine of *Humanism* as one involved with distinctively human ideals and interests in contradiction to religious concerns:

> To replace the conception of man as the subject of a heavenly king . . . *humanism* takes as its dominant pattern the progress of the individual from infancy to self-governing maturity.

But *humanist* has also the entirely dissociated meaning of "classical scholar," one versed in the study of the "humanities," either classical Greek and Latin language and literature, or the liberal arts generally (philosophy, art, literature, etc.) as opposed to the sciences. *Humanist* is not to be confused with *humanitarian*, one engaged in the promotion of human welfare, either through service or as a philanthropist. The Latin basis of both words is *humanus* (human), but *humanist* itself is from the Italian noun *umanista*.

hundredweight (HUN drid wate) *n.* It depends upon where you're doing the weighing. A *hundredweight* in the U.S. = 100 lbs., or ¹/₂₀ of a U.S. ton, which = 2,000 lbs. A *hundredweight* in the U.K. is 112 lbs., because in the U.K. a ton = 2,240 lbs., and ¹/₂₀ of that is 112. The U.S. ton is known as the "short ton," the U.K. ton as the "long ton." So, when you hear or read *hundred-*

weight, pay attention to the geography. Incidentally, in the U.K., despite the introduction of the metric system, the custom still persists in expressing people's weights in "stones," a stone being 14 lbs. ("I'm slimming, dear; my doctor insists I lose at least a stone!") For an extended study of British weights and measures, see this author's *British English, A to Zed* (Facts on File, 1987), particularly Appendix II.C.1.

hyalography (hye uh LOG ruh fee) *n.* This is the art or technique of lettering or drawing on glass by etching or engraving. *Hyalos* is *glass* in Greek, and gave rise to the adjective *hyaline*, glasslike or vitreous, which is also used as a literary noun for "smooth sea" or "clear sky." *Hyaloid* is a term used in anatomy for "glassy" in the sense of "thin and transparent," like the membrane covering the jelly-like tissue filling the eyeball. But away from anatomy and back to glass and etching: *hyalo-* is the prefix from *hyalos*, and that prefix, plus the suffix *-graphy*, from Greek *graphia*, based on *graphein* (to draw or write) add up to *hyalography*, the technique first mentioned above, now a vanishing art, practiced only here and there, especially in Venice, Italy, where one can still see beautiful designs and lettering engraved on glass vases, goblets, and pitchers.

hydromel (HYE druh mel) *n.* Just as the word is a combination of the Greek words *hydro* (water; in combining form, *hydro-*, as in *hydrogen, hydroplane, hydroelectric*, etc.) and *meli* (honey), *hydromel* is a mixture of water and honey, a word taken from the Greek noun *hydromeli*. This liquor, left to ferment, turns into mead, an alcoholic beverage popular in olden times and still found in some English pubs. *Mead* was *mede* in Middle English, *me(o)du* in Old English, and is related to the Greek noun *methy* (wine). Mead, made from *hydromel* (with the addition of yeast, malt, etc.), was a favorite breakfast drink in Merrie Olde long before the introduction of tea or coffee, and that may account for some of the strange happenings and goings-on there in days of yore.

hyenine, see **accipitrine**

hylobatine, see **accipitrine**

hymeneal (hye muh NEE ul) *n.*, *adj.* As an adjective, *hymeneal* describes anything relating to marriage. As a noun, a *hymeneal* is a marriage song. This word is derived, via Latin *hymenaeus*, from Greek *hymenaios*, based on *Hymen*, in classical mythology the god of marriage, shown as a beautiful youth bearing a torch and a veil, said to be a more mature Eros or Amor or Cupid. With a lower case *h*, the *hymen* is the anatomical term for the membrane that partially closes the mouth of the vagina, a word taken intact from the Greek, a symbol of virginity and obviously related to the concept of the very marriage which deprives the bride of it (at least in the old days). A word related to *hymeneal* is *epithalamion* (ep uh thuh LAY mee un), also *epithalamium* (ep uh thuh LAY mee um), a song or poem honoring the bride and bridegroom. The origin of this word is the Greek *epithalamion*, the neuter form of the adjective *epithalamios* (nuptial), based on *thalamos* (bedroom). Apparently, with *hymeneals* and *epithalamia*, there was a great deal of singing at ancient Greek and Latin weddings. Nowadays it seems to be limited to a wedding march and the rather insipid *Oh Promise Me* . . .

hyperbaton (hy PUR buh ton) *n.* Based on the Greek prefix *hyper-* (excessive) plus *baton*, the root of *bainein* (to go), *hyperbaton* is a figure of speech in which natural word order is changed, usually for emphasis or effect. Example: ''That I have to see!'' The English poet Robert Browning (1812–1889) wrote a poem entitled ''Wanting—is What?''

> Wanting—is what?
> Summer redundant,
> Blueness abundant,
> —Where is the blot?

This poem was satirized by an anonymous poet in the English comic weekly *Punch*, issue of April 21, 1883, raising the ante from three to four:

> Browning is—what?
> Riddle redundant,
> Baldness abundant
> Sense, who can spot?

Fowler gives the example: "That whiter skin of hers than now."
This poetic kind of word order inversion leads to—what? Mainly
confusion.

hypocoristic (hye puh kuh RIS tik, hip uh-) *adj. Hypocorism*
(hye POK uh riz um, hih-) is the use of a pet name, or of baby talk
by a grown-up; a *hypocorism* is a pet name or a diminutive, an
endearment, from Greek *hypokorisma* (pet name), related to the
verb *hypokorizesthai* (to use baby talk or pet or endearing names,
or to play the child), based on the Greek prefix *hypo-* (under) plus
koros (boy) and *kore* (girl). *Hypocoristic*, from Greek *hypokoris-*
tikos (diminutive) is the adjective, meaning "endearing," and applicable to pet names, diminutives, and euphemisms in general.
The letter -*y* used as a suffix has several functions, one of which is
hypocoristic: Bill becomes *Billy, John Johnny, Fred Freddy*, etc.;
kitty, pussy, and *doggy* become important members of the family;
-*ie* often takes the place of the *hypocoristic* -*y*, as in *birdie, horsie,*
lassie, laddie, etc.

hysteron proteron (HIS tuh ron PROT uh ron). These Greek
words, the neuter forms of the adjectives *hysteros* (latter) and *pro-*
teros (former), form a phrase that means, literally, "latter, former"
or "later, earlier" and has two uses in our language. Both, to quote
Fowler, put the cart before the horse. In rhetoric, *hysteron proteron*
is a figure of speech in which the rational or logical order of two
or more elements is reversed, as in *bred and born*; (an economist's
description of the British coal industry) *a prosperous and viable*
industry; (from *The Indian Serenade*, by the English poet Shelley,
1792–1822) *I die! I faint! I fail!; then came the thunder and the*
lightning. In the branch of philosophy known as logic, *hysteron*
proteron is the label of a defective argument or logical fallacy that
begs the question by assuming as a premise the very conclusion
that is to be proved. Thus, in Shakespeare's *Much Ado About Noth-*
ing (Act IV, Scene 2), Dogberry, the constable of great dignity but
no sense, addresses the prisoners Borachio and Conrade in these
terms: "Masters, it is proved already that you are little better than
false knaves; and it will go near to be thought so shortly . . . I say
to you, it is thought you are false knaves."

hystricine, see **accipitrine**

■ ▣ ▣ ◼

iatric (eye A trik, ee-) *adj. Iatric* applies to anything relating to a physician, or medicine in general. *Iatros* is *physician* in Greek; *iatrikos* is the adjective. *Iatrogenic* (eye a truh JEN ik) applies to an illness or neurosis caused by a doctor's examination, treatment for the wrong illness, or mistaken diagnosis; from prefix *iatro-*, based on *iatros*, plus suffix *-genic*, producing. *Iatrogenic* ailments are often the subject of medical malpractice suits, which have become so common that medical malpractice insurance rates have gone sky high and, proportionately, doctors' fees. *Iatrogenic* ailments are often the basis for the cliché about the "cure" being worse than the illness.

iatrogenic, see **iatric**

ibidine, see **accipitrine**

icarian (ih KAR ee un) *adj*. As we shall see, *icarian* means "inadequate," in certain contexts. Icarus, in Greek mythology, was the son of Daedalus, the Athenian architect who built the labyrinth for King Minos of Crete. His name in Greek was Daidalos, which, with a lower case *d*, means "skillful." Minos imprisoned both father and son. For their escape, the ingenious Daedalus fashioned a pair of wings for each of them, from bird feathers and wax. Daedalus was successful, but, though warned by his father, Icarus flew too close to the sun, which melted his wings, and he plunged into the sea and drowned. According to the Humez brothers, American authors of *Alpha to Omega* (David R. Godine, Publisher, Inc., Boston, 1981), Icarus's fate was "a lesson to subsequent centuries of children who might otherwise have seriously considered disobeying their wise and prudent parents." The brothers Humez point

228

out the parallel with the tale of Phaeton, son of Apollo, the god who drove his chariot daily across the sky. Phaeton pestered Apollo to let him do the driving for a day ("Pop, can I have the car tonight?"), got his way, lost control, swooped too close to earth, fell out, and was killed—another case history of children who aren't ready to assume control of daddy's business. Shakespeare mentions Phaeton in *King Richard II* (Act III, Scene 3), where Richard, sensing the approach of doom, cries:

> Down, down I come, like glistering Phaeton
> Wanting the manage of unruly jades.

(Like glistening Phaeton, unable to control the wild horses). After all this, we finally come to the adjective *icarian*, as in *an icarian method*, one inadequate for the accomplishment of an ambitious goal. Then what about Daedalus? He gave us the adjective *daedal* (DEE dul) or *daedalian* (dee DAY lee un, -lyun), a description of anything displaying artistic or inventive skill, particularly if it is of an ingenious or intricate nature. In *Prometheus Unbound*, the English poet Shelley (1792–1822) wrote these lines:

> Language is a perpetual Orphic song,
> Which rules with *Daedal* harmony a throng
> Of thoughts and forms, which else senseless and shapeless were.

As to *Orphic* (OR fik): it comes from *Orpheus*, also of Greek mythology, who, with his music, charmed Hades, King of the Underworld, into letting him lead his dead wife Eurydice away, but broke his promise not to look back at her until they got to earth and thus lost her forever. *Orphic* music is music that casts a spell. We've delved quite deeply into Greek mythology, but just remember: *icarian* is over-ambitious and inadequate and *daedal* is ingenious and inventive.

iconodule   (eye KON uh doohl, -dyoohl) *n.* An *iconodule*, literally, is one who venerates *icons* (in the Eastern Church, images of sacred persons), and the practice is known as *iconoduly* (eye KON uh dooh lee, -dyooh-). We are more familiar with the words that denote their antithesis: *iconoclast* (eye KON uh klast) and *iconoclasm* (eye KON uh klas um). Literally, an *iconolcast* is a destroyer of icons and *iconoclasm* is the practice. In the eighth century, reformers in the Eastern Church led a movement against the veneration of icons which was opposed by monks and popes. The struggle took a political turn, and was finally resolved in 843 by the Empress Theodora in favor of the icons. The opposing parties were known as *Iconoclasts* and *Iconodules*. All that is fairly ancient stuff, and, except in history books, *iconoclast* denotes one who attacks traditional beliefs and *iconodule* (a far less common word) one who clings to them. An *iconodule* is, so to speak, a fundamentalist. The *iconoclast-iconodule*, or modernist-fundamentalist, controversy broke into the limelight with the 1925 Scopes evolution trial. That year, Tennessee enacted a statue making unlawful the teaching in public schools of any theory that ran counter to belief in the divine creation of man according to Genesis. John T. Scopes, a biology teacher, was tried for teaching Darwinian evolution in a Tennessee school. The American political leader William Jennings Bryan (1860–1925) appeared for the prosecution, the famous American lawyer Clarence Darrow (1857–1938) for the defense. Bryan won his case (later reversed on a technicality) but Darrow's examination of him went far to discredit fundamentalist interpretation of the Bible and no other state followed Tennessee's example. Darrow was an *iconoclast*, Bryan an *iconodule*. *Iconoclast* is from Greek *icon* (image) and *klastes* (breaker); the suffix in *iconodule* is from Greek *loudos* (slave, servant).

ideate   (EYE dee ate, eye DEE ate) *vb. Ideate* can be used **transitively** or **intransitively**. One can simply *ideate*, i.e., think, like the *Thinker*, the masterpiece by the French sculptor Rodin (1840–1917): or one can *ideate* something, form or have an *idea* of it, imagine it, preconceive it. *Idea* comes, via Late Latin, from the Greek noun *idea* (pattern), related to the verb *idein* (to see); *ideate* is from Late Latin *ideatus*, past participle of *ideare* (to form an idea). Inventors are *ideaters*. The English inventor Thomas Newcomen (1663–1729) *ideated* the steam engine. The legend that the Scotsman James Watt (1736–1819) *ideated* the steam engine while watching the lid of his mother's kettle rattle up and down on the kitchen stove is apocryphal. While repairing a model of Newcomen's engine at the University of Glasgow, Watt *ideated* a new and better type. Edison (1847–1931) was a prolific *ideater* of practical instruments, while Einstein (1879–1955) *ideated* in the abstract.

idiographic,   see **nomology**
230

idiopathic (id ee oh PATH ik) *adj*. This is a medical term applicable to a disease of an unknown cause, a state peculiar to the individual patient, a pathological condition the physician cannot diagnose. He looks you over, asks you a lot of questions, says it might be this or might be that, and winds up baffled and leaving you unsolaced. It's one of those terms like "essential," as used in *essential hypertension*, where *essential* doesn't mean "necessary" or "indispensable" or anything like that, but merely "what it is by its very nature," i.e., it's there because it's there, going right to the root of *essential*, the first four letters: *esse*, Latin for "to be." *Idiopathy* (id ee OP uh thee), denoting a disease existing all on its own, a primary ailment not the result of an identifiable previous condition, is from Greek *idiopatheia* (a subjective feeling, peculiar to oneself), based on *idios* (own, private) plus *pathos* (suffering).

ilk (ilk) *n*. The common use *of ilk* is in the phrase *of that ilk*, and, correctly employed, has a distinctly limited use. It applies properly only when the surname of a person is the same as the name of his estate or the place he's from. In a series of letters to *The Times* (London), Sir Iain Moncreiffe, of Easter Moncreiffe, Perthshire, signed himself "Iain Moncreiffe, Of That Ilk," meaning "Iain Moncreiffe of Moncreiffe." Quoting from *British English, A to Zed* (Facts on File, 1987) by this author: "A friend of the author named Hector Cameron was a Cameron of Cameron, and once announced himself over the telephone as 'Cameron of that ilk.' The uneducated (at that time) author, to his shame, ascribed it to drink. There are MacDonalds of *that ilk* (MacDonalds of MacDonald), Guthries *of that ilk* (Guthries of Guthrie) and so on. From a Sassenach misunderstanding of usage, *ilk* has acquired the meaning 'sort' or 'kind'; used generally in a pejorative sense: *Al Capone, and people of that ilk*, or even (heaven forfend!) *Freudians* (or *communists*, etc.) *and their ilk*." The use of *ilk* is now expanded to include "family," "class," or "set" as well as "kind." Fowler says of *ilk*: "This SLIPSHOD EXTENSION has become so common that the OED [Oxford English Dictionary] Supp[lement] was constrained to add to its definitions 'also by further extension, often in trivial use,—kind, sort.' " The COD [Concise Oxford Dictionary] calls it "vulgar." *Ilk* is, via Middle English *ilke*, from Old English *ilca*. Incidentally, the adjective *Sassenach*

231

mentioned above is defined in *British English, A to Zed* as follows:
"From the Gaelic for *Saxon*, an opprobrious term used by Scots, and sometimes by the Irish as well, to designate and derogate the English."

illation   (ih LAY shun) *n.* *Illation* is the act of inferring from data or the resulting inference or conclusion drawn. The adjective, *illative* (IL u tiv, ih LAY tiv), applies to anything that pertains to or introduces or expresses an inference. The word *therefore* is an *illative* word: It introduces a conclusion drawn from what has gone before. *Illation* is from Late Latin *illatio* (a carrying in), related to *illatus*, past participle of *inferre* (to infer), based on the prefix *il-* (in; a variant of *in-* before *l*) plus *latus* (carried). One must not jump to *illations*, though some people say it's the only exercise they get.

illative,   see **illation**

illuminati   (ih looh mu NAY tye, -NA tee) *n. pl.* The *illuminati* are those endowed with superior knowledge, information, or enlightenment, or who claim to possess it. Historically, the term was applied to a sect of Spanish heretics of the 16th century and later to the members of a German secret society, established in 1776 along the lines of Freemasonry. But *illuminati* is used today as a somewhat pejorative term applied to those whose claim to superior enlightenment may be far from justified. *Illuminati* is the masculine plural of Latin *illuminatus*, past participle of *illuminare* (to light up), used as a noun.

imbroglio   (im BROHL yoh) *n.*; **intaglio** (in TAL yoh) *n.*; **seraglio** (sih RAL yoh) *n.* If you should happen to come across an *intaglio* of an *imbroglio* occurring in a *seraglio*, you would be looking at an incised carving of a bitter row arising in a harem; and if you wanted to announce your discovery with the correct pronunciation, you would be careful to keep all the *g*'s mute (like the one in Modigliani, the Italian painter, 1884–1920, who was also a sculptor but never incised a row in a harem). One justification for lumping these three words in one entry is that they are all taken from the Italian and therefore follow the pronunciation rule given above. Another is that, however unlike the event, an *intaglio* of an *imbroglio* in a *seraglio* makes a nice sound. *Imbroglio*, in Italian, is

232

associated with the verb *imbrogliare* (to embroil). In English, an *imbroglio* is a difficult situation, a complicated disagreement or misunderstanding, leading to a bitter dispute. *Intaglio*, in Italian, is associated with the verb *intagliare* (to cut in, engrave). An *intaglio* is an incised carving, one on which the design or figure is below the surface of the material, thus the antithesis of a relief. In both cases, the English word has the same meaning as its Italian forebear. *Seraglio* presents a somewhat different story. Its common meaning in English is "harem," and one of its meanings in Italian is the same, but there are two *r*s in the Italian *serraglio*, and its primary meaning ("harem" came later) is "menagerie, cage for wild beasts." Draw your own conclusions.

imbrue (im BROOH) *vb*. To *imbrue* something is to soak or drench it, especially with blood. It is not to be confused with *imbue* (im BYOOH), used in connection with inspiring a person with opinions or sentiments (e.g., to *imbue* someone with patriotism). According to the dictionaries, it, too, can mean to "drench with blood," but this must be a rare use indeed. The English poet John Milton (1608–1674) wrote of "Derwen stream [the River Derwen] in Lancashire with blood of Scots *imbrued*." The hands of both Macbeth and his Lady were *imbrued* after the slaughter of King Duncan (Shakespeare's *Macbeth*, Act II, Scene 3). In *Pyramus and Thisbe*, the play within a play in *Midsummer Night's Dream* (Act V, Scene 1), Thisbe, finding Pyramus dead, moans:

> Asleep, my love?
>> What, dead, my dove?
> O Pyramus, arise!
>> Speak, speak! Quite dumb?
>> Dead, dead! A tomb
> Must cover thy sweet eyes. . . .
>> Come, trusty sword:
> Come, blade, my breast *imbrue* . . .

and, true to the stage directions, stabs herself. In Shakespeare's *Henry IV, Part 2* (Act II, Scene 4), in a brawl scene, Falstaff tells Bardolph to quoit [throw] Pistol downstairs, and Pistol, snatching up his sword, cries: "What! Shall we have incision? Shall we *imbrue*?" *Imbrue* is, via Old French *embreuver*, from Late Latin *imbiberare*, based on Latin *imbibere* (to drink in), whereas *imbue* is from Latin *imbuere* (to steep, soak).

imprimatur (im prih MA tur, -MAY-, -prye-) *n.* An *imprimatur* is an official license to print and publish a book or tract, especially as issued by the Roman Catholic Church in the case of a religious work; often followed by the Latin phrase *nihil obstat* (there is no objection) issued by the religious censor, negating any unorthodox pronouncement. *Imprimatur* is Latin for "Let it be printed," and can be used in the more general figurative sense of any sanction, license, or authoritative approval. Do not confuse it with *imprint*, the name of the publisher or printer or place of publication or printing appearing at the front or end of a book, or with *imprimatura* (im pree muh TOOR uh), a term in painting taken from the Italian for a colored wash or underpainting made in connection with the preliminary drawing.

incunabula (in kyooh NAB yuh luh) *n. pl. Incunabula*, in the commonest use of the word, are extant copies of books printed before 1500, during the early stages of the use of movable type. The word is rarely found in the singular: *incunabulum*. The Gutenberg Bible, printed at Mainz, Germany, about 1455 (so called because it is ascribed to Johannes Gutenberg, 1397–1468, said to be the inventor of printing with movable type) is the most famous example of an *incunabulum*. The word is used, but rarely, in the literal sense of the "first stages" or "infancy" of anything. Thus, cylindrical phonograph records or old one-sided 78s might be described as the *incunabula* of the recording industry. *Incunabula* has a complex and interesting derivation. *Cunae* is a Latin noun, plural in form but singular in meaning, for "cradle"; *-bula* is a neuter plural diminutive suffix, so that *cuna-* (stem of *cunae*) plus *-bula* produced *cunabula*, another word for "cradle," and by prefixing *in-* (in), the Romans created *incunabula*, meaning literally "swaddling clothes," and figuratively "infancy." Thus, books produced in the *infancy* of printing from movable type are called *incunabula*. The term was first applied to printing by one Bernard von Mallinckrodt in a 1630 tract on printing. He characterized the era from Gutenberg to 1500 as "prima typographiae *incunabula*," the period when typography was in its "swaddling clothes." *Incunabula* are rare and valuable. Don't waste time looking for them in secondhand bookstores.

indefectible (in dih FEK tuh bul) *adj.* What is *indefectible* is unfailing, not subject to defect, failure, or imperfection; faultless;

the negative form of *defectible* (liable to defect, failure, or error). Both stem from *defect*, derived from Latin *defectus*, past participle of *deficere* (to fail, be wanting), whose present participle *deficiens* gave us *deficient*. To the true Catholic believer, God is *indefectible*, whereas the Pope is merely infallible.

inexpugnable (in ik SPUG nuh bul) *adj. Inexpugnable* means "impregnable, unassailable, invincible," and can be used both literally and figuratively. It is from Latin prefix *in-* (not, un-) plus *expugnabilis* (capable of being taken by storm), based on *expugnare* (to capture, take by storm), and it all goes back to *pugna* (fight, battle), which eventually gave us *pugnacious, pugilist*, etc. *Inexpugnable* is not to be confused with the look-alike *inexpungible* (in ik SPUN juh bul), meaning "ineffaceable, indestructible," from Latin *in-* plus *expungere* (to cancel, obliterate). The American psychologist and philosopher William James (1842–1910), in *The Will to Believe—Reflex Action and Theism*, wrote:

> Man's chief difference from the brute lies in the exuberant excess of his subjective propensities—his preeminence over them simply and solely in the number and in the fantastic and unnecessary character of his wants, physical, moral, aesthetic, and intellectual. Had his whole life not been a quest for the superfluous, he would never have established himself as *inexpugnably* as he has done in the necessary.

"*Inexpugnably*," says James; i.e., unassailably, invincibly, impregnably. (But that was before the H-bomb.) *Inexpungible*, on the other hand, might well describe an ineffaceable memory of a never-to-be-forgotten sight, or experience, like one's first view of the Piazza San Marco in Venice or of the Grand Canyon, or better still, of one's sensation of love at first sight.

inexpungible, see **inexpugnable**

infelicitous, see **felicitous**

inspissate (in SPIS ate) *vb.* To *inspissate* is to thicken; to make or become thicker or denser, as by evaporation. It is from Latin *inspissatus*, past participle of *inspissare*, based on *spissare* (to thicken), related to *spissus* (thick). The English lexicographer, poet, and critic Samuel Johnson ("Dr. Johnson," 1709–1784) used the evocative expression "*inspissated* gloom," much more moving than *inspissated oatmeal*, for instance, thickened by being allowed to stand too long on top of a cold stove.

instate (in STATE) *vb*. It is strange how much more familiar the verb *reinstate* is than *instate*, for persons and things can't be *reinstated* without first having been *instated*. True it is that things get *repeated* without first having been "peated," and there may well be other such cases, but somehow *instate* is a perfectly good verb: to put or place someone or something into a certain state, condition, or position. Yet *instate* has just about completely given way to *install*. A new official is *installed*, his assistants are *installed*, something goes wrong, out they go, things clear up, and they are *reinstated* rather than *reinstalled*. Strange are the ways of language. It's like what the Roman poet Virgil (70–19 B.C.) said about woman: "Varium et mutabile semper/Femina" ("A fickle thing and changeful is woman always!"). Just substitute *lingua* (language) for *femina*, though the sentence becomes a thousand times less dramatic. Or sexist.

intaglio, see **imbroglio**

intercalary, see **intercalate**

intercalate (in TUR kuh late) *vb*. To *intercalate* is to interpolate, and is a term used in the insertion of an extra day or month in a caldendar, in the way February 29 is *intercalated* each leap year in our calendar, or five extra days were added to the French Revolutionary calendar (see **pluvious**) or an additional month to the Jewish calendar in certain years. Such complementary days or months are labeled "intercalary." *Intercalate* is from Latin *intercalatus*, past participle of *intercalare* (to insert, especially a day or month in the calendar); *intercalary* is from Latin *intercalaris* (inserted) or *intercalarius* (intercalary).

internecine (in tur NEE seen, -sine; -NES een, -ine) *adj*. *Internecine* has had a curious history, in having come to mean "mutually destructive," applicable to conflicts arising within families, political parties or other groups. It is from Latin *internecinus* (murderous, deadly—nothing "mutual" involved here), based on the prefix *inter*, which, to be sure, usually means "between" and connotes

236

mutuality, exchange, etc., plus *necare* (to kill). But in certain Latin words, the *inter-* prefix has nothing to do with "betweenness" and has instead the force of "extermination." Examples: *interire* (to perish), *intercidere* (to demolish), *interimere* (to annihilate), *interscindere* (to tear asunder). In no one of these Latin verbs does *inter-* have the force of mutuality, but only that of utter destruction. Be that as it may, since *inter-* implies exchange and mutuality in English (and usually in Latin), the true force of our *inter-* and its Latin forebear has been in this case misinterpreted; hence the current meaning of *internecine*.

intransitive, see **transitive**

invaginate (in VAJ uh nate) *vb. Invaginate* has three distinct meanings, none of them sexual. **Transitively**, to *invaginate* an object is to ensheath it, to push it into a close-fitting cover, such as one made to receive a tool or a sword. **Intransitively**, to *invaginate* is to *become invaginated*, i.e., to receive something *invaginated*. To *invaginate* a tube is to turn it inside out. *Invaginate* is from Latin prefix *in-* (in, into) plus *vagina* (sheath, scabbard); *vagina* in Latin, like *invaginate* in English, has no sexual meaning or connotation. That came from our imaginative English linguists. When you watch those duelling scenes in adventure films and Shakespearean stage productions, there's a great deal of the drawing and *invaginating* of swords, with nary a female in sight.

iota, see **alpha and omega**

irenic (eye REN ik, -REE-) *adj.* At first glance, one might assume that *irenic* was part of the *ire, ireful, irate, irascible* family based on the Latin noun *ira* (wrath), but the assumption would be wrong. Quite the contrary: We are dealing with an adjective derived from *Irene*, the classical goddess of peace and wealth (Eirene in the original transliteration), usually represented as a beautiful young woman carrying on one arm the infant Plutus, the god of wealth (who lent his name to our word *plutocrat*). This representation is in accordance with the statue by Cephisodotus the Elder (fl. fourth century B.C., believed to be either the father or the brother of the greatest of Greek sculptors, Praxiteles, fl. c. 370–333 B.C.) erected in Athens c. 370 B.C. on the occasion of the peace with Sparta. The alliterative phrase *peace and plenty* arose from that combination of Eirene and Plutus—an abundance of goods and luxuries in a time of peace.

irrefragable   (ih REF ruh guh bul) *adj*. Not to be confused with **irrefrangible**, this adjective applies to whatever cannot be refuted or denied. It is from Latin *irrefragabilis*, based on the prefix *ir-* (not; a variant of *in-* before *r*) plus *refragari* (to oppose, resist); or possibly based on *ir-* plus the prefix *re-* (backwards) plus *frangere* (to break). *The Irrefragable Doctor* was an epithet given to Alexander of Hales (died 1245; also known as "The Unanswerable Doctor"), a Franciscan, a lecturer at the University of Paris, the author of the first exposition of Christian doctrine introducing the teachings of the Greek philosopher Aristotle (384–322 B.C.) as a prime authority, and an important influence on St. Thomas Aquinas (1225–1274). Persons who believe their opinions or arguments are *irrefragable* are extremely hard to deal with.

irrefrangible   (ir ih FRAN juh bul) *adj*. Not to be confused with **irrefragable**, *irrefrangible* means "inviolable," applying to anything that should never be broken or violated. The positive form, *refrangible* (rih FRAN juh bul), means "refractable," as rays of light, i.e., deflectible at certain angles when entering obliquely from another medium of different density, e.g., from air into water. Thus, *irrefrangible* has the special meaning in optics of "incapable of being refracted," but the common meaning "inviolable" would apply to a vow or an oath or a secret that must be kept. *Irrefrangible* comes from the Latin prefix *ir-* (not; a variant of *in-* before *r*) plus *refrangibilis*, based on *refringere* (to break), whose past participle *refractus* gave us *refract*; and that goes back to *frangere* (to break), whose past participle *fractus* produced *fractio* (a breaking in pieces), and that gave us *fraction*.

ithyphallic   (ith uh FAL ik) *n.*, *adj*. In the Bacchanalia, ancient festivals of Bacchus (god of wine in classical mythology), where drunkenness and licentiousness were rampant, a large statue of an erect penis was carried in the line of the procession. In its original and literal use, *ithyphallic* pertained to that artifact, but it came to mean "lewd, obscene, grossly indecent, shameless" in general usage. As a noun, *ithyphallic* was the name for a licentious poem.

238

The noun *ithyphallus* (ith uh FAL us) means "erect penis" (in the flesh, not a statue). *Ithyphallic* is from Greek *ithyphallikos*, based on *ithys* (straight) plus *phallos* (phallus). *Ithyphallic* jokes should not be told at the dinner table in the presence of ladies.

izzat (IZ ut) *n. Izzat* is personal dignity, honor, self-respect, prestige, credit, reputation. It comes, via Hindi and Persian *'izzat*, from Arabic *'izzah* (glory). Who can forget the *izzat* maintained by Jacqueline, widow of the slain President Kennedy, during the ordeal of the swearing-in of Johnson in Dallas and throughout the ordeal of the funeral in Washington? *Izzat* is a virtue much to be commended, showing man at his best under the most painful of circumstances. *Man?* Mankind! No sexual distinctions here! *Izzat* has nothing to do with *izard*, the ibex that lives in the Pyrenees, or *izzard*, a British dialectical name for the letter z, called *zed* in standard British English.

jactation (jak TAY shun) *n. Jactation* has two totally distinct meanings. It is bragging, boasting, like **braggadocio, fanfaronade, gasconade, rodomontade,** and **thrasonical** behavior in general. There would seem to be no end of words for this human weakness. *Jactation* comes from Latin *jactatio* (boasting, ostentation), related to *jactatus*, past participle of *jactare* (to boast). But *jactate* and its Latin sources all wear another hat: In pathology, *jactation* is nervous, restless tossing about, convulsive body movements, because Latin *jactare* also means to "fling about, toss," and only by transference to "broadcast" words, to fling them about, and thus, to "boast." To complicate matters, there is a confusingly similar term, *jactitation* (jak tih TAY shun), which is a legal term for a false boast or claim that causes harm to another and can lead to a lawsuit; and this word, too, has a distinct meaning identical with that second meaning of *jactation*: "tossing about." Here the source is Middle Latin *jactitatio* (tossing), related to *jactitatus*, past participle of *jactitare* (to keep tossing about). To sum up: *jactation* and *jactitation* are identical in the terminology of pathology: to "toss about"; otherwise, *jactation* is boasting, pure and simple, while *jactitation* is the false and harmful variety. Apart from the

239

medical symptoms, *jactate* all you want, if you're silly enough to brag; but stop short of *jactitating* or you may land in court.

jactitation,   see **jactation**

jehu   (JEE hyooh) *n.* A *jehu* is a fast driver, with the implication of recklessness and disregard of danger to others. *Jehu* was a king of Israel, a bloodthirsty warrior noted for his wild chariot attacks. We read in II Kings 9:20,

> . . . he driveth furiously.

There were no traffic rules or constraints in those days; there are many now who drive as though that were still the case.

jeremiad   (jer uh MYE ud) *n.* A *jeremiad* is a tale of woe, a lamentation, a doleful complaint, a plea for compassion, deriving its name from the *Lamentations of Jeremiah*, the Old Testament prophet of the sixth and seventh centuries B.C. A book of the Bible attributed to him bears his name. He called for moral reform, threatening doom if his message went unheeded. It is the prediction of doom and disaster that we associate with his name. "How doth the city sit solitary, that was full of people! how is she become as a widow! . . . She weepeth sore in the night . . . all her friends . . . are become her enemies . . . Jerusalem hath grievously sinned . . . The joy of our heart is ceased . . . O Lord . . . wherefore dost thou . . . forsake us . . . thou art very wroth against us." Thus spake Jeremiah; but how very boring it can be to be forced to listen to the *jeremiads* of one's trouble-prone acquaintances! *Jeremiah* is a name given to any person who takes a gloomy view of his times and denounces what is going on in the world.

jorum   (JOR um) *n.* A *jorum* is a large drinking-bowl, the kind generally used for serving punch. (*Punch*, incidentally, is said to be derived from *puncheon*, a large cask—an instance of **metonymy**?) *Jorum* can be used as well to denote the contents of that type of bowl or any great amount of drink, as in *We drank a jorum of wine*. Figuratively, *jorum* may be used to describe a great lot of anything: *With that second Rolls, those people must have a jorum of money*, and *Lot had a jorum of woes*. The word came from the

240

name of Joram, son of King Toi of Hamath, who, according to II Samuel 8:10, "sent Joram his son unto King David . . . And Joram brought with him vessels of silver, and vessels of gold, and vessels of brass . . ."

jugulate (JOOH gyuh late) *vb.* To *jugulate* someone is to cut his throat or strangle him, both rather unpleasant procedures and obviously related (etymologically, not sociologically) to the jugular vein. But the word has a figurative and much more merciful use: to check or suppress by drastic measures, usually applied in medical parlance to the treatment of diseases. One case might be the amputation of an affected part, often the leg. Putting a gag into the mouth of a logorrhea sufferer would be less drastic, but might do the trick. *Jugulate* comes from Latin *jugulatus*, past participle of *jugulare* (to cut the throat of), based on *jugulum* (throat).

jussive (JUS iv) *n.*, *adj.* *Jussive* describes a word or phrase expressing a command, usually a mild one, or having the effect of a command. As a noun, *jussive* is a grammatical term for a word, form, or mood expressing a command. "May I come in?" "Do!" The *Do!* is a mild command. "Halt! Who goes there?" *Halt!* is much less mild (the man uttering it has a gun on him) but both are *jussives*. Any verb in the imperative mood (used in commands, requests, etc.) is *jussive*. *Stay*, in "Stay a while," is *jussive*. Polite people introduce *jussives* with *Please* . . . *Jussive* is from Latin *jussus*, past participle of the verb *jubere* (to command). The neuter form, *jussum*, means "command." It comes as a surprise to a Latinist that the first syllable is pronounced *jus-* rather than *joohs*, the Latin pronunciation (as far as we know—no recordings or tapes in those days).

justiciable (ju STISH ee uh bul) *adj.* A *justiciable* issue or controversy is one within the jurisdiction of a court; one that can be resolved or settled pursuant to law, or in judicial proceedings. The adjective is from Middle Latin *justitiabilis*, based on Latin *justitia* (justice). What would an *unjusticiable* or *nonjusticiable* issue be? In disputes between governments and trade unions, particularly in Britain, the unions sometimes claim that resort by the government to the courts can have no effect because the dispute is not *justiciable*, i.e., that there are aspects of the controversy that must be

241

resolved by negotiation, basic issues lying outside the jurisdiction of the courts, so that a court ruling would be of no effect and could be disregarded by the union.

juvenescence (jooh vuh NES uns) *n. Juvenescence* is the transition from infancy or early childhood to youth. It comes from Latin *juvenescens*, present participle of *juvenescence* (to attain youth—in the sense of "growing up" or "regaining youth"). *Juvenescence*, as well as the common word *juvenile*, and **juvenilia**, all go back to the Latin adjective *juvenis* (young), which may be familiar from the medieval students' song, "Gaudeamus igitur, *Juvenes* dum sumus . . ." (Let us rejoice, then, while we are young . . .)—*juvenes* is the plural of *juvenis*. There is a story about the United States Supreme Court Justices Oliver Wendell Holmes (1841–1935) and Louis D. Brandeis (1856–1941) tarrying on the warm summer day the session ended for the seasonal break. Brandeis, trying to interest Holmes in the details of a complicated case he was going to work on during the vacation, noticed that Holmes's attention was wandering: He was watching the girls go by in their summer dresses. "Ollie!" cried Louis, "you're not listening!" "Oh to be seventy again!" sighed the octogenarian Ollie. He wanted to *juvenesce* in the second sense—to regain youth, à la Ponce de León (c. 1460–1521), the Spanish explorer who searched for the Fountain of Youth. A good story, even if it didn't happen. *Juvenescence* is one of a series of nouns formed from present participles of Latin verbs having to do with the ages of man: *pubescence*, the attaining of puberty, from *pubescens*, present participle of *pubescere* (to attain puberty), and *senescence*, aging, from *senescens*, present participle of *senescere* (to grow old), both, like *juvenescence*, accented on the penultimate syllable. Each of these three words has a corresponding adjective ending in *-ent: juvenescent, pubescent, senescent*. If this is beginning to remind you of the *Seven Ages of Man* speech of Jaques in Shakespeare's *As You Like It* (Act II, Scene 7), so much the better.

juvenilia (jooh vuh NIL ee uh) *n. pl. Juvenile*, from Latin *juvenilis* (youthful), is a familiar word. *Juvenilia* is the neuter plural of that Latin adjective and means, literally, "youthful things." It is a term for either artistic works produced in youth or those suitable for the young, applied primarily to literary output but applicable to the other arts as well. The youthful music of Purcell (c. 1659–

1695), Mozart (1756–1791), and Mendelssohn (1809–1847), and the poetry of Keats (1795–1821) and Shelley (1792–1822), as well as the youthful novels ("The Italian Girl," "A Room with a View") of E. M. Forster (1879–1970), written in his early twenties, qualify as *juvenilia* in the sense of youthful production. *Alice in Wonderland* and *Through the Looking-Glass*, by Lewis Carroll (Charles Lutwidge Dodgson, 1832–1898), *Stuart Little* and *Charlotte's Web*, by E. B. White, the American humorist and poet (1899–1985), as well as the countless "children's books" that flood the market year after year, qualify as *juvenilia* in the second sense.

kame, see **quarrel**

katabasis (catabasis), see **anabasis**

kedgeree (KEJ uh ree) *n. Kedgeree* is a delicious concoction of Indian origin: rice, cooked with butter and dal (a puree of beans, peas, lentils, known collectively as *pulse*), flavored with spices, shredded onions, and other **ad hoc** ingredients. Imported into England and Europe, the dish was enhanced with flakes of fish and hard-boiled eggs, as well as other ingredients to taste—a very useful employment of fish left over from a previous meal. The word (like the dish) comes from India: *khichri*, based on Sanskrit *k'rsara* (dish of rice and sesame). Under the entry *haggis* in this author's *British English, A to Zed* (Facts on File, 1987), we read: "In one dictionary after another the definitions are strewn with *etc.*'s: *hearts, liver, etc., stomach of a sheep, etc.*, etc. This sort of thing tends to make one suspicious. There are fierce partisans on both sides of this *de gustibus* specialty." The dictionaries (and cookbooks) give the same treatment to *kedgeree*, but should not arouse your suspicions; it's delicious.

kern (kurn) *n.* In printing, a *kern* is the part of the face of a letter that projects beyond its body, like the part that makes a *Q* out of an *O*, or a *y* out of a *v.* In italics, the projecting parts of *f* and *j*, for example, are *kerns*. The word is derived, via French *carne* (corner), from Latin *cardo* (hinge).

243

kickshaw (KIK shaw) *n.* *Kickshaw* has a number of distinct meanings: tidbit, delicacy, fancy dish (the last usually derogatory); or toy, trifle, trinket, something showy but worthless. It is a corruption of the French *quelque chose* (something) as the result of popular etymological development. It happened a long time ago, but in more recent times, we have seen the *blanc* of *vin blanc* (white wine) brought back by the British soldiers from France as *plonk*, which has now become British slang for any cheap wine, regardless of color, so the corruption continues. Originally, there was an *s* at the end of *kickshaw*, making the second syllable closer to *chose*, but it became "singular" by back formation. In Shakespeare's *Henry IV, Part 2* (Act V, Scene 1), Justice Shallow is telling his servant Davy what compensation he demands from William the cook for some lost sack (wine: another corruption from the French *sec*, dry): "Some pigeons, Davy, a couple of short-legged hens, a joint of mutton, and any pretty little *kickshaws* . . . ." That was in the sense of "fancy dish" or "delicacy." Shakespeare used it in the other sense ("trifle") in *Twelfth Night* (Act I, Scene 3), when Sir Andrew Aguecheek tells Sir Toby Belch: "I delight in masques and revels . . . ," and Sir Toby asks, "Art thou good at these *kickshawses* . . . ?" and Sir Andrew answers, "As any man in Illyria . . ." and relates how well he dances the galliard and backtrick (contemporary dances).

kinesics (kih NEE siks) *n.* Treated as a singular noun (like *economics*, etc.), *kinesics* is the study of body language, body movements and gestures as a method of communication without speech. It is derived from Greek *kinesis* (movement), related to the verb *kineein* (to move), and *kinesics* can mean "body movement" itself, as well as its study. Nodding to indicate the affirmative and turning the head from side to side to indicate the opposite are examples of *kinesics*. Waving as a gesture of greeting or farewell, raising a clenched fist as one of defiance or solidarity with a group, the rude gestures of thumbing or holding one's nose, the V-for-victory sign— these are all examples and there are many more. In cricket the umpire never speaks; he has gestures for "no-ball" (the bowler overstepping the crease, like a foot-fault in tennis) and "wide" (roughly the equivalent of a "ball" in baseball), and by pointing, indicates to a batsman that he is "out" for protecting his wicket by putting "leg before wicket." The umpire in baseball likewise uses *kinesics* to indicate whether a runner is safe or out at base. The fluttering eyes of a maiden send her gentleman friend a message of consuming interest: *kinesics* indeed.

koniology   (koh nee OL uh gee) *n*. This is the study of dust, germs, pollen, and other allergenic impurities suspended in the atmosphere. A *konimeter* (kon IM ih tur) is an instrument for measuring the dust in the air. A *koniscope* (KON ih skope) estimates the amount of suspended dust. *Koniology* is a field explored by allergists. The source of all these words is Greek *konis* (dust).

lacertine,   see **accipitrine**

laches   (LACH iz) *n*. *Laches*, which looks like a plural noun but is singular, is a term used in law to denote such a degree of delay in the assertion of a claim or the bringing of a lawsuit as will bar the claimant or plaintiff from further proceeding. This is a concept in "equity," that area of the law dealing with the application of principles of natural justice in the determination of the rights of the parties and the disposition of controversies. *Laches* is a general defense, as opposed to specific and rigid statutes of limitation that vary from state to state and as to varying types of lawsuit (e.g., torts as opposed to breach of contract) and in express terms bar the bringing of a legal action after the lapse of a specific period, for example, six years for the institution of suit based on a promissory note, which becomes "outlawed" after that lapse of time beyond the maturity date. *Laches* was derived from Anglo-French *lachesse*, which came from Latin *laxus* (lax, loose, relaxed, postponed).

laconism   (LAK uh niz um) *n*. Or **laconicism** (luh KON uh siz um). *Laconism* may be considered an example of **haplology;** see also **aph(a)eresis.** We are more familiar with the adjective *laconic* (luh KON ik) than the noun *laconism*, a concise style of language, brevity; also applied to a short, pithy statement. Laconia was long ago a country in the southern part of Greece, with Sparta as its capital. The Spartans were concise, brusque, and pithy in their

245

speech, hence *laconic*, under which entry in this author's *1000 Most Important Words* (Ballantine, New York, 1982; Facts On File, New York, 1985) we read: "Philip of Macedonia wrote to the Spartan officials: 'If I enter Laconia, I will level Sparta to the ground.' Their answer: 'If.' Caesar's famous 'Veni, vidi, vici' ('I came, I saw, I conquered') is a famous example of *laconic* speech—not a word wasted." When General Sir Charles Napier (1782–1855) finally completed the conquest of Sind, a province of India, the story goes, he cabled the War Office one word: "Peccavi" (Latin for "I have sinned"). Quite a *laconism*, and quite a **paronomasia** in the bargain, even though the cable is generally believed to be apocryphal. And finally, the message radioed by an American pilot in World War II: "Sighted sub, sank same," an alliterative *laconism*.

lacustrine   (luh KUS trin) *adj. Lacustrine* applies to things having to do with lakes; animals, fish, and plants living and growing in lakes, and geological strata formed at the bottom or along the shores of lakes. *Lacustrine* ecology has suffered enormously as a result of pollution from the disposal of chemical waste matter into lakes by nearby factories devoid of conscience in such matters. The *Lacustrian* Age was the age of lake-dwellings built on piles driven into the beds or shores of lakes. Remains of them have been found in Africa and Asia, but the most renowned are those of the Neolithic (Stone Age) peoples of the Alpine areas of Europe, especially Switzerland, who developed a high degree of skill in agriculture and the arts. Discoveries have been made of numerous village clusters, up to as many as 50, on a single lake where *lacustrine* people dwelt from c. 2500 B.C. until the seventh century B.C., when their territory was invaded by the Celts. The *lacustrine* way of life provided a ready supply of fish, marsh fowl, and fertile open crop land. The adjective comes, via Italian *lacustre*, from Latin *lacus* (lake).

lamia   (LAY mee uh) *n.* The *lamiae* (LAY mee eye), in classical mythology, were a race of monsters with female heads and breasts and the bodies of serpents, who enticed young people and little children in order to devour them. The story went that the original *lamia* was a Queen of Libya with whom Jupiter fell in love. Juno became furiously jealous and stole the children of the queen, who went mad and vowed vengeance on all children. *Lamia* became a term for any vampire or she-demon. The literal meaning of *lamia* in Greek is "female man-eater." In medieval times, witches were sometimes called *lamiae*. The English poet John Keats (1795–1821) wrote a poem entitled *Lamia* a short time before his untimely death. In it, a bride, recognized as a *lamia* by the philosopher Apollonius of Tyana (born shortly before the birth of Christ), vanishes instantaneously. Keats based his theme on an incident related in *The Anatomy of Melancholy* of the English churchman and writer Robert Burton (1577–1640), who took it from *The Life of Apollonius* by the Greek philosopher Flavius Philostratus (born c. 170). The enticement or devouring of the young has long been a theme in legend, all the way from the Minotaur of Crete to the Pied Piper of Hamelin. There were no Missing Persons Bureaus in those days to trace the Hamelin kiddies.

Laodicean (lay od ih SEE un) *n.*, *adj.* As an adjective, this word describes anyone who is generally indifferent, uninterested, and lackadaisical, and especially so in matters of religion. As a noun, *Laodicean* is a label for such a person. *Laodicea* is the ancient name of Latakia, a seaport in northwestern Syria. In Revelations 1:11, John was told: "What thou seest, write in a book and send it unto the seven churches which are in Asia . . ." of which the church of Laodicea was one. In 3:14–16, John was directed: ". . . Unto the angel of the church of the Laodiceans, write . . . 'Thou art neither cold nor hot . . . So then because thou art lukewarm . . . I will spue thee out of my mouth . . .' " It is from those words that *Laodicean* acquired the meaning given above.

lapidary (LAP ih der ee), also **lapidist** (LAP ih dist) *n.* Both forms of this noun denote a cutter and polisher of gemstones. *Lapidary* is also the name of the art itself, as well as that of engraving inscriptions on stone monuments. A *lapidarist* (luh PID uh rist: note change of stress) is a gem expert, a connoisseur of precious stones, also known as a *gem(m)ologist* (je MOL uh jist); and *gem(m)ology* (je MOL uh jee) is the study and science of gemstones. The *gem-* words come from Latin *gemma* (bud, jewel); the *lapid-* words from *lapid-*, the stem of Latin *lapis* (stone), and none of the latter should ever be confused or associated with **lapidate**.

247

lapidate (LAP ih date) *vb.* To *lapidate* is to stone to death, an old Biblical penalty first suggested by the Lord to Moses, as set forth in Leviticus, for various crimes including adultery, incest, homosexuality, and other such naughty practices, and latterly instituted by the Ayatollah Khomeini of Iran for similar offenses. Jesus was gentler: "He that is without sin among you, let him first cast a stone at her." (John 8:7.) Whatever one's views may be on the question of capital punishment, *lapidation* (lap ih DAY shun) is beyond the pale; and never, never associate it with those honest gem cutters and stone engravers discussed under **lapidary**, even though it comes from the same source, *lapid-*, the stem of the Latin noun *lapis* (stone). Further, *lapidate* has nothing to do with *dilapidate* or its more familiar form *dilapidated*, which comes from Latin *dilapidatus*, past participle of *dilapidare* (to demolish), based on the prefix *di-* (asunder; variant of *dis-* before certain consonants) plus the same old *lapid-*. From "dismantled, stone by stone," *dilapidated* has come to mean "fallen into decay," through neglect or abuse, and can apply to things having no connection with stones, from wooden houses to clothing in rags to moldy furniture and books, to say nothing of ravaged bodies.

lapine, see **accipitrine**

lari(di)ne, see **accipitrine**

latitudinarian (lat ih toohd uh NAR ee un, -tyoohd-) *n., adj.* *Latitude*, apart from its use in geography, used figuratively denotes tolerance of freedom of belief or action, freedom from dogma or narrow restrictions of any sort. It is from Latin *latitudo* (breadth), based on *latus* (wide). *Latitudinarian*, as an adjective, applies to those permitting or characterized by such an attitude, in opinion or behavior, and as a noun, to persons of *latitudinarian* persuasion. It has a special significance in matters of religion, describing a person allowing latitude in that field, indifferent as to creed, dogma, and ritual. In the Church of England, the label *latitudinarian* was first applied in the middle of the 17th century as a term of opprobrium to members of the clergy who underrated dogma and practice and came to favor and encourage laxity in that area. *Latitudinarianism* in religion was opposed and eventually checked by the emergence of the Evangelicals, who emphasized the Gospel and the importance of scriptural authority. The term is now applied generally to people who attach little importance to dogma and orthodoxy, like David Jenkins, the current bishop of Durham, who was installed, over wide protest, by the archbishop of York despite the bishop's previous statements disavowing belief in the Virgin Birth or the Resurrection. (Lightning struck the roof of York Minster, the cathedral of York, a few days later. Form your own conclusions.)

lazar, see **lazaretto**

lazaretto (laz uh RET o) *n.* A *lazaretto* is a hospital for patients suffering from contagious diseases, especially leprosy. The term is applied as well to any building or ship maintained for those detained in quarantine. It is also a nautical term for a small storeroom in the hull of a ship, especially one at the very stern. Context should make it clear which kind of *lazaretto* one is dealing with. It is from an Italian word in the Venetian dialect, *lazareto*, formed from *lazar* (LAZ ur), a leper or anyone suffering from a loathsome disease, plus *(N)azareto*, a hospital in Venice maintained by the Church of Santa Maria di Nazaret (St. Mary of Nazareth). *Lazar* comes from the name of Lazarus, the diseased beggar in the Bible parable of the rich man and the beggar in Luke 16:19–31.

legerdemain (lej ur duh MANE) *n.* Legerdemain (which used to be written as three words, *léger de main*, meaning "light of hand" in Middle French) is sleight of hand, prestidigitation, the practice of magic tricks like pulling rabbits out of hats, jugglery, etc., all very fine things; but by extension, trickery, deceit, duplicity, chicanery, all very bad things. The American magician Harry Houdini (Erich Weiss, 1874–1926) was a world-famous practitioner of the art of *legerdemain* in its literal, good sense. Politicians, especially diplomats, are experts in verbal *legerdemain*, also known as word twisting, double talk and gobbledegook. Lawyers who put excessive strains on the Queen's English out of extreme zeal in the practice of advocacy have been known to practice this type of linguistic *legerdemain*, more's the pity, doing violence not only to language, but, on occasion, to justice.

leiotrichous, see **cymotrichous**

leitmotif, -tiv (LEIT moh teef) *n.* This noun is taken from the German noun *Leitmotiv*; the prefix *leit-* is based on the verb *leiten* (to lead); *motiv* is German for *motif*. First applied to the music drama of Wagner, the term denoted a melodic passage accompanying and associated with each appearance of a particular character or each occurrence of a particular situation. Thus, the same musical theme was heard with each appearance of Siegfried, Sieglinde, et al., or with each approach of danger or climactic violence, or a love scene. The term was later extended to music generally, and finally to any life experience, to signify a dominant motive, a controlling emotion, any driving force. In this extended usage, the *leitmotif* of one person's career may be the accumulation of great wealth, while in the case of another it may be the attainment of fame or power, and in the life of still another, the creation of lasting art. People do not always accomplish their *leitmotifs*. The *leitmotif* of Hitler's career was to build a Reich that would last 1,000 years. He failed by about 988. Columbus's *leitmotif* was to find a western passage to Asia. He missed by a good many thousand miles. Napoleon . . . Shall we go on?

lemma (LEM uh) *n.* We are all too often faced with—or on the horns of—a *dilemma* (dih LEM uh, dye-), a quandary or predicament involving a choice between two unsatisfactory courses of action. *Dilemma* was taken intact from the Greek, based on the prefix *di-* (from *dis*, twice) plus *lemma* in the sense of "assumption." The literal meaning of *lemma* in Greek is "anything received, an assumption, a premise taken for granted," based on the verb *lambanein* (to take, assume). If you are faced with two *lemmas*, you are in a dilemma: If I go out in this weather, I'll get soaked; if I don't, I'll miss the concert. Two *lemmas* = one *dilemma*. If there is a third possible choice (if I stay in and get it on the radio, I'll hear it but the sound won't be as good and I won't see Maestro X conduct), you are in a *trilemma*, where there is the choice among three unsatisfactory alternatives. Three *lemmas* = one *trilemma*. What about four? Yes, *tetralemmas* exist, in both life and dictionary (Greek prefix *tetra-*, four, plus old friend *lemma*) and wouldn't it be hell to be on the horns of one of those? But there it stops. You may have five unacceptable choices (one of those confusing restaurant menus), but *pentalemma* (*penta-* is a combining form of *pente*, Greek for "five") still remains to be concocted.

lemurine,   see **accipitrine**

lenis,   see **fortis**

leonine,   see **accipitrine**

leporine,   see **accipitrine**

leptocephalic   (lep tuh suh FAL ik) *adj*. This adjective describes persons with narrow skulls. It is formed from the Greek prefix *lepto-*, based on the adjective *leptos* (narrow) plus the noun *kephale* (head). There are other *lepto-* adjectives: *leptocercal* (lep tuh SERK ul), describing animals with slender tails (*kerkos*, tail); *leptodactylous* (lep tuh DAK tuh lus), for those with slender toes (*daktylos*, finger, toe); *leptorrhine* (LEP tuh reen), for narrow-nosed beings (*rhis*, nose); *leptosome* (LEP tuh some), for those of slender build (*soma*, body), cf. **asthenic**. Quite a family, these *lepto-* adjectives. There appears to be no *lepto-* word for *thin-skinned*, i.e., *sensitive*, such as *leptodermatous*, using *derma* (skin), as an antonym of **pachydermatous** in the figurative sense. Well, you can't have everything.

leptocercal,   see **leptocephalic**

leptodactylous,   see **leptocephalic**

leptorrhine,   see **leptocephalic**

leptosome,   see **leptocephalic**

lethe   (LEE thee) *n. Lethe* is oblivion, forgetfulness of the past; a word arising from *Lethe*, a river of the underworld in classical mythology, of whose waters the souls of all the dead had to drink, in order for them to forget the past. The River Lethe gave rise to another word, *lethargy*, from Greek *lethargia* (drowsy forgetfulness), based on *lethargos* (drowsy), from *lethe* plus *argos* (idle). *Lethe* and oblivion were on the minds of many poets and writers. In *The Dunciad*, the English poet Alexander Pope (1688–1744) wrote:

Here, in a dusky vale where *Lethe* rolls . . .
Old Bavius sits, to dip poetic souls,
And blunt the senses.

Bavius was a first centry **poetaster**, rescued from oblivion by the contempt of the greatest of Roman poets, Virgil (70–19 B.C.). The English poet John Keats (1795–1821), in his *Ode to Melancholy*, warned:

No, no, go not to *Lethe*, neither twist
Wolf's-bane, tight-rooted, for its poisonous wine.

Wolfsbane is aconite, a poisonous plant. Keats again, in his *Ode to a Nightingale*:

My heart aches, and a drowsy numbness pains
My sense, as though of hemlock I had drunk,
Or emptied some dull opiate to the drains
One minute past, and *Lethe*-wards had sunk.

When, in Shakespeare's *Hamlet* (Act I, Scene 5), Hamlet assures the ghost of his father that he will seek revenge, the Ghost answers:

I find thee apt;
And duller shouldst thou be than the fat weed
That rots itself in ease on *Lethe* wharf,
Wouldst thou not stir in this.

The English poet Thomas Campbell (1777–1844), in the poem *Absence*, wrote:

'Tis *Lethe*'s gloom, but not its quiet,—
The pain without the peace of death.

The Roman poet Horace (65–8 B.C.), in an epode, wrote of ". . . a deep oblivion, as though with thirsty throat I'd drained the cup that brings the sleep of *Lethe*." John Milton (1608–1674), in *Paradise Lost*, speaks of ". . . a slow and silent stream,/*Lethe* the river of oblivion . . ." and more recently, the German novelist Thomas Mann (1875–1955), in *The Magic Mountain*, says: "Time, we say, is *Lethe* . . ."

licentiate   (lye SEN shee it, -ate) *n. Licentiate* is the title con-
252

ferred upon one who has been granted a *license* from an institution, especially a university, to practice a profession or art. Some European universities give degrees somewhere between those of bachelor and doctor. Graduates holding such degrees are known as *licentiates*. *Licentiate* is from Middle Latin *licentiatus*, past participle of *licentiare* (to license), derived from Latin *licentia* (freedom, leave). Being a *licentiate* has nothing to do with being *licentious* (from Latin *licentiosus*, arbitrary), though one can, of course, be both, and both words go back ultimately to *licentia*, which is related to Latin *licet* (it is allowed), a form of the verb *licere*, whose present participle is *licens* (unrestrained).

lilliputian (lil ih PYOOH shun) *n.*, *adj.*; **brobdingnagian** (brob ding NAG ee un) *adj.* Both these words, often capitalized, come from *Gulliver's Travels*, the 1726 satirical masterpiece of the English author Jonathan Swift (1667–1745), which describes the visits of his hero Lemuel Gulliver to the imaginary countries of Lilliput, Brobdingnag, and other places whose names have not given rise to adjectives in common use. Lilliput was inhabited by tiny people, the Lilliputians. Hence *lilliputian*, as an adjective, means "extremely small," and by extension, "petty, small-minded, narrow, insignificant, picayune." Dinky toys are *lilliputian* models of the original cars, trucks, etc., and a friend of the author quite appropriately (if somewhat obviously) named his chihuahua "Lilliput." The American journalist William Allen White (1868–1944, the "sage of Emporia"), wrote of the "lilliputian senators," referring to their pettifogging ways. The imaginary land of Brobdingnag was peopled by giants; hence the adjective *brobdingnagian* means "huge, vast, tremendous, mammoth, gigantic." It is sometimes said that Italy, on the map, resembles a *brobdingnagian* boot. A hummingbird is *lilliputian*; a whale is *brobdingnagian*.

limen,   see **algesia**

limnology,   see **genethlialogy**

lingua franca,   see **pidgin**

literati (lit uh RAH tee, -RAY-) *n. pl.* The *literati* are the intelligentsia, the intellectuals, men of letters, the learned, the scholars.

253

Litterati, in Latin, is the plural of *litteratus* (lettered, learned, educated). The *literati* are miles above the merely *literate*, though that word comes from the same Latin source. There are many other *liter-* words: *literacy, literal(ly), literature;* they all go back to Latin *lit(t)era* (letter of the alphabet) and prefer the single *l*, while *letter* kept both.

logogram, see **grammalogue**

logogriph (LO guh grif) *n.* A *logogriph* is a word puzzle, sometimes an anagram, at other times a riddle in which one is supposed to discover a word from other words made up of its letters (example supplied by *Webster's Unabridged*, Second Edition: *chatter*, from *cat, hat, rat, hate, rate*, etc.—they could have given (chatterer), or (what's worse) from synonyms of other word, or (what's even worse than that) verses containing such synonyms. Whatever the riddle, *logogriph* comes from Greek *logos* (word) plus *griphos* (net, fishing basket, riddle—the connection among these meanings being, one supposes, that the riddle is made up of a basket of other words). Submitted, in category 3: "This is the forest primeval," (opening line of *Evangeline*, by the American poet Henry Wadsworth Longfellow, 1807–1882). *Forest = grove; primeval = earliest;* from *grove* and *earliest* select the letters that make up the answer: *overeager*. There must be easier ways to make a living.

logomachy (lo GOM uh kee) *n. Logomachy* is a controversy (usually literary) about words (the kind readers of this book may engage in with the author), or a dispute marked by the incorrect use of words (the kind readers and the author will never engage in); and *logomachy* is also the name of a game played with a set of cards each bearing one letter of the alphabet, for the formation of words. It comes from Greek *logomachia*, based on *logos* (word) plus suffix *-machia* (-fighting), from *mache* (fight). Imagine a hot dispute about the connection between the words *sorrow* and *sorry*. Jones maintains that they come from the same root. Smith says nay. They put it to Green, a philologist, who points out that *sorrow* is from Old English *sorg*, cognate with German *Sorge* (grief, sorrow, worry), while *sorry* is from Old English *sarig*, cognate with Low German *serig* and Old High German *serag*. Smith wins, whereupon Jones gets sore (which comes from Old English *sar*, cognate with Dutch

254

zeer, if you must know) and indulges in a dispute with both Smith and Green in which he recklessly uses incorrect expressions like "the both of you" and "equally as illiterate." Then they all calm down and play a game with a set of those one-letter cards. Three *logomachies* for the price of one.

louche (loohsh) *adj.* A *louche* person, or *louche* conduct, is devious, perverse, untrustworthy, sinister. *Louche* was taken over from the French as is. In French, its literal meaning is "squint-eyed," but the French use it in a figurative sense to describe persons or behavior of dubious character, equivocal, disreputable, shifty, shady, or more informally, fishy. They got *louche* from the Latin *luscus*, which means "one-eyed," and the figurative use of *louche* to mean "shifty" or "fishy" seems quite unfair to perfectly honorable people who happen to have lost an eye somewhere along the line. Like Caesar's wife, who "must be above suspicion" (a traditional saying, based on an alleged remark by Caesar according to the Roman historian Plutarch, 46–120)—Caesar divorced Pompeia not because he believed her guilty, but on mere suspicion of guilt, when her name came up in an accusation against a public figure named Publius Clodius, according to another Roman historian, Suetonius (75–150)—we should all be careful not even to appear *louche*. If you think it discursive to drag in a bit of possibly apocryphal Roman history or gossip in a discussion of *louche*, you're right.

lubricious (looh BRISH us), also **lubricous** (LOOH brih kus) *adj. Lubricious*, describing a surface, means "oily, slippery"; applied to a person, "unstable, shifty," or more commonly, "lewd, lascivious, lecherous." The source is Latin *lubricus* (slippery), which in Middle Latin came to mean "unstable." The noun *lubricitas* in Middle Latin means "lechery." *Lubricious* well describes the smooth, oily, slippery, lewd, lascivious, and lecherous old-time movie villain who hissed at the terrified young slip of a girl, "Aha, my proud beauty!" and strove with might and main to take unfair advantage of the poor thing. Next week *East Lynne*.

lucubrate (LOOH kyoo brate) *vb.* To *lucubrate* (not to be confused with *lubricate*) is to toil, study, or write painstakingly, laboriously, especially at night; to burn the midnight oil, as it were. If the word is used in the context of writing, the implication is one of erudition and scholarship. In the writing of this book, the author has indeed *lucubrated*. The noun is *lucubration* (looh kyoo BRAY shun), signifying toil, study, or writing, especially at night. *Lucubrate* comes from Latin *lucubratus*, past participle of *lucubrare* (to work by night) and the noun is from *lucubratio* (nocturnal study, working by night, or by lamplight). These Latin words are based upon *lux* (light), whose stem is *luc-*. A related word is *luculent* (LOOH kyoo lunt), an adjective meaning "clear, lucid," that comes from Latin *luculentus* (bright, full of light). A good teacher will be able to furnish *luculent* explanations and interpretations to his students, who can then go on to praiseworthy *lucubration* and lots of A's. *Luculent* sometimes has the force of "convincing." A *luculent* explanation would normally be convincing and cogent.

luculent, see **lucubrate**

Lucullan (looh KUL un), **Lucullean** (looh ku LEE un), **Lucullic** (looh KUl ik) *adj*. The usual form is *Lucullan*. A *Lucullan* meal is profusely lavish and luxurious, elegant enough for any epicure, a meal, in fact, fit for the gods. The adjective derives from Lucius Licinius Lucullus (c. 110–57 B.C.), a Roman general and politician who devoted his later years to a rich, elegant way of life, with the emphasis on gourmet food and drink of the highest standard of elegance. He was famed for his banquets, but once, while a lavish supper was in preparation, a friend inquiring who were to be his guests that evening received the answer: "Lucullus will sup tonight with Lucullus." This has come to be quoted of any gourmet who, though dining alone, is as fussy about the meal as though royalty were expected. The sentence, rightly or wrongly, is sometimes applied to gluttonous feeding, though Lucullus himself was a gourmet rather than a gourmand. The highest praise you can give your hostess after a superb meal is to extol it as *Lucullan*. If she doesn't understand, send her a copy of this book with an inscription calling attention to page 256 together with your thanks for a *Lucullan* feast.

Luddite (LUD ite) *n*. Under the leadership of Ned Ludd, a semi-mythical 18th-century worker also known as "King Ludd" from Leicestershire, a county in the midlands of England, bands of English textile workers, during the years 1811–1816, rioted and smashed new industrial machinery in the manufacturing districts of the northern counties of Nottinghamshire, Lancashire, Cheshire, and Yorkshire. They blamed the machinery for their unemployment and distress. Ned Ludd was said to have originated the idea and his followers were called *Luddites*. Their doctrine was given the name of *Luddism* or *Ludditism*. The *Luddites* were right in their belief that the introduction of the machinery eliminated jobs and caused unemployment, but their methods of combating the evil were on the crude side. A similar situation arose in the southern counties in the period 1830–1833, when the "Swing Riots" of the agricultural laborers were touched off by the introduction of new threshing machinery, causing unemployment and distress. Machines were smashed and hay and grain ricks set afire. A "Captain Swing" was held to be the leader of the movement, but unlike the semi-mythical Ned Ludd he appears to have been a wholly imaginary character. The English humorist Richard Harris Barham (1788–1845), in *The Ingoldsby Legends*, wrote about the legendary captain:

> The neighbors thought all was not right,
> Scarcely one with him ventured to parley,
> And Captain Swing came in the night,
> And burnt all his beans and his barley.

Many an unemployed worker today believes Ludd and Swing were right, and blames his condition on "progress."

lumbricine, see **accipitrine**

lupine, see **accipitrine**

lustral, lustrate, lustration, see **lustrum**

lustrum (LUS trum) *n.* also **luster** (LUS tur). A *lustrum* is a period of five years. In ancient Rome, the census was taken every five years, after which the authorities performed a *lustrum* (lustration), a ceremonial purification, a purificatory sacrifice conducted by the censors for the population. To *lustrate* (LUS trate) is to purify ceremonially, and *lustral* (LUS trul), literally "pertaining to the *lustrum* ceremony," acquired the meaning "occurring every five years," synonymous with *quinquennial* (kwin KWEN ee ul), based on Latin *quinque* (five) plus *annus* (year). Lustrum is a Latin word, based on the verb *lustrare* (to purify). The president of the United States is elected for a *quadrennium*, a period of four years (from a New Latin alteration of the Latin *quadriennium*); the prime minister of Britain serves for a *lustrum*, or *quinquennium*, i.e., five years—unless something happens to cause the Government to fall, or the Government, to test public opinion in a crisis, thinks the time is ripe to hold a general election (called a "snap election") before the *lustrum* expires. The British don't call it a *lustrum*, though there's no reason why they shouldn't, except that nobody gets purified at its conclusion.

lutrine,   see **accipitrine**

lycanthropy   (lye KAN thruh pee) *n.* This is a type of madness in which a human being imagines himself to be a wolf (at times, another animal) and acts and sounds like one. *Lycanthropy* also applies to the case of a person's assuming the form of a wolf—in old legend. One affected with this form of insanity is a *lycanthrope* (LYE kun thrope, lye KAN thrope) or a werewolf in folklore. The words come from Greek *lykanthropia* and *lykanthropos*, based on *lykos* (wolf) plus *anthropos* (man), adding up to *wolf-man*. The *were-* in *werewolf* comes from Old English *wer* (man), cognate with Latin *vir*, from which we get *virile, virility*, etc., so that *werewolf* changes the order of the components to *man-wolf*. *Wolf-man* or *man-wolf*, this has nothing to do with the unpleasant kind of wolf that some men turn into in the presence of an attractive woman.

lyncine,   see **accipitrine**

macaronic   (mak uh RON ik) *adj.* This peculiar word, a jocular concoction from *macaroni*, is applied, in a narrow sense, to language characterized by a mixture of Latin and non-Latin words, or by non-Latin words given phony Latin endings; in a broader sense, to prose or verse composed of any mixture of languages; in its broadest sense, to anything mixed or jumbled. As a noun, *macaronics* (plural in form, singular in meaning, like *economics*) means "*macaronic* language," particularly in verse form. *Omnium gatherum*, a bit of British mock Latin meaning "mixture," any motley

258

collection of persons or things, or sometimes "open house," a party open to all comers, is a sample of *macaronic* language (*omnium* is the genitive plural of *omnis*, Latin for "all"; *gatherum* is a phony Latinization of *gather*.) Merlinus Coccaius (1491–1544), a monk of Mantua, Italy, wrote a poetical rhapsody using words of various languages, entitled *Liber Macaronicorum* (Book of Macaronics). An example of *macaronic* verse of mixed Latin and English, from *The Elderly Gentleman* by J. A. Morgan:

> Prope ripam fluvii solus [By the bank of the river alone]
> A senex [old man] silently sat,
> Super capitum ecce [On his head behold] his wig
> Et wig super, ecce [And on the top of his wig, behold] his hat.

Eventually, Zephyrus . . . in rivum projecit (the wind blew into the stream) his hat! In the third line, *capitum* is an incorrect form; the *-um* should be *-e*, though it serves the meter. In his lecture on Pepys's diaries (Samuel Pepys, English diarist, 1633–1703), at the Royal Society of Arts, recorded in its *Journal* of May 1984, Robert Latham, a fellow of Magdalene College, Cambridge, and editor of the most recent edition of the diaries, described the "amorous passages" as "written in a *macaronic* mixture of language—English, French and Spanish for the most part."

machicolation (muh chik uh LAY shun) *n.* This is an architectural term for an opening in a castle parapet (defensive wall) or balcony floor through which molten lead, boiling oil, miscellaneous missiles, and other charming weapons could be cast down upon the heads of the hapless attackers. The term was also applied to a balcony or parapet provided with such openings. To *machicolate* (muh CHIK uh late) a parapet or projecting gallery floor is to provide it with *machicolations*. These words are, via French *mâchicoulis*, from Middle Latin *machicol(l)atus*, past participle of *machicol(l)are*, a Latinization of Old French *machecoller*, derived from the *mache-* of Old French *macher* (to mash, crush) plus *coller* (to flow) or *col* (neck). Whatever the derivation, and however quaint these military devices and tactics may seem in the atomic age, *machicolations* were very effective in their day, and novelists like the Scottish Sir Walter Scott (1771–1832) and France's Victor Hugo (1802–1885), with their castles and cathedrals and rousing battle scenes, could hardly have done without them.

macropine,   see **accipitrine**

macropodine,   see **accipitrine**

maggot   (MAG ut) *n.* Those nasty little squirmy creepy-crawly
things are legless grubs, the larvae of certain insects of the order
Diptera, the common members of which are the housefly, mos-
quito, and gnat. They are used for bait in England, where they are
called "gentles." But *maggot* has another quite distinct meaning,
possibly archaic in America, but not in Britain: "whimsical fancy,
odd fad, **crotchet**." It comes from Old English *magot*, an unex-
plained variant of *maddock*. There would seem to be no possible
connection between the two disparate meanings, but there is one:
The strange notion in olden times that odd or whimsical people had
maggots (the creepy-crawly variety) in their brains. In *Women
Pleased*, a play by the English dramatist John Fletcher (1579–1625;
he was the collaborator of Francis Beaumont, 1584–1616; *Beaumont and Fletcher* is a linkage as established as *Gilbert and Sullivan*), we find this bit of dialogue:

> Are you not mad, my friend? What time o' th' moon is't?
> Have you not *maggots* in your brain?

Maggots in the brain has the ring of *bats in the belfry* or *rats in the
garret*, and *Brewer's Phrase & Fable* mentions the Scottish *head
full of bees*, the French *rats in the head*, and the Dutch *mouse's
nest in the head*. So, going back to old Fletcher, we do come up
with a logical connection between *maggots* and whimsies. The English novelist and poet Sylvia Townsend Warner (1893–1978), a
constant contributor to *The New Yorker* magazine (and, incidentally, a good friend of this author), wrote a wonderful short novel
published by Viking Press in 1927 entitled *Mr. Fortune's Maggot*.
But Miss Warner and the special quaint meaning of *maggot* were
unknown to the author at that time. Idle curiosity in a bookshop
quickly established that the slim volume was neither a work on
entomology nor a follow-up on *The Compleat Angler* of Izaak Walton (1593–1683). Right under the title, on a flyleaf, there is printed:

> MAGGOT 2. A nonsensical or perverse fancy;
> a **crotchet**.

magisterial   (maj ih STEER ee ul) *adj.* What is *magisterial* is authoritative, important, weighty, a matter of consequence, or, in a different context, domineering, overbearing, high-handed. The first meaning is laudatory; the second, far less flattering and in fact pejorative, and one must be careful to distinguish. We get the word from Middle Latin *magisterialis*, based on Latin *magister* (master), which goes back to the Latin comparative adverb *magis* (more, more so, to a greater extent). In *Law and Literature*, a lecture given in 1931, the great jurist and Supreme Court Justice Benjamin Cardozo (1870–1938) described six types of judicial writing. The first was ". . . the type *magisterial* or imperative . . . ," and it is difficult to know just how he was using the word. But it is clear that the word expresses praise in a passage about Winston Churchill (1874–1965) by the English writer, editor, and columnist Godfrey Smith (b. 1926) in *The English Companion* (Pavilion Books, London, 1984): "He not only led his nation to a triumphant victory in the Second World War; he wrote a *magisterial* six-volume history of it."

maieutic   (may YOOH tik) *adj.* This word has an interesting meaning and an amusing derivation. It comes from Greek *maieutikos* (pertaining to midwifery), related to the verb *maieuesthai* (to act as midwife), based on the noun *maia* (midwife). It applies, however, to the performance of a "midwife's" services in the realm of thoughts or ideas, especially the method employed by the Greek philosopher Socrates (c. 469–399 B.C.) in creating knowledge by questioning, a procedure known as the "Socratic method." Socrates considered himself a "midwife" in bringing to birth the ideas and thoughts of others by means of his questions. Fowler says that *educative* (Ed oo kay tiv, ED yoo-), "contains the same notion, but much overlaid with different ones, and the literary critic and the pedagogue consequently find *maieutic* useful enough to pass in spite of its touch of pedantry." Don't automatically scoff at pedantry, or for that matter, snobbery, both of which can serve a useful purpose in small doses.

malacology   (mal uh KOL uh jee) *n.* This is the study of mollusks and the science dealing with them. The term *mollusk* covers snails, oysters, clams, and mussels, which are hard on the outside but soft inside, as well as octopuses and squids, which are soft all over. It is this softness that explains the derivation of *mollusk* from Latin *molluscus* (softish—from *mollis*, soft). The *malaco-* is from Greek *malakos* (soft), plus *logos* (study, discourse). Thus we see the etymological connection between *malacology* and *mollusks*. (See also **genethlialogy**.)

mallecho (MAL ih choh) *n.* As the play within the play begins in Shakespeare's *Hamlet* (Act III, Scene 2) and the players act out the poisoning of the king and the wooing and winning of the queen by the poisoner, Ophelia enters and cries, "What means this, my lord?" and Hamlet answers, "Marry, this is miching *mallecho*; it means mischief." Thus Shakespeare himself supplies the definition: mischief. *Mallecho* was derived from the Spanish noun *malhecho* (evil deed), based on the prefix *mal-* (evil) plus *hecho* (deed). *Miching* (MICH ing) is an adjective made of the present participle of the verb *miche*, meaning to "skulk" or "slink," thought to be a variant of *mooch* (British slang for "slouch about" or "skulk," differing from the American slang usage, to "scrounge," both, however, coming from the same source, Middle English *michen*, to skulk or hide). The English poet Robert Herrick (1591–1674), in a lovely poem about his domestic animals, included:

> A cat
> I keep, that plays about the house
> Grown fat
> With eating many a *miching* mouse.

Micher appears in Shakespeare in the sense of "thief" or "truant." In *Henry IV, Part I* (Act II, Scene 4), Falstaff asks Prince Henry,

> Shall the blessed son of heaven prove a *micher* and eat blackberries? a question not to be asked. Shall the son of England prove a thief and take purses? a question to be asked.

Thus, *miching mallecho* means "sneaky mischief." You may never run into this eloquent phrase in contemporary literature, unless you happen to read *An Awkward Lie* by the English whodunitist Michael Innes (b. 1906), where his detective Sir John Appleby, considering the mysterious disappearance of a corpse from a golf bunker, wonders about this "elaborate piece of *miching malicho*." *Malicho* is a variant of *mallecho*, or vice versa. Some authorities say that it is

262

vice versa, *mallecho*, influenced by the Spanish, being a learned emendation of *malicho*, the form favored by Michael Innes.

manatine, see **accipitrine**

manes (MAY neez) *n. Manes* can be treated as a plural noun for the shades of the departed, the spirits of the dead, or as a singular noun for the shade or spirit of an individual. It is a Latin word whose literal meaning is "the good ones" (from Old Latin *manus*, good), and was applied figuratively, as now in English, to the spirits of the dead or the spirit of a single departed one. In Latin it was always treated as a plural grammatically. To appease a person's *manes* is to do what would have pleased him or what was his due in his lifetime. The *manes* of a deceased could not sleep quietly, it used to be believed, until his survivors fulfilled his wishes. On February 19 of each year, the Romans made sacrifices to the shades of their family and friends, in the same way that Roman Catholics are supposed to devote November 2 to prayer for the souls of the faithful departed.

mangonel (MANG guh nel) *n.* A *mangonel* was a huge military apparatus for hurling stones, darts, javelins, etc., operated by a large crew and involving huge wheels, pulleys, etc. The name of the machine is, via Latin *manganum*, from Greek *manganon* (engine of war). However naive and quaint the *mangonel* appears to us in this day of rocket artillery (cf. **machicolation** and the military tactics discussed thereunder), it did a respectable amount of damage to walls, fortifications, and personnel in its day.

mansuetude (MAN swih toohd, -tyoohd) *n. Mansuetude* is meekness, gentleness, mildness, docility. The word comes from Latin *mansuetudo* (tameness), related to *mansuetus* (tamed), based on *manus* (hand) plus *suetus* (tame), past participle of *suescere* (to grow accustomed). An animal *accustomed* to the *hand* is tame, gentle, docile. In John 13:34 we read: "A new commandment I give unto you, That ye love one another,"and in Romans 13:8, "Owe no man anything, but to love one another." This is the doctrine of the *mansuetude* of Christian love. What a world it would be if . . .

mantic   (MAN tik) *n.*, *adj. Mantic* applies to things relating to augury and prophesy. A *mantic* person has the gift of **divination**, of foretelling the future. ("Beware the Ides of March!" etc.) The word comes from Greek *mantikos* (prophetic), an adjective from *manteia* (divination), which gave us our suffix *-mancy*, as in **myomancy**, **rhabdomancy**, etc. Used as a noun, a *mantic* is one possessed of prophetic powers, a seer. There have been many *mantics* in folklore and history, like **Cassandra**, Nostradamus (the French astrologer Michel de Nostredame, 1503–1566), to say nothing of our very own Jeanne Dixon, whose stuff (and nonsense?) is taken seriously by millions.

mariticide,   see **aborticide**

matrilocal   (MA truh loh kul) *adj.* In the science of anthropology (the study of man, including his social customs), the term *matrilocal* applies to the custom of the newlyweds' going to live with the wife's family. *Uxorilocal* (uk SOR uh loh kul, ug ZOR-) means the same thing. *Patrilocal* (PA truh loh kul, pay-) covers the converse arrangement of the new couple's residing with the husband's family. In primitive cultures, one can substitute *tribe* for *family* in these definitions. All three words are based on combinations of the Latin prefixes *matri-*, from *mater* (mother), *uxori-*, from *uxor* (wife), and *patri-*, from *pater* (father), with *-local*, from *locus* (place). Apparently, the in-law problem and attendant bad jokes were not a part of earlier cultures.

matutinal   (muh TOOHT un ul, -TYOOHT-) *adj.* A *matutinal* event is one occurring in the morning, early in the day. *Matutinal* describes anything relating to the morning, or happening in the morning. It comes from Late Latin *matutinalis* (early), derived from Latin *matutinus* (of the morning), based on Matuta (muh TOOH tuh, -TYOOH-), in Roman mythology the goddess of the dawn, as well as childbirth, and the oceans and harbors (a busy goddess!), sometimes known as *Mater* (Mother) *Matuta*. After performing his *matutinal* **ablutions** and perhaps saying his *matutinal* **orisons**, eating his *matutinal* **refection**, and, if he has a job, *matutinally* departing for work, interrupted only by his **meridional** repast, our polysyllabic protagonist (unless it's one of those late nights at the office) **crepuscularly** returns home to the wife and
264

kiddies. Changing the subject: The lark is a *matutinal* bird. Shakespeare gives us the saddest parting of lovers in *Romeo and Juliet* (Act III, Scene 5), when morning is heralded by the singing of a bird. "It was the nightingale, and not the lark," says Juliet, though she knows better, and Romeo faces reality and says, "It was the lark, the herald of the morn . . . ."

maudit (moh DEE) *n.*, *adj.* *Maudit* applies to a lost soul, a loser, a person beyond redemption, beset by unearned bad luck. The French poet Paul Verlaine (1844–1896) wrote a prose work entitled *Les Poètes Maudits* (literally, The Accursed Poets), consisting of sketches of six fellow poets, including Stéphane Mallarmé (1842–1898) and Arthur Rimbaud (1854–1891) among the six whose art went neglected and unappreciated in their day. They were symbolists, influenced greatly by Charles Pierre Baudelaire (1821–1867), conveying impressions by suggestion rather than literal statement, experimenting with form, particularly free verse. Verlaine and his contemporaries led wretched lives; hence the epithet *maudit*. The term could well be applied to the hopeless drug addicts and other derelicts who live on the streets. *Maudit* is the past participle of the French verb *maudire* (to curse).

maunder (MAWN dur) *vb.* To *maunder* is to drivel, to talk aimlessly, in a silly, dreamy, meaningless way, or to move or act in a confused, listless, rambling way. Most dictionaries give its etymology as "unknown," but the *Concise Oxford* takes a "perhaps" shot at the obsolete *maunder* (beggar, beg). Fowler says that the etymology is uncertain, but ". . . it is clear that it is not a corruption of *meander* . . . But it is also clear from the way some people use *meander* that they take the two words to be merely variant pronunciations. *Meander* means to follow a winding course, was originally used of rivers, is still often so used, describes frequent but not violent change of direction rather than aimlessness, and is applied more often to actual locomotion than to vagaries of the tongue. *Maunder* is best confined to speech, and suggests futility rather than digression, dull discontent rather than quiet enjoyment, and failure to reach an end rather than loitering on the way to it." *Meander* does have a well-known etymology, and an interesting one: via Latin *maeander*, from Greek *maiandros* (a winding), from

Maiandros, the Greek name for the Menderes River, famous for its tortuous course.

mediatize (MEE dee uh tize) *vb*. To mediatize a state is to annex it. The *mediatized* state is usually a smaller one than the annexing power. The former government is permitted to keep certain local governing powers. When Great Britain was expanding its empire, most of the provinces of India were *mediatized*, and the former sovereigns were allowed to retain some governing rights; they became "*mediatized* princes." The word was formed after the model of the German verb *mediatisieren*. The annexed state held its powers *mediately*, i.e., subject to the annexing power, rather than *immediately*, i.e., on its own, independently; in other words, indirectly rather than directly. Great Britain's imperial expansion involved many parts of the world other than India, and in more recent times, the USSR and Hitler's Germany did a fair amount of *mediatizing*, which would appear to be a euphemism for . . . shall we say, *grabbing*?

medicaster, see **poetaster**

megapterine, see **accipitrine**

megillah (muh GIL uh) *n*. *Megillah*, in Hebrew, means "scroll," in particular one that contains the Book of Esther, Ecclesiastes, the Song of Solomon, the Book of Ruth, or the Book of Lamentations. Megillah became Yiddish, later American slang for any long-winded account. In Yiddish, it was often preceded by *ganze* (GAHN tse), from German *ganz* (whole, complete). A *ganze megillah* is an exhaustive (and usually exhausting) account, the implication being that the long and elaborately detailed narrative concerned a minor matter worthy of only a much more condensed report. *Megillah* is one of a number of Yiddish words that have been naturalized into the American slang vocabulary: *meshugah* (muh SHOO guh) for "crazy, nuts"; *nosh* for "snack"; *chutspah* (CHOOT spuh—*ch* as in German *ach*) for "brazen cheek, unmitigated gall"; *shlepp* (shlep) for "carry," to name a few that have emigrated far and wide from Brooklyn and the Bronx.

meleagrine, see **accipitrine**

266

melioration, see **meliorism**

meliorism (MEEL yuh riz um, MEE lee uh-) *n. Meliorism* is the belief that everything tends to get better and better. One who lives by this doctrine is a *meliorist* (MEEL yuh rist, MEE lee uh-). These words are derived from Latin *melior* (better), the comparative of *bonus* (good). The superlative is *optimus* (best), which gave us *optimism* and *optimist*. It may be hard to find much difference between the attitudes of *meliorists* and *optimists*, but the English novelist George Eliot (1819–1880) did find a shade of difference: The English poet A. E. Housman (1859–1936) wrote, in an autobiographical note: "I am not a pessimist but a pejorist (as George Eliot said she was not an optimist but a meliorist) . . ." In Latin, *pejor* means "worse" and *pessimus* means "worst." A pejorist (whose doctrine is known as *pejorism*) believes that everything is getting worse; a pessimist thinks that it's all going to be as bad as possible: superlatively bad, shall we say, in this atomic age? In any event, George Eliot thought that the world was going to get better— but not as good as possible; and that is the fine difference between *meliorism* and *optimism*. Other words from *melior* are *ameliorate* (uh MEEL yuh rate, -ee uh-), to improve; *amelioration* (uh meel yuh RAY shun), improvement generally, but with a special use in linguistics: semantic change to a better, i.e., more favorable meaning, the way *Okie*, once a pejorative term for a migrant farm worker, usually from Oklahoma, became merely a colloquial nickname for any Oklahoman, and exactly opposite to the way *egregious* (from Latin *egregius*, extraordinary, preeminent, based on prefix *e-*, out of, plus *grege*, a form of *grex*, herd, i.e., out of the herd) changed from *preeminent* to *glaring, flagrant, notorious*, as in *an egregious blunder*. But caution: *meliority* (meel YOR ih tee, mee lee OR-) has nothing to do with attitudes about which way the world is moving; it is only an uncommon synonym for *superiority*.

meliority, see **meliorism**

menology (mih NOL uh jee) *n.* A *menology* is a calendar or register of saints' day, especially of the Greek Church; from Late Greek *menologion*, based on *men* (month) plus *logos* (discourse, account). We are familiar with the use of the prefix *meno-*, in such words as *menopause*, for instance. A *menology* shows all the fes-

267

tivals celebrated during the year honoring saints and martyrs, with brief biographical notes of each.

mensal, see **hebdomadal**

mephitine, see **accipitrine**

mephitis   (muh FYE tis) *n.* This is the term for a noxious emanation from the earth, such as a poison gas, but the word is also applied to something less deadly, like any foul, noisome stench, even if not actually poisonous. The adjective is *mephitic* (muh FIT ik), describing any offensive odor, noxious or not. Exposure to *mephitic* exhalations are to be avoided; they may or may not be poisonous, but they certainly are exceedingly offensive. Swamps give off *mephitic* odors. Living within smelling range of the *mephitic* emanations from certain industrial operations, like oil refineries, can be unhealthful, and is undoubtedly unpleasant. It is often not worthwhile putting up with the *mephitic* odors of a compost pile, despite its value as fertilizer. *Mephitis* was taken over as is from Latin; *mephitic* from Late Latin *mephiticus.* Appropriately enough, *mephitine* (see **accipitrine** and list of *-ine* adjectives attached) means "pertaining to skunks."

merkin   (MUR kun) *n.* A *merkin* is a sort of pubic wig consisting of false hair for the female pudenda. Some authorities say that *merkin* is a variant of *malkin*, a noun with several meanings, including "mop" (especially the kind used by bakers for cleaning out ovens) and "cat." Other authorities are content with "origin unknown." Whether or not there is a connection between *merkin* and *malkin* meaning "cat" (there is a close connection between *cat* and *pussy*), and however unlikely it is that you will run across this word in your reading, the burning question remains: What is or ever was the occasion for the use of this commodity? The early stages of retirement from the profession of modeling bikinis? On this, the dictionaries are silent.

metalinguistics   (met uh ling GWIS tiks) *n.* As with other *-ics* words (*economics, politics,* etc.) *metalinguistics* is construed as a singular noun. It is the study of the relationship between a language and other aspects of a particular culture, of language in relation to

268

meaning, of "body-language," i.e., expression or gesture accompanying speech, etc. It is a hybrid (derived in part from Greek, in part from Latin), based on the Greek prefix *meta-* (along with, beyond) plus the Latin noun *lingua* (tongue, language). Fowler defines *hybrids* (in the context of language) as "words formed from a stem or word belonging to one language by applying to it a suffix or prefix belonging to another." *Television* is a good example: *tele-* (a Greek prefix meaning "distant," especially "transmitting over a distance") plus *vision*, from Latin *visio*, meaning "a seeing" or "view," based on *visus*, past particle of *videre* (to see).

metathesis   (muh TATH ih sis) *n*. This is the name applied to the transposition of letters or sounds in words. It was taken over intact from the Greek, where it means "transposition," based on prefix *meta-* (beyond) plus *thesis* (something set down). Examples: *aks* for *ask*; chaise *lounge* for chaise *longue*. In Old English, *bird* was *bridd* and third was *thrid*. The modern forms were the result of *metathesis*. Similar transposition turned Spanish *tronada* (thunderstorm) into *tornado*. Spoonerism is a type of *metathesis*, in that the initial sounds of two words are transposed. *Spoiled brat* becomes *broiled sprat*; *half-formed wish* comes out as *half-warmed fish*; *loving shepherd* turns up as *shoving leopard*. Spoonerisms were named after the absentminded Rev. Canon W. A. Spooner (1844–1930), warden of New College, Oxford. *Kinkering Kongs* was his *metathesis* of *Conquering Kings*. Other kinds of tampering with words are discussed under **epenthesis** and **paragoge**.

metempsychosis   (muh tem suh KOH sis, -temp:, met um sye-) *n*. This word has nothing to do with *psychosis*, despite its last three syllables. *Metempsychosis* is transmigration of a soul, its passage after the death of a human being or an animal into the body of another human being or animal. It is taken intact, via Late Latin, from the Greek, based on the verb *metempsychousthai* (to pass from one body into another), constructed of the prefix *meta-* (indicating change) plus *en-*, which becomes *em-* before *p* and other consonants (in) plus *psyche* (soul). *Metempsychosis* is an ancient belief in the transition of the soul into another body. The Brahmins of India, worshipers of Brahma (the Absolute, God conceived as wholly impersonal, later as the Creator of the universe), and Buddhists expanded the belief to include *metempsychosis* into plants as well as animals. In the play *Faustus* by the English dramatist Christopher Marlowe (1564–1593) we read the lines:

> Ah, Pythagoras' *metempsychosis* . . .
> O soul, be changed into little water drops
> And fall into the ocean, ne'er be found . . .

It is to Pythagoras, the Greek philosopher and mathematician (c. 582–c.500 B.C.) that the doctrine of *metempsychosis* is attributed.

metonymy   (mih TON uh mee) *n. Metonymy* is a figure of speech, a rhetorical device, in which a suggestive word is substituted for the name of a related person or thing, like *the Crown* or *the Scepter* for the sovereign, *wealth* for people of means, *the bottle* for alcoholic spirits, strong drink, *a good table* for lavish food, *the ring* for boxing, *Virgil* or *Homer* for their works. *Metonymy*, like the names of most figures of speech, has a Greek origin, in this case *metonymia* (change of name), based on *met-* (shortened form of *meta-*, a prefix usually signifying change) plus *onyma* (name). *Metonymy* is a rhetorical term, but it is not reserved for rhetoricians; we use it all the time in common speech: "He hits *the bottle*"; "We counted *noses*" or "*heads*"; "We went to *the track*." In an article entitled "On the Stump," in the June 1, 1983 issue of the English magazine *Punch*, Roy Hattersley, of the British Labour Party, writes about cricket periodicals, including the *Wisden Cricket Monthly*, ". . . the real voice of the cricket establishment . . . Indeed, the very name of *Wisden* is indivisible from cricket. [Note: John Wisden was a great cricketer of the 1850s. In 1864 he produced the first issue of the *Wisden Cricketers' Almanack*, still published annually and the Bible of English and international cricket.] It is—together with *Hansard* [the official report of British parliamentary proceedings—their equivalent of the U.S. *Congressional Record*—initiated by Luke Hansard in 1774], *Debrett* [*Debrett's Peerage, Baronetage, Knightage, and Companionage*, first compiled by John Debrett in 1802 and published continually ever since] and *Burke* [*Burke's Peerage, Baronetage and Knightage*, first compiled by John Burke in 1826 and published continuously to date]—one of those words which stand *metonymy* on its head. The name of a person has turned into the name of an institution . . ." One must admire Mr. Hattersley's insight into *metonymy*. In the field of etymology, there is a phenomenon known as "*metonymic* transference," the process by which a word changes its meaning in a "metonymic" way. In Latin, *arena* (usually in the form *harena*) means "sand." The sports field in the amphitheater was covered with sand, and eventually, *(h)arena* came to mean what it means in English today: a sports center or, more widely, the scene of any contest or struggle (e.g., the "political arena"). By *metonymy*, the suggestive word was substituted for a related thing in the original language, and by the time it got to us, the original meaning was lost through *metonymic* transference.

miching, see **mallecho**

micturate (MIK chuh rate) *vb. Micturate* is another word for *urinate*, from the Latin *micturire* (to want to urinate), a **desiderative** verb based on *mictus*, past participle of *mingere* (to urinate). *Micturition* (mik chuh RIH shun) is urination. There are several euphemisms for this bodily function: *pass water, make water, use the powder room* or *boys' or gents'* or *girls' room, wash one's hands, go to the bathroom* ("Look daddy, Fido went to the bathroom on the petunias!"), etc., and in British English *spend a penny*—a reference to the insertion of a coin (it once was a penny) to unlock those little cabinets in ladies' rooms. *Micturate* is not a euphemism, just a synonym.

millenarian (mil uh NAR ee un) *n.* A *millennium* (note double *n*) is a thousand years (Latin *mille*, one thousand, plus combining form of *annus*, year). In Revelations 20:1-7, the *millennium* is the period of a thousand years during which Jesus will return to earth and live with His saints and then take them up to heaven. A *millenarian* is a believer in that *millennium*, and this belief of early Christians is now held by Mormons and Adventists. The spelling of *millenarian* with a single *n* shows that it is not directly based on *millennium*, but is a word in its own right, formed independently of *annus*. A synonym of *millenarian* is *chiliast*, based on the Greek equivalent of *mille*, *chilioi*.

milvine, see **accipitrine**

mimesis (mih MEE sis, mye-) *n.* In rhetoric, *mimesis* is the reproduction of a person's supposed or imaginable words, a device much resorted to by the writers of "historical" novels, in the reconstruction of events and the thoughts and sayings of personages. (Then Abe turned to his mother and said: "Some day, I'm goin' to live in that big white house . . .") It happens all the time in historical plays. ("I am dying, Egypt, dying . . .") In zoology, *mimesis* is quite a different story, the mimicry by one animal of the appearance of another that is distasteful to the predators of the imitator, or the imitation of a natural object like a leaf, or bark, that would be ignored by a predator. *Mimesis* is intact from the Greek, where it is related to the verb *mimeesthai* (to copy). Related words are *mime* (from Greek *mimos*, imitator); *mimetic* (from Greek *mimetikos*, imitative); *mimic* (from Greek *mimikos*, mime-like); *mimicry*; and *mimeograph*, tacking on the Greek suffix *-graph*, based on the verb *graphein* (to write).

mimetic, see **mimesis**

minacious (min AY shus) *adj.*; **minatory** (MIN uh tor ee) *adj.* Both these words mean "threatening," and both are of Latin ancestry: *minacious* from *minax* (menacing, threatening), *minatory* from *minatus*, past participle of *minari* (to threaten). Of the two, *minatory* is the more common. The primary meaning in Latin of *minax* is "projecting, jutting out," and of *minari* is to "project, jut out," and the concepts of *jutting out* and *threatening* must have merged in the past from the threat posed by an overhanging cliff or balcony that might collapse or from which rocks and other projectiles might be cast down. Projection and threat certainly merged in the position of Mussolini's chin when he was riding high and making those speeches from the balcony of the Palazzo Chigi in Rome, witnessed by this author when he was a graduate student at the University of Rome.

minatory, see **minacious**

misocapnic, see **philogyny**

misoclere, see **philogyny**

272

misogamy,   see **philogyny**

misogyny, misogynous, misogynic, misogynistic,   see **philogyny**

misology,   see **philogyny**

misoneism,   see **philogyny**

misprision   (mis PRIZH un) *n.* This is a legal term that has a number of technical meanings, but its principal use is to denote failure to notify the authorities of another person's felony. *Misprision* is in itself a crime. It comes, via Old French *mesprision*, from the prefix *mis-* (in the sense of *non-*) plus Latin *prensio*, a variant of *prehensio* (seizure, arrest). This noun has nothing to do with *misprize* (mis PRIZE), to scorn or undervalue, which has a different derivation: via Middle English from Middle French *mépriser* (to scorn).

misprize,   see **misprision**

monolithic   (MON uh LITH ik) *adj.* A *monolith* (MON uh lith), literally, is a large single block of solidly uniform stone, usually a pillar or column constructed of one piece. Figuratively, the term is applied to anything suggestive of a *monolith* because of its massiveness and uniform solidity, top to bottom, and hence of its intractability. The adjective *monolithic* is often applied to nations, particularly of the communistic persuasion, that are massive and uniform throughout in their political structure, and therefore tend to be intractable in their international dealings. Senator James W. Fulbright (b. 1905), in a memorable speech in the Senate in 1964, dared to differ from the prevailing view when he said, "The master myth of the cold war is that the communist block is a *monolith* . . ." The intervening history of Sino-Russian relations appears to have borne him out. One speaks also of a *monolithic* company or organization that is self-sufficient, in that it commands the source of its raw materials, its labor supply, its manufacturing facilities and sales outlets. The United States Government often uses legal means to break up *monolithic* organizations. The derivation from the Greek *monos* (alone) and *lithos* (stone) speaks for itself. We

273

find *monos* in many words: *monogamy, monopoly, monotony;* like-wise *lithos: lithography, lithoid, lithosphere.*

morphology   (mor FOL uh jee) *n. Morphology* has several mean-ings, all dealing with *form*, and in its broadest use, applies to the study of the form and structure of anything. The prefix *morpho-* is the combining form of the Greek noun *morphe* (form). In biology, *morphology* is the aspect dealing with the forms of animals and plants. In geology, it is the study of the features, origin, and de-velopment of land forms, and is known as *geomorphology* (jee oh mor FOL uh jee), *geo-* being the combining form of Greek *ge* (earth). In grammar, *morphology* is the study of word formations, their makeup, etymology, and inflection (changes in their endings or form depending on syntactic function, as in *boy, boys, boy's, boys'* or *go, goes, going, gone, went;* much more complex in other languages).

mortmain   (MORT mane) *n.* From Middle English *morte mayne*, based on Middle Latin *mortua manus* (dead hand), this term in law applies to the perpetual holding of title to land by a corporation or charitable trust, such as a church. The term originally described the holding of land by a religious body, but today it covers such holding by any charitable or business corporation. In medieval times, the church and monasteries acquired vast amounts of land, which were exempt from taxation and other feudal dues, a fact which laid an enormous burden on secular property. Beginning as far back as the reign of Edward I (1272–1307) and continuing right up to the 1800s, laws were enacted in England and other countries to restrict *mortmain* holdings by religious bodies, limiting that type of ownership to what was absolutely necessary. This has never been a serious problem in the United States.

moschine,   see **accipitrine**

mote   (mote) *n.* A *mote* is a speck or tiny particle, usually in the context of dust. Geoffrey Chaucer, one of England's earliest poets (c.1340–1400), wrote, in the *Tale of the Wyf of Bathe* [Wife of Bath], of "hooly freres . . . /As thikke as *motes* in the sonne-beem . . ." [as thick as *motes* in the sunbeam]. "Sudden in a shaft of sunlight/Even when the dust moves/There arises the hidden laughter/

of children in the foliage . . . ," from the poem *Burnt Norton*, by
the American-born British poet T. S. Eliot (1888–1965) is a modern
reference to Chaucer's lovely simile. In Shakespeare's *King John*
(Act IV, Scene 1), Hubert de Burgh goes through the motions of
preparing to put out, with hot irons, the eyes of young Arthur, at
the command of Arthur's uncle, King John, and says:

> Come, boy, prepare yourself.
> *Arthur.* Is there no remedy?
> *Hubert.* None, but to lose your eyes.
> *Arthur.* O heaven! that there were but a *mote* in yours.
> A grain, a dust, a gnat, a wandering hair,
> Any annoyance in that precious sense;
> Then feeling what small things are boisterous
> [rough, massive] there,
> Your vile intent must needs seem horrible.

The best known use of *mote* appears in the Bible, at Matthew 7:1–4:

> Judge not, that ye be not judged . . . And why beholdest thou the *mote*
> that is in thy brother's eye, but considerest not the beam that is in thine
> own eye? . . . Or how wilt thou say to thy brother, Let me pull out the
> *mote* out of thine eye; and, behold, a beam is in thine own eye? Thou
> hypocrite, first cast out the beam out of thine own eye; and then shalt
> thou see clearly to cast out the *mote* out of thy brother's eye.

This excellent advice is couched in quite different terms in the *New
English Bible*:

> Pass no judgment, and you will not be judged . . . Why do you look
> at the speck of sawdust in your brother's eye, with never a thought of
> the great plank in your own? Etc., etc.

This new version may be far less poetic than the old familiar language, but since *beam* in the King James must mean "plank," *mote*
would logically refer to a speck of sawdust. In either case—plain
dust or sawdust—a *mote in the eye* is a trifling fault one finds in
someone else, while blind to a much greater fault in oneself. *Mote*
is from Old and Middle English *mot* (speck).

muliebrity   (myooh lee EB rih tee) *n. Muliebrity* is womanhood,
the female nature, the characteristics of a woman; more abstractly,

275

effeminacy, softness. The word is, via Late Latin *muliebritas*, from Latin *muliebris* (womanly), based on *mulier* (woman). Its counterpart is *virility*, from Latin *virilis* (male), based on *vir* (man), but whereas *muliebrity* is most often used in the literal sense of "womanhood," *virility* is commonly understood to indicate the abstract qualities of vigor, strength, and ruggedness associated with "the stronger sex." 'Twas ever thus: the sexual chauvinism of language. *Man* and *mankind* embrace the whole human race, including *woman* and *womankind*. We hear about *homo sapiens*; how about *mulier sapiens*? In chess, even the queen is a *man*. And even an all-female crew of a lifeboat would *man* it! Up the E.R.A. !

murine, see **accipitrine**

mussitation (mus ih TAY shun) *n. Mussitation* is muttering to oneself, in a very low voice, if any, soundlessly making speaking movements. Lots of people *mussitate* while thinking things over, solving problems, planning the next move or the day's activities, cooking with exact measures of numerous components, rehearsing excuses. *Mussitation* is the converse of ventriloquism, where one speaks without making any speaking movements. The word is from Latin *mussitatus*, past participle of *mussitare* (to grumble inaudibly, keep muttering to oneself). *Mussitare* is what the grammarians call a **frequentative** of *mussare* (to murmur, mutter).

musteline, see **accipitrine**

myocardium, see **myomancy**

mygenic, see **myomancy**

myology, see **myomancy**

myomancy (MYE o man see) *n.* The Greek prefix *myo-* appears in a number of words pertaining to *muscle*, since *myo-* is the combining form of the noun *mys* (muscle). Thus we have *myocardium* (heart muscle), *myogenic* (originating in a muscle, said of a physical sensation), *myology* (the study of muscles), and other *myo-* words having to do with muscles. What about *myomancy*, then? Well, we said *myo-* was based on the noun *mys*—but *mys* has a second and
276

entirely distinct meaning: it means "mouse" as well as "muscle." And -*mancy* is a suffix based on the Greek noun *manteia* (**divination**, prophecy). All this, with the result that *myomancy*—surprise!—is divination or prophecy based on watching the movements of mice. With all due respect to palmists, astrologers, and the readers of tea leaves and tarot cards—why not?

myrmidon (MUR mih don, -dun) *n.* A *myrmidon* is any follower or servant or underling who carries out his superior's orders remorselessly, blindly, without pity or fear or merest thought of contradiction. The word was taken from the *Myrmidons*, in classical mythology a fierce, warlike people of ancient Thessaly, in northern Greece, whose king was Achilles. They accompanied him to the siege of Troy. Shakespeare makes much of Achilles's *Myrmidons* in *Troilus and Cressida*. In Act V, Scene 5, Ulysses says:

> . . . great Achilles
> Is arming, weeping, cursing, vowing vengeance . . .
> Together with his mangled *Myrmidons*.

In Scene 7, Achilles commands:

> Come here about me, you my *Myrmidons* . . .

and gives them orders to slay Hector where they find him. Again, in Scene 7, he cries:

> Strike, fellows, strike! . . .
> On! *Myrmidons*, and cry you all amain
> 'Achilles hath the mighty Hector slain.'

A chief characteristic of the *Myrmidons* was their fierce, unflinching devotion to their leader, whom they obeyed without scruple. Hence *myrmidon*, with a lower case *m*. The prime example in modern times is Adolf Eichmann, who was executed by the Israelis as a war criminal despite his defense that he was "simply" carrying out his masters' orders—the common defense of war criminals on trial. The British use *myrmidon* in a somewhat wider sense: to denote any hired ruffian or thug, and *myrmidon of the law* as a pejorative to signify "policeman" or other officers of the law employed to execute writs of attachment and the like.

mythicize, see **mythopoeic**

mythomania, see **mythopoeic**

mythopoeic (mith uh PEE ik) *adj. Mythopoeic* describes anything related to myth-making, or giving rise to a myth. *Myth* comes from Greek *mythos* (story), and *mythopoeic* from Greek *mythopoios* (making stories), based on *mytho-*, the combining form of *mythos*, plus the suffix *-poios* (making), from the verb *poiein* (to make). We are familiar with the noun *mythology*, but not with *mythomania* (mith uh MAY nee uh), which is not a craze for reading or hearing myths, but a psychiatric term for excessive exaggeration or lying to an abnormal degree. To *mythicize* (MITH ih size) an event is to treat or explain it as a myth, and this practice is known as *mythicization* (mith uh sye ZAY shun). The controversial Bishop Jenkins of Durham, England, scandalized adherents to the Anglican faith by *mythicizing* the Virgin Birth and the Resurrection. See also **historicity**.

naiad, see **nereid**

neologism (nee OL uh jiz um), **neology** (nee OL uh jee) *n.* A *neologism* or *neology* is a new-coined word or phrase, or a new usage. The term can also be applied to the introduction or use of a new word or a new meaning of a word or phrase. One who indulges in that practice is a *neologist* (nee OL uh jist); the practice can be described as *neologistic* (nee ol uh JIS tik) or *neologistical* (nee ol uh JIST uh kul). *Neologism* comes from the French *néologisme*, derived from the Greek prefix *neo-* (new) plus the Greek noun *logos* (word). The Irish writer James Joyce (1882–1941) made masterful uses of *neologisms* in the linguistic inventions introduced in his great novel *Ulysses*, published in 1921, and went even further in his extremely difficult last major work *Finnegans Wake*, published in 1939. A friend of the author, Henry Morton Robinson (1898–1961), a writer himself, coauthored with Joseph Campbell a *Skeleton Key to Finnegan's Wake*, and was somewhat miffed when this author suggested he then write a *Key to the Key*. Both Joyce's novels

278

are rich in their play with words and are the quintessence of *neologism*. Another use of the terms *neologism* and *neology* is to denote the adoption of new or rationalistic religious views or doctrines, or new interpretations of holy writings. Some examples of contemporary *neologisms*: guesstimate; cheesecake (photographs of female shapeliness); *snafu* (acronym for "situation normal: all fucked up"); *corny*; *wolf* (male who makes amorous advances to lots of women); *soap opera*; *baloney*, *applesauce*, *eyewash* and *banana oil* (nonsense); *grapevine* (unofficial communication system or rumor); *piece of cake* (task easily accomplished); *chicken* (young girl, or scared); *sexpertease*, from a 1950 short short story entitled *Great in the Hay* by the American writer Norman Mailer (b. 1923).

neoteric   (nee uh TER ik) *n.*, *adj.* The adjective means "modern, of recent origin, new." A *neoteric* is a modernist, one who admires modern ideas, ways, art forms; a modern writer, thinker, etc. *Neoteric* comes, via Late Latin *neotericus*, from Greek *neoterikos* (youthful), equivalent to *neoteros* (newer, younger), the comparative of *neos* (new), which gave us the familiar prefix *neo-* (new, recent), as found in words like *neologism*, *neophyte*, *neoclassic*, etc. *Neon*, the neuter form of *neos*, was the name given to the inert gas discovered by Sir William Ramsey and M. W. Travers in 1898, and is Greek for "something new." Apparently, they didn't know what else to call it. "Nuisance," they should have called it, when you consider the look of our urban streets at night.

nepenthe   (nih PEN thee) *n.* This is the name of an Egyptian drug taken by the ancients to banish sorrow or care and make people forget their woes. *Nepenthe* has now been applied to anything that has that effect. The name comes from Greek *nepenthes* (soothing herb), noun use of the adjective meaning "without sorrow," based on prefix *ne-* (not) plus *penthos* (grief). It is mentioned in the *Odyssey*—a drug given by Polydamna, wife of King Thonis of Egypt, to Helen (daughter of Jupiter, in the guise of a swan, and Leda), wife of Menelaus, King of Sparta. Her elopement with Paris, Prince of Troy, resulted in its siege and destruction by the Greeks. The English poet John Milton (1608–1674) mentions this incident in *Comus*:

> That *nepenthes* which the wife of Thone
> In Egypt gave to Jove-born Helena . . .

Fowler says: "The -*s* is part of the Greek word and should have been retained in English; but it has very commonly been dropped, probably from being mistaken for the plural sign, cf. *pea* for *pease* etc. . . . But in ordinary use the word has been superseded by *tranquilliser*." (Note double *l*, and *s* for *z*, in British English spelling, though -*ize* has taken over in some words in Britain. And our *inning* for their *innings* is another example of the dropping of an -*s* mistakenly taken as the sign of a plural.)

nephalism (NEF uh liz um) *n. Nephalism* is the creed of the teetotaler, the complete abstinence from alcohol. It is from Greek *nephalios* (sober), related to the verb *nephein* (to be sober). A teetotaler is a *nephalist* (NEF uh list). An alcoholic friend of the author, trained in the classics and redeemed by Alcoholics Anonymous, now refers to *nephalism* as *neverlism*, and who can begrudge him his little pun?

nereid (NEER ee id) *n.* A *nereid*, in classical mythology, is a sea nymph, one of the 50 or 100 daughters, by the Oceanid (see **oread**) Doris, of Nereus, an old sea god who lived with his *nereids* in the depths of the sea, particularly the Aegean. Do not confuse the saltwater *nereids*, who live in the ocean, with the freshwater *naiads*, who inhabit lakes and streams, or you may be in trouble with Nereus, who not only can transform himself into fire, water, and many other shapes, but is strong enough to wrestle with Hercules. One must be careful about these things.

nescience (NESH uns, -ee, uns) *n. Nescience* is ignorance, lack of knowledge. It comes from Late Latin *nescientia*, based on the prefix ne- (not) plus Latin *scienta* (knowledge), which gave us our noun *science*. *Nescience* is one of a group of words composed of a prefix plus -*science: omniscience* (om NISH uns—universal knowledge); *prescience* (PREE shee uns, -shuns, PRESH ee uns, PRESH uns—foreknowledge). All these words have related adjectives: *nescient* (ignorant), *omniscient* (all-knowing), *prescient* (clairvoyant, prophetic). It is the *nescience* of the masses that permits the rise of demagogues. In Shakespeare's *Julius Caesar* (Act I, Scene 1),

280

the Tribune Marullus, disgusted with the *nescient* common throng, calls them "You blocks, you stones, you worse than senseless things . . ." In these days when reading has so much given way to sitting in front of the boob tube (awake or asleep), *nescience* is fast becoming epidemic.

nestorine,   see **accipitrine**

nictitate   (NIK tih tate), also **nictate** (NIK tate) *vb*. To *nictitate* (or *nictate*) is to close and open one's eyes, i.e., to wink. It is from Middle Latin *nictitatus*, past participle of *nictitare*, the **frequentative** of Latin *nictare* (to wink), itself the frequentative of *nicere* (to beckon). *Nictitation* (nik tih TAY shun) is winking, a time-honored method of flirting (old-fashioned), or showing one is wise to what's happening, or simply beckoning, as indicated by the connection between the Latin verbs *nicere* (beckon) and *nictare* (wink). For some reason, *nictitation*, with a little shake of the head, evokes the image of Mae West and "Why doncha c'm up an' see me some time?"

nimiety   (nih MYE ih tee) *n*. A *nimiety* of something is too much of it, an overabundance, the opposite of a *paucity*. *Nimiety* is from Late Latin *nimietas*, based on the Latin adjective *nimius* and adverb *nimis* (very much, too much). *Paucity* is from Latin *paucitas* (scarcity), based on the adjective *pauci* (few; plural of *paucus*). The Roman playwright Terence (c. 190–159 B.C.), in his comedy *Andria*, expressed the view that ". . . the most important thing in life was never to have too much *(nimis)* of anything," while the English lexicographer and writer Samuel Johnson (1709–1784) wrote: "It is very strange, and very melancholy, that the *paucity* of human pleasures should persuade us ever to call hunting one of them," which brings to mind the words of the Irish playwright and poet Oscar Wilde (1854–1900): "The English country gentleman galloping after a fox—the unspeakable in full pursuit of the uneatable." The next time your host asks how much vermouth you want in your martini, reply: "Neither a *nimiety* nor a *paucity*," and see what happens. You may never be invited there again.

noctambulism   (nok TAM byuh liz um) *n*. *Noctambulism*, like its more familiar synonym *somnambulism*, is another word for "sleepwalking." *Noctambulation* (nok tam byuh LAY shun), like

281

somnambulation, means the same thing, and a *noctambulist* (nok TAM byuh list), like a *somnambulist*, is a sleepwalker. All the *noct-* words are based on Latin *nox* (night) plus *ambulare* (to walk), while *somnabulism* and its associated words are built on Latin *somnus* (sleep) and *ambulare*. Another *noct-* word is *noctivagant* (nok TIV uh gunt), night-wandering, involving Latin *vagari* (to wander). *Noctuary* (NOK tooh uh ree), a record of night happenings or thoughts, is built on the model of *diary*, the *u* being borrowed from Latin *nocturnus* (by night), and where would Chopin have been without that word? Freudian psychoanalysts set great store by dreams, and often advise patients to enter them in a *noctuary* on awakening, though they never seem to use that word.

noctilionine, see **accipitrine**

noctivagant, see **noctambulism**

noctuary, see **noctambulism**

nodus (NO dus) *n. A* nodus is a knotty point, a difficult situation, a complication in the plot of a play or story. In *De Arte Poetica* (on the Art of Poetry), the Roman poet Horace (65–8 B.C.) warns against those convenient coincidences that writers sometimes grasp at: "A god should not intervene unless a *nodus* develops worthy of his interference."

noesis (noh EE sis) *n.* Noesis is intellectual activity, the exercise of reason. It was taken intact from the Greek, where it means "intelligence" or "thought," based on the verb *noein* (to think). The adjective *noetic* (noh ET ik) describes things pertaining to the intellect, as does the Greek source, *noetikos*, and is used as well to mean "purely intellectual" (as opposed to emotional or intuitive) or "abstract." *Noetics*, treated as a singular noun, is the science of the mind or intellect. Scientists must put aside bias, preference, or emotion, and determine results purely *noetically*.

nomology (no MOL uh jee) *n.* Nomology is the science of law. The word comes from the Greek prefix *nomo-*, the combining form of *nomos* (law), related to the verb *nemein* (to control, manage). *Nomothetic* (nom uh THET ik) means "legislative, lawgiving" or "based on law," or applies to the study or formulation of universal

282

laws, as opposed to *idiographic*, which relates to the study of individual cases. *Nomothetic* is from Greek *nomothetikos: nomo-* plus *-thetikos*, from *thetos* (set), past participle of *tithenai* (to lay down), while *idiographic* involves the Greek prefix *idio-* (peculiar, individual), plus *-graphikos*, related to *graphein* (to write). Our word *thetic* (THET ik), meaning "positive," also comes from *thetikos*.

nomothetic, see **nomology**

notchel (NOCH ul) *n.*, *vb.* To cry someone *notchel* is to give notice, usually by advertisement, of refusal of responsibility for that person's debts. To *notchel* someone means the same thing. These are dialectical colloquial terms of unknown origin. The person whose debts are involved is generally the wife who has left the bed and board of the *notcheler* (serves her right). Occasionally, the *notchelee* is an ex-business partner.

noumenon (NOOH muh non, NOU-) *n.* A *noumenon* is a thing whose existence can be assumed only by purely intellectual nonphysical intuition, conceived by reason as opposed to perception by any of the physical senses. A *noumenon* is an unknowable object whose actual existence is theoretically problematic, especially God and the soul. The concept of the *noumenon* is part and parcel of the philosophical system of the German philosopher Immanuel Kant (1724–1804), the antithesis of a *phenomenon*, a thing as it appears in actual experience. *Noumenon* is from Greek *nooumenon* (thing being perceived), a noun use of the neuter form of the present participle passive of *noein* (to think). See also **noesis, nous**.

noun of assembly, see **collective noun**

noun of multitude, see **collective noun**

nous (noohs, nous) *n.* In Greek philosophy, *nous* was the Platonic term for *mind, intellect, intelligence;* now, in upper-class colloquial usage, *nous* is *common sense, horse-sense, understanding*; in slang, *savvy*; sometimes it is used for "gumption." It is a Greek word, (related to **noesis**) taken into English. In *The Dunciad*, a bitter satire on dunces and literary hacks aimed principally at the English poet and critic Lewis Theobald (1688–1744) who in his *Shakespeare Restored* pointed out errors in the edition of Shakespeare by the English poet Alexander Pope (1688–1744), Pope wrote a couplet demonstrating *his* pronunciation of *nous*:

> Thine is the genuine head of many a house,
> And much divinity without a NOUS.

According to *Brewer's Phrase & Fable*, ". . . the system of divinity referred to . . . is that which springs from blind nature," i.e., "without a *NOUS*."

novercal (noh VUR kul) *adj.* Legend has it that stepmothers are harsh and cruel to their stepchildren: Snow White and Cinderella and that crowd had very tough going. That was because of the *novercal* aspect of the relationship with daddy's new wife. *Noverca* is "step mother" in Latin, and *novercalis* describes anything pertaining to stepmothers. There must, of course, be good, kind, loving stepmothers, who don't exhibit the fearful *novercal* qualities celebrated by the Brothers Grimm and Hans Christian Andersen. *Vitricus* is Latin for "stepfather," but the expectable "vitrical" never made it into the English language.

numen, see **numinous**

numinous (NOOH muh nus, NYOOH-) *n.*, *adj.* Anything described as *numinous* is spiritual, has a sacred quality, is mysterious and awe-inspiring. *Numen* (NOOH mun) is literally "nod" in Latin, related to the verb *nutare* (to nod, or keep nodding), and by extension came to mean "divine will" (as indicated by the *nod* of a god). *Numen* was taken over intact, to mean "divine power" or "spirit," and gave rise to the adjective *numinous*, which denotes a quality that is divine, especially in the sense that it is beyond human understanding. There is something *numinous* in the late quartets of Beethoven. Dark forests have a *numinous* quality that inspires reverence and awe. The Roman satirist Juvenal (60–c. 130) wrote that if people had foresight, Fortuna wouldn't be a goddess—she would have no *numen*.

nuncupative (NUNG kyuh pay tiv, nung KYOOH puh tiv) *adj.* This adjective means "oral" and is more or less confined to the term *nuncupative will*, denoting a last will and testament spoken aloud to a witness or witnesses, rather than one in written form executed with the usual formalities. The word comes from Late Latin *nuncupativus*, derived from Latin *nuncupatus*, past participle of the verb *nuncupare* (to name, call by name; in connection with wills, to nominate as heir or legatee), probably based on the phrase *nomen capere* (literally, to take a name; figuratively, to utter a name publicly). *Nuncupative* wills are usually recognized if made by a person in extremis, i.e., in anticipation of imminent death, or by soldiers on the battlefield or sailors engaged in battle—those unable to get to lawyer Jones's office, talk things over, and come back to sign a document in the presence of witnesses with the customary rigmarole—but statutory rules differ in various jurisdictions. *Nuncupative* wills are rare. Even if you are young and healthy, find a lawyer to prepare a will, execute it at his or her office, put it in a safe place, preferably with your lawyer, but not in your safe deposit box, because that might necessitate getting a court order to open the box in order to get the will for probate. Incidentally, *nuncupative* is all too often misspelt *noncupative*, the *nun-* degenerating into *non-* under the influence of the *un-* in *unwritten*.

nympholepsy (NIM fuh lep see) *n*. The ancients believed that a kind of ecstasy or frenzy took hold of a person who had caught sight of a nymph. Such a person was known as a *nympholept* (NIM fuh lept), in Greek, *nympholeptos* (one caught by nymphs), based on *nymphe* (nymph) and *leptos* (seized). *Nympholepsy* was formed of a blend of *nympholept* and *epilepsy* in the sense of "seizure." Apart from the delightful world of nymphs, *nympholepsy* denotes any frenzied yearning for the unattainable, and a *nympholept* is a person with such a yearning, someone inspired by violent enthusiasm for an unattainable ideal.

obeah (O bee uh), **obi** (O bee) *n*. This is a West African word for a type of voodoo, sorcery, or witchcraft engaged in among black persons mainly in Africa and the West Indies, particularly Haiti. The words are also applied to any charm or fetish employed in the ceremony. The original West African meaning of these words was an object buried in the ground to cause illness, death, or other grave misfortune.

obi, see **obeah**

obiter dictum (OB ih tur DIK tum). This expression applies generally to any incidental or cursory remark not necessarily germane to the subject under discussion, but its use is practically confined to the law, to describe a judge's incidental expression of opinion, not essential to his decision in giving judgment, and therefore not binding as setting a precedent. In Latin, *obiter* is an adverb meaning "in passing, by the way, incidentally," and *dictum*, the neuter form of *dictus*, the past participle of *dicere* (to say), means, literally, "a thing said," so that an *obiter dictum* is a thing said incidentally, not constituting a point essential to the decision reached. The English politician and writer Augustine Birrel (1850–1933), professor of law at University College, London, wrote a series of witty and polished essays published in 1884 under the title *Obiter Dicta*. His name gave rise to the term *birrellism*, a name for a good-humored but thoughtful comment tinged with irony. *Obiter* is formed from the Latin prefix *ob-* (toward) plus *iter* (way): *toward the way*, as it were, but not *to the point*.

objurgate (OB jur gate) *vb*. To *objurgate* is to denounce harshly, to upbraid vigorously, to berate sharply, to reproach in no uncertain terms, to give 'em hell. *Objurgate* is from Latin *objurgatus*, past participle of *objurgare* (to scold, chide, reprove), based on prefix *ob-* (against) plus *jurgare* (to rebuke), based in turn on *jur-*, stem of *jus* (law, right) plus *agere* (to drive). *Objurgation* (ob jur GAY shun) is the noun, and a great deal of it is heard at the United Nations (which is given as an example of **oxymoron** in another part of this book).

oblate (OB late, ob LATE) *n*. An *oblate* is a layman residing and serving in a monastery, not under monastic vows or regulations. There are various Roman Catholic organizations to which laymen, known as *oblates*, devote their services in special religious or charitable work. The term is from Latin *oblatus*, past participle of *offerre* (to offer). *Oblation* (o BLAY shun), as a general term, applies to any offering for charitable or religious purposes; specifically, in the Eucharist, it denotes the offering of bread and wine. One of the novels of the French writer Joris Karl Huysmans (1848–1907) is entitled "The Oblate."

Occam's razor   (OK umz RAY zur). This is the popular name of a maxim originated by William of Ockham (d. 1349), the Franciscan scholastic philosopher, born, it is believed, at Ockham, Surrey, England. He was known as the *Doctor Singularis et Invincibilis* (Singular and Invincible Doctor) because of his remarkable intellectual prowess. His maxim: All superfluous assumptions raised in the discussion of a subject under analysis should be eliminated, i.e., the fewest possible assumptions are to be made in explaining a thing. William "dissected" all questions as with a razor; hence the expression *Occam's razor*. He argued that many questions previously considered accessible to human knowledge (immortality, God's existence, the soul) were objects exclusively of faith and must be excluded from the fund of man's intellectual knowledge. William was of Ockham, and from Missouri as well.

oceanid,   see **oread**

octopine,   see **accipitrine**

odyssey   (OD ih see) *n*. An *odyssey* is a long, adventurous journey, a wandering full of hardships and notable experiences. The word comes from the epic poem *The Odyssey*, attributed to the eighth century B.C. Greek poet Homer, also the reputed author of *The Iliad*, the epic poem about the siege of Troy, whose Latin name was *Ilium*. Odysseus, the hero of *The Odyssey*, was King of Ithaca and the greatest, most valorous, and wisest of the Greek leaders in the Trojan war. His Latin name was *Ulysses*. *The Odyssey* celebrated the trials and tribulations of Odysseus during his ten years' journey *(odyssey)* to return to Ithaca at the conclusion of the Trojan war, and eventually lent its name to any long, trying journey marked by memorable experiences.

oeillade   (u(r)-ee AD) *n*. This is a French word taken into English, whose meaning depends on the circumstances. It can denote an innocent glance, or a less than innocent ogle or leer with amorous implications. *Oeil* (u(r)-EE, pronounced as one syllable) is

French for "eye" and the -*ade* suffix is common in both French and English nouns denoting action (*blockade*, *renegade*, *tirade*, etc.). In Shakespeare's *King Lear* (Act IV, Scene 5), Regan says to Oswald, her sister Goneril's steward:

> I know your lady does not love her husband;
> I am sure of that; and at her late being here
> She gave strange *oeillades* and most speaking looks
> To noble Edmund . . .

And in *Merry Wives of Windsor* (Act I, Scene 3), Falstaff, speaking to Pistol of Mistress Page, says: " . . . who even now gave me good eyes too, examined my parts with most judicious *oeillades*; sometimes the beam of her view gilded my foot, sometimes my portly belly . . ." In *Lear*, *oeillades* takes the form *eliads*, in *Merry Wives*, *iliads*; *oeillades* is the form in modern editions. Elizabethan spelling leeves mutch to bee deezyr'd.

oenologist,   see **oenology**

oenology   (ee NOL uh jee) *n.* *Oenology* is the science of viniculture, the knowledge and study of wines. An *oenologist* (ee NOL uh jist), as you might expect, is one engaged in that field. There are a great many would-be *oenologists*, amateurs in the field, who on the slightest provocation, or none at all, will gladly tell you rather more than you care to know about wines, châteaux, regions, which slope, etc. There is a whole series of *oeno-* words, based on the Latin prefix *oeno-*, from the Greek *oino-*, based on *oinos* (wine). Thus, in addition to *oenologist*, we have *oenophilist* (ee NOF uh list), combining *oeno-* and the suffix -*phil*, from Greek *philos* (dear, loving)—a lover of wine; *oenophobist* (ee NOF uh bist), *oeno-* plus -*phob*, from the Greek *phobos* (fearing)—a hater of wine; *oenopoetic* (ee nuh poh ET ik), *oeno-* plus *poetic*, from Greek *poetikos* (productive)—describing anything relating to the making of wine; and *oenomel* (EE nuh mel), *oeno-* plus *mel*, from Greek *meli* (honey)—a mixture of wine and honey, a word which has as well the meaning of "somethine combining strength and sweetness," used in a figurative sense, especially in the field of language or thought. Perhaps, as in the case of the quasi-*oenologist* mentioned above, you have been told more than you cared to know about *oeno-*; it is to be hoped that it is not so. But we must say something about the word *wine* itself, which presents an interesting etymological problem: Is it related to German *Wein* or to Latin *vinum* and Greek *oinos*? Probably all of them. Incidentally, Oeno, the daughter of Anius, a son of Apollo and the king of Delos, was empowered by Dionysus to change *anything* into wine. This has nothing to do with the miracle at Cana (John 2:1–11).

oenomel, see **oenology**

oenophilist, see **oenology**

oenophobist, see **oenology**

oenopoetic, see **oenology**

oligopoly (ol uh GOP uh lee) *n.*; **oligopsony** (ol uh GOP suh nee) *n.* These words that sound confusingly alike are taken together for that reason, and because they are the converse of each other and both relate to market conditions. An *oligopoly* is a sellers' market, the condition that obtains when there is a dearth of sellers and a small group of firms control the market, producing a state of limited competition. Prices go up. An *oligopsony* is a buyers' market, when there are few buyers and each competitive buyer influences the market. Prices go down. *Oligopoly* comes from the Greek prefix *oligo-*, a combining form of *oligos* (little, few) plus the Greek verb *polein* (to sell). *Oligopsony* is derived from the Greek prefix *olig-*, combining form of *oligos* before a vowel, and the Greek noun *opsonia* (purchase of food).

oligopsony, see **oligopoly**

olio (OH lee oh) *n.* An *olio*, literally, is a stew made up of a large number of ingredients. Figuratively, *olio* is used for a medley, whether of musical pieces or literary passages. *Olio*, going further, can cover any miscellany, whether of styles, colors, ideas, or whatever. See **gallimaufry**. *Olio* comes from the Spanish noun *olla* (pot, stew), which is derived from Late Latin, where it means "jar" or "pot."

omphalos (OM fuh lus) *n.* The literal meaning of this word, taken intact from the Greek, is "navel." It is used figuratively to mean "central point" or "hub." *Omphalos* was the name originally applied to a conical stone in the temple of Apollo at Delphi that was reputed among the ancients to mark the exact center of the earth (then thought to be flat). Legend had it that when Zeus, in his quest for the earth's center, started two eagles of equal speed simultaneously, one from the eastern rim of the earth, the other from the western, they met at Delphi. Any centrally located place came to be called the *omphalos* of its region. In addition to denoting the geographical center, *omphalos* can be understood in the sense of a spiritual hub, so that Rome or the Vatican is the *omphalos* of Roman Catholicism, while Jerusalem is the *omphalos* of Judaism.

onager (ON uh jur) *n.* This word has two distinct meanings, which appear at first to have nothing whatever to do with each other, and indeed, the connection is tenuous. An *onager* is a wild ass, habitat central and southwestern Asia. It is from Greek *onagros*, based on *onos* (ass) plus *agrios* (wild), related to *agros* (field). *Onager* is also the name of an ancient and medieval war machine in the nature of a great catapult operated as a sling for throwing large stones loaded into a bag or wooden bucket. *Onager* was a colloquial term in Late Latin for *scorpion*, a Biblical name (I Kings 12:11) for a *whip* or *scourge*, figurative for that military device with a "tail" that "stung." A wholly different word, *trebuchet* (TREB yoo shet) was also the name of a medieval engine of war for launching heavy missiles. *Trebuchet* was derived from Old French *trebucher* (to overturn). Both *onagers* and *trebuchets* served to make breaches in defense walls, with sorry results for the defenders.

oneiric (oh NYE rik) *adj.* *Oneiric* describes anything relating to dreams. There is a group of *oneiro-* words based on the Greek noun *oneiros* (dream) and the ancient Greek god of dreams *On(e)iros*. The *e* in *oneiro-* is optional. An *oneirocritic* is an interpreter of dreams and *oneirocriticism* is the interpretation of dreams, from *oneirokritikos* (pertaining to dream interpretation), based on *oneiro-* plus *kritikos* (judging, skilled in judgment). *Oneiromancy* is prophecy based on dreams, *oneiro-* plus *manteia* (**divination**). *Oneirodynia* is troubled sleep, nightmare, *oneiro-* plus *odyne* (pain). *Oneirology* is the study of dreams, *oneiro-* plus *logos* (word, dis-

290

course). An *oneiroscopist*, like an *oneirocritic*, is an interpreter of dreams, *oneiro-* plus *skopia* (watching). Altogether, a very dreamy subject, and an oneirodynia-free night's sleep to you.

oneirocritic,   see **oneiric**

oneirodynia,   see **oneiric**

oneirology,   see **oneiric**

oneiromancy,   see **oneiric**

oneiroscopist,   see **oneiric**

oniomania   (oh nee uh MAY nee uh) *n.* A *mania*, we know, is a craze; from the Greek, via Latin, *mania* (madness). *Onios* is Greek for "for sale," hence *oniomania*, a mania or craze for buying things, abnormal acquisitivenss, and one afflicted with it is an *oniomaniac* (oh nee uh MAY nee ak). One of the most renowned *oniomaniacs* of modern times was the American newspaper publisher William Randolph Hearst (1863–1951), whose ranch and castle in San Simeon, California, were famous as a depository of art, antiques, objets d'art, and miscellanea of every description. A more recent *oniomaniac* was the subject of a BBC (London) documentary shown on July 14, 1985 on the *Great Collections* series, described in the previous day's (London) *Times* program notes as follows: "Henry P. McHenny . . . admits that he cannot resist buying things and has the money to indulge his passion . . . bolstered by funds provided by his mother, he began a lifetime's buying spree . . ." The film showed him "surrounded by one of the finest collections of 19th century French paintings." *That's* real *oniomania*!

onomastic   (on uh MAS tik) *adj. Onomastic* applies to anything pertaining to proper names. *Onomastics*, as a noun construed as singular (cf. *economics*, *politics*, etc.), is the study of proper names, their origin and history. *Onomatology* (on uh muh TOL uh jee) is synonymous with *onomastics*. An *onomasticon* (on uh MAS tuh kon) is a dictionary of proper names. All these words are based on

the Greek adjective *onomastikos*, equivalent to *onomasos* (named), **past** participle of *onomazein* (to name), stemming from *onoma* **(name).** *Onomastic* has a special use in law, describing a signature **to** a handwritten document written in handwriting different from **that** in which the document itself is written.

onomasticon,   see **onomastic**

onomatology,   see **onomastic**

ophidian,   see **herpetology**

ophiolatry,   see **herpetology**

ophiology,   see **herpetology**

oread   (OR ee ad) *n.* An *oread*, in classical mythology, is a mountain nymph. The *oreads* were the companions of the Greek goddess Artemis, whose Roman name was Diana, goddess of the hunt and the woodlands, and considered sacred to the moon. The name *oread* is derived from the Greek noun *oros* (mountain); in *oread*, *naiad*, etc., *-ad* is a Greek suffix with the effect of "related to." The *oreads* are mentioned by the English poet Shelley (1792–1822; alas, so young!) in the *Witch of Atlas*, along with other nymphs:

> The Ocean-nymphs and Hamadryades,
> *Oreads* and Naiads, with long weedy locks . . .

The naiads were water-nymphs who populated lakes and streams. The dryads or hamadryads were tree-nymphs. The ocean-nymphs Shelley mentions were the oceanids. Lots of nymphs, lots of romance; what innocence! See also **nereid.**

orison   (OR i zun) *n.* An *orison* is a prayer. Rarely met with nowadays, it was much favored by Shakespeare. Perhaps the most familiar use of it by anyone is from Hamlet's speech to Ophelia in Act III, Scene 1, as she enters at the end of the "To be, or not to be . . ." soliloquy:

Soft you now!
The fair Ophelia! Nymph, in thy *orisons*
Be all my sins remember'd . . .

In *Romeo and Juliet* (Act IV, Scene 3), Juliet says to her nurse:

I pray thee, leave me to myself tonight;
For I have need of many *orisons*
To move the heavens to smile upon my state,
Which, well thou know'st, is cross and full of sin.

In Act I, Scene 4 of *Henry VI, Part 3,* as Lord Clifford is about to carry out Queen Margaret's command to kill the Duke of York, she says:

Nay, stay; let's hear the *orisons* he makes.

Orison is from French *oraison* (oration, prayer), derived from Latin *oratio*, based on *orare* (to speak, pray).

orogeny, see **orography**

orography (oh ROG ruh fee) *n. Oro-* is a Greek prefix, the combining form of *oros* (mountain), and our suffix *-graphy* is from *-graphia*, a Greek suffix based on the verb *graphein* (to write), denoting drawing, writing, and describing, as well as an art or science, as in *geography*, *photography*, etc. Together *oro-* and *-graphy* make *orography*, the earth science dealing with mountains. The related word, *orogeny* (oh ROJ uh nee, or-) covers the study of the origin and formation of mountains; from the same *oro-*, plus the suffix *-geny*, from the Greek suffix *-genia*, based on *genes* (born, produced). Logically enough, an *orometer* (oh ROM ih tur) is a barometer showing elevation above sea level, used in the measurement of the heights of mountains and volcanoes.

orometer, see **orography**

orotund (OR uh tund) *adj.* This is an adjective descriptive of a full, rich, articulate voice or speech, but it has acquired as well the pejorative meaning of "pompous" when applied to a style of speaking. It comes from the Latin phrase *ore rotundo* (with a round mouth; figuratively, well-turned speech). That quality of voice or speech is known as *orotundity* (or uh TUN dih tee). The Roman poet Horace (65-8 B.C.) in *Ars Poetica (The Art of Poetry*, Wickham translation), wrote; "It was the Greeks who had at the Muse's hand the native gift, the Greeks who had the utterance of finished grace." The Latin for the last four words is "ore rotundo . . . loqui," literally "to speak with a round mouth." *Ars Poetica* brings to mind the couplet from *Prologue to the University of Oxford* by the English poet John Dryden (1631–1700):

> So poetry, which is in Oxford made
> An art, in London only is a trade.

orphic   see **icarian**

orthoepy,   see **cacoepy**

orthography   (or THOG ruh fee) *n. Orthography* is correct conventional spelling, and is also the name of that section of grammar dealing with letters generally and spelling. *Orthography* comes, via Latin, from Greek *orthographia* (correct writing), based on the prefix *ortho-*, from the adjective *orthos* (straight, correct) and the verb *graphein* (to write). *Orthography* has a special meaning in drafting, for a technique of perspective projection used in maps and elevations in which the viewer is in theory infinitely far away so that the projection lines are parallel and a scale drawing results. In this technical sense, *orthography* is also called *orthogonal* (or THOG uh nul) *projection*.

oscine,   see **accipitrine**

oscitance, oscitancy, oscitation,   see **oscitant**

oscitant   (OS ih tuhnt) *adj. Oscitant*, literally, describes a person yawning with drowsiness, but figuratively, it is used to mean "drowsy," or "inattentive, dreamy, off in a world of one's own, oblivious, wool-gathering," and that sort of thing. Its use has been expanded to include "dull, lazy, unmindful, neglectful." The daydreaming youngster who forgets his chores may well be described as *oscitant*. The word is from Latin *oscitans* (yawning), the present participle of *oscitare* (to yawn, gape), based on *os* (mouth) plus

294

citare (to put into violent motion). To be in an *oscitant* state is *oscitance* (OS ih tuhns) or *oscitancy* (OS ih tuhn see); *oscitancy* means "yawning" or "sleepiness," but its use has been extended to include "stupidity." *Oscitation* (os ih TAY shuhn) means "yawning" or "sleepiness," depending on the context. If the context includes a political speech, it could mean either or both.

osseous (OS ee uhs) *adj. Osseous* describes things consisting of bones, containing bones, or bonelike. Anything bony can be described as *osseous*, or *osteal* (OS tee uhl). *Osseous* comes from the Latin *osseus* (bony), based on the noun *os* (bone), the basis of many medical terms starting with the prefix *osteo-. Ossiferous* (o SIF uhr uhs) applies to anything containing bones, and often refers to fossil bones. An *ossuary* (OSH ooh air ee), also known as a *charnel house* (a repository for corpses, from Late Latin *carnale*, noun formed from the neuter of Latin *carnalis*, based on *carn-*, stem of *caro*, flesh) is a receptacle for the bones of the dead, from Late Latin *ossuarium*; also a bone-urn, or a cave in which ancient bones are discovered.

ossiferous, see **osseous**

ossuary, see **osseous**

osteal, see **osseous**

ostracine, see **accipitrine**

oubliette (ooh blee ET) *n.* This rather pleasant-sounding word, taken from the French, suggests a fragile piece of Louis XV furniture or a lovely old-fashioned flower out of a cottage garden—but not so! It is, in fact, the name of something quite dreadful: a secret pit in the floor of a dungeon, enclosed by four thick walls, accessible only through a trap door at the top, through which the wretched prisoner would be flung—and forgotten. Hence the name: *oubliette* comes from the French verb *oublier* (forget). Horrid thought! The French use *oubliette* methaphorically in the expression *mettre aux oubliettes*, meaning "assign to oblivion."

ovibovine, see **accipitrine**

ovine, see **accipitrine**

oviparous, see **viviparous**

ovoviviparous, see **viviparous**

oxymoron (ok sih MOR on) *n.* An *oxymoron* is a figure of speech utilizing the joining of seemingly self-contradictory terms to produce the effect of irony through paradox. The word was taken intact from the Greek neuter form of the adjective *oxymoros* (pointedly foolish), based on the adjectives *oxys* (sharp) plus *moros* (foolish—from which we get *moron*). Examples: to *make haste slowly*, to *kill with kindness, benign neglect, interesting bore;* and the famous lines from *Lancelot and Elaine*, by the English poet Alfred Lord Tennyson (1809–1892):

> The shackles of an old love straiten'd him,
> His honour rooted in dishonour stood,
> And faith unfaithful kept him falsely true.

Honour rooted in dishonour—faith unfaithful—falsely true! Now, there's a collection of *oxymora* if there ever was one. A waggish friend of this author, disillusioned by the news of the day, has suggested, as *oxymora, United Nations* and *peace-keeping force.* A few additional suggestions: *civil service; military intelligence; jumbo shrimp.*

pachydermatous (pak ih DUR muh tuhs) *adj. Pachyderm* (PAK ih durm) is a familiar term for *elephant* and certain other thick-skinned animals that are hoofed and do not chew their cud. The derivation is from Greek *pachys* (thick) and *derma* (skin). *Pachydermatous* is the adjective. The word *pachyderm* is applied figuratively to a person who is "thick-skinned," i.e., insensitive, especially to criticism, insults, or ridicule, or to his surroundings, and *pachydermatous* describes a person or a personality of that sort. There are ham actors who have somehow developed a *pachydermatous* indifference to boos, jeers, and ridicule. *Pachyder-*
296

matous people are more than uncouth or boorish; they are simply impervious to the reactions they produce.

palimpsest   (PAL imp sest) *n.* This is the name for a piece of parchment, vellum, or other writing surface from which the original writing has been completely or partially erased to provide room for another writing—a common practice in ancient times because of the scarcity of material. We owe the discovery of certain ancient texts, notably the *De Republica* of the Roman statesman and writer Cicero (106-43 B.C.), to *palimpsests* on which enough of the original writing has remained to make possible the restoration of the entire text. In the case of the Ciceronian work, the partial erasure had been made to provide room for a discourse by St. Augustine on the Psalms. There exist interpolated *palimpsests*, where the new text is inserted between the lines of the original writing. *Palimpsest* comes, via Latin *palimpsestus*, from Greek *palimpsestos* (rubbed again), based on *palin* (again) plus *psestos*, past participle of *psen* (to rub off, scrape).

palindrome   (PAL in drome) *n.* A *palindrome* is a word or a series of words that reads the same way backward or forward. It is from Greek *palindromos* (running back, recurring), based on *palin* (again) plus *dromos* (running, course). Here are some examples: *rotator; nurses run;* (what Adam said to Eve—herself a *palindrome*—when he first made her acquaintance): "Madam, I'm Adam"; (what Napoleon said when his luck ran out): "Able was I ere I saw Elba"; (a campaign slogan apocryphally credited to Teddy Roosevelt's speechwriters): "A man, a plan, a canal, Panama"; *deified*, and a couplet in which it appears: "Dog as a devil deified/ Deified lived as a god." The first recorded *palindrome* in the English language is ascribed to the poet John Taylor (1580-1653) and goes: "Lewd did I live & evil did I dwel," but he, with characteristic Elizabethan scope in spelling, chose to spell *dwell* with one *l* and used an **ampersand.** *Palindromes* exist in other languages. For example, the French give us: "Léon n'osa rêver à son Noël" (Leon didn't dare dream about his Christmas), but you have to ignore the diacritics. One who dreams up these things is a *palindromist* (pal IN dro mist). The adjective is *palindromic* (pal in DROM ik, -DROH mik). *Palindrome* applies to numbers, too: e.g., 2270722. *'Nuf fun* with *palindromes*?

palinode (PAL uh node) *n.* A *palinode*, literally, is a poem in which the poet retracts something expressed in an earlier poem, but *palinode* has come to denote any retraction or recantation or disavowal. This noun comes, via Late Latin *palinodia*, from Greek *palinoidia* (singing anew, recanting), based on *palin* (again, back) plus *oide* (song). There are *palinodes* famed in history. The Greek lyric poet Stesichorus (fl. c. 600 B.C.), of whose works only fragments survive, wrote a *palinode* to Helen of Troy recanting a previous poem describing her as evil, for which he had been struck blind by the gods. The Roman poet Horace (65–8 B.C.) wrote an ode (Book I, Ode 16) in which he apologized for an earlier scurrilous peom, ending his *palinode*: "Now I am anxious to replace bitter taunts with soothing strains, if only, after I recant my taunts, you become my friend and restore my peace of mind." The English poet Isaac Watts (1674–1748) wrote a *palinode* retracting earlier praise for Queen Anne and expressing his disillusionment because of her acts in the later part of her reign. More latterly, Patrick Leigh Fermor, the English writer (b. 1915), in his travel-memoir *A Time of Gifts* (Harper & Row, New York, 1977), speaks of the "disillusioned *palinodes* that lay in wait for most of [his] . . . friends" who had earlier succumbed to left-wing opinions. Here, *palinode* was used in its general sense of "retraction" or "disavowal."

pallium (PAL ee um) *n. Pallium* (a Latin word) is the name of the large rectangular cloak worn as an outer garment in classical times by Greek men, and in imitation, by learned Roman men. In matters of church dress, the *pallium* is the woolen garment worn by the pope and conferred by him upon bishops, as a symbol of office. It consists of a narrow band resting on the shoulders, with loosely hanging flaps in front and behind. The verb to *palliate* and the noun *palliative* come from Late Latin *palliatus* (cloaked, covered), related to the *pallium* that cloaked the body.

palmary (PAL muh ree) *adj.* The leaf of the palm tree has long been considered a symbol of victory, excellence, preeminence. The motto of Admiral Nelson (1785–1805) was "Palmam qui meruit, ferat" (Let him bear the palm who merits it). From this symbolism came the word *palmary*, meaning "praiseworthy, preeminent," derived from Latin *palmaris* (deserving the palm; excellent, admirable), based on *palmarius* (pertaining to the palm tree, *palma* in Latin). A *palmary* achievement, like the landing of the men on the moon, or the winning of a Nobel Prize, is a notable one, deserving reward and acclaim.

paludal   (puh LOOHD ul) *adj*. *Paludal* applies to anything having to do with swamps or marshes, or produced by marshes, like diseases, especially malaria, or miasma, noxious atmosphere arising from rotting organic matter. *Paludal* comes from Latin *palud-*, the stem of *palus* (swamp). *Paludism* (PAL yuh diz um) is a medical term for malaria. The *paludal* countryside was one of the main problems encountered in the digging of the Panama Canal, producing malarial conditions that had to be overcome so that construction could continue.

paludism,   see **paludal**

pandemic   (pan DEM ik) *adj*. *Pandemic* means "universal" or "general." Applied to a disease, it describes a condition prevalent throughout a country, a continent, or the entire world, like smallpox in the old days. There is now a *pandemic* dread of an atomic war. Starvation is *pandemic* in some African countries. *Pandemic* is from Greek *pandemos* (common), basd on the prefix *pan-* (all) plus *demos* (people). It is a long step further than *epidemic* (from Greek *epidemia*, among the people, based on the prefix *epi-*, upon, plus *demos*), which describes unhappy conditions prevalent in a community, rather than the entire world or a very large part of it.

panjandrum   (pan JAN drum) *n*. This is a mock title used of a self-important, pompous, pretentious person, a burlesque of a self-imagined potentate. The word is a piece of pseudo-classical nonsense consisting of the Greek prefix *pan-* (all) plus the humbug-Latin *-jandrum*, so that the word is not only nonsense but hybrid in the bargain. *Panjandrum* was concocted by the English playwright and actor Samuel Foote (1720–1777) in a bit of gibberish composed to test the memory of the old actor Charles Macklin (c. 1697–1797). who had boasted that he could remember anything after reading it once. He was so angry when he saw the passage that he refused to have anything to do with it. Here is the passage, with certain variations in spelling indicated in parenthesis:

So she went into the garden to cut a cabbage leaf (cabbage-leaf) to make an apple pie (apple-pie), (;) and at the same time a great she-bear, coming up the street, pops its head into the shop (came running up the street and popped its head into the shop). "What! No soap?" So he died, and she (—) very imprudently—married the barber. (;) And (and) there were present the Picninnies, (and the) Joblillies, (and) the Garyalies (Garyulies), and the grand (Grand) *Panjandrum* himself, with the little round (red) button at top (a-top), and they all fell to playing the game of catch as catch can (catch-as-catch-can) (,) till the gunpowder ran out at the heels of their boots.

Panjandrum is now used as a jocular pejorative to signify a person in high position who takes himself too seriously.

panoptic (pan OP tik) *adj*. Literally, *panoptic* applies to anything that makes it possible to view all parts of something, the way a *panoptic* aerial view of enemy emplacements reveals all the elements. Figuratively, *panoptic* can be used in the sense of "exhaustive, all-inclusive," describing something that considers all the aspects of a given subject, like a *panoptic* treatment of a particular era, or a *panoptic* view of the contemporary novel. The name *panopticon* (pan OP tuh kon) was applied by one Jeremy Bentham to a prison of his design, circular in form, with a warden's room in the center permitting him to oversee all inmates' cells from a single vantage point. *Panoptic* is from the Greek adjective *panoptes* (all-seeing); *panopticon* is from Greek prefix *pan-* (all) plus *optikon* (sight).

panopticon, see **panoptic**

pantagruelian (pan tag rooh EL eeun) *adj*. This term may be applied to the conduct of any jolly, drunken, coarse, boisterous boon companion of the nature of Pantagruel, the son of Gargantua (see **gargantuan**) and the hero of the satirical novel bearing his name by the French novelist François Rabelais (1495–1553). Like his father, Pantagruel was a giant of incredible proportions, under whose tongue there was room enough to shelter a whole army from the rain, and in whose mouth and throat there was space enough for entire cities. Pantagruel's name came from the Greek *pan* (all—cf. the *pan-* in *panorama*, *pantheism*, etc.) plus Arabian *gruel* (thirsty), based on the fact that he was born during a drought that lasted more than three years. *Pantagruelism* is coarse, lusty, bois-

300

terous humor and clowning, but in reality (as the novel shows), behavior of serious purpose.

pantherine, see **accipitrine**

parachronism (pa RAK ruh niz um) *n.*; **prochronism** (PROH kruh niz um, PROK ruh -) *n.* These words are taken together because they are both types of *anachronism* in the sense of "error in chronology." A *parachronism* is the assignment of a date that is too late; a *prochronism* the assignment of a date that is too early, and this word is a synonym of **prolepsis** used in that sense. *Parachronism* is derived from the Greek prefix *para-* (beyond) plus *chronos* (time); *prochronism* is from the Greek prefix *pro-* (before) plus *chronos*. Both are incorrect time references, or *anachronisms* (from Greek *anachronismos*, formed of prefix *ana-* backwards, plus our old friend *chronos*). *A Connecticut Yankee in King Arthur's Court*, by the American humorist Mark Twain (Samuel Langhorne Clemens, 1835–1910), is an example of a *prochronistic* spoof. Shakespearean plays done in modern dress are *parachronistically* disturbing. *The Time Machine* of the English novelist H. G. Wells (1866–1946) worked both ways.

paraclete (PAR uh kleet) *n.* A *paraclete* is a person called upon for aid or support in time of need; an advocate or intercessor. With an upper case *P*, *Paraclete* is used as a title of the Holy Ghost, the Comforter, in John 14:26, when Jesus, comforting his disciples, says: ". . . The Comforter, which is the Holy Ghost, whom the Father will send in my name, he shall teach you all things . . ." (In the *New English Bible*, the Holy Ghost is called "your Advocate, the Holy Spirit.") *Paraclete* is from the Late Greek *parakletos* (comforter: literally, one called in to aid), related to the verb *parakaleein* (to call in), based on the prefix *para-* (beside) plus *kaleein* (to call). In the poem *Veni, Creator Spiritus* of the English poet John Dryden (1631–1700), we read the lines:

> O source of uncreated light
> The Father's promised *Paraclete*!

The French scholar, philosopher, and theologian Peter Abelard (1079–1142), of Abelard and Héloïse fame, founded a school called

Paraclete, where he and Héloïse were buried until their remains were removed to Père-Lachaise cemetery, Paris, in 1817.

paradigm (PAR uh dim, -dime) *n.* In grammar, a *paradigm* is a complete set of the inflected forms that can be built on a single stem, e.g.: *girl, girl's, girls, girls'; love, loves, loving, loved.* In highly inflected languages, the list would be many, many times longer: in nouns, all the cases, singular and plural, sometimes also dual; in verbs, all the persons, tenses, voices, moods, participles, and their inflections. As a general term apart from grammar, *paradigm* can mean "example, pattern, model." It is from Greek *paradigma* (pattern), related to the verb *paradeiknynai* (to show side by side), based on the prefix *para-* (beside) plus *deiknynai* (to show—also discussed under **elenchus** with respect to *deictic*).

paragoge (par uh GOH jee) *n.* A *paragoge* is the addition of one or more letters, or a sound, to the end of a word, whether as language develops (among*st*, amid*st*, again*st*; peasan*t*—cf. French *paysan*), or as a result of illiteracy (drown*d*, acros*t*, heigh*tth*, chance*t*—pronounced *chanst*). *Paragoge* was taken intact, via Late Latin, meaning "lengthening of a word," from the same word in Greek, meaning "leading by" or "change," based on *paragein* (to lead past), formed of prefix *para-, par-* before a vowel (beside), plus *agein* (to lead). See also **epenthesis** and **methathesis.**

paralipsis, see **apophasis**

paranymph (PAR uh nimf) *n.* A *paranymph* is a bridesmaid, or (surprisingly enough!) a best man, also known as a *groomsman*, at a wedding. The one word can apply to either sex. The Greek source of this word, *paranymphos*, could do for either the friend of the groom who accompanied him when he went forth to fetch the bride, or the bridesmaid who escorted the bride on her way to the groom, in accordance with the customs of ancient Greece. This is strange in view of the etymological basis of the word: *para- (beside)* plus *nymphe* (bride), but it can be supposed that the context would eliminate any ambiguity. All the English news reports of the marriage of England's Prince Andrew (now Duke of York) to Sarah Ferguson referred to Andrew's younger brother Prince Edward as

Andrew's *supporter*, the term replacing *best man* in the case of a royal wedding.

paraph (PAR uf) *n*. A *paraph* is a flourish after a signature to a document, originally to prevent forgery, later merely for decorative purposes and sometimes to lend importance. *Paraph* was taken from the French *paraphe*, based on Middle Latin *paragraphus* (the paragraph symbol:) shortened from *paragraph* to *paraph* by **syncope**. Never confuse *paraph* with **paraphilia**! People who indulge in fancy flourishes after their signatures may have quite normal sexual appetites.

paraphilia (par uh FIL ee uh) *n*. *Paraphilia* is sexual perversion, and a *paraphiliac* is a person who indulges in abnormal sexual practices. (Just what is "normal" and what isn't is another matter; some would understand *paraphilia* to signify any sexual activity other than the missionary position, but one man's meat . . . This subject is for a quite different book.) *Paraphilia* comes from the Greek prefix *para-* (beside, amiss, abnormal) plus *philia* (liking for).

parapraxis, parapraxia, parapraxic, see **praxis**

pararhotacism, see **rhotacism**

parataxis (par uh TAK sis) *n*. This is a grammatical term for putting together clauses or sentences without a connective. Examples: *Don't worry, I'll see to everything. You're so kind, I don't know what I'd have done without you. Come along, dear, we'll be late. Parataxis* is from the Greek prefix *para-* (beyond) plus *taxis* (arrangement).

pardine, see **accipitrine**

parietal (puh RYE ih tul) *adj*. If you said *parietal* to a doctor, he would think of a medical problem having to do with the skull, and *parietal* has other meanings in biology and botany too technical to go into here. The sense of *parietal* you are apt to come across pertains to the rules and regulations of a college with respect to what goes on within its walls, *parietal* being from Late Latin *par-*

ietalis (pertaining to walls) based on Latin *paries* (wall). When this author was at college (then an all-male institution, whose *parietal* adornment was ivy), it was a *parietal* rule that no one appeared in class or dining-hall without jacket and tie. ("This rule is not negotiable," the rule book stated.) A very serious *parietal* mandate pertained to the presence of a female in a dormitory room outside of closely restricted occasions (even at those the door had to remain open): penalty, nothing less than expulsion. Nowadays, with most institutions coeducational and dormitories unisex, anything goes. (Are there any surviving *parietal* rules?)

paronomasia (par uh noh MAY zhuh, -zhee uh) *n. Paronomasia* covers puns and other types of plays on words, like jokes based on **homophones** and **homonyms**, etc. Fowler points out the "best known of all (though concealed in English,)" in Matthew 16:18: "*Thou art Peter* (Greek *Petros*), *and upon this rock* (Greek *petra*) I will build my church.*" Another pun "concealed in English" was uttered by the English classical scholar Richard Porson (1759–1805), who, returning home at night somewhat in his cups, seeking both whiskey and a candle, muttered: "Oude tode oude tallo" ("Neither one nor the other," in Greek), *tode* being a pun on *toddy* and *tallo* one on *tallow*. Complicated, but ingenious. Porson, incidentally, drank too much and there is a tale about the start of an after-dinner speech made by the English poet A. E. Housman (1859–1936) at Trinity, Cambridge, where Porson taught: "Cambridge has seen strange sights. It has seen Wordsworth [the English poet, 1770–1850] drunk and Porson sober. Tonight, gentlemen, you see a better scholar than Wordsworth and a better poet than Porson, neither drunk nor sober, just betwixt and between." What Housman really meant was that he was a better poet than Wordsworth and a better scholar than Porson! And how's this for a concealed pun? After two years of fighting in India, the British General Sir Charles Napier (1782–1853), in 1843, sent home a dispatch announcing his conquest of the elusive province of *Sind*—in a single word: "Peccavi." This is Latin for "I have *sinned*." Fun, even if apocryphal; and it is to be presumed that the boys at the War Office had worked hard at their classics at Eton and Harrow. *Paronomasia* is from Greek, where it means "slight name-change," based on prefix *para-*, *par-* before a vowel (beside) plus *onoma* (name). Shakespeare did not hesitate to use puns, even under horrendous circumstances. In *Romeo and Juliet* (Act III, Scene 1), after Mercutio is hurt in the duel with Tybalt, dying, he jests: ". . . ask for me tomorrow, and you shall find me a *grave* man . . ." And in *Macbeth* (Act II, Scene 2), Lady Macbeth tells Macbeth to "smear/The sleepy grooms with blood," and when he refuses, she says, "If he [Duncan] do bleed/I'll *gild* the faces of the grooms withal;/For it must seem their guilt." Under lighter circumstances, in *Merry Wives of Windsor* (Act I, Scene 3), the fat, boastful Falstaff says to his cronies Pistol et al.: "My honest lads, I will tell you what I am *about*," and Pistol puns: "Two yards, and more." Falstaff responds: "No quips, now, Pistol. Indeed, I am in the *waist* two yards *about*, but I am now *about* no *waste*; I am *about* thrift." See, too, Shakespeare's puns in *Henry IV, Part I*, discussed under **termagant**. The Austrian pianist Artur Schnabel (1882–1951) invented a spoonerism in German that (like the Lord's pun to Matthew and Porson's in Greek) is "concealed" in English:

> Von vierzig Jahr' war *Schnabel nur*
> Am Ende einer *Nabelschnur.*

(Forty years ago Schnabel was only—*war Schnabel nur*—at the end of an umbilical cord—*Nabelschnur.*) The English writer Laurence Sterne came up with a "concelaed" pun in French. Having dined in a French inn with a fair French companion, he was asked for payment after he had already paid, and had to pay again. He said, "Sur mon *foie*, j'ai *déchargé* deux fois." This was bad French for "Sur ma *foi*, j'ai *payé* deux fois." What he meant to say, in English, was "Upon my faith (*ma foi*), I've paid (*payé*) twice." Instead, in his bad French, he said: "Upon my liver (*mon foie*) I've *discharged* twice." The witty lady came back with a pun: "Mieux que sur mon *con*." She said *con* (cunt) instead of *compte* (account). In other words, "Good thing you didn't discharge twice upon my cunt." Naughty lady. Can we say that Sterne con-cock-ted that one? Writing in *The Listener*, the BBC weekly program magazine, of August 8, 1985, Fritz Spiegel discusses word-plays, intentional and accidental, involving dat ole debbil sex. "With 'organ'," he writes, "you never know whether the user is being innocent . . . But surely Dickens cannot have been so innocent when he wrote (in *Martin Chuzzlewit*): 'She touched his organ, and from that bright epoch, even it, the old champion of his happiest days, incapable as

305

he had thought of elevation, began a new and deified existence.' ''
And ''E. M. Forster apparently had no misgivings about writing (in
A Room with a View): '. . . I do detest conventional intercourse.
Nasty! . . . Oh, the Britisher abroad!' '' We could continue in this
vein, but space does not permit further intercourse. However, see
also **collective noun**.

paronym (PAR uh nim) *n.* A *paronym* is a word based upon
the same root, i.e., having the same derivation, as another. It is
from Greek *paronymon*, the neuter form of *paronymos*, based on
par- (*para-* before a vowel) plus *onoma* (name). The adjective is
paronymic (par uh NIM ik) or *paronymous* (puh RON uh mus).
Examples of *paronymous* pairs or groups: *wise, wisdom*; *dote, do-
tage, dotard*; *will* (noun), *willing* (adjective); *free, freedom*; **paronomasia**, *paronym*. One must not assume that words that sound
alike and are somewhat related in meaning are *paronyms*. *Sorrow*
and *sorry* may appear to be *paronymous*, but *sorry* is from Old
English *sarig*, Low German *serig*, while *sorrow* is from Old English *sorg*, German *Sorge*.

parrhesia (pa REE syuh, -zyuh) *n.* *Parrhesia* is boldness of
speech. In oratorical rhetoric, i.e., the art of influencing an audience, *parrhesia*, in the words of William Safire (*On Language*, in
The New York Times Magazine of October 21, 1984), ''has a specialized meaning: 'warning of potential offense, and asking pardon
in advance.' '' The expression *with all due respect* (in Britain, they
shorten it to *with respect*) is an example of *parrhesia*: What it really
means is, ''I haven't the slightest respect for you and certainly not
for what you just said, and I'm going to show you up before this
prestigious audience for the blithering idiot you are . . . !'' In *Words
Fail Me* (Hamish Hamilton, London, 1980), the English linguist
and columnist Philip Howard calls *with (all) respect* a ''Benedict
Arnold phrase,'' and goes on: ''In academic circles, the man who
begins his remarks *with respect* means 'I am about to demolish
your argument and if possible you with a buzz-saw of disre-
spect.' '' Mr. Howard then quotes Alfred Friendly, the witty *Washington Post* journalist: ''When, in argument, an Englishman says
to me, 'With all respect . . . ,' I know he means that he has no
respect at all for what I have said . . . I rather like it. In telegraphing
the punch, it gives me a moment to prepare myself for the fact that

he is about to knock the neck off a bottle and ream me a new arsehole with what remains." Mr. Safire quotes President Reagan's frequent oratorical use of "Forgive me, but . . ." as an example of *parrhesia*, which amounts to a warning that he is about to follow up his plea for forgiveness with a withering blast at his political adversary. The word comes from the Greek prefix *para-* (beside, beyond—as in, e.g., *parapsychology*) plus *rhesis* (speech). Forgive me, but you ought to pay more attention to the derivation of our wonderful English words.

parricide, see **aborticide**

parturient, see **parturition**

parturition (par too RISH un, -tyoo-, -choo-) *n. Parturition* is childbirth, the act of producing offspring. It is from Late Latin *parturitio* (labor in childbirth), from Latin *parturitus*, past participle of *parturire* (to have labor pains), related to *parere* (to give birth to, to bring forth). *Parturient* (par TOOR ee unt, -TYOOR-) describes the state of being in labor, about to give birth; figuratively, it can apply to producing ideas (offspring of the mind), concepts, inventions. *Parturient* is from the present participle of *parturire, parturiens.* Related words are *postpartum* (post PAR tum) and *antepartum* (AN tee par tum). *Postpartum* pertains to the period after childbirth, derived from Latin *post* (after) plus *partum*, accusative form of *partus* (birth); *antepartum* to the period preceding childbirth, derived from Latin *ante* (before) plus *partum. Postpartum* (or its more familiar synonym *postnatal*) depression is a condition sometimes experienced by women after childbirth, resulting from a sudden drop in the hormone progesterone.

pasquinade (pas kwuh NADE) *n., vb.* This word has an amusing history. A *pasquinade* is an anonymous satirical and sometimes scurrilous attack or lampoon posted in a public place. To *pasquinade* a person is to attack him in that way. The attack is most often political in nature. The story runs that in the 15th century there lived in Rome a tailor (some say barber) named Pasquino, who was famous for his stinging, sharp-tongued wit. After his death, a mutilated ancient Roman statue was unearthed and put up in the vicinity of the Piazza Navona, opposite Pasquino's house. Nobody knew whom the statue represented, so the people called it *Pasquino*, and thereafter annually affixed political, religious, and personal satires to it which were given the name *pasquinata* in Italian, and from that came *pasquinade*. The story goes on to tell us that in another part of Rome there stood a statue of Mars called *Marforio*, to which those attacked in *pasquinades* affixed their replies if so inclined. Both the *pasquinades* and the replies were in verse, mostly doggerel.

passel (PAS ul) *n.* A *passel* is a group, of indeterminate number but with the implication that the number is somewhat large. The funeral of John F. Kennedy was attended by a *passel* of heads of state. Summit meetings usually involve a *passel* of expert advisers. A *passel* is not necessarily a *swarm*, a term that would more aptly apply to the clique or claque that surrounds professional boxers and rock stars when they appear out of the ring or off the stage. *Passel* is simply a modification of *parcel*, which comes, via French *parcelle* (portion, particle) from Latin *particula* (particle; diminutive of *pars*, part). Strange, that a word whose ancestor meant "small part" should come to have the implication of a large mass.

passerine, see **accipitrine**

passim, see **sic**

pathetic fallacy (puh THET ik FAL uh see). We are familiar with both words, but in this phrase, their individual meanings go off in unusual directions: *Pathetic* means "produced by one's feelings" and *fallacy* means "figure of speech" or "literary license." The phrase was coined by the English writer and art critic John Ruskin (1819–1900) in his work *Modern Painters* and denotes the tendency to ascribe human emotions to nature, to anthropomorphize, to endow animals and inanimate objects with human characteristics. (*Anthropomorphize*, from Greek *anthropos*, man plus *morphe*, form.) Examples: The American marine biologist and writer Rachel Carson (1907–1964) wrote *The Sea Around Us*. The Scottish poet Robert Burns (1759–1796) wrote: "How can ye chant, ye little birds,/And I sae weary fu' o' care!" The "friendly skies" of a certain airline was dreamt up by an advertising agency. In *pathetic fallacies*, flames devour, tempests are pitiless, and mountains challenge. There is nothing "pathetic" or "fallacious," in the ordinary sense, about *pathetic fallacies*.

patrilocal, see **matrilocal**

paucity, see **nimiety**

pavonine, see **accipitrine**

pecksniffian (pek SNIF ee un) *adj.* This wonderfully expressive word is applicable to any hypocrite endeavoring to impress upon his fellows that he is a person of great benevolence or high moral standards. It comes from a character named Seth Pecksniff, in *Martin Chuzzlewit* (another great name) by the English novelist Charles Dickens (1812–1870), who described Pecksniff as having ". . . affection beaming in one eye, and calculation shining out of the other." The American writer and critic H. L. Mencken (1880–1956), in *The American Language*, called Philadelphia "the most *pecksniffian* of cities." He was quite an inventor of words; for example, *bibliobibulus*, meaning "one who gets drunk on books" (*biblio*-, as in *bibliophile*, plus *bibulous*, addicted to drink): "There are some people who read too much: the bibliobibuli. I know some who are constantly drunk on books, as other men who are drunk on whiskey or religion." This passage is from his *Mencken Chrestomathy* (see **chrestomathy**).

peculate (PEK yuh late) *vb.* To *peculate*, or engage in *peculation* (pek yuh LAY shun), is to embezzle, i.e., to appropriate someone else's money or other asset entrusted to one's care. *Peculate* is from Latin *peculatus*, past participle of *peculari* (to embezzle: literally, to make public property "private"). *Peculate* is etymologically related to *peculiar*, from Latin *peculiaris* (as one's own), in the sense of "distinctly characteristic of" or "belonging exclusively to" someone or something, as in the *peculiar* (characteristic) sounds of the music of a certain composer, or the *peculiar* properties or effects of a certain drug. When a person *peculates*, he makes someone else's property *peculiar*, so to speak, to himself (temporarily, we hope—until the cops catch up with him).

peculation, see **defalcation**

pedicular, see **pediculosis**

pediculicide, see **aborticide**

pediculosis (puh dik yuh LOH sis) *n.* This word denotes the unhappy state of being infested with lice. The adjective is *pediculous* (peh DIK yuh lus). *Pedicular* (puh DIK yuh lur) describes anything pertaining to lice. All these words are from Latin *pediculus*, diminutive of *pedis* (louse).

pedology, see **genethlialogy**

pedophile, pedophilia, see **catamite**

pejorism, see **meliorism**

pelagic (puh LAJ ik) *adj. Pelagic* means "pertaining to the ocean." In biology, *pelagic* is the term applied to plants and animals inhabiting the surface of the sea, far from land. The word comes, via Latin *pelagicus*, from Greek *pelagikos*, based on the noun *pelagos* (sea). *Pelagic* is synonymous with *thalassic* (thuh LAS ik), which too means "pertaining to the ocean," although it is sometimes distinguished from *pelagic* (or *oceanic*) as applying to seas, gulfs, etc., rather than oceans—a rather thin distinction. *Thalassic* is somewhat wider than *pelagic* as a biological term, meaning "marine" generally, so that it applies to plants and animals growing and living in the sea, whether or not at or near the surface. The Greek noun *thalassa* (ocean) is the source here. In *The Anabasis* of the Greek historian Xenophon (c. 430–c. 355 B.C.), he reports that when the ten thousand Greeks, in their retreat (*katabasis*: see **anabasis**) from the interior of Babylonia first caught sight of the sea, they cried out, in their relief, "Thalatta! Thalatta!" (The sea! The sea!), *thalatta* being an Attic form of *thalassa*. The German poet Heinrich Heine (1797–1856) wrote a poem entitled "Thalatta! Thalatta!" with the lines "Thalatta! Thalatta! Hail to thee O Sea, ageless and eternal." The English poet Barry Cornwall (1787–1874) in his poem *The Sea* wrote the lines:

> The sea! the sea! the open sea!
> The blue, the fresh, the ever free!

310

And the English novelist Iris Murdoch (b. 1919 and still going strong, God bless her!) wrote a novel entitled *The Sea! The Sea!* in which her hero lives in a house by the edge of the sea, which plays an important role in the story.

pelf (pelf) *n*. This is a contemptuous pejorative for "money, riches," or "filthy lucre," from *lucrum*, Latin for "profit"; in slang—"loot," and appropriately so, for *pelf* is from Middle English and Old French *pelfre* (booty) and is probably connected with *pilfer* (to steal in small quantities, acquire through petty theft). Money is often regarded contemptuously: 'It's only money"; or "Who steals my purse steals trash," says Iago (Shakespeare's *Othello*, Act III, Scene 3) to Othello, " 'tis nothing . . .''; and from the First Epistle of Paul to Timothy: "The love of money is the root of all evil." "I have arrived at a **flocci-pauci-nihili-pili-fication** of money," wrote the Scottish novelist Sir Walter Scott (1771–1832) in his *Journal*, "and I thank Shenstone [the English poet William Shenstone (1714–1763) in a 1777 letter] for inventing that long word." (But see **floccinaucinihilipilification** for the true authorship and spelling of that word.) Scott harps again on the belittling of money in *The Lay of The Last Minstrel* ("Breathes there a man with soul so dead" etc.): "High though his titles, proud his name,/Boundless his wealth as wish can claim;/Despite those titles, power and *pelf*,/The wretch concentered all in self,/Living shall forfeit fair renown,/And doubly dying shall go down/ . . . Unwept, unhonour'd, and unsung." So much for *pelf*! In *Timon of Athens*, Shakespeare uses *pelf* when, in Act I, Scene 2, the "churlish philosopher" Apemantus, spurning Timon's food and drink, poetizes: "Immortal god, I crave no *pelf*;/I pray for no man but myself . . ." So much for *pelf* again!

pellucid (puh LOOH sid) *adj*. *Pellucid* means "clear," both physically, as in a *pellucid stream* or *lake*, and figuratively, as in *pellucid prose*, i.e., writing that is explicit in meaning. *Pellucid* is from Latin *pellucidus*, a variant of *perlucidus*, based on the prefix *per-* (thoroughly, utterly) plus the adjective *lucidus* (light, clear, lucid). The waters off Caribbean shores are all unusually beautiful in color and *pellucid*. The writings of the American novelist Henry James (1843–1916), and those of the English poet and novelist Thomas Hardy (1840–1928) are notable for their *pellucid* quality.

American author Edgar Rice Burroughs (1875-1950), the creator of Tarzan, wrote a screwball fantasy, called *Pellucidar*, about a hollow inner earth with a small, perpetually shining (naturally) sun at its center—all accessible through a polar opening.

Pelmanism (PEL muh niz um) *n.* This is the name quite arbitrarily given to a memory-training system known as the Pelman Institute, established about 1900 by its founder, W. J. Ennever. He chose that name because he thought it easy to remember. The wide advertising of the course led to the coining of the verb to *pelmanize*, to get good results through memory training. A similar system instituted by a man named Cody swept the United States not long thereafter. His ubiquitous advertisements showed a salesman making a terribly good impression on a potential customer by greeting him (he had only met him once, and some time previously) with: "Mr. Addison Sims of Seattle!" This became a jocular greeting among the enlightened, along with "Dr. Livingstone, I presume?" *Pelmanism* became as well the name of a children's card game that depended largely on mental concentration and memory.

penelopize (pih NEL uh pyze) *vb.* to *penelopize* is to act like Penelope (pih NEL uh pee), the wife of Ulysses (Odysseus, in Greek mythology) and the model of all domestic virtues. According to Homer, she was beset by suitors at Ithaca, of which her husband was king, while he was away at the siege of Troy. To get rid of them and their pestering, she promised to choose one of them as soon as she had finished making a shroud for her father-in-law, Laertes. Each night she unraveled what she had produced the previous day, and thus succeeded in postponing her choice until Ulysses came home, whereupon he slew all the suitors. The "Web of Penelope" is a piece of work never-ending, but always in progress. Cf. **sisyphean**, but Penelope's never-ending task was self-imposed.

pentimento (pen tuh MEN toh) *n.* A *pentimento* is the emergence or reappearance of earlier underlying painting (part of a "first draft," as it were) which eventually shows through the finished painting because of the increasing translucence, through aging, of the superimposed layer. *Pentimento* means "repentence" or "regret" in Italian, related to the reflexive verb *pentirsi* (to repent), from Latin *paenitere* (to regret). The artist "repents" or "regrets"

312

what he first painted, changes his mind, and corrects it by painting over it, but the original brush strokes show through in the course of time. The American dramatist Lillian Hellman (1905–1984) wrote an autobiographical work entitled *Pentimento*, subtitled "A Book of Portraits" (Little, Brown & Co., Boston, 1973) which explains the titles in these moving words:

> Old paint on canvas, as it ages, sometimes becomes transparent. When that happens it is possible, in some pictures, to see the original lines: a tree will show through a woman's dress, a child makes way for a dog, a large boat is no longer on an open sea. That is called pentimento because the painter "repented," changed his mind. Perhaps it would be as well to say that the old conception, replaced by a later choice, is a way of seeing and then seeing again.
>
> That is all I mean about the people in this book. The paint has aged now and I wanted to see what was there for me once, what is there for me now.

perigee, see **apogee**

periphrase, see **periphrasis**

periphrasis (puh RIF ruh sis), also **periphrase** (PER uh fraze) *n.* Either of these words means "circumlocution," a roundabout way of expressing oneself, or a phrase so expressed. The adjective is *periphrastic* (per uh FRAS tik). *Periphrasis* was taken as is from the Greek, based on the prefix *peri-* (around) plus *phrasis* (speech), related to *phrazein* (to speak). In a *periphrasis*, one uses a longer expression when a shorter and plainer one would do, introducing double negatives, passives, superfluous descriptive epithets, abstract generalities, and the like. The young mother was pushing her baby along in a *little four-wheeled carriage fitted with a mattress, pillows and a coverlet.* All that is *periphrasis* for *baby carriage*, and the British make it even shorter with "pram," an abbreviation of *perambulator.* In his *Les Précieuses ridicules* (The Ridiculous Precious Ladies), a comedy by the French dramatist Molière (1622–1673) satirizing the affected intellectualism and preciosity of the ladies of fashion, he has them using ridiculous *periphrases* for common objects too "vulgar" to mention by name, e.g., "conveniences for sitting" for *chairs*. The manuscript for this book was first written with a writing instrument using a built-in reservoir of ink, and then copied on a machine in which keys are pressed to transfer letters and words and punctuation marks to paper.

perlustration (pur lus TRAY shun) *n.* A *perlustration* is a thorough survey or inspection, whether of a document or collection of documents or an institution such as a museum or an installation. The verb is *perlustrate* (to traverse, wander through, survey, examine), based on Latin prefix *per-* (through, thoroughly) plus *lustrare* (review, observe, examine). In the foreword to *The Birds Fall Down*, a novel by the English writer Rebecca West (1892–1983), we read of the Tsarist government's ". . . astounding interference with liberty such as the violation of the mails, known as *perlustration.*"

perspicuous (pur PSIK yooh us) *adj.* A *perspicuous* person, *perspicuous* language, or a *perspicuous* argument is clear, lucid, readily understandable, unambiguous. The noun is *perspicuity* (pur spuh KYOOH ih tee), meaning "clarity, intelligibility." Do not confuse this pair with *perspicacious* and *perspicacity*, which express sharp mental perception and discernment. *Perspicacity* has to do with seeing clearly, *perspicuity* with clarity of style, freedom from obscurity. A look at their Latin ancestors will make the distinction clear. *Perspicuous* is from *perspicuus* (transparent), related to the verb *perspicere* (to look through), based on prefix *per-* (through) plus *specere* (to look), while *perspicacious* is from *perspicax* (sharp-sighted), based on the same two elements but *perspicuous* is passive, as it were (look through-able) while *perspicacious* is active (look-through-ing). Fowler has this to say: "*Perspicacious, -acity*, mean having or showing insight; *perspicuous, -uity*, mean being easy to get a clear idea of. *Shrewd* and *shrewdness*, *clear* and *clearness*, or other short words, are used in preference by those neither learned nor pretentious. The learned can safely venture on the *perspic-* pair . . . The usual mistake is to write *-uity* for *-acity* . . ." and examples follow. From the pen of the Arabian writer Hariri (1054–1122), in *Makamet*, about the adventures of the old rogue Abu Zaid who lives by his wits through clever talk, we find this prayer:

> We praise Thee, O God,
> For whatever *perspicuity* of langauge Thou has taught us
> And whatever eloquence Thou hast inspired us with.

petard (pi TARD) *n*. A *petard* was a heavy explosive engine of war, filled with gunpowder and fastened to gates to blow them in or to walls, barricades, etc., to smash them and form a breach. The soldier whose job it was to fire the device was always in danger of blowing himself up as well, in which case he would wind up *hoist with his own petard*. In Shakespeare's *Hamlet* (Act III, Scene 4) the prince says to the queen:

> . . . 'tis the sport to have the engineer
> Hoist with his own *petar* . . .
> But I will delve one yard below their mines,
> And blow them at the moon.

(Shakespeare spelt it *petar*, possibly influenced by the French pronunciation of *petard* in which the *-d* is silent.) Hamlet was speaking of Rosencrantz and Guildenstern, commissioned by King Claudius to escort him to England and see to his death; but as the play develops, it is they who will be done in, and thus *hoist with their own petard*. To be thus hoist is to be caught in the trap laid for someone else. This was indeed the fate of certain inventors of torture devices and dreadful places of imprisonment, like the Bastille built by Hugh Aubriot, Provost of Paris c. 1360, where he was the first to be imprisoned. In the *Book of Esther* 7:9, Haman was hanged on the high gallows he had devised for the hanging of Mordecai, and the witch-hunter Matthew Hopkins, tried for witchcraft under the rules he had set up, was himself executed as a wizard in 1647. *Petard* has an amusing derivation: via Middle French *petard*, related to *peter* (to fart), from the Latin *peditum* (breaking wind), neuter form of *peditus*, past participle of *pedere* (to fart). In this age of jet propulsion, doesn't that derivation give *hoist with one's own petard* a new twist?

peteman (PEET mun) *n*. A *peteman* is a safecracker, in American thieves' slang. *Peterman* is the British form, based on British slang for safe: *peter*. Eric Partridge (1894–1978), the British lexicographer who specialized in slang, in his *Dictionary of Slang and Unconventional English*, quotes from *Limey Breaks In* by one James Spenser, published in 1934, as follows: "A 'peter' is a safe made from tool-proof steel and usually has safety linings made from a special sort of cement." Partridge goes on to say: "? origin: perhaps because 'netted' by thieves: in allusion to Simon Peter's occupation.'' Partridge was ingenious in matters of troublesome derivation. This one seems far-fetched.

pharisee   (FAR ih see) *n.* A *pharisee* (with a lower case *p*) is a sanctimonious hypocrite, narrow-minded and self-righteous. The word derives from the *Pharisees*, a Hebrew sect that flourished during the first century B.C. and the first century A.D. in Judea. They sought to ensure that the nation was governed in strict conformity to religious law. Jesus denounced them for their fundamentalist hypocrisy. Their name came from the Hebrew word *perusim* (the separate ones—based on the verb *perash*, to separate or set apart); it became *pharisaios* in Greek, and came to be applied to any self-righteous person. The adjective is *pharisaic* (far ih SAY ik) or *pharisaical* (far ih SAY ih kul), and characterizes anyone who insists on strict observance of religious law without regard to the spirit behind it, or any self-righteous hypocrite. There are unbearable people with narrow, *pharisaical* views, who think they are the sole possessors of virtue. In The Acts of the Apostles 26:5, Paul, defending himself before King Agrippa, says: ". . . After the most straitest sect of our religion I lived a *Pharisee*.'' The American poet James Russell Lowell (1819–1891), in *The Pious Editor's Creed* (*The Bigelow Papers*, First Series), has this to say:

> I do believe in Freedom's cause,
>   Ez fur away ez Payris is;
> I love to see her stick her claws
>   In them infarnal *Phayrisees* . . .

The Russian poet and novelist Boris Pasternak (1890–1960) wrote in his poem *Hamlet*:

> I am alone; all drowns in the *Pharisees'* hypocrisy.
> To live your life is not as simple as to cross a field.

(The second line is from an anonymous Russian proverb: To live a life through is not like crossing a field.)

pharos   (FAR os) *n.* A *pharos* is a lighthouse, or any beacon for the guidance of mariners. The word comes from the Greek name

316

of the island off Alexandria, Egypt, where Ptolemy Philadelphus (Ptolemy II, c. 309–c. 247 B.C., king of Egypt 285–c. 247 B.C.) built a lighthouse 450 feet high and visible at a distance of 42 miles. Some of it fell in 793 and the rest was destroyed by an earthquake in 1375. Ptolemy's *pharos* was one of the Seven Wonders of the (ancient) World.

phasianine, see **accipitrine**

phatic (FAT ik) *adj.* A *phatic* communication is one that uses speech to express feelings and sociability rather than information, ideas, or specific meaning. The adverb is *phatically* (FAT ik ul ee), the noun *phasis* (FAY sis). The adjective appears mostly in the expression *phatic communion*. Friends who meet on the street often wind up their conversations with a bit of *phatic* communion: "Well, take care of yourself." "Have a nice day!" has become a bit of automatic *phasis* that has replaced "So long!" or "Bye now!" In the novel *Rates of Exchange* (Secker & Warburg, London, 1983), the English writer Malcolm Bradbury (b. 1932) places his protagonist, Prof. Petworth, in an imaginary Iron Curtain country whose language Petworth, though a linguist, doesn't understand. He is having difficulty communicating with the unattractive stewardess in a dingy plane, and thinks about the delights of air travel back home where " . . . stewardesses . . . offer smiles and adulterous glances, promises of intimate excess, display made-up faces and nice legs, utter cries of 'Enjoy your flight' and 'Fly us again' and 'Have a nice day.' Indeed, they transmit what a linguist . . . calls *phatic* communion, which is to say, non-verbal intercourse, speechless communication, the kind of thing babies and lovers . . . constantly use." Speechless, yes, in the special sense of non-communication. *Phatic* comes from Greek *phatos* (spoken), past participle of *phanai* (to speak). *Phasis* (utterance) was taken intact from the Greek. Anyway, have a nice day.

philanderer (fih LAN dur ur) *n.* Sometimes too great familiarity with classical roots may be misleading, strange as it seems. *Phil-*, a variation of *philo-* used before vowels, is a common Greek prefix, the combining form of the adjective *philos* (loving), as found in many English words derived from Greek: *philanthropy* (*anthropos*, man), *philology* (*logos*, word), *philosophy* (*sophia*, wisdom). So it would seem that *philanderer*, composed of *phil-* plus *andros*, another Greek noun for "man" or "husband," should mean "one who loves men," but it doesn't, for it has been altered from its original Greek meaning—a term of praise for a loving wife, who, like Frankie of Frankie and Johnnie, loved her man—and misapplied as a pejorative for a "faithless husband," or at least a woman-chaser who makes love without serious or honorable intentions. This inversion may have come about as a result of the use of *Philander* by the Italian poet Ariosto (1474–1533) as the name of a lover in his poem *Orlando Furioso*, the epic treatment of the *Roland* legend, and later by the collaborating English playwrights Beaumont (1584–1616) and Fletcher (1579–1625) in their play *The Laws of Candy*. To *philander*, as a verb, is to act as the *philanderer*, the rake, womanizer, Don Juan, Lothario, Casanova—there is no end of them in literature in this naughty world.

philately, see **philogyny**

philippic (fih LIP ik) *n.* A *philippic* is a **diatribe**, a speech or writing of extremely bitter denunciation and vilification, a tirade, a tongue-lashing loaded with invective. The word arose from the general application of the term originally applied to the orations of the Greek statesman and orator Demosthenes (c. 384–322 B.C.) to rouse the Athenians against the encroachments of Philip II of Macedon (382–336 B.C.), the father of Alexander the Great (356–323 B.C.). Other examples of *philippics* are the orations of the Roman philosopher, statesman, and orator Cicero (106–43 B.C.) against the Roman politican and conspirator Catiline (c. 108–62 B.C.)—the four *Catilinarian Orations* familiar to high school students of Latin. More recently, Senator Joseph McCarthy (1908–1957) was on the receiving end of a *philippic* delivered during the "Army Trials" by defense counsel Joseph N. Welch (1890–1960), of Boston, Massachusetts, which did much to condemn McCarthy as a dangerous and irresponsible demagogue and witch-hunter and to damage his career. ("Senator, have you no shame . . . ?" etc., etc.)

phillumeny, see **philomath**

philogyny (fih LOJ uh nee) *n. Philogyny* is love of women. The adjective is *philogynous* (fih LOJ uh nus). One who loves women

318

is a *philogynist* (fih LOJ uh nist). *Philogynia* is Greek for "love of women," based on the prefix *philo-* (loving), *phil-* before a vowel, from the Greek adjective *philos* (loving) plus *gyne* (woman). The opposite of *philogyny* is *misogyny* (mih SOJ uh nee, mye-), hatred of women, from Greek *misogynia*, based on the prefix *miso-* (referring to hate), *mis-* before a vowel, the combining form of *misein* (to hate) or *misos* (hatred), plus the same *gyne*. The adjectives are *misogynous* (mih SOJ uh nus), or *misogynic* (mih SOJ uh nik), or *misogynistic* (mih soj uh NIS tik), with *my-* as an alternative first syllable in all three. (Women-hating was and is widespread enough for the adjective to take three forms.) There are a good many Greek-based *philo-* and *miso-* (sometimes *phil-* and *mis-*) words. To name a few: *philology* (*logos,* word); *philosophy* (*sophia,* wisdom); *philanthropy* (*anthropos,* man); *philately* (*ateleia,* freedom from delivery charges); *misanthropy* (*anthropos,* man); *misocapnic* (mih so KAP nik), smoke-hating, particularly tobacco smoke—a burning (?) issue today—(*kapnos,* smoke); *misoclere* (MIS o kleer), clergy-hating (*kleros,* clergy); *misogamy* (mih SOG uh mee), hatred of marriage (*gamos,* marriage); *misology* (mih SOL uh jee), hatred of reason or knowledge (*logos,* reason); *misoneism* (mih so NEE iz um), hatred of novelty (*neos,* new). *My-* is an alternative first syllable in all those. There appear to be more things to hate than to love in this world. Getting back to a *phil-* word, Fowler has this to say about *philately* and *philatelist:* "The derivation is, through French, from Greek *ateleia,* exemption from tax; the word thus means fondness for the symbols that vouch for no charge being payable, namely stamps. It is a pity that for one of the most popular scientific pursuits one of the least popularly intelligible names should have been found. The best remedy now is to avoid the official titles whenever *stamp-collecting* and *-collector* will do." ". . . least popularly intelligible . . ." indeed: That is why *philately* and 999 other words have been included in this book!

philomath (FIL uh math) *n.* A *philomath* is a lover of learning, an enthusiast for study and knowledge; not especially concerned with *math*, short for *mathematics*, though that comes from Greek *mathematike* (scientific), related to *math-*, the root of *mathanein* (to learn), the same *-math* as that in *philomath*. *Philomathes* is Greek for "fond of learning." *Philo-* (*phil-* before a vowel) is a common prefix consisting of the combining form of *philos* (loving), related to the verb *phileein* (to love), while *-phile* is a common suffix from the same source (*philanthropy*, *philology*, *philosophy*; **ailurophile**, *bibliophile*, *Francophile*). In the *philo-* department, we also have **philately** (fih LAT uh lee), stamp-collecting (literally, love of postage stamps), the *-ately* being from *ateleia* (literally, freedom from taxation, i.e., cost-free, showing the addressee's freedom from delivery charges by affixing a stamp) and *phillumeny* (fin LOOH muh nee), the collection of matchbox labels (what will they think of next?), a hybrid word, with a Greek prefix tacked onto a Latin noun (*lumen*, light), formed, e.g., like *television* (Greek *tele-*, far, as in *telegraph*, *telephone*, etc.) plus Latin *visio* (view).

philosophaster, see **poetaster**

phocaenine, see **accipitrine**

phocine, see **accipitrine**

phylactery (fuh LAK tuh ree) *n*. During daily morning prayers (except on Saturday—the sabbath—and religious holidays), orthodox Jewish males past the age of 13 wear *phylacteries*, small black leather cubes containing verses of the Old Testament inscribed on parchment. One is strapped to the left arm, the other to the forehead, in a manner prescribed by religious law. One cube contains a square of parchment with passages from Exodus 13:1–10 (Moses said to the people: "And it shall be for a sign unto thee upon thine hand, and for frontlets between thine eyes . . ."). The other contains passages from Deuteronomy 6:4–9 ("And thou shalt bind them for a sign unto thee upon thine hand, and they shall be frontlets between thine eyes.") and 11:13–21 ("Therefore shall ye lay up these my words in your heart and in your soul, and bind them for a sign upon your hand, that they may be as frontlets between your eyes." *Phylactery* is from Greek *phylakterion* (safeguard, amulet), related to the verb *phylassein* (to watch). The term for *phylacteries* in Yiddish is *t'fillin*, from Hebrew *tefilla* (prayer).

picaresque (pik uh RESK) *adj*. This adjective generally applies to a certain type of novel dealing sympathetically with attractive rogues and adventurers; full of entertaining, sometimes satirical episodes, often involving vagabonds and other social parasites, and incidentally painting a picture of the everyday life of the common people. The *picaresque* novel was first developed in Spain; *picaresque* was taken, via French, from Spanish *picaresco* (roguish, knavish), based on *picaro* (not only roguish and knavish but low and vile as well, malicious, mendacious, mischievous, crafty, and sly), which as a noun means "rascal, rogue, knave." The earliest example of this type of Spanish novel is *Lazarillo de Tormes*, anonymously issued in Spain c. 1553, the prototype of *picaresque* fiction. *Gil Blas*, from the pen of the French novelist Alain René Le Sage (1668–1747), followed in 1715 and *Moll Flanders*, by the English writer Daniel Defoe (1660–1731), appeared in 1722. The *picaresque* novel still flourishes, for example, in works like *Fanny* (New American Library, New York, 1980) by the American poet and writer Erica Jong (b. 1942), who is a neighbor of the author and had photographs taken of her in costume in his 1710 house as part of *Fanny*'s advance publicity campaign.

picine, see **accipitrine**

pidgin (PIJ un) *n.*, *adj.* Pidgin is a *lingua franca* (see definition below), a supplementary language, developed by peoples speaking different languages, usually a simplified form of one of the languages, corrupted as to pronunciation, with its syntax a combination of grammatical features common to the languages involved. *Pidgin* sometimes takes the form *pigeon*. The word *pidgin* is the best the Chinese could do with the word *business*, and is usually found in the expression *pidgin* (or *pigeon*) *English*, a jargon consisting for the most part of a combination of mispronounced English words and elements of Chinese syntax, used primarily in commercial circles in Chinese ports but also in other parts of the Far Eastern world. The *pidgin English* word most familiar to Western ears is *chop-chop*, meaning "quick(ly)." This familiarity is based chiefly on grade-B movies set in allegedly exotic parts of the Far East. The Chinese have a hard time with the sound of the letter *r*, usually converting it into the sound of *l*, so that *sorry* becomes *solly*, *marry mally*, *tree te-lee*, etc. Also, the sound -*ee* is often added to an English word, as in *nye-fee* for *knife*. In Chinese grammar, a word (called "classifier") is inserted between a number and the noun it modifies. This becomes *piece* in *pidgin English*: *one piece* means "one," *two piece* "two," etc. *Pidgin*, by itself as a

321

noun, covers any combination and distortion of two languages with elements of both in a simplified grammar. English-speaking people confused the (to them) nonsensical word *pidgin* with the familiar *pigeon*, so that one runs across the term *pigeon* (or *Pigeon*) *English* occasionally. This explains the expression "That's not my pigeon" or "This isn't my pigeon," meaning "This is not my business, not my affair, not my responsibility; this has nothing to do with me." *Pidgin* can be classified as a *lingua franca* (literally, Italian for "Frankish language"): originally a jargon or mixed language consisting of simplified Italian combined with elements of Provençal, French, Spanish, and a bit of Greek and Arabic, spoken in ports of the Mediterranean; but the expression came to be applied to any hybrid language used over a wide area as a common means of communication, especially in commercial circles, among peoples who speak different languages. In the novel *Rates of Exchange* by the English novelist Malcolm Bradbury (b. 1932; Secker & Warburg, London, 1983), the wife of a British Embassy official in an obscure Iron Curtain country is giving a party. She doesn't speak the very difficult native tongue, and Magda, the native cook, doesn't speak a word of English. Magda approaches, and the hostess has to give her some instructions. She excuses herself to a guest, saying, ". . . I'm afraid I must try my *pidgin*." It works: the soup gets to the table on time. Prince Charles of England is known in Fiji as "Number 1 pickaninny him belong Mrs. Queen." The noun *pickaninny* is itself taken from *pidgin*, which got it from Portuguese *pequenino* (very small). *Brush Up Your Pidgin*, a slim volume by Dorgan Rushton (Willow Books, Collins, London, 1983), is informative on this subject and amusing as well. (Note: *brush up* is British English for *brush up on*.)

pilgarlic (pil GAR lik) *n.* This curious old word, now no longer current, comes from *peeled garlic*, an old metaphor for a bald-headed person, whose pate looks like a peeled garlic bulb. In addition, an obsolete verb *pill* meant, among other things, "make or become hairless." The English chronicler John Snow (c. 1525–1605) said of an acquaintance who was losing his hair: "He will soon be peeled garlic like myself." *Pilgarlic* is also used as a facetious term of contempt or pity, to describe a person as a poor wretch or a sad sack, especially one abandoned by his friends, and was used of oneself as a term of self-pity. We find it so used in a passage from *Pantagruel*, from the pen of the French satirist Rabelais (c. 1490–1553): ". . . we jogged off to bed for the night; but never a bit could poor *pilgarlic* sleep one wink, for the everlasting jingle of bells."

piscifauna, see **avifauna**

piscine, see **accipitrine**

pismire (PIS mire, PIZ-) *n*. A *pismire* is an ant, but the term has been applied contemptuously to a despicable individual. Robert Penn Warren, the American poet and novelist (b. 1905), used it that way. "What do you think I'd do with a young *pismire* like you?" Shakespeare knew the word. In *Henry IV, Part I* (Act I, Scene 3), the impetuous young Harry Percy, known as Hotspur, cannot bear to hear the name of Bolingbroke:

> Why, look you, I am whipped and scourged with rods,
> Nettled and stung with *pismires*, when I hear
> Of this vile politician, Bolingbroke.

In the same play (Act III, Scene 1) the same Hotspur uses the word *ant*. In reviling Mortimer's father, he says:

> . . . sometimes he angers me
> With telling me of the moldwarp [mole] and the *ant* . . .

In the earlier speech, the Bard obviously needed a two-syllable synonym for *ant. Pismire* is derived from Middle English *pissemyre* (a urinating ant, based on Middle English *pisse*, urinate, plus obsolete *mire*, ant). A *pismire*, then, is a urinating ant, i.e., an ant exuding formic acid. See **formication.**

plantigrade (PLAN tih grade) *n., adj. Plantigrade* applies to animals that walk on the whole sole of the foot, as opposed to *digitigrade* (DIJ ih tuh grade), describing animals that walk on toes. *Plantigrade* is from New Latin *plantigradus*, based on Latin *planta* (sole) plus *gradus* (step) or *gradi* (to walk). *Digitigrade* is from Latin *digitus* (finger, toe) plus *gradus* or *gradi*. The human race and bears are *plantigrade*, while most mammals are *digitigrade*, especially horses and cattle, which walk on the tips of one or two digits of each foot. Ballerinas walk *plantigradely* and dance *digitigradely.*

pleonasm   (PLEE uh naz um) *n. Pleonasm* is the use of more words than are required to give sense; in short, redundancy. Examples: *free gift; hear with one's own ears, see with one's own eyes; save and except; of any sort or kind; in any way or manner; equanimity of mind; alas and alack; rags and tatters; shape or form; obviate the necessity of. Alas and alack*, like *lo and behold*, if not overdone, may be permissible for emphasis; perhaps the same may be said for *rags and tatters*. When Mr. Jones *makes, publishes and declares* this to be his *Last Will and Testament*, his lawyer is guilty of two *pleonasms* (or should we say *not one but two*?), and legal *verbiage* (defined as "overabundance or superfluity of words," also known as "verbosity") is notorious. This is not so much a case of the *care, concern and solicitude* of the lawyer as it is a result of tradition and the ancient practice of hiring scribes who were paid by the word. Lord *save me and preserve me* from that *practice, custom and convention*! And from all *redundancies, tautologies and pleonasms*! The adjective is *pleonastic* (plee uh NAS tik). *Pleonasm* comes, via Late Latin *pleonasmus*, from Greek *pleonasmos* (redundancy), **verbid** of *pleonazein* (to be, or have, more than enough), based on prefix *pleo-*, a variant of *plio-* (more), combining form of *pleion* (more), comparative of *polys* (much), from which we get our many *poly-* words.

plethoric   (ple THOR ik, PLETH uh rik) *adj. Plethoric* is based upon the fairly familiar word *plethora* (PLETH uh ruh), meaning "superabundance," taken intact from the Greek, where it means "fullness." *Plethoric* is its adjective, meaning "excessive, overfull, turgid." When pompous, garrulous Polonius, in Shakespeare's *Hamlet* (Act I, Scene 3), utters his long string of moral maxims to his son Laertes who is leaving for France ("Give thy thoughts no tongue . . ." etc., etc., etc., he gives him a *plethora* of paternal advice; it is, to say the least, a *plethoric* speech. Some of the discussions in this here book may seem *plethoric* to some readers, but too much, let us hope, is preferable to too little.

Plutonian   (plooh TOH nee un) *adj.*; also **Plutonic** (plooh TON ik). *Pluto*, in classical mythology, was the god of the underworld (Hades, not cosa nostra). *Plutonian* describes anything relating to Pluto or his underworld, and can be used as a synonym of *infernal*. Pluto is also the name of the planet ninth in order from the sun, the outermost in the solar system. It is next beyond the planet Neptune, which gave its name to the element neptunium, atomic number 93; and so Pluto gave its name to the element plutonium, that substance of horrendous overtones. *Plutonian*, with either upper or lower case *p*, is the name of the geological theory that the condition of the earth's crust today is the result of subterranean heat (the fires of hell?). In any case, plutonium is one helluvan element. The American poet Edgar Allan Poe (1809–1849) used *Plutonian* in his famous poem *The Raven*:

> "Ghastly grim and ancient Raven wandering
>   from the nightly shore—
> Tell me what thy lordly name is on the
>   Night's *Plutonian* shore!"
> Quoth the Raven, "Nevermore."

His countryman James Russell Lowell (1819–1891), in *A Fable for Critics*, published in 1848 while poor Poe was still alive, expressed mixed feelings about him:

> There comes Poe, with his raven, like Barnaby Rudge,
> Three fifths of him genius and two fifths sheer fudge.

pluvious (PLOOH vee us) *adj. Pluvious* means "rainy" and can be applied to anything pertaining to rain, like *pluvious conditions* or *pluvious areas*. The related adjective *pluvial* (PLOOH vee ul) is synonymous, often with the implication of a very rainy condition, and in geology is used to describe conditions caused by rain, such as *pluvial erosion* or *pluvial flooding*. *Pluvia* is Latin for "rain," coming by back formation from the adjective *pluvius* (rainy)—*pluvia* being the feminine form modifying *aqua* (water) understood. A related Latin adjective, *pluvialis* (pertaining to rain), gave us *pluvial*. The Roman god Jupiter was described by the Roman poet Tibullus (c. 54–c. 18 B.C.) as "Jupiter pluvius" (Jupiter the rainbringer.) That Jupiter certainly got around and had a finger in lots of pies. *Pluviôse* was the name assigned to the fifth month (January 20 to February 18) in the French Revolutionary calendar, adopted on October 5, 1793, as of September 22, 1792, by the National Convention. It remained in force until January 1, 1806, when Napoleon restored the Gregorian calendar. The Revolutionary calendar (designed by one Gilbert Romme, 1750–1795) was composed of 12 30-day months plus five intercalary (see **intercalate** and **bissextile**) or complementary days called "sansculottides," so named in honor of the "sans culottes' (French for "without breeches"), the French revolutionary name for the extremists of the working class. These extra days were nonworking holidays. Every fourth year a sixth extra day was added. It was the French poet Fabre d'Eglantine (1775–1794) who gave the months their names, including *Pluviôse*.

pococurante (poh koh kooh RAN tee) *n.*, *adj.* A *pococurante* is an easygoing, nonchalant, indifferent person, who exhibits a minimum of interest in anything. As an adjective, it describes that type of individual, for whom the popular slang of the moment is "laid back." *Pococuranti* are relaxed and unharried, enjoy a carefree life-style, aren't bothered by social pressures or responsibilities. *Poco curante* is Italian for "caring little." The term for this attitude is *pococurantism* (poh koh kooh RAN tiz um). The Italians have an enviable flair for the *mot juste* in this department. It is to them we owe the *dolce far niente*, literally, the *sweet-do-nothing*—pleasant idleness, complete relaxation—untroubled by the so-called Judeo-Protestant work ethic; and they presented us with the expression *la dolce vita*, the sweet life—devoted to luxurious sensuality. The Spanish gave us *mañana*, tomorrow—never do today what you can put off to tomorrow—or indefinitely—or forever!

poetaster (POH it as tur) *n.* This is the label bestowed upon a second rate poet, a writer of inferior verse. A great deal of doggerel issues from the pens of *poetasters*, who are also called "rhymesters" or "versifiers." The suffix *-aster*, taken from Latin, is used to form nouns that denote inferior versions of the real thing. Thus, a *criticaster* (KRIT ih kas tur) is an incompetent, inferior critic, in whatever field he covers; a *grammaticaster* is a grammatical pedant, a petty grammarian; a *medicaster* is a quack; a *philosophaster* is a superficial philosopher, one who poses as a philosopher; the *oleaster* is the wild olive tree which bear inedible bitter fruit—olive-shaped, but of no use (*olea* is Latin for "olive tree"). There is also an *oleaster* which resembles it bearing yellow flowers but no fruit. You are welcome to make your own *-aster* words (acrobaster? educaster? artistaster?), but a *disaster* is not an inferior *dis*. In the long (1,070 lines) poem *English Bards and Scotch Reviewers* (1809) in which the English poet Lord Byron (1788–1824) reviled a long list of English poets and Scottish critics, we read, as just one sample, this couplet:

> Let simple Wordsworth chime his childish verse,
> And brother Coleridge lull the babe at nurse . . .

and later on, toward the end:

> Nay more, though all my rival rhymesters frown,
> I too can hunt a *poetaster* down . . .

And the English novelist Thackeray (1811–1863) exclaimed: "Away with *poetastering* at dinner parties!"

pogonology (poh goh NOL uh jee) *n.* *Pogonology* has nothing whatever to do with the art of using the pogo stick, a long upright stick with a crossbar on a strong spring; one stands on the crossbar and propels oneself along the ground in a series of leaps. But to get back (without leaping) to *pogonology*; it is the study of beards, from Greek *pogon* (beard) and the common suffix *-ology* to indicate science or study, as in *geology*, *theology*, etc. *Pogonotomy* (poh goh NOT uh mee) is shaving, from *pogon* plus *tome* (cutting). *Pogonotrophy* (poh goh NO truh fee) is beard growing, from *pogon* plus suffix *-trophia* (growth, nourishment), related to *trophe* (food). Beards are back in fashion, so that all these *pogo-* words have become quite important.

pogonotomy, see **pogonology**

pogonotrophy, see **pogonology**

polder (POHL dur) *n.*, *vb.* A *polder* is a tract of low-lying land reclaimed from the sea and thereafter protected against flooding by a system of dikes, an operation that occurs quite frequently in the Netherlands, where so much of the land is nether. *Polder* is a Dutch word, taken over intact, and is also a verb denoting this operation.

polity   (POL ih tee) *n. Polity* has nothing to do with *policy* or *politics* or *politeness. Polity* is a form or system of civil government, for example, a democratic *polity*, a communist *polity. Polity* has another meaning as well: "state," or any other organized community or body of people living under a system of government, unlike an **ad hoc** group. *Polity* comes, via Latin *politia*, from Greek *politeia* (citizenship, form of government), related to *polites* (citizen). In *The Republic* of the Greek philosopher Plato (c. 428-348 B.C.), we read (Jowett translation): "Let there be one man who has a city obedient to his will, and he might bring into existence the ideal *polity* about which the world is so incredulous."

polyhistor,   see **polymath**

polymath   (POL ee math) *n.* A *polymath* is a person of great and varied learning. The same goes for a *polyhistor* (pol ee HIS tur). *Polymathic* (pol ee MATH ik) and *polyhistoric* (pol ee his TOR ik) are the respective adjectives. *Polymathy* (pol IM uh thee) and *polyhistory* (pol ee HIS tuh ree) both mean "great and varied learning." *Poly-* (much, many) is the familiar Greek prefix taken over into many of our words (*polygamous, polychrome, polygon,* etc.); the *-math* in *polymath* is based on the Greek verb *manthanein* (to learn), while the *histor-* in *polyhistor* is based on the Greek verb *historeein* (to inquire, learn). Note that the two meanings of that verb support the aphorism (St. Matthew 7:7): "Seek and ye shall find." The old radio quiz show *Information Please* (1932-1947; briefly on TV, 1952) involved a panel that included those famous *polymaths* Franklin P. Adams ("F.P.A.," the American author and columnist, 1881-1960), John Kieran (the American writer, naturalist, and sports columnist, 1892-1981), the American pianist Oscar Levant (1906-1972) and other wits and pundits who could answer almost any question on any subject. Then there was the general knowledge quiz program *The $64,000 Question* (a phrase that has passed into our language) which achieved notoriety when it was discovered that a "winner" had been fed the answers in advance, and became famous as a *pseudopolymath*. Current in Great Britain is a TV program similar—without the fraud—to *The $64,000 Question*, called *Mastermind. Polymaths* and *polyhistors* are convenient to have around if you lack encyclopedias.

polysyndeton, see **asyndeton**

porcine, see **accipitrine**

porlock (POR lok) *vb.* To *porlock* is to interrupt an artist engaged in aesthetic creation. This word, as a verb, appeared in print for the first time in *Bruno's Dream* (Chatto & Windus, London, 1969), a novel by the great contemporary English novelist Iris Murdoch (b. 1919). This author suspected that *porlock*, as a verb, was an invention of Miss Murdoch, and dictionary research revealed only the following entry in Volume 3 (O to Sez) of the Supplement (1982) to the Oxford English Dictionary:

> **Porlock** . . . The name of a town in Somerset [an English county], used allusively (see quot. 1816) in phr. *a person* etc. *from Porlock,* a person who interrupts at an inconvenient moment.
>
> [**1816** COLERIDGE *Kubla Khan* in *Christabel* 53 At this moment he [sc. Coleridge] was unfortunately called out by a person on business from Porlock, and detained by him above an hour.] **1959** *Listener* 1 Jan. 37/3 All the incidental distractions—the telephone-bell, the Christmas carollers at the door, the gentleman or lady 'from Porlock'—to which one is subject.

It seemed, therefore, that to *porlock* was to interrupt at an inconvenient moment. But correspondence with Miss Murdoch brought forth a graciously prompt fuller explanation, if a narrower definition (her letter posted February 7, 1985):

> The verb "to porlock"is my coinage. (I know of no other use of it.) It fills a terminological gap and I hope it will pass into general usage! The Coleridge story, upon which the idea entirely rests, and not on the characteristics of people in Porlock generally (!), is of course that Coleridge 'dreamt' *Kubla Khan* and on awaking started to write it down but was interrupted by the person on business from Porlock—and later on could remember no more of his 'dream poem'. Strictly, 'to porlock' should mean to interrupt an artist engaged in aesthetic creation. One *might* extend it to the interruption of any sustained serious theoretical or scholarly reflection or activity (e.g., that of a philosopher or historian). I would be against weakening it to mean any sort of unwelcome interruption. . . . One or two of my philosopher friends have already,

with my encouragement, adopted it—in light-hearted conversation only.
I haven't seen it yet in print!

This author can only express the hope that in this (and former)
correspondence with Miss Murdoch, he has not been guilty of
porlocking—and delaying even for a moment the completion of her
next and eagerly awaited novel! A reference to the rather obscure
village of Porlock appears in *The Kingdom by the Sea*, a travel book
by the American writer Paul Theroux (b. 1946) (Hamish Hamilton,
London, 1983):

> I left Lynton on the Cliff Railway, a cable car that descended to Lyn-
> mouth [incidentally, a short but terrifying ride experienced by this
> author and his wife many years ago]. I took a bus to Porlock, ten miles
> away. The road cut across the north of Exmoor, a rather brown forbid-
> ding place, and down the long Porlock Hill . . . Porlock, the home of
> the man who interrupted the writing of 'Kubla Khan', was one street
> of small cottages, with a continuous line of cars trailing through it.
> Below it, on the west side of the bay, was Porlock Weir . . . A hundred
> and seventy years ago a man came to Porlock and found it quiet. But
> he did not find fault. He wrote: 'There are periods of comparative
> stagnation, when we say, even in London, that there is nothing stirring;
> it is therefore not surprising that there should be some seasons of the
> year when things are rather quiet in West Porlock.'

Porlock seems to be on writers' minds, undoubtedly because of
the Coleridge incident. In his *Diaries, 1920–1922* (Faber & Faber,
London, 1981), Siegfried Sassoon (1886–1967) notes under dates
April 27, 1921, ff.:

> ". . . Thinking of taking Gabriel [Gabriel Atkin, the English artist and
> Sassoon's great friend] to Porlock next week."

And he did so on May 5 following. Ten days later, he sent this
poem to the English poet and critic Edmund Blunden (1896–1974)

> KNOW YOU EXMOOR? Have ye heard tell of PORLOCK?
> Whence started out, one morn in 1800 (?),
> A man, on *business* bent, at Nether Stowey.
> Sought there one Samuel Coleridge; knocked and blundered
> Through green-leaf-shuttered parlour into garden;
> Coughed; made his errand palpable; surmised
> Tomorrow's rain or rainlessness. 'Beg pardon
> If I've disturbed your nap, sir!' Coleridge smiled;

Seemed half-attentive. Murmured like the stream
Descending Quantock, sloping toward the Channel.
And is he known in Hell—that oaf from Porlock?
Do flames attend him? Is he crucified
Upon Mount Abora? Plagued from feet to forelock
By parasitic friends? Or has he tried
To earn atonement? Did his phantom go,
With necroscopic clichés simplified,
To irritate poor Edgar Allan Poe?

postiche   (paw STEESH) *n.*, *adj.* A superfluous and inappropriate addition to a finished work, like a sculpture or other ornament
stuck onto a building, may be described as *postiche*. More generally, *postiche* applies to things counterfeit or false. As a noun, a
postiche is a superfluous and unbecoming addition, a sham, an
imitation of or substitute for the real thing, a pretense, and in a
special use, a wig or hairpiece, a particular type of replacement of
the genuine article. *Postiche* was taken from the French, where it
has all those meanings; they got it from the Italian *posticcio* or
apposticcio (artificial, sham; *capelli posticci* means "false hair");
and they took it from Late Latin *apposticius* (false, put on).

postil,   see **apostil(le)**

postliminy   (pohst LIM uh nee) *n.* This is a term in international
law, defined as the restoration to their original status of people or
things captured in war, when they are returned into the power of
their own nation. Under Roman law, the term covered the right of
a war captive to resume his civil rights and privileges on his release
and return to his native land, or of a banished citizen on his return
after a pardon. The Latin term is *postliminium*, literally the condition of being "behind the theshold," i.e., at home, based on the
prefix *post-* plus *limen* (threshold), the same *limen* that figures in
subliminal, describing stimuli that operate *sub-* (under, below) the
threshold of consciousness.

postpartum,   see **parturition**

postprandial   see **preprandial**

potsherd   (POT shurd) *n.* A *postsherd* is a fragment of broken
pottery. It is a term commonly used to denote those that are of

interest to archeologists, the kind found in digs all over the world, in ancient sites. It is from the gathering and piecing together of *potsherds* that the archeologists have been able to reconstruct samples of prehistoric and ancient pottery, which often reveals much about the respective cultures. A *shard*, also spelt *sherd*, is a fragment of broken earthenware, and, combined with *pot*, gives us *potsherd*. *Shard* is from Middle English, which got it from Old English *sceard*.

prandial, see **preprandial**

praxis (PRAK sis) *n. Praxis*, from the Greek for "deed, action," is practice as opposed to theory, the actual use of one's skills and knowledge. *Praxis*, the Greek noun, is related to the verb *prassein* (to do), and involves really *doing something* (Don't just sit there; *do* something!). But *praxis*, in English, can also mean "practice" in the sense of "convention" or "custom," i.e., the usual or accepted *practice* in a given profession or set of circumstances: what the British colloquially call the "drill," or the "right" or "usual drill," to denote the *praxis*, the usual and correct way of doing things, the normal and accepted procedure. *Parapraxis* (par uh PRAK sis), on the other hand, is an error, blunder, lapse, e.g., a slip of the tongue, a sudden blank in memory, and *prapraxia* is erroneous, faulty blundering action in general. *Parapraxic* (pair uh PRAK sik) is the adjective, and all three come from the Greek prefix *para-* (beside, amiss) plus *praxis*. The language of writers like the Irishman James Joyce (1882–1941) and the American Gertrude Stein (1874–1946) was intentionally *parapraxic*, employing invented words and unconventional constructions. This author, in his days as a student in Paris, under their influence, had a couple of *parapraxically* concocted poems accepted by the long-since defunct magazine *transition* (lower case *t* intentional), devoted to the "Revolution of the Word"; the compensation was $1.00 per page paid *to* the magazine *by* the poet. Hardly fair publishing *praxis*.

prelapsarian (pree lap SAIR ee un) *adj.* This adjective is descriptive of the time or state of things before the fall of man, the degeneration of the human race resulting from Adam's disobedience of the Lord's injunction forbidding the eating of the fruit of the tree of knowledge. Adam, the unredeemed man, is a symbol of original sin, for which he was cast out of the Garden of Eden and the state of innocence. We have been suffering from that sin ever since. Remember how sweet a time it was before we suffered from the knowledge of the power of the atom? *Prelapsarian* is from *pre-* (before) plus Latin *lapsus* (fall).

preprandial (pree PRAN dee ul) *adj. Preprandial* and *anteprandial* (an tee PRAN dee ul) mean "before a meal" and *postprandial* (pohst PRAN dee ul) means "after a meal"; the meal in question may be any meal, but the one referred to in all these words is usually dinner, despite the fact that the Latin noun *prandium* means "lunch" or "late breakfast," and the related Latin verb *prandere* means to "take lunch." This disparity probably has to do with the difference beween the eating habits of the ancient Romans and those of our contemporary society. Even today, country people have "dinner" at midday, when city people eat "lunch." It is pleasant to have a *preprandial* apéritif or a *postprandial* liqueur (and even pleasanter to have both). Alcoholic beverages are not the only things *pre-* or *ante-* or *postprandial*: you can have a *preprandial* chat with a friend, or a *postprandial* business talk with an associate. *Postprandial* oratory or eloquence can be quite oppressive, or (much better) soporific after a heavy meal. The English novelist, poet, and dramatist Robert Williams Buchanan (1841–1901) wrote of enjoying "the sweet *post-prandial* cigar" (the British are lavish in the use of hyphens). A *postprandial* nap can be of great comfort. *Prandial*, without benefit of prepositional prefix, applies to anything pertaining to a meal, like *prandial* conversation, or *prandial* pleasure, but it is a word you won't come across often.

presbyopia (prez bee OH pee uh, pres-) *n. Presbyopia* is farsightedness, not the good kind that wisely foresees future developments, but the annoying affliction of advancing age, when people develop the defect in vision in which near objects are hard to see clearly. There's the tired old joke: "My arms aren't long enough to hold the newspaper where I can read it." The remedy for *presbyopia* is, of course, reading glasses, which change the focus to accommodate the defect. *Presbyopia* is formed of the Greek prefix *presby-*, the combining form of the adjective *presbys* (old; also found in *Pres-*

byterian, based on *presbyteros*, older or elder) plus the suffix *-opia*, based on *ops* (eye; cf. *myopia*, formed of *mys*, muscle, plus *ops*).

prescriptive (prih SKRIP tiv) *adj.* In law, a *prescriptive right* is one attained by long, unchallenged use or tenure of property, like an easement over land or title to land (the period of use conferring the right varies from state to state). *Prescriptive*, as opposed to *descriptive*, has a special application in the field of lexicography. A *prescriptive* dictionary is one that *prescribes* rules for the proper spelling, meaning, and use of words. A *descriptive* one "tells it like it is," to use the idiom of sports announcers, which in some cases has already earned the blessing of the descriptivists; it *describes* words as to current spelling, usage, etc. For example, *Webster's Unabridged*, Second Edition, lists and defines *chaise longue* with its proper pronunciation, while the *Random House Unabridged* does the same, but then adds (the unthinkable!) "Also **chaise lounge.**" *Webster's* is prescriptive, Random House descriptive. Another example: *Webster* lists and defines *lingerie* with its correct pronunciation *à la française*, points out that it applies to women's linen underwear, and adds *prescriptively*: "also, underwear of any fabric; as silk *lingerie*. This is a commercial misuse," while *Random House* descriptively gives in its system, what would be lahn zhu RAY. To sum up, if enough people do it wrong, it becomes right in a descriptive dictionary. Both these examples happen to involve aspects of the boudoir, but no sexual chauvinism is intended. *Prescriptive* is modeled after *descriptive*, which is from Late Latin *descriptivus*, based on Latin *descriptus*, past participle of *describere* (to describe). The Roman poet Horace (65–8 B.C.), in *De Arte Poetica* (On the Art of Poetry), favors the descriptive side: "Many terms that have fallen from use will be reborn, and some now honored will fall, if that is the will of usage, which controls the law and standards of speech." Well, Horace, you pays your money and you takes your choice.

prestidigitation (pres tih dij ih TAY shun) *n. Prestidigitation* is sleight of hand, a synonym of **legerdemain** in its literal, good sense. This word was taken over intact from the French, where it means, literally, "ready-fingerness." The French got it from the Latin *praestigiae* (juggler's tricks), adding the *-digitation* from the Latin noun *digitus* (finger—whence we get *digit*). *Prestidigitation* is *not* light-fingeredness, which means, literally, "having nimble fingers," but is almost always used in the sense of "thievish," especially with reference to expertise in the art of pickpocketing. Thus, unlike *legerdemain*, which has both a good sense and a bad sense, *prestidigitation* has only a good sense, and is in fact a noble art, affording much enjoyment to children of all ages.

preterhuman, see **preternatural**

preterit, see **preternatural**

preterition, see **preternatural**

pretermit, see **preternatural**

preternatural (pree tur NACH ur ul) *adj.* Anyone or anything so described is exceptional, outstanding, outside the ordinary course of nature, even abnormal. In context, this word can also mean "supernatural." It is from *praeternaturalis*, a Middle Latin adjective based on two Latin words, *praeter* (beyond) and *natura* (nature). *Praeter* has given us the prefix *preter-* (beyond, past, outside the range of, more than), as in *preterhuman* (beyond what is human, superhuman); *pretermit* (pree tur MIT), to disregard, neglect, leave undone, from Latin *praetermittere* (to let pass), based on *praeter* plus *mittere* (to send, to let go): *preterit* (PRET ur it), past tense, from Latin *praeteritus*, past participle of *praeterire* (to go by); *preterition* (pret uh RISH un), passing over, disregard—in law, the passing over, i.e., disinheriting of an heir, from Late Latin *praeteritio* (passing by). The general concept of *preter* words is *going beyond*, *exceeding* (as in *preterhuman*, *preternatural*) or *passing by* or *over* (as in *pretermit*, *preterition*).

prevaricate (prih VAR uh kate) *vb.* To *prevaricate* is to lie, to speak falsely with intent to mislead. A *prevaricator* (prih VAR uh kay tur) is a liar; a *prevarication* (prih var uh KAY shun) is a lie, a falsehood. The English poet and writer of hymns William Cowper (1731–1800) wrote of "the august tribunal of the skies, where no *prevarication* shall avail" (i.e., it won't do you any good to lie in heaven). In his mock-heroic satirical poem *Hudibras*, the English poet Samuel Butler (1612–1680—not the Samuel Butler, 1835–1902,

335

who wrote *Erewhon*), with a fine disregard for pronunciation and the help of a terrible pun (*rat*, *cat*), wrote this couplet:

> Quoth Hudibras, I smell a rat;
> Ralpho, thou dost *prevaricate*.

Prevaricate comes from *prevaricatus*, past participle of Latin *prevaricari* (to lie; literally, to walk crookedly, as if straddling something).

priapean,   see **priapic**

priapic   (prye AP ik) *adj*. A *priapic* man is one exaggeratedly preoccupied with male sexuality and maleness generally. *Priapism* (PRYE uh piz um) is lascivious behavior, lewd display. The word is also used as a medical term for continuous erection of the penis, especially when due to a physical disorder. Priapus (prye AY pus), in classical mythology, was the god of male procreative power, who eventually came to be regarded as the principal deity of lasciviousness. The phallus was his chief symbol. He was the son of the great Aphrodite (af ruh DYE tee), the ancient Greek goddess of love and beauty (Venus in Roman mythology), and Dionysus (dye uh NYE sus), the classical god of fertility, wine, and drama, whose other name was Bacchus (BAK us). That was quite a family! A modern word for *priapic* is *oversexed* (sounds weak in comparison) or *macho* (MAH cho), describing one who is excessively virile, full of swagger and bravado. *Macho* is simply the Spanish word for "male." A *priapic* man has a one-track mind; his primary concern is with his virility and potency. Don Juan, the legendary Spanish nobleman, and the Italian sexual adventurer Giovanni Jacopo Casanova (1725–1798), famous for their many sexual exploits, are prototypes of *priapic* males, insatiable amorists, obsessed roués, rakes, and libertines. In Mozart's opera *Don Giovanni* (Don Juan), the hero's valet asserts that his master had "in Italy 700 mistresses, in Germany 800, in Turkey and France 91, in Spain 1,003." That's *priapic*! *Priapean* (prye uh PEE uh) is a synonym of *priapic*. In the *New York Times* of October 10, 1984, there is a review of *Parachutes and Kisses* (NAL Books, New York, 1984) by Erica Jong (b. 1942), an author whose previous books were much concerned with sex. Says the reviewer: "In the new novel, the *priapean* Central Park West princess [Isadora Wing, Miss Jong's protagonist] has changed her venue but not her style . . . Miss Wing is one long sexual advertisement of herself . . ." It would seem that in his characterization of a female as "priapean," the reviewer showed a fine disregard for human comparative anatomy. Even the proposed Equal Rights Amendment doesn't go that far. Vive la différence!

pristine   (PRIS teen, -tin, -tine) *adj. Pristine* is a much abused and misused word. It comes from Latin *pristinus* (former, earlier) and does *not* mean "spotless" or "pure" or "fresh." It is properly used to describe something still in its original state, with its original purity. The American historian William Hickling Prescott (1796–1859), in his *Conquest of Mexico*, wrote: "What, then, must have been the emotions of the Spaniards, when, after working their toilsome way into the upper air . . . they beheld these fair scenes in all their *pristine* magnificence and beauty! . . ." The Spanish historian Bernal Diaz del Castillo (c. 1492–1581), in his *Authentic History of the Conquest of New Spain*, tells us: "From this summit [Popocatepetl] could be seen the great city of Mexico, and the whole of the lake, and all the towns which were built in it."

prochronism,   see **parachronism**

Procrustean   (pro KRUS tee un) *adj*. This adjective, based on the legend of Procrustes (discussed hereafter) applies to anyone intent on promoting conformity at any cost, arbitrarily and even violently. According to classical mythology, Procrustes was an Attican robber who captured wayfarers and placed them on his iron bed. If they were longer than the bed, he amputated their overhanging limbs. If they were shorter, he stretched them until they fit the bed. Nasty chap! Thus, the attempt to reduce all people to a standard belief or pattern of behavior is known as placing them on Procrustes's bed, and *Procrustean* describes this radical type of enforced conformity. In his poem *Verbal Criticism*, the English poet David Mallet (c. 1705–1765) wrote:

> Tyrants more cruel than Procrustes old,
> Who to his iron-bed by torture fits
> Their nobler parts, the souls of suffering wits.

337

It does seem something of an exaggeration to label an attempt to procure conformity with a reference to old Procrustes. Would one thus characterize the legend at the bottom of a dinner invitation "Formal"?

procyonine, see **accipitrine**

prodrome (PO drome) *n.* A *prodrome* is a forewarning symptom of a disease, a warning signal, the way a scratchy throat is a *prodrome* of a cold. The word comes from the Greek *prodromos* (literally, running before), based on the prefix *pro-* (before) plus the suffix *-drome*, combining form of *dromos* (running), related to *dromein* (to run). This word suggests comparison with the more familiar word *syndrome*, from Greek *syndrome* (combination), formed from the prefix *syn-* (with) plus *drom-*, a variant stem of *dramein* (to run) plus the noun suffix *-e* which explains why an alternative pronunciation of *syndrome* is SIN druh mee. A *prodrome* is a warning symptom; a *syndrome* is a combination of symptoms. There can, of course, be a *syndrome* of *prodromes*. Why not?

proem (PRO em) *n.* A *proem* is an introductory piece, preface, or preamble to a book or speech. The adjective applicable to an introductory discourse is *proemial* (pro EE mee ul). *Proem* comes from Greek *prooimion*, based on the prefix *pro-* (before) plus *oime* (song) plus diminutive suffix *-ion*. Fowler characterizes *proem* and *proemial* as " . . . not having made their way like *poem* and *poetic* into common use," and says that they "remain puzzling to the unlearned and are better avoided in general writing." They are. The same would certainly go for *prolegomenon* (pro luh GOM uh non, -nun), a preface or prologue (though *prologue* is from *prologos*, based on *pro-*, before, plus *logos*, word or discourse). In *The Life and Opinions of Tristram Shandy*, the English writer Laurence Sterne (1713–1768) speaks of a "pithy *prolegomenon*" handed to Tristram by the commissary of the post-office in France, regarding the rules and regulations of travel by post-chaise in that country.

prolegomenon, see **proem**

prolepsis (pro LEP sis) *n. Prolepsis*, in Greek, means "anticipation," and is a **verbid** of the verb *prolambanein* (to anticipate),
338

based on prefix *pro-* (before) plus *lambanein* (to take). In argument, *prolepsis* is the anticipation of objections from one's opponent in order to reply to them in advance. "But, you will complain, that cannot be because . . . To that I can only reply . . ." *Prolepsis* is used in other senses as well: the assignment of an event to too early a date (in this it is a synonym of **prochronism**); or the use of an adjective describing a condition which has not yet occurred. Fowler calls it the "anticipatory use of an epithet," and gives the example of a passage from *Isabella*, by the English poet John Keats (1795–1821):

> So the two brothers and their *murder'd* man
> Rode past fair Florence.

Murder'd was applied to one who was only later their victim. Other examples: He struck him *dead*, Fill *full* the cup, Paint the town *red*. In each case, the adjective anticipates something that will happen later, and is therefore used *proleptically*.

Promethean   (pruh MEE thee un) *adj.* A *Promethean* person is inventive, creative, courageously original. The adjective comes from *Prometheus*, a Titan in Greek mythology, a famous benefactor of mankind. His name means "forethinker" in Greek. Prometheus was a master craftsman who could construct men of clay and mud and water and bits of other animals. His creativity led to the meanings given above. Zeus had hidden fire from man, but Prometheus tricked him by stealing it and giving it to man, whereupon Zeus chained him to a mountainside and sent down an eagle to eat his liver by day. But his liver was wholly renewed at night. Prometheus remained in torment until Hercules slew the eagle and released him. An early form of match (1828) was called a "Prometheus." It consisted of a tiny glass bulb of sulphuric acid coated with potassium chlorate, sugar, and gum, wrapped in a twist of paper. One bit the bulb with the teeth and the chlorate set the paper on fire. Sounds dangerous! The English naturalist Charles Darwin (1809–1882), in his *Voyage of the Beagle*, wrote: "I carried with me some *promethean* matches, which I ignited by biting; it was thought so wonderful that a man strike fire with his teeth, that it was usual to collect the whole family to see it." In Shakespeare's *Othello* (Act

V, Scene 2), Othello, finding Desdemona asleep, and deciding that she must die by his hand, cries:

> Yet she must die . . .
> I know not where is that *Promethean* heat
> That can thy light relume . . .

The "heat" was the *Promethean* fire with which Prometheus had given life to his figures of clay.

prosody (PROS uh dee) *n.* This word starts out looking like something that has to do with *prose*, but not so: *prosody* is the science or study of the metrical structure of poetry and verse form generally. The *prosody* of a particular poet is his distinctive form of versification. *The Divine Comedy* of the Italian poet Dante Alighieri (1265–1321) is written in a special, quite complex *prosody*, called "terza rima" (literally, third rhyme), in which the middle line of each triplet (series of three lines) rhymes with the first and third lines of the following triplet, with an odd line to complete the canto (main division of a long poem). It is a very difficult *prosody*, not to be recommended to lazy poets. In linguistics, the stress patterns of a statement are its *prosody*. The word is from Greek *prosoidia* (tone, accent, voice modulation, song), based on *pros* (toward) plus *oide*, a contraction of *aoide* (song), related to *aeidein* (to sing).

protasis, see **apodosis**

protopathic, see **epicrisis**

proximate (PROK suh mit) *adj.* By itself, *proximate*, from Latin *proximatus*, past participle of *proximare* (to come near, approach), in either the abstract or physical sense, describes something very near or close in time, order, or meaning, or immediately before or after. It has a special significance in legal parlance, in the expression *proximate cause*: a cause that, in the natural sequence of things, with no independent intervening agency, produces a specific effect or consequence. If A punches B on the nose and B, losing his balance, falls backward and dies of a broken skull, A is guilty of manslaughter even though never intended—there is no intervening act, and A's action was the *proximate cause* of B's death. In a 1930 case, a woman was waiting for a train. A different train came in and started to pull out. A man carrying a package ran for the departing train. A conductor leaned out in an attempt to help the running man jump aboard, dislodging the package, which fell to the track. The train wheels hit it, and, since it contained explosives, there was an explosion. The shock dislodged a heavy baggage scale from its hook and it dropped down onto the woman, who was injured. She sued the railroad company, and lost: no *proximate cause*. A plantiff suing for resulting damages must show that they were the *proximate* result of the defendant's act. Class dismissed.

psittacine,   see **accipitrine**

pteropine,   see **accipitrine**

pubescent,   see **juvenescence**

puissant   (PYOOH ih suhnt, pyooh IS unt; PWIS unt) *adj.* This is a literary adjective for "powerful, potent, mighty." It is a French word with all those meanings, and *le Tout-Puissant*, in French, means "the All-Powerful," i.e., "the Almighty." The ultimate source of *puissant*, via Vulgar Latin *possens*, is Latin *potens*, present participle of *posse* (to be able or powerful). In his *Areopagitica*, an attack on censorship and a stirring argument for freedom of the press, the English poet John Milton (1608–1674) wrote: "Methinks I see in my mind a noble and *puissant* nation rousing herself like a strong man after sleep . . ." The noun, with the same variations of pronunciation, is *puissance*.

pullulate   (PUL yuh late) *vb.* As a special term in botany, to *pullulate* is to grow sprouts or buds. As a general term, to *pullulate* is to breed, to be fruitful and multiply (as enjoined by God in Genesis 1:28), or to exist in abundance, to teem. *Pullulate* is from Latin *pullulatus*, past participle of *pullulare* (to sprout), related to *pullulus* (sprout, young animal), diminutive form of *pullus* (young animal), which gave us *pullet*, a young hen. Excessive *pullulation* is a problem in many nations of the third world, a burden that the one-to-a-family campaign of China aims to curb; but no siblings . . . ?

pyknic, see **asthenic**

Pyrrhic, see **Cadmean**

Pyrrhonism, see **dubiety**

quarrel (KWOR ul) *n*. Besides its common use to denote an angry outburst of hostilities, *quarrel* has two other distinct meanings: a short, square-headed arrow used with a crossbow, or a small diamond-shaped or square pane of glass used in a latticed window. The narrow bar of lead that holds the *quarrels* together is known as a "came"—another example of a special and distinct use of a very common word, the past tense of *come*. *Quarrel*, in this use, is from Middle Latin *quadrellus*, the diminutive of Latin *quadrus* (square). *Came*, in this application, is a special use of *came* or *kame*, a term in physical geography meaning "ridge," especially one of detrital material left by a retreating ice sheet, from Middle English *camb* (comb). *Cames* are used in stained-glass windows as well as plain ones. One mustn't jump to conclusions about the meanings of English words: *quarrel*? *came*?

quasi (KWAY zye, -sye, KWAH zee, -see) *adj.*, *adv.*, *prefix*. As an adjective, *quasi* is the equivalent of "seeming (but not real)," as in a *quasi revolutionary* (who goes through the motions but really doesn't mean it). As an adverb, it means "seemingly (but not really)" and as such, is usually hyphenated as a prefix to an adjective, as in *quasi-authoritative*, *quasi-serious*, *quasi-historical*, like a "historical" novel that takes too many liberties. A *quasi-scientific* experiment is not the real thing; it pretends to be scientific, but there were no controls or checks providing a standard of comparison. *Quasi* is derived from the Latin *quam* (as) plus *si* (if): *quam si* became *quasi*, i.e., *as if* (but not actually). As to the use of the hyphen after *quasi*: treat it as a separate word before a noun (a *quasi alliance*, *a quasi authority*); use the hyphen when *quasi* is used with an adjective, adverb or verb: *quasi-authentic*, *quasi-willingly*, *quasi-believing*.

342

quiddity (KWID ih tee) *n. Quiddity* has two remarkably distinct meanings. First, *quiddity* is the essence of a thing or person, the whatever-it-is that makes a thing or person what he, she, or it is *Quid?*, in Latin, is *what?* and Middle Latin invented *quidditas* (quiddity; literally, "whatness"). The other meaning is "quibble," a nit-picking subtlety or nicety in argument. Shakespeare used it in the second sense in *Henry IV, Part I* (Act I, Scene 2) in the scene where the Prince and Falstaff are having a boisterously non-sensical argument, and Falstaff says to Prince Henry: "How now, how now, mad wag! what, in thy quips and thy *quiddities*? what in a plague have I to do with a buff jerkin?" Again, in *Hamlet* (Act V, Scene 1), Hamlet, gazing at a skull (Yorick's, but Hamlet doesn't know that yet), says: "Why may not that be the skull of a lawyer? Where be his *quiddities* now . . . ?" But in *Hudibras*, the English poet Samuel Butler (1612–1680) used *quiddity* in the first sense, "whatness, essence," whatever it is that differentiates a person or thing from all others:

> He knew
> Where entity and *quiddity*
> (The ghosts of defunct bodies) fly.

The English novelist Laurence Sterne (1713–1768) gave an example of *quiddity* without using the word: " . . . the *corregiescity* of Corregio." The English historian Thomas Carlyle (1795–1881), in *Frederick the Great*, quoted Sterne (without credit) but corrected his spelling: ".. the *correggiosity* of Correggio." They were both referring to the *quiddity* of the Italian painter Antonio Allegri da Correggio (1494–1534), but they might as well have written of the Michelangelosity of Michelangelo or the Shakespeareosity of Shakespeare. Today, *quiddity*, in that sense, is a pet word of literary critics, who discuss the *quiddity*, for instance, of T. S. Eliot or John Updike, i.e., the special quality that makes Eliot Eliot and Updike Updike. In this sense, *quiddity* has a synonym: *haecceity* (hek SEE ih tee, heek-), denoting that which gives something its unique quality or characteristic. It is a "partial synonym," in that *quiddity* applies to persons as well as things, and *haecceity* appears to apply only to things. Its derivation is from Middle Latin *haecceitas* (literally, "thisness"), based on Latin *haecce*, a variant of *haec* (this—

the feminine form of *hic;* feminine because it modifies the feminine noun *res*, thing, understood).

quidnunc   (KWID nunk) *n.* A *quidnunc* is a gossip, a busybody, a nosy individual, a pretentious and over-eager collector and connoisseur of the latest tidbits of news. It comes from two Latin words: *quid nunc* (what now?). A *quidnunc* wants to know what's going on, and sometimes pretends to know it. John Lothrop Motley, the American historian and diplomat (1814–1877) wrote of "the idle stories of *quidnuncs,*" and *Quidnunc* is the name of the hero of *The Upholsterer, or What News?* by the American playwright C. W. Murphy (d. 1931).

quincunx   (KWING kungks, KWIN-) *n.* A *quincunx* is an arrangement of five objects, one at each corner of a square or rectangle and one in the center. The term is used mainly in landscaping, with reference to the arrangement of trees. The adjective is *quincuncial* (kwin KUN shul). *Quincunx* has an interesting derivation: *quinque,* Latin for "five" plus *uncia,* Latin for "twelfth." What have *five* and *twelfth* to do with the arrangement of trees, or anything else? Well, there was once a Roman coin called an "as," which originally consisted of a pound of copper (later reduced), and another Roman coin worth *five-twelfths* of an *as,* and that one was marked with a *quincunx* of spots, to indicate its value. Incidentally, *uncia* gave us *ounce* (one-twelfth of a pound) and *inch* (one-twelth of a foot). The English writer Patrick Leigh Fermor (b. 1915), in *A Time of Gifts* (John Murray, London, 1977), made a dramatic use of *quincunx* in this passage: "Pruned to the bone, the dark vine-shoots stuck out of the snow in rows of skeleton fists which shrank to *quincunxes* of black commas along snow-covered contour-lines of the vineyards . . ."

quinquennial,   see **lustrum**

quoin   (koin, kwoin) *n.*, *vb.* This little word has serveral uses, depending on context. In printing, a *quoin* is a wedge for locking type on a frame (called a "chase"). In architecture, it is an external angle of a wall or one of the stones forming the angle; a cornerstone (not necessarily the kind laid by governors and other celebrities), or a *voussoir* (vooh SWAR), a wedge-shaped stone forming part of an arch (derived, via French and Late Latin, from Latin *volutus*, past participle of *volvere*, to roll). Apart from these special uses, a *quoin* is any wedge-shaped piece of material used for a variety of purposes, like steadying a table in one of those restaurants where it's too dark to read the menu, keeping a door open, etc. To *quoin* is to wedge or secure or raise by wedging. *Quoin* is a variant of *coin* in the sense of "cornerstone," which is, via French *coin*, from Latin *cuncus* (wedge). *Cuncus* is the basis of the term *cuneiform* as to which see **cuneal**, **cuneate**.

quondam (KWON dam) *adj. Quondam* means "former" or "sometime," describing something that used to be, or someone who once bore a certain relationship to a person, or a title to an office that no longer exists. It was taken intact from the Latin, where it is an adverb meaning "formerly, once upon a time," although the Latin poets used it also in the senses of "some time in the future" and "at times." In English, *quondam* is not an adverb but an adjective that looks only at the past, pointing to something or someone that at one time had a certain role or character that now has ended, like a *quondam* dynasty or a *quondam* friend, associate, or partner. Shakespeare was fond of *quondam*. He used it twice in *Henry VI, Part 3*. In Act III, Scene 1, King Henry, in disguise, enters a chase (an unenclosed hunting-ground), where, unknown to him, two gamekeepers stand. He laments his fate. One of the keepers recognizes him and says: "This is the *quondam* king; let's seize upon him," and they finally arrest him. In Act III, Scene 2, the Earl of Warwick addresses King Henry's wife, Queen Margaret, as "our *quondam* queen." And in *Troilus and Cressida* (Act IV, Scene 5), Hector, addressing Menelaus, refers to Helen in these terms:

> Your *quondam* wife swears still by Venus' glove;
> She's well, but bade me not commend her to you.

quotidian (kwoh TID ee un) *adj. Quotidian* means "daily," i.e., recurring every day, as in a *quotdian report,* and in that sense is synonymous with **diurnal** but only in the first meaning given under that entry, i.e., "daily," as opposed to "daytime" used attributively. By extension, *quotidian* has acquired the second meaning of "everyday" in the sense of "ordinary, commonplace," and in certain contexts, "trivial." In this extension, it follows its Latin antecedent *quotidianus* (daily), which acquired the meaning "common, ordinary." Things that go on day after day do become run-of-the-mill after a while. Variety is the spice, etc. The American poet Wallace Stevens (1879–1955), in *The Comedian as the Letter C*, wrote: " . . . The *quotidian* saps philosophers."

ralline, see **accipitrine**

rangiferine, see **accipitrine**

ranine, see **accipitrine**

rapscallion (rap SKAL yun) *n.* This picturesque word means "rascal" or "rogue" or "scamp." It is based on *rascal*, which comes from Old French *rascaille* (rabble) and gave modern French *racaille* (rabble, riffraff, scum). In *The Adventures of Huckleberry Finn*, the American author Mark Twain (Samuel Langhorne Clemens, 1835–1910) tells us, "All kings is mostly *rapscallions*," a bird's-eye view of history, and rather a sweeping generalization. But don't let's get started on Richard III (1452–1485), king of England 1483–1485), who this author firmly believes was a good guy and whom he stoutly defends against the libels of the English statesman and writer Sir Thomas More (1478–1535 and only three years old when Richard died), the English chronicler Holinshed (died c. 1580—a firm follower of Sir Thomas More and a public relations man for Richard's foe and successor Henry VII (1457–1509), king of England 1485–1509, the first Tudor king), and William Shakespeare, who, after all, writing in the time of the Tudor Queen Elizabeth I, couldn't very well make Richard anything but a villain. Richard was *not* a *rapscallion*. Suggested reading on this disputed matter: *The Daughter of Time*, a most original piece of historical detection (first published by Peter Davies, London, 1951, by Penguin Books, Harmondsworth, 1954 and oft-reprinted by Penguin) by the Scottish writer and playwright Elizabeth MacKintosh under the pseudonym Josephine Tey (1896–1952).

raptorial (rap TOR ee ul) *adj.* A *raptorial* animal is a predator, one that preys upon other animals for its sustenance and that of its young. Eagles and hawks, for example, are *raptorial* birds; tigers and lions *raptorial* animals; almost all fish, reptiles, and insects are *raptorial*. *Raptorial* can apply as well to parts of the body adapted for seizing prey, like claws and teeth. Thus far, *raptorial* has not been used to describe those conglomerates that like to swallow defenseless corporations. It comes from Latin *raptor* (robber, plunderer, one who seizes), related to the verb *rapere* (to seize), *raptare* (**frequentative** of *rapere*), and *raptus* (tearing off, carrying off), from which we derive *rape*, a most unlovely crime.

ratiocinate (rash ee OS uh nate) *vb.* To *ratiocinate* (note the pronunciation of the first syllable) is to reason, and the process is *ratiocination* (rash ee os uh NAY shun). The Latin verb *ratiocinari* has a number of related meanings, all having to do with brainwork: to compute, consider, deliberate, infer, conclude, and it all goes back to *ratus*, the past participle of the verb *reri* (to think). The Latin noun *ratio* means "reckoning" and *accountant*, in Latin, is *ratiocinator*, which speaks well for the profession of accountancy. *Ratiocinatio* is Latin for "reasoning." It is only by discarding our biases and preconceptions that we can *ratiocinate*, and reach sane and *reason*able conclusions. Pure *rationcination*, the exercise of the intellect alone, without interference from the emotions, is extremely difficult to achieve. The English novelist and satirist Samuel Butler (1612–1680), in his mock-heroic poem *Hudibras*—a venomous satire against the Puritans, represented by the "Presbyterian knight" Sir Hudibras—wrote:

> He was in logic a great critic
> Profoundly skill'd in analytic.
> He could distinguish, and divide
> A hair 'twixt south and south-west side.
> On either which he would dispute,
> Confute, change hands, and still confute.
>
> He'd run in debt by disputation,
> And pay with *ratiocination*.

(This poem gave rise to the adjective Hudibrastic [hyooh duh BRAS tik], which came to describe anything written in a mock-heroic, sportively burlesque style.)

razzia (RAZ ee uh) *n*. This is a word, not much heard these days, to denote a pillaging incursion or a plundering or slave-collecting raid of the sort we read about in the history books and romantic novels. *Razzia* also applies to a piratical takeover of a ship at sea. The term was used originally of the raids carried out by African Muslims, but would not be applicable to the October 1985 hijacking of the Italian cruise ship *Achille Lauro* by a small Palestinian force, because the four hijackers, though in cold blood they shot and killed an innocent crippled elderly gentleman as he sat in his wheelchair, were kind enough to refrain from plundering or slave-collecting. *Razzia*, via French and the Algerian Arabic word *ghaziah* or *gazia*, is from Arabic *ġazwa*, related to the verb *ġazw* (to make raids), the Arabic *g* being pronounced like the gutteral French *r*.

realpolitik (ree AL paw lih teek) *n*. This is a word from the German, with the effect of "political realism, practical politics," international policy based on national interests and on material rather than moral considerations; a cynical term for the "might is right" school of international conduct that eschews any hint of idealism. The traditional policy of the "Drang nach Osten" (the thrust to the East), the age-old urge of German politicians to annex territories in the East, and *Lebensraum* (room for living), space for an expanding population, a Nazi slogan, have been German concepts and policies that have disturbed peace again and again. *Realpolitik* is only one of a series of words coined in Germany, alas.

rebarbative (ree BAR buh tiv) *adj*. What is *rebarbative* is unattractive, annoying, irritating, distasteful, even repellent or downright repulsive. It comes, via French *rébarbatif* (stern, surly, grim, forbidding) from Old French *rébarber* (to be unattractive). The dictionaries all relate *rébarber* and *rebarbative* to French *barbe* (beard), based on Latin *barba*, but it is hard to see the connection, especially among the French who often wore beards long before they became as common as they are now in England and America; and in any case, beards can be attractive or unattractive, as the case may be. Whose beard are they talking about? Bluebeard's?

reboant (REB oh unt) *adj*. Anything so described is resounding, reechoing, reverberating loudly. This is a poetical term, from Latin

348

reboans, present participle of *reboare* (to echo, resound), based on prefix *re-*, indicating repetition, plus *boare* (to shout, roar, cry aloud; when describing places, to echo). The sound of a bass drum can be described as *reboant*. The voices of **spelunkers** shouting at one another in the far reaches of a huge cave are *reboant*.

rebus (REE bus) *n.* A *rebus* is a riddle, wholly or partly hieroglyphical, an enigmatic representation of a word, phrase, or sentence by a series of pictures or symbols or a combination of both. A dot (*speck*) followed by pictures of a *tack* and a *yule* log and the letter *r* add up to *spectacular. I C U R Y Y 4* before a picture of a *hymn* book gives us "I see you are too wise for him." An English *rebus: If the B m t put: If it b.* means: "If the grate be empty, put coal on. If it be full, stop." Explanation (if needed): In British English, *great*, modifying a letter of the alphabet (now archaic in this sense), meant "capital, upper case," so that *B* was "great *b*"; and a period (punctuation ending a sentence) is usually called "full stop." *Rebus* is a form of Latin *res* (thing) and means "by means of things," i.e., represented by things rather than words.

recension (rih SEN shun) *n.* *Recension* is the critical revision of a literary work based on close examination of both text and source material—the kind this author expected (and got) from his **diaskeuast** in the course of the writing of this book. *Recension* is derived from Latin *recensio* (reviewing), related to the verb *recensere* (to examine, review), based on prefix *re-* (again) plus *censere* (to assess, estimate). It is to be hoped that the *recension* of this manuscript will not result in too many changes and corrections.

redact (rih DAKT) *vb.* To *redact* a piece of writing is to edit and revise it, work it into shape, put it into literary form suitable for publication. To *redact* a proclamation or a formal written statement is to frame it. *Redact* is from Latin *redactus*, past particple of the verb *redigere* (to bring back), based on *red-*, variant of *re-*, before a vowel, plus *agere* (to drive). The editor is the *redactor* (rih DAK tur); the activity is *redaction* (rih DAK shun), and the adjective is *redactional* (rih DAK shun ul). *Redaction*, a vital step in the preparation of a writing for publication, can lead to serious disagreement between the *redactor* and an author who considers his every word sacred. In the case of writing that is too verbose, *redaction* can lead to *reduction*. Suffice it to say that there has been nothing short of peace and harmony between this author and his *redactrix*!

reify (REE uh fye) *vb.* To *reify* an abstraction is to turn it into, or consider it as a concrete or material thing, to materialize it. *Space* is an abstract concept. It can be *reified* into a finite distance between two objects, and in that sense made concrete, or materialized. Time, too, can be *reified* from a concept to an objective, concrete thing, like the time between one event and another. *Reify* and *reification* (ree if uh KAY shun), the act or result of *reifying*, are based upon the Latin noun *res* (thing) and its stem, *re-*. One can *reify* an endless number of abstract concepts, like *love* (think of Dante's love for Beatrice or Petrarch's for Laura), or hate (Macduff's for Macbeth, Lady Anne's for Richard III). One can *reify* the concept of communication into concrete systems such as speech, writing, the telephone, television, and all the other contemporary physical means of communicating information.

repine (rih PINE) *vb.* To *repine* is to fret, complain, unhappily and nervously express discontent. The word is made up of the prefix *re-* (repeatedly) plus *pine* (to suffer and languish with yearning and longing, to waste away under emotional distress); via Old English *pinean* (to torment) and Latin *poena* (penalty, pain), from Greek *poine* (penalty). *Repine* may have been formed after the model of *repent*. In *Martin Chuzzlewit*, the English novelist Charles Dickens (1812–1870) has Mr. Pecksniff tenderly say: "Do not *repine*, my friends. Do not weep for me . . ." The American poet and essayist Ralph Waldo Emerson (1803–1882), in his poem *Sacrifice*, wrote:

> Though love *repine*, and reason chafe,
> There came a voice without reply—
> " 'Tis man's perdition to be safe,
> When for the truth he ought to die."

restive (RES tiv) *adj.* A *restive* person is impatient and fidgety; he cannot easily bear control or restraint or delay, but always wants to get moving. A *restive* horse, on the other hand, stubbornly refuses to get moving, and keeps shifting sideways or backwards, jibbing and balking. Whether man or beast, *restive* indicates fidgeting and resistance to control; the person wants to get going, while

350

the horse refuses to move. Fowler warns against the use of *restive* as a synonym of *restless*. "*Restive* implies resistance," says Fowler. The use of *restive* for *restless* would be an instance of **catachresis**. The derivation of *restive* is a complicated story. Originally it meant "at rest"; then, "obstinate"; then, "impatient," especially under restraint—the opposite of its original meaning. These things happen in language: *Egregious* originally meant "distinguished, noble, eminent, outstanding, out of the ordinary"; now, "glaring, flagrant," always pejorative, as in *an egregious blunder, an egregious liar*. *Restive*'s predecesor is Middle English *restif* (stationary, or balking).

revanchism (rih VAN shiz um) *n. Revanche*, French for "revenge," has given rise to the noun *revanchism*, the policy of a nation seeking to regain territory lost to another nation, such as France's attitude and policy towards Alsace and Lorraine, lost to Prussia after the Franco-Prussian War of 1870–71. The adjective describing the policy is *revanchist* (rih VAN shist). The revanchist attitude of the Arab states as to territory lost to Israel after the Six Day War of 1967 has played a prominent part in causing the turmoil of the Middle East.

rhabdomancy (RAB duh man see) *n. Rhabdomancy* is another name for "dowsing," whether for water or metal ores, through the use of a forked rod. The source of the word is Late Greek *rhabdomanteia*, based on *rhabdos* (wand, rod) plus *manteia* (**divination**, prophecy). The rod in question is known as a "divining rod." This ancient form of divination, dowsing, or *rhabdomancy* was imported from Germany to Cornwall, England, for use in the Cornish mines, some time in the 16th century. People still discuss the question whether the use of *rhabdomancy* is an art, a skill, a gift, or a fake. If you are interested in the possibility of discovering oil under your lawn, there are available a number of modern scientific techniques.

rhinocerine, see **accipitrine**

rhotacism (ROH tuh siz um) *n. Rho* is the equivalent of our letter *r* in the Greek alphabet. The Greeks had a word for just about everything, and came up with the verb *rhotakizein* (to make exces-

351

sive use of the letter *rho*). Why the need for such a highly specialized word? Obviously, because the *r* sound was often unduly substituted for some other sound. *Rhotacism*, from Greek *rhotakismos* via Latin *rhotacismus*, based on that peculiar Greek verb, is the excessive use or misuse or mispronunciation of the letter *r*. The converse, i.e., the substitution of some other sound for that of *r*, is known as *pararhotacism*. In philology, the tendency to change *s* or *z* to *r*, especially between vowels, is a common form of *rhotacism*, as in the case of *lose* becoming *-lorn* in the word *forlorn*, and the genitive of the Sanskrit word *janasas* (race, people) taking the form *generis* in Latin. A common form of *rhotacism* in the way of mispronunciation or misarticulation is the burring sound of *r* in French speech and that of many inhabitants of Northumberland, a county in the northeast of England. In speaking English, the Japanese commonly practice *rhotacism* by substituting the sound of *r* for that of *l*, while the Chinese indulge in *pararhotacism* by substituting the sound of *l* for that of *r*. The verb is *rhotacise* (ROH tuh size). Talk about minding your *p*'s and *q*'s!

rodomontade   (rod uh mon TADE, -tad, roe duh-, -mun-) *n.*, *adj.*, *vb.* This interesting word, which can be used as an adjective (boastful) or a verb (to boast, brag, talk big) is, however, almost always found as a noun, denoting extravagant boasting, vainglorious bragging, blustery self-glorification. The Italian fascist leader Benito Mussolini (1883–1945), whom the author saw (1926) in military trappings, addressing the multitudes from the balcony of the Palazzo Chigi in Rome, with jutting jaw and flailing arms, was the embodiment of *rodomontade*. His pal of later days, Adolf Hitler (1889–1945), wasn't bad at *rodomontade* either. That year, 1945, seems to have been a bad one for these two leading exponents of *rodomontade* following in the footsteps of Rodomonte, the vainglorious, bragging king of Algiers, who figured in the unfinished epic poem *Orlando Innamorato* by the Italian poet Matteo Maria Boiardo (1434–1494) and its sequel *Orlando Furioso* by his successor Ludovico Ariosto (1474–1553). Both works were based on Roland, the great French hero of medieval legend celebrated in the 11th century *Chanson de Roland*. The name *Orlando* is the Italian equivalent of *Roland*, but both Italian poets took advantage of their poetic license to transform Roland beyond recognition. What has survived of the *Chanson* and both *Orlandos* to become part of our language is *rodomontade*, nothing less than old Rodomonte with the *e* cut off and the suffix *-ade* stuck on, as often happens to nouns denoting action, like *fusillade*, *renegade*, *promenade* and *cannon-ade*. Cf. **braggadocio**, **fanfaronade**, **gasconade**, **thrasonical**. Next time you run into an irritating braggart, just point your finger and cry: "High time to stop your *rodomontade*, your *gasconade*, your *braggadocio*, your *fanfaronade*, you *thrasonical* churl!"

roorback (ROOR bak) *n.* A *roorback* is a smear, a defamatory lie published as a political "dirty trick" à la Nixon campaign. When James K. Polk (1795–1849, 11th president of the United States) was running for that office, a spurious and damaging article was published in 1844 purporting to be an extract from *Roorback's Tour through the Western and Southern States in 1836.* Baron von Roorback was a pretended traveler whose alleged notes included an account of an incident damaging to Polk's character. From this the word *roorback* (lower case *r*), sometimes *roorbach*, came to signify any damaging falsehood circulated for political effect.

Roscian (ROSH ee un) *n.*, *adj.* As an adjective, *Roscian* may be used to describe anything having to do with actors or acting, but its special use is to describe a highly talented actor or performance. One can safely say of Laurence Olivier (b. 1907) that he is an actor of *Roscian* proportions, or that he always gives a *Roscian* perform-ance. As a noun, a *Roscian* is an actor of uncommon, outstanding ability. John Gielgud (b. 1904) can be described as a *Roscian*. This word is derived from the name of the actor Roscius (126–62 B.C.), the sensation of the Roman stage. Shakespeare refers to him in *Henry VI, Part 3*, when (Act V, Scene 6) King Henry says to Gloucester, who is about to kill him, "What scene of death hath Roscius now to act?" (How am I to die?), and again, in *Hamlet* (Act II, Scene 2), when Hamlet, mocking the long-winded Polon-ius, who is about to announce the arrival of the players (which is old news to Hamlet) and make a long, long story of it, puts words into Polonius's mouth and starts to recite: "When Roscius was an actor in Rome . . ." It was the great fame of Roscius that gave us this interesting word *Roscian*.

rubric (ROOH brik) *n.* A *rubric* is a heading in a book or man-uscript, a title or other distinguishing caption at the beginning of a

353

chapter, section, etc. The *rubric* is written or printed in red or in special type that sets it apart from the general text. In older books and manuscripts it was customary for the *rubric* to be in red; hence its name, from the Latin *rubrica* (red earth, red ochre), based on *ruber* (red), from whose kindred adjective *rubeus* we get *ruby*. The adjective *rubrical* (ROOH brik ul) means "reddish" or "marked with red." To *rubricate* (ROOH bruh kate) something is to mark or color it with red. In the translation by the English poet and painter Dante Gabriel Rossetti (1828–1882), the opening words of *La Vita Nuova* (The New Life), an early work in prose and poetry of the great Italian poet Dante Alighieri (1265–1321), are these: "In that part of the book of my memory before which is little that can be read, there is a *rubric*, saying, 'Incipit Vita Nuova [The New Life Begins].' " Dante goes on to say, in the translation of Professor Mark Musa (Indiana University Press, Bloomington, Indiana, 1973): "It is my intention to copy into this little book the words I find written under that *heading*—if not all of them, at least the essence of their meaning."

rubrical, see **rubric**

rubricate, see **rubric**

rucervine, see **accipitrine**

ruddle (RUD ul) *n.*, *vb. Ruddle* is red ochre, used principally in sheep-marking for purposes of identification of the owner, a much less painful process than cow-branding. To *ruddle* is to mark sheep in that way. *Ruddle* has two variants, *raddle* and *reddle*. The latter is used as a pejorative for rouge and its application. *Raddled* is slang for the description of a face treated with an excess of make-up.

ruminant (ROOH mu nunt) *n.*, *adj. Ruminant*, as a noun, embraces all even-toed hoofed animals, comprising cloven-hoofed cud-chewing quadrupeds, including cattle, deer, camels, etc. As an adjective, *ruminant* means, literally, "cud-chewing" and figuratively, "meditative, contemplative." The related verb, to *ruminate*, means to "chew the cud"; figuratively, to reflect, meditate, ponder, muse. *Ruminant* is from Latin *ruminans*, present participle of *ruminare* (to chew over, chew the cud), and *ruminate* is from *ruminatus*, the past participle of that verb. All these words go back to Latin *rumen* (throat, gullet), which is English for the first of the two stomachs of a *ruminating* animal. The English novelist Charles Dickens (1812–1870), in *Pickwick Papers*, has Mr. Pickwick say: "I am *ruminating* on the strange mutability of human affairs." In Shakespeare's *Othello* (Act III, Scene 3), Othello says to Iago: ". . . Speak to me as to thy thinkings,/As thou dost *ruminate* . . ." The German philosopher Friedrich Nietzsche (1844–1900) gave this advice in *Thus Spake Zarathustra*: "We ought to learn from the kine [cattle] one thing: *ruminating*." He was right.

rupicaprine, see **accipitrine**

rusticate (RUS tuh kate) *vb.* To *rusticate* is to live in the countryside or take a trip to the country. To *rusticate* someone is to send him to the country. To *rusticate* something is to give it a rustic finish, like *rusticating* the surface of a piece of furniture to make it look countryish, or *rusticating* a wall to produce a rural effect. *Rusticate* has a special meaning in Britain: to *rusticate* a university student is to suspend him as punishment for an offense; not to *expel* him, which, in British English, is to *send him down*. Rustic, *rusticity*, *rural*, etc., are all based on Latin *rus* (country); *rusticate* is from Latin *rusticatus*, past participle of *rusticari* (to live in the countryside).

ruth (roohth) *n.* Where do you suppose the common adjective *ruthless* comes from? Answer: from the uncommon noun *ruth*, meaning "pity, compassion," or "sorrow, grief"; from Middle English *ruthe*. Our verb and noun *rue* is from the related Middle English verb *ruen*. It often happens, as in the case of *ruth* and *ruthless*, that the negative is used far more commonly than the positive, and often has a positive effect. To describe the Macbeths as *ruthless* is to impact a quite positive impression. *Impeccable conduct* or *dress* presents a positive image; and how often have you run across *peccable*? *Impervious/pervious*: If you ran into the rarely used *pervious*, you might think it was a misprint for *previous*.

■ ■ ■ ■

sabelline, see **accipitrine**

sacerdotal (sas ur DOTE ul) *adj. Sacerdotal* means "priestly" and applies to anything having to do with priests and priesthood. *Sacerdotalism* (sas ur DOTE u liz um) is the spirit of the priesthood, devotion to priestly matters, priestcraft, and in context, the claim of excessive, even supernatural authority for the priesthood. *Sacerdotal* is from Latin *sacerdotalis*, based on *sacerdos* (priest), formed of *sacer* (sacred) plus *dare* (to give). When asked, in a test at school, "What is rabies, and what can be done about it?" a young student replied, "Rabies is Jewish priests and nothing can be done about it."

salamandrine, see **accipitrine**

salmagundi (sal muh GUN dee) *n.* This peculiar word describes, in its narrow sense, a dish, usually served as a salad, consisting of a mixture of chopped cooked meat, onions, hard-boiled eggs, anchovies, pickled vegetables, radishes, olives, watercress, and other ingredients, with salad dressing, sometimes arranged in rows to form a color pattern. The term, however, is sometimes applied to a much simpler concoction: a meat and vegetable stew. It can also be spelt with a final -*y* instead of an -*i*. *Salmagundi* has a much wider figurative application, as a term denoting any heterogeneous mixture or miscellany, and in this sense it is a synonym for **gallimaufry** or **olio** or *hodge-podge*, a medley, a potpourri, a mishmash, a farrago. A painting, for instance, or any work of art, for that matter, revealing a mixture of many influences may be referred to as a *salmagundi* or pastiche. There is a jocular saying that a camel is a horse designed by a committee. That would make the poor beast a sort of *salmagundi* of an animal—a little of this and a little of that. Any creation in which too many cooks have had a hand may sadly turn out to be a *salmagundi*. The word is derived from the French noun *salmigondis*, said to be based, in turn, on the Italian for "pickled salami," known as *salami conditi*. Though it has nothing to do with the old nursery rhyme, the sound of *salmagundi* brings to mind the sad tale of

> Solomon Grundy
> Born on a Monday
> Christened on Tuesday
> Married on Wednesday
> Took ill on Thursday
> Worse on Friday
> Died on Saturday
> Buried on Sunday
> This is the end
> of Solomon Grundy

and the end of *salmagundi*.

sanguinary (SANG gwuh nair ee) *adj. Sanguis* is Latin for "blood" and is the basis of several Latin adjectives having to do with *blood, bloodiness, bloodstained* and *bloodthirstiness*. We, too, have a number of derivatives having to do with *blood*: *sanguinary*, meaning "bloodthirsty, delighting in bloodshed or slaughter," or "characterized by bloodshed"; *sanguineous* (san GWIN ee us) or *sanguinous* (SANG gwuh nus), pertaining to blood, blood-colored, involving bloodshed; *sanguinolent* (sang GWIN uh lunt), pertaining to blood, tinged with blood; and finally *sanguine* (SANG gwin)—of all things, after this bloody mess, cheerful, hopeful, confident, disposed to thinking that all is going to go well. This nonconforming meaning arose from the belief, in old physiology, that there were four basic body fluids, known as "humors," blood, phlegm, black bile, and yellow bile or **choler,** which determined, by their relative proportion, one's mental as well as physical make-up, and if blood predominated, that person was of cheerful disposition. This belief gave rise to the terms *sanguine*, phlegmatic, melancholic, and *choleric* and the theory that a good balance made for "good humor" and an imbalance for "ill humor." All this leads to the conclusion that one should not confuse *sanguinary* with *sanguine*, even though people out for bloodshed can, one supposes, be cheerful, hopeful, and confident about their mission and thus be *sanguinary* and *sanguine* at the same time. (See also **consanguinity**).

sanguineous, sanguinous,   see **sanguinary**

sanguinolent,   see **sanguinary**

sapid   (SAP id) *adj. Sapid* describes anything having flavor, the implication being that it is agreeable flavor, palatable and appetizing. Applied to things other than food, like conversation, writing, etc., *sapid* takes on the flavor of "interesting," even "exhilarating." *Sapid* is, of course, the opposite of *insipid*, i.e., *not sapid. Sapid* is from Latin *sapidus* (flavored); *insipid* from Latin *insipidus*. The change from the *a* of *sapid* to the *i-* of *-sipid* in *insipid* is an instance of **ablaut** in related words—in this case, antonyms.

saprogenic   (sap roh JEN ik) *adj.* This is a word with unpleasant associations. *Sapro-* is the combining form of Greek *sapros* (rotten, putrid); *-genic* is an adjectival suffix meaning "producing," from the root of the Greek verb *gignesthai* (to produce). *Saprogenic*, then, means, "producing decay or putrefaction," as caused, for example, by certain bacteria; or "produced from putrefaction," like organisms growing on decaying matter, like maggots thriving on rotting flesh. Another form of *saprogenic* is *saprogenous* (suh PROJ uh nus). Other *sapro-* words are *saprophagous* (suh PROF uh gus), a biological term for a plant or animal feeding on dead or rotting animal matter, with suffix *-phagous* based on the Greek verb *phagein* (to eat, devour); *saprophyte* (SAP ruh fite), an organism, like certain bacteria and fungi, that lives on dead plant or animal matter, with suffix *-phyte* from Greek *phyton* (plant). Ugh!

saprophagous,   see **saprogenic**

saprophyte,   see **saprogenic**

sarcophagus   (sar KOF uh gus) *n.* A *sarcophagus* is a stone coffin, often adorned with sculpture and inscriptions. The ancient Greeks called limestone *lithos sarkophagos: lithos* (stone), *sarkophagos* (flesh-eating) based on prefix *sarko-*, combining form of *sarx* (flesh), plus suffix *-phagos* (eating), combining form of *phagein* (to eat, devour). *Lithos sarkophagos* meant "corrosive limestone," which was used to build coffins that would dissolve corpses.

Later the *lithos* was dropped, and the *sarkophagos* was retained to mean "stone coffin" even after the Greeks began to use ordinary non-corrosive stone for their coffins. After all this gruesome stuff, let us get on to something a little less eerie—*subreption*. The use of *sarkophagos* is an example of *subreption*, a semantic change or shift occurring when a word continues in use though what it signifies undergoes change. *Subreption* denotes, literally, the obtaining of something by surprise, stealth, or misrepresentation. It comes from Latin *subreptio* (purloining), based on the verb *subrepere* (to crawl up from below), which has the variant *surrepere* and is related to the adjective *subrepticius*, variant *surrepticius*, from which we get *surreptitious*. Here are some examples of *subreption*: *pen* is derived from *penna* (feather) and was used originally when pens were made of quills. The name stuck even after the object underwent change. A *horn* was originally made of an animal's horn. A drinking *straw* was originally made of a straw. The word *volume* originated from the fact that, once, reading matter was in the form of a scroll or roll of papyrus or parchment, and the *vol-* of volume is related to *revolve*.

Sassenach, see **ilk**

satyriasis (say tuh RYE uh sis) *n.* A *satyr* (SAY tur, SAT ur), in classical mythology, was a forest deity, lustful and riotous, an attendant on the god Bacchus, the god of wine (the Roman counterpart of Greek Dionysus). Satyrs were half man, half goat. *Satyr* has acquired the figurative meaning of "lecher," and so has *goat*, in slang usage. Hamlet didn't think much of satyrs. In the famous soliloquy "O! that this too too solid flesh would melt . . ." (Shakespeare's *Hamlet*, Act I, Scene 2), in his contempt of King Claudius, he cries that his father, compared with Claudius, ". . . was Hyperion to a satyr . . ." (Hyperion was a Titan, later identified with Apollo; his name was an epithet of the Sun god himself.) It will come as no surprise, then, that *satyriasis*, taken intact from the Greek, is the name for pathological uncontrollable lust among males. *Satyromania* (say tuh roh MAY nee uh) is a synonym of *satyriasis*.

satyromania, see **satyriasis**

saveloy (SAV uh loy) *n.* A *saveloy* is a highly seasoned, cooked, and dried sausage, originally containing pig's brains. The name comes, via French *cervelas* and Italian *cervellata* (a Milanese variety), based on *cervello* (brain), from Latin *cerebellum*, diminutive of *cerebrum* (brain). In the *Pickwick Papers* of the English novelist Charles Dickens (1812–1870), we read of "Mr. Solomon Pell . . . regaling himself . . . with a cold collation of an Abernethy biscuit [a hard biscuit flavored with caraway seeds, probably originated by John Abernethy, a English surgeon who died in 1831] and a *saveloy*." And in *Life and Labour*, by an English writer named Smiles—the book came out in 1887—we discover that "Sawyer, the gastronomist [see **gastronome**] . . . would stop at a stall in the Haymarket [a street in London] and luxuriate in eating a penny *saveloy*." As to the present status of the *saveloy*, a search through a large number of cookbooks in various languages has failed to produce any information. This must now be an obsolete delicacy.

sc. (no pronunciation given—used only in writing). *Sc.* is the abbreviation of Latin *scilicet*, a contraction of *scire licet* (it is permitted to know), an explanatory word meaning "namely." *Scilicet* is practically never used in full. If spoken, it is pronounced SIL ih set. *Sc.* is used to clarify, as in *I saw him (sc., the accused) running down the alley*, or *I had heard the opera (sc. Cosi Fan Tutte) in Milan*. Another use is to introduce a word to replace one already used, as in *I could (sc. couldn't) care less*, or *I couldn't of (sc. have) done that without your help*. In short, *sc.* explains an ambiguous word or introduces a word to be supplied, e.g., to establish the sense of a word used incorrectly.

scaphocephalic (skaf oh sih FAL ik) *adj.* A *scaphocephalic* person is one with a boat-shaped head. The unfortunate owner of this undesirable feature might also be described as *scaphocephalous* (skaf oh SEF uh lus), his head as a *scaphocephalus* (same pronunciation), and his condition as *scaphocephaly* (skaf oh SEF uh lee). These words are from Greek *skaphe* (boat) plus *kephale* (head). *Scaphocephalic* persons are rare, and if you come across one, don't stare, just mutter "scaphocephalic" to yourself, quietly.

scatology (skuh TOL uh jee) *n.* *Scatology* is obscenity, generally understood to be of the kind associated with aspects of excrement and obsessive interest in it. *Scatological* (skat uh LOJ uh kul) humor is based on some reference to excrement—"bathroom humor," as it were. *Scatological* language is the type preoccupied with excrement, but *scatology* has, in context, a more dignified meaning: the study of fossil excrement, also known as *coprology* (kah PROL uh jee). *Scatology* is derived from Greek *skato-*, the combining form of *skor* (dung), plus the familiar suffix *-logy*, from Greek *-logia* used in the name of sciences, as in *geology*, *philology*, etc. *Coprology* comes from the Greek *kopro-*, the combining form of *kopros* (dung), a synonym of *skor*, plus the suffix *-logia*. *Coprology*, like *scatology*, can mean "obscenity" generally, but in particular the type preoccupied with excrement. *Scatological* sometimes drops the *-al* and is met with much more often than *coprologic(al)*. Whichever of these words is used, this type of humor is a consummation devoutly to be ditched.

sciamachy   (sye AM uh kee, skye-) *n.* Based on the Greek nouns *skia* (shadow) and *mache* (battle), the Greeks formed *skiamachia* from which we took *sciamachy*, fighting with a shadow, a futile combat with an imaginary foe. Shadow-boxing, against an imaginary opponent in training for the ring, is a specialized form of *sciamachy*, a label which exponents of the art would be unlikely to recognize. When Don Quixote de la Mancha, in the novel by the Spanish writer Cervantes (1547–1616), tilted at windmills, he was engaging in *sciamachy*. His famous fight has become part of the language: To *tilt at windmills* is to contend with an imaginary enemy, or imagined injustices or wrongs. Paranoids, in mental conflict with the imagined hostility of others, are involved in involuntary *sciamachy* of still another sort.

sciolism,   see **sciosophy**

sciosophy   (sye OS uh fee) *n.* This term covers any field claiming to constitute knowledge, but without basis in proven fact. Astrology and numerology are prime examples of *sciosophy*, a word formed of two Greek words: *skia* (shadow) and *sophia* (wisdom)—in other words, "shadow-wisdom," i.e., unsubstantiated theory, hypothesis, supposition, and guess-work, posing as knowledge, as opposed to scientifically ascertained fact. It is different in both meaning and derivation from another "scio-" word: *sciolism* (SYE uh liz um), which is pretension to knowledge, and is derived via Late Latin

361

sciolus (one with only a smattering of knowledge), from Latin *sciolus*, a diminutive of *scius* (knowing), based on the verb *scire* (to know). A *sciolist* (SYE uh list) is a pretender to knowledge or science; and *sciolistic* (sy uh LIS tik) and *sciolus* (SYE uh lus) describe such pretension. Palmists, phrenologists and readers of tea-leaves are all *sciolists*.

sciurine, see **accipitrine**

scot (skot) *n.* A *scot*, in olden times, was a charge, a fee, a payment, or a tax assessment. That explains why we say *scot-free*. (He got off *scot-free*, i.e., without penalty or other harm, or I got it *scot-free*, i.e., for nothing, without having to pay anything.) *Scot* is from Old Norse *skot* (contribution). There was also a Saxon coin called *sceat*, which gave rise to the term *church-scot*, a contribution in grain or poultry paid to support parish priests in those days. People who didn't chip in went *scot-free*, the cheapskates. See Falstaff's pun on *scot* mentioned under **termagant**.

scumble (SKUM bul) *n.*, *vb.* To *scumble*, in painting or drawing, is to soften the brilliance of the finish by overlaying it with a thin coat of opaque or semiopaque color, applied with an almost dry brush. In the case of a drawing, this effect can be obtained by rubbing the surface lightly with a stump or a finger. As a noun, *scumble* is the act of scumbling, or its result, the softened effect thus produced. This technique is called *scumbling*. The word is believed to be a **frequentative** of the verb *scum* in the sense of to "form scum."

secern (sih SURN) *vb.* To *secern* is to discriminate, separate in thought, distinguish, discern; from Latin *secernere* (literally, to sever, divide, separate), based on prefix *se-* (apart) plus *cernere* (to sift). The Roman poet Horace (65–8 B.C.) used *secernere* in the sense of "distinguishing" the just from the unjust, and a flatterer from a true friend. *Secernere* is synonymous with *discernere*, which gave us *discern*, one of the meanings of *secern*.

semiology (see mye OL uh jee) *n.* Also *semeiology* (pronounced the same way), which, with the second *e*, is closer to its Greek source, *semeion* (sign), with the ubiquitous suffix *-logy*, from Greek *logos* (word, discourse, thought). *Semiology* is the science of signs and symbols or sign language itself. *Semiotic* (see mee OT ik, -mye-, sem ee-, sem eye-), *adj.*, means "relating to signs," and *semiotics* (treated as a singular noun, like *economics* or *politics*) is the theory of signs and symbols, which includes (and is not to be confused with) semantics (sih MAN tiks), the study of meaning, as well as pragmatics and syntactics—all quite complex and unnecessary to go into here. This is fairly technical stuff, but if you run into these words, don't think that the *semi-* part has anything to do with the prefix *semi-*, meaning "half," as in *semiannual, semicircle*, etc. Perhaps the spelling *semeiology* is preferable, because it would avoid any such misconception. And you will run into *semiology* and related words if you read the works of the English novelist Malcolm Bradbury (b. 1932). In *The History Man* (Secker & Warburg, London, 1975), we read: "The route to the children's school [Daddy is driving them from home in the morning] is a track of familiar lanes, arrows and pointers, lines and halts, a routed *semiology*." And in *Rates of Exchange* (Secker & Warburg, London, 1983): "Some *semiotician* [Bradbury's concoction, but of obvious meaning; the scene is an airport terminal] has designed a system of wordless signs—arrows through squares, crosses in circles, ladders in oblongs—to guide bemused strangers through the labyrinth . . ." This lovely writing should give you a clear idea of the meaning of *semiology* and *semiotics*.

semiotic,   see **semiology**

sempiternal   (sem pih TUR nul) *adj.* This is a literary term for "eternal, everlasting, imperishable," and is from Latin *sempiternus*, based on *semper* (always) plus *eternus* (eternal). It would seem that *eternal* should suffice and that *sempiternal* is tautological. How can something be "occasionally eternal"? "To gild refined gold, to paint the lily," says the Earl of Salisbury (*King John*, Act IV, Scene 2), ". . . Is wasteful and ridiculous excess." (Usually misquoted ". . . to gild the lily . . .") The same may be said of *reiterate* (to "rerepeat," if you take your etymology seriously), and *sempiternal* is a clear case of painting the lily—too much of a muchness.

senescent,   see **juvenescence**

seraglio,   see **imbroglio**

seraph (SER uf) *n*. We read in Isaiah 6:1–2 ". . . I saw . . . the Lord sitting upon a throne . . . Above it stood the *seraphims*: each one had six wings . . ." According to the *Heavenly Hierarchy (De Hierarchia Celesti)* popularized in the fifth century, these *seraphim* were superior angels, the highest of the nine choirs or orders. *Seraphim* is a Hebrew word (-im is a masculine plural ending) from which, by back formation, *seraph*, the singular form, developed. The form *seraphims* in the King James version has been corrected in the New English Bible with the dropping of the -*s*, *seraphim*, as is, being already plural. A *seraph* has three pairs of wings, one more than mere *cherubim*. In Isaiah's vision, as to each *seraph*: ". . . with twain he covered his face, and with twain he covered his feet, and with twain he did fly." The adjective *seraphic* (suh RAF ik) can be applied not only to *seraphs* but also, figuratively, to mortals of angelic or sublime character, those pure in heart. The English poet Thomas Gray (1716–1771), in *The Progress of Poesy*, praised John Milton (1608–1674) as one ". . . that rode sublime/ Upon the *seraph*-wings of ecstasy." In the following century, the English novelist and poet George Meredith (1828–1909), in his poem *The Lark Ascending*, described the music of that bird celebrated in literature as "The song *seraphically* free/Of taint of personality."

seriatim (seer ee AY tim, ser-) *adv.*, *adj*. This is a word taken intact from Middle Latin, based on Latin *series* (row, chain, series), related to the verb *serere* (to connect, link). *Seriatim* means "point by point, taking up one subject or point after another in order." If you receive a letter covering a number of subjects, or hear an opponent's argument involving a series of points, you will do well to take them up *seriatim*, i.e., in the order in which they were served up. *Seriatim* can be used as an adjective (e.g., a *seriatim* listing, a *seriatim* response), but is most commonly used as an adverb, with verbs like *answer*, *consider*, *discuss*, *examine*, *look into*, *respond to*. The pattern of *seriatim* follows that of Middle Latin *litteratim* (letter by letter, i.e., literally), based on *littera* (letter of the alphabet).

serpentine, see **accipitrine**

sesquipedalian (ses kwih pih DAY lee un, -DAYL yun) *adj*. *Sesquipedalian* words are very long words. *Sesquipedalian* means, literally, "a foot and a half long." Julius Caesar (100–44 B.C.), in his *Gallic Wars*, wrote of *sesquipedalian beams*. The Roman poet Horace (65–8 B.C.) used this lovely adjective ironically when he wrote of *sesquipedalian words*, and another Roman poet, Catullus (c. 84–c. 54 B.C.) used it the same way, writing of *sesquipedalian teeth*. This adjective is applied ironically to pedantic words of inordinate length, like some of the entries in this book: e.g., **floccinaucinihilipilification**—a preposterous bit of *sesquipedalianism*. *Sesqui* is a Latin adverb meaning "half as much again"; *pedalis* (based on *ped*, the stem of *pes*, foot) means "a foot long"; hence *sesquipedalis* (a foot and a half long), and all perfectly logical. *Antidisestablishmentarianism* is often cited as a *sesquipedalian* word. (It means "opposition to a state's withdrawal of recognition or support of an established church," with special reference to the Anglican church in 19th-century England.) *Disarcivescovocostantinopolizzarsi* is a *sesquipedalian* Italian word meaning "to cease being the Archbishop of Constantinople," a word that you won't run into very often unless you do a lot of reading about ecclesiastical matters in that part of the world that happened before they changed the name of the city to *Istanbul*. The German language, of course, is full of *sesquipedalian* words because of the German habit of endless tacking on and making one word when other languages would use a phrase. Thus, *Feuerversicherungsgesellschaftspräsident* means "president of a fire insurance company"—and so on and so on. *Sesquipedalian* is itself a *sesquipedalian* word. In a learned article entitled "Learned Length and Thund'ring Sound: A Word-Lover's Panegyric" in Volume X, No. 3, of *Verbatim, The Language Quarterly*, Bryan A. Garner invented a lovely *sesquipedalian* word: *sesquipedalophobia* ("hatred or fear of big words").

shallop   (SHAL up) *n.* A *shallop* was a fore-and-aft rigged vessel, used in the 17th and 18th centuries for sailing in shallow waters. The term is now applied to any dinghy or small or light boat, used chiefly on rivers, propelled by oars or sails. *Shallop* comes from French *chaloupe* (launch), taken from German *Schaluppe*, archaic forerunner of *Schlup*, from which, together with Dutch *sloep*, we got *sloop*.

shivaree   (shiv uh REE) *n.*, *vb.* This word has a number of variant forms and pronunciations: *charivari* and *charivaree* (shuh riv uh REE, sha ruh VAR ee), *chivari* and *chivaree* (shiv uh REE). *Charivari* was taken from the French (where the verb is *charivariser*), which got it from the Late Latin *caribaria* (headache); that came from the Greek *karebaria*, based on *kare* (head) plus *baria* (heaviness). However you spell or pronounce it, a *shivari* or *charivari* is a din or uproar, a cacophonous mock serenade produced by banging kettles, pans, trays, with the accompaniment of other noisemakers and hissing and shouting, for the purpose of expressing disapproval. The connection between its meaning and its derivation becomes abundantly clear. Originally, *charivari* was a common practice at weddings in medieval France, a bit of fun in the way of a noisy serenade to the newlyweds, but as time went on, the practice was continued only as an expression of derision and disapproval at unpopular weddings, and eventually, as a means of expressing ill will toward any unpopular person. Yet, according to Virginia writer Earl Hamner, Jr. (b. 1923), author of *Spencer's Mountain* and creator of the television series *The Waltons, shivarees*, as late as 50 years ago, were still a time-honored way to treat newlyweds in the rural Shenandoah. Another name for *shivaree* is *cat's concert. Charivari* was adopted as the name of a Paris satirical journal in 1832, and later, *The London Charivari* was taken as a subtitle for the English satirical weekly magazine *Punch*. As a verb, to *shivaree* is to engage in producing one.

sibyl (SIB il) *n.* A *sibyl* (often misspelt *Sybil*, as a girl's given name) is a fortune-teller, a prophetess, a medium, sometimes a witch. It was the name (*Sibylla* in Greek, *Sibilla* in Latin) given in ancient times to a number of women in various parts of the world who were thought to be qualified to make prophecies and utter oracles under the guidance of a god and pursuant to divine inspiration. The adjective *sibyllene* (SIB uh leen, -line, -lin), from Latin *Sibyllinus*, means "oracular, prophetic." The political and economic pundits of the day are much given to making *sibylline* utterances for our guidance, but where are the customers' yachts? The *Sibylline Books* were a collection of oracular pronouncements owned by the ancient Roman state and were consulted by magistrates, and in emergencies and times of disaster by the Roman Senate. When a prediction is characterized as *sibylline*, there is a strong implication that the utterance is considered cryptic and ambiguous, like those of the Delphic Oracle.

sic (sik, unless you prefer the Latin pronunciation, seek) *adv. Sic* has been taken over from Latin, where it means "thus," "so," "in this manner." It is found in two famous sentences: *Sic transit gloria mundi* ("Thus passes away the glory of the world." First written by Thomas à Kempis, 1380–1471, in *Imitation of Christ*, this sentence is included in the ceremony of the crowning of the pope.) and *Sic semper tyrannis!* ("Thus always to tyrants!" i.e., this is always the fate of tyrants. This anonymous Latin saying was adopted by John Wilkes Booth [1838–1865] after shooting Abraham Lincoln on April 14, 1865). However, used by itself in parentheses after a quoted word or passage, it indicates that the word or passage is being quoted (e.g., by a reviewer, or in an essay) exactly as it appeared in the original, where it was incorrectly used or spelt. *Sic*, thus used, calls attention to the error in the original and makes it clear that it is not the quoter's mistake. In short, *sic* means "Thus in the original; I found it this way, and am leaving it exactly as I found it, though I know it is incorrect. Don't blame it on me!" One receives a note reading: "You wernt in I'll try again tomorow" and wants to quote it in a letter to a friend. One writes, "I got a note from Jennie reading: 'You wernt *(sic)* in (no punctuation) I'll try again tomorrow *(sic)*.' " Thus one calls attention to the errors and makes sure that they are not attributed to him. Sometimes the phrase *sic passim* is used. *Passim* (PAS im) is Latin for "here and there, in various places." *Sic passim*, inserted in parentheses, means "Thus throughout the original," to indicate that the error in the original occurs repeatedly in the work referred to. If a student spelt James Joyce *James Joyse* repeatedly in an essay, a teacher quoting a passage in which the misspelling occurred would (or should) write "(sic passim)" after the error. The language quarterly *Verbatim*, published by the eminent American lexicographer Laurence Urdang (b. 1918) of Old Lyme, Connecticut, and Aylesbury, Buckinghamshire, England, has a department listing errors in spelling, usage, grammar, etc., discovered in advertisements, public notices, etc., and sent in by readers. Mr. Urdang, a scholar much given to puns, heads the column "Sic! Sic! Sic!"

simulacrum (sim yuh LAY krum) *n.* This word, in Latin, means "exact image, effigy, representation," or, figuratively, a semblance, imitation, counterfeit, illusion, phantasm," depending on the context. Its principal use in English is to denote a superficial

367

likeness or semblance, as might be expected from its relation to the Latin verb *simulare* (to imitate, pretend, counterfeit), from whose past participle, *simulatus*, we got *simulate*, to feign, make a pretense of (something—like knowledge or innocence). The English physician and writer Thomas Browne (1605–1682), in *The Garden of Cyrus*, wrote: "Life itself is but the shadow of death, and souls departed but the shadows of the living. All things fall under this name. The sun itself is but the dark *simulacrum*, and light but the shadow of God." In his *Religio Medici (Religion of the Physician)*, Browne attempted to reconcile religion and science, which is nice work if you can get it.

sinapism (SIN uh piz um) *n.* *Sinapism* is mustard plaster, an old-fashioned medical remedy consisting of a black powdered mixture of mustard and rubber placed on cloth, applied to the body as a counterirritant. Via Latin *sinapismus*, the word is from Greek *sinapismos* (application of mustard), based on *sinapi* (mustard), and related to *sinapizein* (to apply mustard). Incidentally, the *must-* in *mustard* is from *must* (new wine, pressed but not yet fermented): *must* is from the Latin adjective *mustus* (young, new, fresh), in the neuter ending *mustum*, short for *vinum mustum* (new wine). Originally must was used in mixing mustard paste.

sisyphean (sis uh FEE un) *adj.* A *sisyphean* task is a never-ending fruitless effort. This adjective derives from the sad legend of Sisyphus, in classical mythology the king of Corinth, a man famous for his trickery. For reasons varying with each of several sources, he was punished in Hades by being condemned to roll a huge stone up a steep hill, at the top of which the stone escaped him and rolled all the way down again—forever. Thus, his task was eternal, and totally unavailing. A "labor of Sisyphus" or *sisyphean toil* is endless and heartbreaking. Literate mothers cleaning up the family room for the umpteenth time that day after the children have occupied it for a short while have been known to characterize their task as *sisyphean*. Recurring floods present riparian dwellers with *sisyphean* labors. The attempts of the authorities throughout history to stamp out prostitution would appear to be of *sisyphean* proportions. Penelope, the faithful wife of Ulysses, created for herself a *sisyphean* task: she was beset by suitors while Ulysses was away at the siege of Troy. To get rid of them, she promised to select one as soon as she had finished weaving a shroud for her father-in-law. Each night, she unraveled the work of the previous day, until Ulysses came home—and slew the suitors. Hence the expression *web of Penelope*, a never-ending task; a self-created *sisyphean* labor, as it were.

skimble-scamble, skimble-skamble (SKIM bul SKAM bul, SKIM ul SKAM ul) *adj.* This lively adjective describes things that are confused, rambling, incoherent, like a *skimble-skamble* narration of a frightening experience, or a *skimble-skamble* explanation of something somewhat beyond the speaker's power of comprehension. *Skimble-skamble* is said to have developed as a reduplication of the dialectal word *scamble* (to scramble, shamble, sprawl, struggle, or trample); or it may be simply a union of *scramble* and *shamble*. Shakespeare used it in *Henry IV, Part I* (Act III, Scene 1), when Hotspur, angrily mocking the long-winded Glendower, says:

> . . . sometimes he angers me
> With telling me of the moldwarp [mole] and the ant,
> Of the dreamer Merlin and his prophecies,
> And a dragon and a finless fish,
> A clip-wing'd griffon and a moulten raven,
> A crouching lion and a ramping [rearing] cat,
> And such a deal of *skimble-skamble* stuff
> As puts me from my faith . . .

(Hotspur goes on, and on, and on; it's well worth reading!) In later days, James Morris, in *Farewell the Trumpets* (Faber & Faber, London, 1978), used the expression "treated with *skimble-skamble* deference" to describe the way a throng might treat a great personage. *Skimble-skamble*, in its sound, is reminiscent of *crinkle-crankle*, a word described by this author in his *British English, A to Zed* (Facts On File, 1987) as follows: "A precious, or a least rare, adjective used to describe serpentine red brick garden walls, full of twists and turns . . . *Crinkle-crankle* is an informal variant of *crinkum-crankum*, which describes anything (not only walls) full of twists and turns and is sometimes used by itself as a substantive."

sleuth,   see **slot**

slot (slot) *n.* Apart from its familiar meanings, a *slot* is an animal trail or track, especially that of a deer, marked out by hoofprints. This meaning is derived from Old Norse *sloth* (trail, track), which also produced the noun *sleuth*, likewise a track or trail, or a bloodhound, a tireless tracker; hence a detective, the common meaning. Tireless tracker? A good name for an etymologist.

sockdol(l)ager, also **sockdol(l)oger, slogdollager, stockdol(l)ager,** etc. (sok DOL u gur) *n.* This is a slang word for "something sensational or exceptional," according to the English lexicographer Robert Burchfield (b. 1923) in *The English Language* (Oxford University Press, 1985). He includes it in a list of "American words that remain firmly unborrowed in British English, though they are encountered often enough in magazines like *Time, Newsweek,* and the *New Yorker* . . . Without them one cannot hope to understand the novels of modern American novelists like Bernard Malamud or Saul Bellow, or, for that matter the daily speech of most Americans." Also included in the list was *"honeyfuggle"* (to obtain by cheating or deception). According to the American dictionaries, a *sockdolager* is anything unusually big or heavy, or a heavy finishing blow, a word coined from the slang *sock* (hard blow) plus **doxology,** in the slang sense of "finish," i.e., the closing act of a church service. The English dictionaries include the definition "whopper," and add the meaning "decisive argument" (i.e., the "clincher").

soffit (SOF it) *n.* This is an architectural term for the underside of a building feature like a beam, arch, vault, cornice, staircase, or balcony. *Soffito* is "ceiling" in Italian, but its descendant *soffit* is usually limited to the ornamental underside of an architectural element. The ultimate source is Latin *suffixus,* past participle of *suffigere* (to fasten beneath), based on prefix *suf-,* a variant of *sub-* (under) plus *figere* (to fasten). *Suffixus* also gave us *suffix,* something "fastened on."

sol-fa, see **solmization**

solfeggio, solfège, see **solmization**

solidus (SOL ih dus) *n.* A *solidus* is an oblique stroke (thus: /)

which has a variety of functions: in writing fractions (e.g., ¾); to signify ratios (e.g., miles/minute); in the term *and/or*, used to indicate that either or both of the things enumerated may be involved (e.g., fine and/or imprisonment, or damage to persons and/or property); in Britain, under the former monetary system based on pounds, shillings, and pence, to denote the now obsolete shilling: 7/6 meant "seven shillings six pence"—the *solidus* or oblique stroke being descended from the lengthened form of the *s* that stood for "shilling(s)," the *s* of the still familiar, if now abandoned, L.S.D. (this has nothing to do with the hallucinatory drug *ly*sergic acid *d*imethylamide), L.s.d. or £.s.d., an abbreviation of the Latin *librae* (pounds), *solidi* (shillings), *denarii* (pence). *Solidus* has a number of synonyms: *diagonal*, *oblique*, *slant*, *virgule*, and in British English, simple *stroke*. *Virgule* (VUR gyoohl) is from Latin *virgula* (little rod).

solmization (sol mih ZAY shun) *n*. This is the system of using the *do*, *re*, *mi*, etc., syllables to represent the tones of the scale. The set of syllables is known as *sol-fa* (sohl FAH, SOL fah), which is also used as a verb: to *sol-fa* is to sing a tune in these syllables. *Solfeggio* (sol FEJ oh, -FEJ ee oh), from the Italian, based on *sol* and *fa*, is another name for *solmization*, and for any vocal exercise using the *sol-fa* syllables, but the form *solfège* (sohl FEZH), the French equivalent, is more commonly heard. *Solmization* is derived, via French *solmisation*, from *sol* or *so* (the fifth tone of the diatonic scale—the basic scale in music—known as *G* in the key of *C*) plus *mi* (the third tone of that scale, *E* in that key).

solstice (SOL stis) *n*. This is the astronomical term for either one of the two times each year when the sun is farthest from the equator, either north or south. In the Northern Hemisphere, the summer *solstice*, on or about June 21, the longest day/shortest night, marks the beginning of summer, and the winter *solstice*, on or about December 31, the shortest day/longest night, the beginning of winter. The *ecliptic* (ih KLIP tik) is the "track" in the heavens along which the sun appears to travel. It is, of course, the earth that does the traveling. On the two *solstices*, the sun reaches its north and south points in the ecliptic, i.e., the two points in the ecliptic farthest from the equator, and appears to be standing still. It is that illusion which gives the *solstices* their name, derived from Latin *solstitium*, based on *sol* (sun) plus *-stitium*, from *status*, past participle of *sistere* (to stand still). *Ecliptic* comes, via Old English and Latin, from Greek *ekleiptikos*, based on the verb *ekleipein* (to fail to appear—like the sun or moon during an *eclipse*).

somatic   (soh MAT ik, suh-) *adj. Somatic* means (among other technical senses) "physical" or "bodily," as opposed to *psychic*, having to with the mind. The combination of the two gives us *psychosomatic* (sye koh soh MAT ik, -suh-), based on Greek *psyche* (literally, breath, based on *psychein*, to breathe; figuratively, soul, mind), describing a physical ailment resulting from a mental or emotional disturbance. *Somatic* is from Greek *somatikos* (pertaining to the body), based on *soma* (body, as opposed to soul). *Psyche* and *psychosomatic* have become fairly familiar terms nowadays, but one doesn't run into *soma* or *somatic* very often. A general practitioner friend who feels that *psychosomatic* is used all too glibly by his colleagues likes to greet his patients with a terrible pun: "What's *somatic* with you today?"

sonant,   see **surd**

sopor   (SO pur) *n. Sopor* is a pathological condition of unnaturally deep sleep; from Latin *sopor* (deep sleep, slumber). We are more familiar with the noun and adjective *soporific*, (something) producing sleep, like a sleeping pill or political oratory or after-dinner speeches. ("You may be wondering why you were asked here tonight . . .") *Sopor* can also mean "lethargy," not actual sleep, in certain contexts. In this connection, if you are still awake, see **lethe**.

soricine,   see **accipitrine**

sororicide,   see **aborticide**

soteriology   (su teer ee OL uh jee) *n.* As a general term, *soteriology* is a discourse on health and hygiene, but in Christian theology, it is the doctrine of salvation through Jesus Christ. In Greek, a *soter* is a deliverer or savior, and *soteria* is safety, salvation, or deliverance. *Soter*, in Greek religion, was an epithet of Zeus, Poseidon, and other gods. Ptolemy I (c. 367–285 B.C., king of Egypt

323–285 B.C.), known as Ptolemy *Soter*, was given that surname, meaning "Preserver," because he forced the Macedonian King Demetrius I (c. 337–283 B.C.) to raise the siege of Rhodes in 304 B.C. Saint *Sofer* was pope from c. 166 to 175. Whether they know it or not, today's born-again Christians are practicing *soteriology*.

speleology, see **spelunker**

spelunker (spih LUNG kur) *n*. A *spelunker* is a cave explorer; to *spelunk* (spih LUNGK) is to do the exploring. *Spelaean* or *spelean* (spih LEE un) means "relating to caves," and serves as well to describe a cave-dweller. *Spelunk* comes, via Latin *spelunca*, from Greek *spelynx* (cave); *spel(a)ean* from New Latin *spelaeus*, based on Latin *spelaeum* (cave), which came from Greek *spelation*. *Speleology* or *spelaeology* (spee lee OL uh jee) is the exploration of caves, or, in other contexts, their study and science; likewise based on Latin *spelaeum*, plus *-logy*, from Greek *-logia* (study or science). *Spelunkers* take chances, and sometimes have to be rescued by search parties, experiences that usually make the headlines.

steatopygia (stee uh toh PYE jee uh) *n*. *Stear*, Greek for "fat, grease," gave rise to the prefix *steato-*, while *pyge* is Greek for "buttocks, rump." Together, this prefix and noun gave us *steatopygia*, for fatty accumulation on the buttocks, and *steatopygic* (stee uh to PIJ ik) or *steatopygous* (stee uh toh PYE gus) fat-buttocked, as well as *steatopygy* (stee uh tuh PYE jee, -TOP ih jee), the condition of possessing a very fat rump. Cf. **callipygian, callipygous**, an endowment much to be preferred, except among certain South African peoples, perhaps, where *steatopygy* is very common, especially in women, and is very much admired, and *steatopygous* and *steatopygic* might be considered synonymous with *callipygian* and *callipygous*.

stereotropism, see **haptic**

stertor (STUR tur) *n*. *Stertor* is snoring, the emitting of a rasping sound in breathing, as a result of obstruction of air passages in the head, in sleep or coma. *Stertorous* (STUR tuh rus) is the adjective. A *stertorous* condition is marked by deep snoring or very heavy breathing, especially in certain diseases, including apoplexy. *Ster-*

tor is from the Latin verb *stertere* (to snore). *Stertor* is related to *stridor* (STRYE dur), which has the general meaning of a "harsh, grating sound," but in pathology is a heavy respiratory sound that comes, like *stertor*, from obstruction of breathing passages. *Stridor* is from Latin *stridor* (harsh noise, grating sound), related to *stridere* (to make a shrill sound, to creak, hiss or grate).

stich,   see **stichomythia**

stichomythia   (stik uh MITH ee uh) *n.* Also *stichomythy* (stik KOM uh thee). This word, taken intact from the Greek, denotes a brief dialogue in verse drama in which each character usually utters a single line. This is common in classical Greek drama. Hallmarks of *stichomythia* are antithesis and repetition. There are such passages in all the Greek dramas. Here is an example from *Oedipus Rex* of Sophocles (c. 495–c. 406 B.C.), a dialogue between Oedipus and the seer Tiresias:

> Oedipus: Begone this instant! Away, away! Get you from these doors!
> Tiresias: I had never come but that you sent for me.
> Oedipus: I did not know you were mad.
> Tiresias: I may seem mad to you, but your parents thought me sane.
> Oedipus: My parents! Stop! Who was my father?
> Tiresias: This day shall you know your birth; and it will ruin you.

And so on, and so on; next stop, Sigmund Freud. In the *Prometheus Bound* of Aeschylus (525–456 B.C.):

> Io: Zeus fall from power?
> Prometheus: You would rejoice, I think, to see that happen?
> Io: How could I not, who suffer at his hands?
> Prometheus: Know then that it shall surely be.

And more, and more. *Stichomythia* is based on *stichos* (row, line, verse) plus *mythos* (speech, story). The word *stich* (stik), from Greek *stichos*, means "line of poetry."

stochastic   (stuh KAS tik) *adj.* Also **stochastical**. A *stochastic* study, opinion, or observation is a conjectural one, governed by the laws of probability. The English theologian and philosopher Ralph Cudworth (1617–1688), in a *Treatise on Freewill*, wrote: "We may

374

. . . and often do proceed to make a judgment in the case one way or another, *stochastically* or conjecturally . . . There is need and use of this *stochastical* judging and opining concerning truth and falsehood in human life.'' Pollsters make their predictions *stochastically*, and are at times astonished at how wide of the mark they wind up (remember the headline DEWEY DEFEATS TRUMAN?). The source of this word is Greek *stochastikos* (skilled in aiming), based on the verb *stochasezthai* (to aim at, guess). Antistochastic advice: Don't count your votes before they're cast.

stock,   see **talon**

storiology,   see **genethlialogy**

strabismus   (struh BIZ mus) *n.* A person suffering from *strabismus* is cross-eyed, a vision disorder resulting from the turning of one or both eyes from the normal position. *Strabismus* is derived from Greek *strabos* (squinting) plus the suffix *-ismos*, which gave us our common suffix *-ism*, as in *baptism*, *criticism*, and nuisances like *rheumatism* and *communism*. There are several adjectives meaning "cross-eyed": *strabismal*, *strabismic*, and *strabismical*, all accented on the syllable *-bis-*. *Strabismal* rhymes with *dismal* and limericks are invited.

stridor,   see **stertor**

strigine,   see **accipitrine**

sturnine,   see **accipitrine**

Stygian   (STIJ ee un) *adj. Stygian*, with an upper case *S*, describes anything relating to the River Styx, the river, according to classical mythology, over which Charon ferried the souls of the departed on their journey into the underworld. He charged a fee of one obol, a coin which was placed in the mouth of the deceased, for use in payment of that fee. From that dreadful river, the adjective *stygian* came to mean "dark, gloomy, forbidding," or "infernal," and one may speak of *stygian* night or a *stygian* cave or landscape, or a *stygian* room or hallway, dark, gloomy, forbidding. *Stygian* takes on an entirely different meaning in the expression

Stygian oath: an oath "by the Styx" sworn by a god, a "Stygian oath," is inviolable. The Roman poet Virgil (70–19 B.C.), in *The Aeneid*, writes of "the swamp of the Styx, by which the gods take oath." The adjective in Latin was *Stygius*, in Greek *Stygios*. The English poet John Milton (1608–1674) starts his poem *L'Allegro* with the lines:

> Hence, loathed Melancholy,
>> Of Cerberus, and blackest Midnight born,
> In *Stygian* cave forlorn,
>> 'Midst horrid shapes, and shrieks, and sights unholy . . .

subreption, see **sarcophagus**

sudorific (sooh duh RIF ik) *adj*. This adjective describes anything that produces sweat, whether heat, fright, nervousness, medication, a message that the boss wants to see you, an unopened letter from the Internal Revenue Service, or simply one of those sweaty little afternoon naps. The related adjective *sudoriferous* (sooh duh RIF ur us) means "sweaty," describing a person secreting the stuff. A *sudarium* (sooh DAIR ee um) in ancient Rome was a handkerchief, or any piece of cloth, usually linen, for wiping one's face, and a *sudatorium* (sooh duh TOR ee um) is a hot-air room to produce sweating. All these words are based on the Latin noun *sudor* (sweat) and verb *sudare* (to sweat). *Sudorific* has a synonym from the Greek: *diaphoretic* (dye uh fuh RET ik), which also means "sweat-producing," and comes from *diaphoretikos*; the noun *diaphoretic* means "sweat-producing medicine," and the related noun *diaphoresis* (dye uh fuh REE sis) is the medical term for perspiration, especially when it is artificially produced for health purposes. This batch are all based on the Greek verb *diaphorein* (to carry off). *Hidrosis* (hih DROH sis, hye-) based on Greek *hidros* (sweat), is the term used in pathology for excessive sweating resulting from medication or illness. One must sweat one's way through all these ancient **etymons** (or, if you prefer, *etyma*) to find the *mot juste*.

suilline, see **accipitrine**

sumptuary (SUMP chooh air ee) *adj*. This adjective describes anything relating to or regulating expenditure. It comes from Latin *sumptuarius*, based on *sumptus* (expense), related to the verb *su-mere* (to take, buy). Another Latin word stemming from *sumptus* is *sumptuosus* (very costly), from which we get *sumptuous*. *Sumptuary* is not a common word, but *sumptuous* is, and their etymologically related first two syllables should make it easier to get the sense of *sumptuary* when you run into it. The common use of *sumptuary* is in the term *sumptuary law*, one regulating and limiting personal budgets, especially expenditures for food, dress, and luxuries. Such laws have been enacted in various parts of the world from time to time. Some were in force in Greece and Rome in ancient times. Japan applied that type of regulation to the farming and commercial classes until the middle of the 19th century. In the 14th and 15th centuries, England enforced *sumptuary* statutes relating to dress and diet, imposing much more stringent limitations upon peasants than on the gentry, for the purpose of maintaining class distinctions and keeping the peasants in their place, lest they seek to pass as something superior to their actual status. The English laws were all repealed by James I, who ruled from 1603 to 1625. However, under the exigencies of World Wars I and II, there were returns to *sumptuary* laws for a time. There was food rationing, and limitations were imposed upon the cost and availability of other necessities of life. The alcoholic content of beer and whiskey was reduced, and restaurant meals were subject to a maximum cost of five shillings. This had nothing to do with class distinctions, but rather with the effectiveness of the enemy blockade. The author well remembers dining at the Savoy and the Ritz-Carlton for five "bob" (shillings)—then worth about $1.25—and not enjoying the food one bit!

supposititious,   see **supposititious**

supposititious   (suh poz ih TISH us) *adj.* This word, meaning "spurious, counterfeit," is not to be confused with its lexical close neighbor *supposititious* (sup uh ZISH us), meaning "hypothetical, assumed." They not only look alike; they come from the same Latin source, *suppositus*, past participle of *supponere* (to substitute). But they mean quite different things, despite what some dictionaries say (e.g., the *Random House College Dictionary*, Revised, 1980, which rightly defines *supposititious* as "growing out of supposition," and then gives as a second meaning "supposititious

377

[shortened form of SUPPOSITITIOUS])." As you might expect, Fowler has something to say about this troublesome matter, under the heading **supposititious, supposititious**: "It is often assumed that the first form is no more than an ignorant or wrong variant of the other. Ignorant it often is . . . , but there is no reason to call it wrong. There are two fairly distinct senses to be shared, viz. spurious, and hypothetical. *Supposititious* is directly from the Latin past participle *suppositus* = substituted . . . and therefore has properly the meaning foisted, counterfeit, spurious . . . *supposititious* is from the English supposition = hypothesis, and therefore may properly mean supposed, hypothetical, assumed . . . *Supposititious* should not be given . . . senses proper to the synonyms of *supposititious*; it should be confined to those implying intent to deceive." This argument is supported by the *Oxford Guide to English Usage*, compiled by E. S. C. Weiner (Oxford University Press, 1983): "**supposititious**, hypothetical, conjectural; *supposititious*, fraudulently substituted (especially of a child displacing a real heir), e.g. *Russia . . . is the supposititious child of necessity in the household of theory* (H. G. Wells)." So does the *Chambers Twentieth Century Dictionary*, New Edition, 1973: "**supposititious** . . . usu[ally] a blunder for supposititious."

sural (SOOH rul) *adj. Sural* describes anything relating to the calf of the leg, from *sural* arteries to *sural* cramp to *sural* beauty as in classical Greek statuary, prima ballerinas, and the ladies of the ensemble. The word is from Late Latin *suralis*, based on Latin *sura* (calf).

surd (surd) *n.*, *adj.* A technical term in phonetics for a "voiceless" consonant, the opposite of a sonant. These terms denote pairs of consonants, alike except that they are or are not pronounced with vibrations of vocal cords. Thus, *surd p*, sonant *b*, *s*, and *z*, etc. *Voiced* and *unvoiced* are also used. *Surd* is from Latin *surdus* (deaf, unheard); *sonant* (from Latin *sonans*, present participle of *sonare* (to sound). Incidentally, absurd is from Latin *absurdus*, formed of *ab-* plus *surdus*, with the primary meaning "ear-offending, harsh, inharmonious," and by transference, "foolish, unreasonable."

susurrant, see **susurration**
378

susurration (sooh su RAY shun) *n.* A *susurration* is a whisper, a murmuring, a rustling. *Susurrous* (soo SUR us) describes things with rustling or whispering sounds. *Susurrant* (soo SUR unt) means "whispering, murmuring." A *susurrus* (soo SUR us) is a whisper, a soft rustling or murmuring sound. All these words go back to Latin *susurrus* (whisper) and *susurrare* (to whisper), its present participle *susurrans* and past participle *susurratus*. Both the Latin and the English words are onomatopoeic—words formed by imitation of the sound made by the things they describe or denote, like *boom*, *buzz*, *hiss*, *sizzle*, *cuckoo*, and **tintinnabulation**.

susurrous, see **sussuration**

susurrus, see **susurration**

syllepsis (sih LEP sis) *n.* *Syllepsis* covers two rhetorical situations: where a word functions in a sentence in the same grammatical relation to two or more words but has a different sense in relation to each (example: he took the oath and his seat; for other examples, see **zeugma**), and where a word is applied to two others of which it grammatically suits only one (examples: neither you nor he knows; neither he nor they are happy). *Syllepsis* was taken intact from the Greek, based on the prefix *syl-*, variant of *syn-* before *l*, plus *lep-*, the stem of *lambanein* (to take).

syncope, see **aph(a)eresis**

syncretism (SING krih tiz um) *n.* In philosophy and theology, *syncretism* is the attempt to reconcile or unify opposing schools of thought, principles, practices, etc. The word has been used as a pejorative term for inconsistency in accepting incompatible beliefs or principles. The term is applied especially to the attempt by the German theologian Georg Calixtus (1586–1656) to unite Christian churches, minimizing the importance of doctrine and emphasizing the basic principles of Christian living. The derivation is from Greek *synkretismos* (literally, confederation of Cretan communities; hence, a united front of opposing parties against a common foe), related to *synkretizein* (to unite, or attempt to unite opposing principles), based on prefix *syn-* (together) plus *Kret* (a Cretan).

syndic (SIN dik) *n*. This word has a number of uses. In classical Greece, a *syndic* was a lawyer, a delegate, or a judge, depending on the context. At various places and times, a *syndic* was a mayor. The Italian word for mayor today is *sindaco*. *Syndic* is the title of a member of a special committee of the senate of Cambridge University, England. As a general term, a *syndic* can be an agent to transact business for others, especially an accredited legal representative of a town or corporation. *Syndicate* (SIN dih kate) has the special meaning of "body of *syndics*," but is generally understood to denote a commercial group of firms or individuals with a common interest, or a combined group of newspapers, or a criminal group. *Syndic*, via the French and the Late Latin *syndicus* (city official), is from the Greek *syndikos* (defendant's counsel), based on prefix *syn-* (with) plus *dike* (justice).

synecdoche (sih NEK duh kee) *n*. This is the name of a figure of speech that uses a part for the whole or vice versa, or the general for the special or vice versa. It comes from Greek *synekdoche*, based on the prefix *syn-* (with, together) plus *ekdoche* (receiving from another). Examples: part for whole: 50 *head* (of cattle), lunch at five dollars a *head*; whole for part: *America* won 20 gold medals at the games; general for special: a nasty *creature* (man); special for general; an *Einstein* (genius). *Synecdoche* is one of those things we use all the time without knowing it—the way M. Jourdain, the Bourgeois Gentilhomme in the play of that name by the French writer of comedies Molière (1622–1673), says to the Master of Philosophy: "Good Heavens! For more than forty years I have been speaking prose without knowing it."

synesis (SIN ih sis) *n*. This is a term in grammar for a construction in which meaning takes precedence over strict grammatical form. An example is the use of a plural verb after a singular noun to indicate the action of the individuals who compose a group, like a committee, crew, university, company, athletic team, or political body, as opposed to the action of the entity as a whole. This is common usage in Britain, not usual in America. "Thus," quoting from this author's *British English, A to Zed* (Facts On File, 1987), "Harvard *plays* Yale, but Oxford *play* Cambridge . . . An American would be downright startled to see a sports headline reading 'JESUS ROW TO EASY VICTORY.' " (*Jesus* is the name of an

380

Oxford college, and there is a *Jesus* at Cambridge as well, so we're not sure who won.) Fowler cites a good example of a choice between the singular and plural form of the verb: "*The Cabinet is divided* is better, because in the order of thought a whole must precede division; and *The Cabinet are agreed* is better, because it takes two or more to agree." *Synesis* was taken as is from the Greek, where it means "understanding, sense, intelligence."

synod (SIN ud) *n. Synod* has a number of technical meanings in church parlance: an ecclesiastical council, an offical assembly of church dignitaries meeting to decide on matters of policy or religious doctrine; the entire body of a particular church or denomination; the region or district governed by a church council. *Synod*, however, quite apart from its technical uses in the ecclesiastical world, can be and has been used of any council, assembly, or convention. It has been used rather fancifully by some. The English lexicographer, critic, and poet Dr. Samuel Johnson (1709–1784), passing favorable judgment on a meal he had eaten, said: "Sir, we could not have had a better dinner had there been a *Synod of Cooks*." The Scottish soldier and poet James Graham, Marquess of Montrose (1612–1650), used it in a poem addressed to "My Dear and Only Love":

> My dear and only love, I pray
> This noble word of thee,
> Be govern'd by no other sway
> But purest Monarchy.
> For if confusion have a part,
> Which virtuous souls abhor,
> And hold a *synod* in thy heart,
> I'll never love thee more.

Synod is, via Latin *synodus*, from Greek *synodos* (meeting).

tabes, see **tabescent**

tabescent (tuh BES unt) *adj. Tabescent* describes anyone or anything wasting away, growing emaciated, becoming consumed. A

381

person on a hunger strike becomes *tabescent*; so does a patient in terminal cancer. The noun *tabescence* (tuh BES uns), meaning "emaciation, shriveling," is sadly evocative of those starving millions in Ethiopia and other Third World countries we see on our television screens. *Tabes* (TAY beez) is the name of the pathological condition of progressive emaciation. *Tabes dorsalis* (dor SAY lis) is locomotor ataxia, syphilis of the spinal cord leading to loss of muscular control and paralysis. *Tabes* is Latin for "wasting, decay"; *tabescent* and *tabescence* are from *tabescens*, present participle of Latin *tabescere* (to waste away, decline, decay).

talion,   see **condign**

talon   (TAL un) *n.* Apart from its use to denote the claw of a bird or prey, *talon* has a special use in card games: the *talon* is the cards remaining after the deal. Thus, in cribbage, each of the two players is dealt a hand of six cards, and the thirteenth card is turned up and placed atop the remaining cards. That leaves 39 cards unused (52 – 13), and that is the *talon*, which comes from Latin *talus* (heel). In gin rummy, each player is dealt a hand of ten cards and one is turned up and placed to one side of the rest of the deck, which is the *talon* from which, in this game, unlike cribbage, the players draw in turn. A synonym of *talon* in this sense is *stock*, which, via Middle English, comes from Old English *stoc* (stump).

talpine,   see **accipitrine**

tang,   see **tinnient**

tantivy   (tan TIV ee) *n.*, *adj.*, *adv.*; in the plural—**tantivies**—an *interjection*. A *tantivy* is a gallop. To *ride tantivy* is a hunting term for riding at full gallop. As an adverb, *tantivy* means "swiftly, headlong." *Tantivies* (plural) is a hunting cry when the chase is at full gallop, thought by some to be in imitation of the sound of the hunting-horn, by others in imitation of the sound of hoof-beats. The cry of *tantivies* brings to mind the definition of fox-hunting by the Irish poet and dramatist Oscar Wilde (1854–1900) in his play *A Woman of No Importance*: "The English country gentleman galloping after a fox—the unspeakable in full pursuit of the uneatable." In the late 17th century, *Tantivy* became slang for a High

Church cleric or true-blue Tory, based on a contemporary caricature showing High Church clerics "riding *tantivy*" to Rome; sometimes *Tantivy Man* or *Tantivy Boy*.

tapirine,   see **accipitrine**

tarn   (tarn) *n.* A *tarn* is a small mountain lake or pool. It got its name from Middle English *terne*, which came from Old Norwegian *tjörn* (pond). Weary mountain climbers delight in *tarns*, but one doesn't come across them often in speech or reading. The poets are fond of them. Wrote the English poet Walter de la Mare (1873–1956) in *The Scribe*:

> And still would remain
>   My wit to try—
> My worn reeds broken
>   The dark *tarn* dry,
> All words forgotten—
>   Thou, Lord, and I.

And the American poet Edgar Allan Poe (1809–1849), in *Ulalume*, wrote:

> It was down by the dank *tarn* of Auber,
> In the ghoul-haunted woodland of Weir . . .

Tarns are usually dark, dank, or deep, or all three, and always romantic.

Tarpeian,   see **defenestration**

tatterdemalion   (tat ur deh MALE yun, -MAL-) *n.* A *tatter* is a bit of rag, any torn shred hanging loose from an article of clothing, a banner, a flag, a sheet of paper, etc., and anything *in tatters* like a battle-torn flag, a banner long exposed to the elements, long and arduously worn clothing, poorly laundered washing, is in shreds, about to fall apart. A *tatterdemalion* is a ragamuffin, someone in *tattered* clothes. The *tatter-* part, from Middle English, based on Old English *taetteca* (shred), is obvious; *-demalion* is claimed to be of unknown origin, though *-malion* suggests the Italian noun *maglia* (MAL yuh), meaning "undershirt," something that might

383

well be visible through the *tatters*, no? Tramps, bag-persons combing through litter bins, panhandlers, bindlestiffs, beachcombers, vagabonds, and derelicts in general all fall within the genus *tatterdemalion*—a sad state of affairs.

taurine, see **accipitrine**

taxonomy (tak SON uh mee) *n. Taxonomy* is the technique of classification generally, but it has a special application in biology: the science of identification and classification of animal and plant life. One engaged in this pursuit is a *taxonomist* (tak SON uh mist) or *taxonomer* (tak SON uh mur). *Taxonomy* came from the French *taxonomie*, based on the Greek noun *taxis* (order or arrangement in a physical science), related to the verb *tassein* (to arrange, put in order).

tectonics (tek TON iks) *n. Tectonics* (like *economics, physics, politics,* etc.) is treated as a singular noun; it is the name of the art and science of building in general, sometimes known as the "constructive arts," using *constructive* as an adjective meaning "pertaining to construction," i.e., building. *Tectonic* (tek TON ik), as an adjective, means "pertaining to construction or building." (It has other technical meanings in the fields of geology, relating to the earth's crust.) Both words come from Greek *tektonikos* (relating to construction), based on *tekton* (carpenter).

telegony (tuh LEG uh nee) *n.* In genetics, there is a theory, unsupported by reliable evidence, that a previous male mate exerts an influence upon offspring later born of the same female to a later mate. The word comes from Greek prefix *tele-*(far) plus *gonos* (begetting, seed). There is another unsupported theory, in stock breeding, known as "saturation," according to which the successive offspring of the same parents increasingly resemble the sire. These terms apply to animal genetics, but there is no reason, if the theories are correct, why they shouldn't be effective in human affairs— or is *affairs* an injudicious word in this discussion?

teleology (tel ee OL uh jee, tee lee-) *n.* This is the name applied to a philosophical doctrine serving to explain any series of events in terms of goals, purposes, or ends; the doctrine that final causes
384

exist; the study of purpose and design in nature and the belief that they are a part of and apparent in nature. *Teleologism* (tel ee OL uh jiz um, tee lee-) insists that all phenomena are guided not only by mechanical forces but also by the aim of self-realization. In this sense, *teleology* is opposed to mechanism, the doctrine that all happenings are explainable by mechanical principles of causation. Our word came from New Latin *teleologia*, based on the Greek prefix *tele-* (end, from the noun *telos*), plus the suffix *-logia*. *Dysteleology* (dis tel ee OL uh jee, -tee lee-) is the opposite doctrine, negating the existence of final causes or purposes, and holding that life and nature are random, devoid of purpose. *Teleologists* have equated purpose or cause in the universe with God's will, arguing that since there is design in the universe, there must be a designer, who could only be God, and therefore God exists. The Spanish philosopher and poet Miguel de Unamuno (1864–1936) wrote, in the prologue of *San Manuel Bueno*: "I would say that *teleology* is theology, and that God is not a 'because,' but rather an 'in order to.'" (Unamuno is the man who said, in *The Agony of Christianity*: "Faith which does not doubt is dead faith.")

tellurian   (teh LOOHR ee un) *n.*, *adj.* *Tellurian* is descriptive of anyone or anything having to do with the planet earth, or characteristic of it; it is synonymous with *terrestrial* in that sense. As a noun, a *tellurian* is an earth-creature, a terrestrial, an inhabitant of this planet. *Tellurian* was formed from the Latin noun *tellus* (earth). *Tellus* was the ancient Roman goddess of earth, marriage, and fertility, the counterpart of the Greek goddess Gaea, who was also called *Ge*, *ge* being the Greek noun for "earth" and the basis of the prefix *geo-*, used in compound words having to do with the earth, like *geography*, *geology*, etc. *Tellus* is mentioned in the poem *Hyperion* of the English poet John Keats (1795–1821), when he writes of:

> Asia, born of most enormous Caf,
> Who cost her mother *Tellus* keener pangs,
> Though feminine, than any of her sons.

(*Caf*, also Kaf or Qaf, was the name of the mountain chain that encircled the earth, according to Moslem **cosmology**.)

telpherage (TEL fur ij) *n. Telpherage* is a system of overhead traction operated electrically, utilizing a cable along which cars or carriers travel suspended. These are known as *telphers*; the passage is known as a *telpherway* or *telpherline* and the operator as a *telpherman. Telpherage* and all these related words were coined in 1882 by the British electrical pioneer Fleeming Jenkin (1833–1885), who collaborated with the British physicist Lord Kelvin (1824–1907) in the development of submarine telegraphy cables. Jenkin, who knew his classical Greek, coined the the word from the Greek prefix *tele-* (far, as found, e.g., in *telephone, television*, etc.) plus the Greek *pherein* (to bear).

tenebrous (TEN uh brus), rarely **tenebrious** (tuh NEB ree us) *adj*. A *tenebrous* place is dark and gloomy. *Tenebrae* is a Latin noun (plural in form, singular in meaning) that means "darkness," from which several Latin adjectives, including *tenebrosus*, were formed, all meaning "dark, gloomy." *Tenebrae* is the name given to a Catholic church ritual sung on Thursday, Friday, and Saturday of Holy Week, commemorating the Crucifixion. It is accompanied by the gradual extinguishing of candles, leaving the church in darkness. A landscape can be *tenebrous*; so can the interior of one of those Charles Addams (cartoonist, born 1912) houses. Murder mystery films often use *tenebrous* rooms and hallways for atmosphere. The Roman poet Catullus (c. 87–c. 54 B.C.) wrote of the *iter tenebricosum* (dark and gloomy road) whence, they say, no one returns, beating Hamlet's "bourn" whence "no traveller returns" by more than 16 centuries.

teratism, see **teratology**

teratoid, see **teratology**

teratology (ter uh TOL uh jee) *n*. This is a term used in biology to denote the study and science of malformations and abnormal growths in animals and plants. The word is formed from the Greek noun *teras* (monster) and the suffix *-logia* which gave us the familiar *-logy* used in the names of sciences and bodies of knowledge, as in *biology, geology, theology*, etc. *Teras* gave us also a number of related words: *teratism* (TER uh tiz um), the worship of monstrosities, and *teratoid* (TER uh toid), monstrous, resembling a monster. *Monster*, in these definitions, denotes any malformed animal, including man, that deviates grotesquely from the norm, with the implication that the effect is hideous, frightening, revolting. Ancient religions and legends often involve *teratological* concoctions. The Egyptian goddess Hathor was represented as a woman's body with a cow's head, and Bubashtis as a woman with the head of a cat or lioness, while the god Anubis was shown as a man with a jackal's face, and Thoth had the body of a man and the head of an ibis. Greek legend gave us the one-eyed Cyclops, the winged, snake-haired Medusa and her Gorgons, so hideous that one who gazed at them turned to stone; and the Sphinx, borrowed from Egyptian religion, was a winged lion with a human head, or sometimes the head of a ram or hawk. Hindu religion offers the god Siva or Shiva, a supreme deity endowed with multiple arms and, at times, three heads. Getting to later times, Gulliver, the traveler conceived by the English satirist Jonathan Swift (1667–1745), was faced by *teratoid* creatures, gigantic and infinitesimal. On the subject of actual human beings, though the word *teratology* didn't figure in the newspaper reports, the subject was deeply involved in the hideous results of radiation after the August 1945 A-bombings of Hiroshima and Nagasaki and the resulting malformation of Japanese babies, and later, in the birth of deformed babies as the result of the use of the tranquilizer thalidomide by pregnant women. *The Elephant Man*, the play by the dramatist Bernard Pomerance (b. 1940), concerned the tragic life of a *teratoid man*. Anyone who has braved freak shows at circuses has been exposed to *teratological* phenomena.

tergiversate (TUR jih vur sate) *vb.* To *tergiversate* is to keep reversing one's opinon or attitude with regard to a subject, a theory, a cause, etc. More narrowly, it is to desert one cause or party for another, or become an apostate from one's religious faith. It can be used, as well, where one changes one's principles, equivocates, makes conflicting statements, is evasive. This rather tongue-twisting verb is derived from Latin *tergiversare* (to turn one's back), based on *tergum* (back) plus *versatus*, past participle of *versare* (to turn about often), related to *vertere* (to turn). The practice is *tergiversation* (tur jiv ur SAY shun). The adjective describing this type of behavior is *tergiversatory* (TUR jih vur suh tor ee, -torh ee)— an even greater challenge to the tongue, and one who practices *tergiversation* is a *tergiversator* (TUR jih vur say tur) or a *tergiv-*

387

ersant (TUR jih vur sunt). After all this, one might prefer to remain consistent, but remember the American poet and essayist Ralph Waldo Emerson (1803–1882): "A foolish consistency is the hobgoblin of little minds . . . Speak what you think to-day (sic) in words as hard as cannon-balls (sic), and to-morrow (sic) speak what to-morrow (sic) thinks in hard words again, though it contradict every thing (sic) you said to-day (sic)." Please forgive all the (**sic**)s, but one must preserve the proofreader from criticism, at all costs.

termagant   (TUR muh gunt) *n.*, *adj.* A *termagant* is a shrew, a virago, an overbearing, violent, brawling woman (see **billingsgate**), and *termagant* as an adjective covers all those unlovely qualities. The word has an interesting derivation. With an upper case *T*, it was the name the Crusaders gave a legendary male deity supposedly worshipped by the Saracens who became a figure in the allegorical morality plays of the 15th and 16th centuries. As a character, *Termagant* was violent and rampageous, and dressed in flowing eastern robes that led the public to regard him as a turbulent female. In Shakespeare's *Henry IV, Part I* (Act V, Scene 4), in the heat of battle Falstaff shams death in order to escape being killed, and when young Prince Hal, thinking him dead, makes the pun:

> Death hath not struck so fat a *deer* to-day,
> Though many *dearer*, in this bloody fray,

fat, old Falstaff puns back: ". . . 'twas time to counterfeit, or that *termagant Scot* [the rebellious Archibald, Earl of Douglas] had paid me *scot* [let me have it] . . ." (See **scot**.) *In Hamlet* (Act III, Scene 2), Hamlet advises the players: "Speak the speech, I pray you, trippingly on the tongue . . . O! it offends me to the soul to hear a robustious periwig-pated fellow tear a passion to tatters . . . I would have such a fellow whipped for o'er-doing *Termagant* . . . avoid it."

tertium quid   (TUR shum QUID, -shee um) *phrasal n.* This is the Latin translation of the Greek *triton ti* (literally, third what?) to denote a third something related to two known things but distinct from both, or intermediate beween two things that are opposite or incompatible, like mind and matter, or, euphemistically, the third person in the eternal triangle, as a result of the new twist applied to the expression when the English poet and writer Rudyard Kipling (1865–1936), in *Wee Willie Winkie (At the Pit's Mouth)*, opened with "Once upon a time there was a Man and his Wife and a *Tertium Quid.*" *Tertium quid* can also apply to something that escapes a dichotomy assumed to be exhaustive, or, jocularly, to anyone or anything whose status is anomalous or ambiguous, like a dependent living with the family and helping out—guest or servant?—or to a third thing resulting from the combining of two things but distinct from either, like the chemical result of two substances that produce a third, e.g., an alloy, or a neutral salt resulting from the mixture of an acid and an alkali, or a third party that shall be nameless. *Tertium quid* is said to be the invention of the Greek philosopher and mathematician Pythagoras (c. 582–c. 500 B.C.), who defined *biped* as follows: "A man is a biped, so is a bird, and a *tertium quid*," the last believed to be a reference to Pythagoras himself. Fowler says it has been applied to a "middle course, as the British Liberal Party . . . between the Conservatives and the Socialists." A lovely phrasal noun; choose your own interpretation.

test, see **carapace**

tetragram, see **Tetragrammaton**

Tetragrammaton (teh truh GRAM uh ton) *n.* A *tetragram* is any word of four letters, like *love* or *hate*; from the Greek, based on *tetra* (four) plus *gramma* (letter). *The Tetragrammaton* is the Hebrew name of God, JHVH (transliteration of the four letters of the Hebrew alphabet, *yod* [yood], *he* [hay], *vav* [vov], *he*), too sacred to be pronounced, so that the Jews substituted *Adonai* (ah doh NOY) or *Elohim* (eh loh HIM; the plural of *eloh*, God). The *Tetragrammaton* was transliterated by scholars to *Yahweh* (YAH weh), and eventually corrupted to *Jehovah*. The English poet John Dryden (1631–1700), in *Britannia Rediviva* (Britian Renewed), wrote:

> Such was the sacred *Tetragrammaton*.
> Things worthy silence must not be revealed.

Getting back to *tetragram*, one might think that a *pentagram* is a word of five letters, but one would be mistaken. Though *penta-* is a combining form of *pente* (five), and *gramma* remains "word," a *pentagram* is not a five-lettered word, but a five-pointed star. And while we're at it, the next time you want someone to stop using four-letter words, tell him to cut out the *tetragrams* and see what happens.

tetralemma, see **lemma**

tetraonine, see **accipitrine**

thalassic, see **pelagic**

thaumatrope, see **thaumaturgy**

thaumaturgy (THAU muh tur jee) *n.* *Thaumaturgy* is magic, the working of miracles or wonders. A *thaumaturge* (THAU muh turj) is a miracle-worker. *Thaumatology* (thau muh TOL uh jee) is the study of miracles. A *thaumatrope* (THO muh trope) is a "magic card," one with different pictures on the two sides, which appear to combine when the card is twirled rapidly. Examples: a horse on one side and a rider on the other, so that one gets the image of a rider on horseback; a girl on one side and a boy on the other, giving the image of a couple embracing. All these words are based on the Greek noun *thauma* (wonder, wondrous thing, marvel) and the *-trope* in *thaumatrope* combines it with *tropos* (a turning). *Thaumaturgus* is Greek for "miracle-worker," and is a term applied to certain saints credited with the working of miracles. Bishop Gregory of Neo-Caesaria (c. 213–c. 270) was called "Thaumaturgus" because of the miracles he performed, including the moving of a mountain, no less. St. Bernard, abbott of Clairvaux (1090–1153), known as the "mellifluous doctor" for his wisdom and influence, was so effective in his work for the church that he acquired the title "Thaumaturgus of the West." The next time you employ a magician for a children's party, you may address him as "prestidigitator" (see **prestidigitation**), or "*thaumaturge*," if you really want to compliment him.

theodicy (thee OD ih see) *n.* The German philosopher Gottfried Leibnitz (1646–1716) coined the French word *théodicée*, based on the Greek prefix *theo-* (combining form of *theos*, god) plus *dike*

390

(right, justice), for his theory of vindication of God's justice in permitting the existence of evil. Leibnitz was trying to establish that this was the best of all possible worlds, despite the existence of evil, which is a necessary condition for the existence of the maximum moral good. If there were no evil against which to measure its opposite, how could there be moral good? It is not appropriate here to enter into an argument on this point. Suffice it to say that is what is meant by *theodicy*, for what it is worth.

thetic, see **nomology**

theurgy (THEE ur jee) *n. Theurgy* is miraculous divine action, the operation of a supernatural or divine agency in the management of human activities. The word is derived, via Late Latin *theurgia*, from Greek *theourgeia* (magic), based on *theos* (god) plus *ergon* (work), from which, incidentally, we get our word *erg*, a unit of work in the parlance of physics. The adjective is *theurgic, -al* (thee UR jik, -jih kuhl). One who believes that human affairs are governed by the intervention of a supernatural agency is a *theurgist* (THEE ur jist). The world is in such a mess that a bit (not too much!) of *theurgy* might be welcome.

thew (thyooh) *n.* This word, usually found in the plural, means "muscle" or "sinew"; figuratively, "strength." It comes from Middle English. The English poet Edmund Blunden (1896–1974), in his poem *Forefathers*, wrote:

> These were men of pith and *thew*,
> Whom the city never called;
> Scarce could read or hold a quill,
> Built the barn, the forge, the mill.

Shakespeare used *thews* frequently. In *Hamlet* (Act I, Scene 3), Laertes, advising his sister Ophelia not to take Hamlet too seriously, tells her:

> . . . nature . . . does not grow alone
> In *thews* and bulk; but as this temple waxes,
> The inward service of the mind and soul
> Grows wide withal.

391

Cassius, in *Julius Caesar* (Act I, Scene 3), bemoaning the weakening of the Roman character, says to Casca:

> . . . for Romans now
> Have *thews* and limbs like to their ancestors;
> But, woe the while! our fathers' minds are dead,
> And we are govern'd with our mothers' spirits.

And in *Henry IV, Part 2* (Act III, Scene 2), Falstaff asks Justice Shallow:

> Will you tell me . . . how to choose a man? Care I for the
> limb, the *thewes* . . . the bulk . . . ! Give me the spirit, Master
> Shallow.

The word is still alive: John Russell, the chief art critic of *The New York Times*, in an article on Brittany, writing rhapsodically about a country inn, tells us:

> The service is about as good as it could be, whether by
> strong-*thewed* young women from Moelan or by senior staff
> whose ways are anything but rustic.

Strong-*thewed* young women . . . ? Can't you see those muscles rippling? One can hardly wait . . . As might be expected, *thewless* means "timid, cowardly," or "weak."

thewless, see **thew**

thigmatropism, see **haptic**

thrasonical (thray SON ih kul) *adj.* A *thrasonical* person is a braggart, a vainglorious boaster; a *thrasonical* statement is boastful, blustering, puffed-up, overweening. *Thraso* is the braggart in *Eunuchus (The Eunuch)*, a comedy by the Roman comic dramatist Terence (c. 190–c. 159 B.C.). In Shakespeare's *As You Like It* (Act V, Scene 2), Rosalind, speaking to Orlando of the love-at-first-sight of Oliver and Celia, says: " . . . there never was anything so sudden but the fight of two rams, and Caesar's *thrasonical* brag of 'I came, saw and overcame.' " Shakespeare liked the word: In *Love's Labour's Lost* (Act V, Scene 1), there is a hilarious colloquy between the schoolmaster Holofernes and Sir Nathaniel, a curate. The curate starts: "I praise God for you, sir . . ." and goes on, in pompous language, to praise the schoolmaster, who responds: "Novi hominem tamquam te: [I know a man just like you:] his humour is lofty, his discourse peremptory, his tongue filed, his eye ambitious, his gait majestical, and his general behaviour vain, ridiculous and *thrasonical* . . ." For another adjective derived from another character in the same play, see **gnathonic**. Cf. **braggadocio, fanfaronade, gasconade, rodomontade.**

thremmatology, see **genethlialogy**

threnody (THRED uh dee) *n.* A *threnody* is a lamentation, in the form of a speech, a poem, or a song, especially a dirge or funeral song, and in that sense it is a synonym of **epicedium.** *Threnody* comes from Greek *threnoidia*, based on *threnos* (dirge) plus *oide* (song). The observations with respect to contemporary funeral practices noted under **epicedium** apply here as well.

threpsology, see **genethlialogy**

thwart, see **umiak**

tigrine, **accipitrine**

ting, see **tinnient**

tinnient (TIN ee unt) *adj. Tinnient* describes anything that has a clear ringing or clinking sound; from Latin *tinniens*, present participle of *tinnire* (to clink, jingle). The bells around the neck of a horse trotting as it pulls a sleigh on a clear winter's day (shades of Currier & Ives) have a *tinnient* sound. Good crystal sounds *tinnient* when it is lightly tapped. Related words: a *ting* is a clear ringing sound, and *to ting* is to make such a sound; a *tang* is a sharper ringing sound, and *to tang* is to ring out or clang; *tinnitus* is a pathological ringing in one's ears, from *tinnitus*, past participle of the same *tinnire*. Tinging is pleasant, tinnitus isn't. (See also **tintinnabulation**).

tinnitus, see **tinnient**

tintinnabulation (tin tih nab yuh LAY shun) *n. Tintinnabulation* is the ringing or sounding of bells. This delightful onomatopoeic word comes from the Latin for *bell; tintinnabulum.* The adjective describing the sound is *tintinnabular* (tin tih NAB yu lur). The American writer Janet Flanner (1892–1978) wrote of ". . . church bells [tolling] . . . in a melancholy, quivering *tintinnabulation.*" The word, by extension, can be applied to any belllike sound. The English poet and novelist Sir Osbert Sitwell (1892–1969) used these lovely words: " . . . the splashing and *tintinnabulation* of a hundred country-scented showers," and in his poem *The Bells*, the American poet and short-story writer Edgar Allan Poe (1809–1849) tells of

> Keeping time, time, time
> In a sort of Runic rhyme
> To the *tintinnabulation* that so
> musically wells
> From the bells, bells, bells, bells,
> Bells, bells, bells.

(See also **tinnient**.)

titivate (TIT uh vate) *vb. Titivate* is colloquial for "spruce up, smarten up, put on the finishing touches"; sometimes written *tittivate. Tidivate* is an earlier form, giving rise, despite its initial short *i*, to a supposed derivation from *tidy*, plus the *-vate* from *elevate*, resulting in *tidy up*, or the *-vate* from *cultivate*, according to some authorities. Somehow, all this seems unlikely. A wholly distinct meaning, "titillate," which comes from Latin *titillatus*, past participle of *titillare* (to tickle), must have been the result of confusion, a powerful influence in etymology. In any event, do not confuse *titivate* with *titubate* (TIT ooh bate), meaning "to stumble, or stagger, or totter," from Latin *titubare* (to stagger) whose noun is *titubation* (tit ooh BAY shun), a medical term for "unsteadiness," especially when caused by a nervous disease. There is another *tit*-word that has to do with the way one moves: *tittup* (TIT up), *n.*, *vb.*, that means, as a noun, "moving in an exaggeratedly bouncy way," like a frisky horse, and as a verb, to move in that way, supposedly derived, via *tit* (a dialectal term for "twitch"), from Middle English *tittle*, plus *-up*, taken from the *-op* of *gallop*. Maybe.

In any case, all these *tit-* words have nothing to do with the *tit* or *titty* that means "teat," or the *tit* that you get for *tat* if you're lucky.

tittup,   see **titivate**

titubate,   see **titivate**

tmesis   (tu MEE sis) *n.* *Tmesis* is the grammatical term for the interpolation of a word between the parts of a compound word. *Be thou ware* for *beware; what things soever* for *whatsoever things;* the . . . greatness of his power *to us-ward* for *toward us* (The Epistle of Paul to the Ephesians 1:19) are examples of *tmesis* in olden use. It was done in Roman times: The Roman poet Ennius (236–169 B.C.) separated *cerebrum* (brain) thus: "Saxo *cere* comminuit *brum*" for "Saxo comminuit *cerebrum*" ("He smashed his brain against a rock.") *Tmesis* has been adapted into current slang, especially British: *abso-bloody-lutely, hoo-bloody-ray,* etc. A sort of *tmesis* (though this is, strictly speaking, an unwarranted extension of the term, because the interpolation is between two words, not the parts of one word) is heard in the departing husband's long speech in *Fumed Oak,* by the English dramatist Noel Coward (1889–1973), in which the finally resolute spouse condemns all the things in the dreary household he can't stand a minute longer, including the "A-1 bloody sauce." *No bloody good* is another example of quasi-*tmesis*. *Tmesis*, Greek for "cutting," was taken into Latin intact, and came to us likewise without change.

tolypeutine,   see **accipitrine**

topiary   (TOH pee air ee) *n., adj.* As an adjective, *topiary* describes shrubs and trees clipped into artificial shapes. As a noun, *topiary* is the art of performing such shaping into elaborte "sculpture," including animals, birds, urns, castellation (with turrets and battlements) and abstract geometrical forms. It is an old-fashioned art practiced mainly in older gardens, involving frequent clipping, at least twice a year, starting when a tree or shrub is young. Thickness and uniformity are the aims of such frequent clipping and trimming. The commonest plants used in *topiary* are box, privet and yew. Because of the constant and expert attention required, and the increasing cost and scarcity of the highly special skill involved, this type of gardening is growing ever rarer. *Topiary* is from Latin *topiarus* (pertaining to ornamental gardening), based on *topia* (landscape or landscape gardening—a plural noun, from Greek *topos*, place).

toponym (TOP uh nim) *n.* A *toponym* is not only a place name, but also a noun derived from a place name. There are many examples of such nouns. An extensive collection appears in an article entitled "Around the World by Dictionary", by Stephen E. Hirschberg, in the Spring 1984 edition of *Verbatim, The Language Quarterly*, from which it is a pleasure to cull some illustrations. A 16th-century mint at Sankt Joachimsthal, in Bohemia, produced a coin called the "Joachimsthaler," which was shortened in German to *taler*, from which we got *dollar*. To *meander* is to roam or wander in a rambling course, because that is the way the River *Meandros*, in ancient Phrygia, wound its way; and *frieze*, a decorative feature of stately buildings, goes back to the embroidery of the same *Phrygia*. The Italian town of *Cerreto*, once famous for its quacks, gave the name *ciarlatano* to its natives—whence *charlatan*. *Taranto*, Italy, was a breeding place for big, hairy spiders, now known as *tarantulas*. *Angora* is based on *Ankara*, Turkey; *calico* on *Calicut*, East Indies; *damask* on Damascus, Syria. *Tuxedos* are named for the Tuxedo Park, New Jersey, country club where they first became popular. *Sherry* started in *Jerez*, Spain; *cos* lettuce came from the Greek island of *Kos*; *vichyssoise* from *Vichy*, France; *bourbon* from *Bourbon* County, Kentucky; *china* from China; *delft* from *Delft*, Holland; *bunk* from *Buncombe* County, North Carolina. *Toponym* comes from two Greek words: *topos* (place) and *onoma* (name), and is not to be confused with **eponym,** which is quite a different matter.

toxophilite (tok SOF uh lite) *n.* This is the name for one who uses the bow and arrow, a bowman or archer; *archer* is from Latin *arcarius*, based on *arcus* (bow). The English scholar and tutor of Queen Elizabeth I, Roger Ascham (1515–1568), coined the word *toxophilus* (bow-lover) from the Greek noun *toxon* (bow) and suffix *-philos* (loving), based on the verb *phileein* (to love). A *toxophilite* is a devotee of archery; the study, practice, and love of that skill is *toxophily* (tok SOF uh lee). Archery, a method of hunting since time immemorial, and of primary military importance until the invention of gunpowder, was revived as a sport by King Charles II of England (1630–1685) and became a certified Olympic event in 1972.

traduce   (truh DOOHS,-DYOOHS) *vb.* To *traduce* someone is to slander him, vilify him, malign, defame, and calumniate him, speak falsely and with malice toward him or his character; from Latin *traducere* (to disgrace), a variant of *transducere* (literally, to carry over; figuratively, to expose, "show up"). In Shakespeare's *Othello* (Act V, Scene 2), Othello cries to Lodovico who has come to arrest him:

> . . . in Aleppo once,
> Where a malignant and a turban'd Turk
> Beat a Venetian and *traduc'd* the State,
> I took by the throat the circumcised dog
> And smote him thus.

Whereupon, he obeys Shakespeare's stage directions: *Stabs himself*. Things are tough all around and it's a bloody mess; but getting back to words and definitions, avoid the common error of identifying *slander* or *defame* with *libel*. Without going into legal minutiae and ramifications, *libel* is *slander* in written form and "published," i.e., communicated in that form to a third party or parties. Best advice: Keep your mouth shut and your pen in your pocket.

tra(ns)montane   see **cisalpine**

transalpine,   cisalpine

transitive   (TRAN sih tiv, -zih-) *adj.*; **intransitive** (in TRAN sih tiv, -zih-) *adj.* These are grammatical terms applicable to verbs. A *transitive* verb is one that can take an object, i.e., that expresses an action having a direct effect upon someone or something; examples: *love*, *hate*, *kiss*, *kick*. One doesn't just love or hate or kiss or kick; one loves, hates, kisses, or kicks someone or something. An *intransitive* verb does not take an object, but indicates a complete action by itself; examples: *go*, *stay*, *sit*, *lie*. The same verb, depending upon the use, can be both. After the battle of Marathon in

490 B.C., an unnamed courier ran almost 23 miles from the scene of battle to Athens to announce the victory—and fell dead on his arrival. His name was not Pheidippides, as often stated in error; that individual ran from Athens to Sparta (110 miles) before the battle to ask for help against the Persian foe. In the last two sentences, *ran* is *intransitive*; it is complete in itself, without an object. But when someone runs a business or a factory, *run*, in the sense of "operate" or "manage," is *transitive*. When you open in a play, *open* is *intransitive*; when you open a bottle of champagne (or a can of worms), *open* is *transitive*. To err is human, to forgive divine. Both verbs are *intransitive*. *Err* can't be used *transitively*, but *forgive* can, when, for example, we forgive them that trespass against us. *Transitive* verbs can form a passive; *intransitive* verbs cannot. One can be forgiven, but can't be "erred."

transmarine, see **cisalpine**

trebuchet, see **onager**

trencherman (TREN chur mun) *n.* A *trencherman* is a heavy eater, a person endowed with a hearty appetite, one who would satisfy even the allegedly typical Italian mother who keeps crying, "Mangia, mangia!" or the caricature of the Jewish mother who endlessly inflicts cholesterol on her family. It is based on *trencher* (a plate, platter, or cutting-board; from French *tranchoir*, related to *trancher*, to cut or slice, and *tranche*, a slice or slab). In Shakespeare's *Much Ado About Nothing* (Act I, Scene 1,) Beatrice describes Benedick: ". . . He is a very valiant *trencherman*; he hath an excellent stomach." *Trencherman*, in context, can also apply to a sponger, one who likes to feed at another's table.

tribade, see **tribadism**

tribadism (TRIB u diz um) *n. Tribadism* is lesbianism; a *tribade* (TRIB ud) is a lesbian, usually in the sense of a homosexual female who assumes the male role, the "active" partner. *Tribadic* (trih BAD ik) is the adjective for the person and the practice. All these words go back to the Greek noun *tribas* (rubbing) and verb *tribein* (rub). In view of the anatomical limitations involved, the etymology is self-explanatory.

trigraph, see **digraph**

trilemma, see **lemma**

tringine, see **accipitrine**

triskaidekaphobia (tris kye dek uh FOH bee uh) *n.* This is fear of the number 13, and a person suffering from it is a *triskaidekaphobe* (tris kye DEK uh fobe). *Triskaidekaphobia* is from Greek *triskaideka* (13) plus the suffix *-phobia* (indicating fear or dread), while the suffix *-phobe,* applicable to the affected person, is the combining form of *phobos* (fearing). The superstition revolving around the number 13 is said to have originated from a banquet in Valhalla (in Scandinavian mythology, the hall that housed the souls of heroes slain in battle) where 12 were seated. When Loki, the Norse god of strife and spirit of evil, intruded (12 + 1 = 13), Balder, the Norse god of light, was killed. This was enhanced by the Last Supper, where Christ sat with the 12 Apostles (12 + 1 = 13 again). Friday the 13th is considered by *triskaidekaphobes* as a particularly unlucky day. The English essayist Joseph Addison (1672–1719) wrote in *The Spectator* (the English daily that ran from March 1, 1711 to December 6, 1772 and for a time in 1774) about being in a mixed group when an old lady caused panic by pointing out that it numbered 13. The day was saved when one of them, a friend of Addison, noticed that one of the ladies was pregnant. "Had not my friend found this expedient to break the omen, I question not but half the women in the company would have fallen sick that night." (13 + ? = ?)

triturte, see **comminute**

trochili(di)ne, see **accipitrine**

troglodyte (TROG luh dite) *n.* This is a technical name for a caveman, or one who lives in a cave. The term also covers anyone living in seclusion or in a primitive state, like a hermit. The adjective is *troglodytic* or *troglodytical* (trog luh DIT ik [al]). *Trogle* is Greek for "hole" and *dyein* is Greek for "get into"; hence *troglodyte*. The ancient Greeks gave the name *troglodytes* to uncivilized races who dwelt in holes in the ground or caves. The Greek historian and geographer Strabo (c. 63 B.C.–c. 21 A.D.) wrote of *troglodytes* living in Syria and Arabia, and the Roman naturalist and writer Pliny the Elder (23-79) asserted that *troglodytes* fed on snakes. Southern Egypt and Ethiopia were alleged to be the homes of the best known of the *troglodytes*. (The term has been applied in ornithology to wrens, because they build their nests, for the most part, in holes.) However, there was some confusion among the ancients between *troglodytes* and *Trogodytae*, a primitive people of northern Sudan. *Troglodytes* lived in caves because of the cold; the Trogodytae were located, according to some authorities, in Egypt and points south, where it isn't cold and there are no natural caves. There was predictable confusion because of the similarity of names: the inclusion of the *l* in ancient manuscripts was an understandable error. The Trogodytae went naked, it was said, ate not only the meat of cattle but the bones and hide as well, drank blood mixed with milk, squeaked like bats and kept their women in common. Whatever the case, a *troglodyte* is now understood to be a cave-dweller, a hermit, and in ornithological circles, a wren; and to complicate matters still further, *troglodyte* has gained the figurative sense of anyone primitive in character, coarse, brutal, or degraded in the way they look, live, or behave. To call someone a *troglodyte* is fightin' words.

troilism (TROY liz um) *n.* One ignorant of its pronunciation might have guessed that this had something to do with Troilus, the lovesick Trojan hero, whose exceptional obsession is attested by these lines from Shakespeare's *Troilus and Cressida*: "I am mad/ In Cressid's love/ . . . Her eyes, her hair, her cheek, her gait, her voice;/ . . . her hand/In whose comparison all whites are ink,/ . . . to whose soft seizure/The cygnet's down is harsh" ". . . I am giddy, expectation whirls me round./The imaginary relish is so sweet/That it enchants my sense./Even such a passion doth embrace my bosom;/My heart beats thicker than a fev'rous pulse . . ." and an amateur etymologist might be forgiven for his guess that *troilism* denoted love-enslavement. But no: according to the *Oxford English Dictionary* it is nothing nearly so romantic, but rather "sexual activity in which three persons take part simultaneously"; and the *Collins English Dictionary* defines it as "sexual activity involving three people" (they omit the *simultaneously*) with a reference to *ménage à trois* and *dualism*, apparently with the suggestion that the

400

-l-, far from that in *Troilus*, is nothing more than an echo from the one in *dualism*. (No mention is made of *pluralism, idealism, materialism*, or for that matter, *feudalism*; and there must be many more *-al* adjectives that grew into *-ism* nouns). So we see that *troilism* is based simply on *trois*, and we wonder, did the French invent it—for there is no such word as *threeism, treism, tresism or dreiism* that has come to this author's attention. Whatever the origin of the word, it is a far from common usage (we are not discussing the practice), and since in *Vita (The Life of Vita Sackville-West)* [Dame Victoria Mary, 1892–1962, English novelist and poet] (Weidenfeld and Nicholson, London, 1983) by the English biographer Virginia Glendenning (b. 1937) we find a quotation out of a communication from the English novelist Virginia Woolf (1882–1941) that includes the phrase "emotional troilism," one might conclude that *troilism* is (or was) nothing more than a bit of Bloomsbury cant. The *-l-* in *Troilus*, however seductive a clue to the amateur etymologist, turns out to be, alas, a red herring.

trope   (trope) *n.* A *trope* is any use of language in other than its literal sense; a figure of speech, a rhetorical device such as a metaphor, **metonomy, synecdoche**, irony, etc. *Trope* is, via Latin *tropus* (figure of speech), from Greek *tropos* (a turning), related to *trepein* (to turn). *Tropology* (troh POL uh jee) is the use or study of figurative language or a treatise on the subject of figures of speech, from Greek *tropologia*. The overuse of *tropes* has been a frequent subject of satire. In *Hudibras*, the English poet and satirist Samuel Butler (1621–1680) mocked the subject of his satire in a number of different ways, including this:

> For rhetoric, he could not ope
> His mouth, but out there flew a *trope*.

Another English poet, Matthew Prior (1664–1721), in the poem *Paulo Purganti and his Wife*, satirized his subject with:

> He ranged his *tropes*, and preached up patience;
> Backed his opinions with quotations.

tropology,   see **trope**

trumpery   (TRUM puh ree) *n.*, *adj.* *Trumpery* is worthless stuff. In context, it can mean "nonsense, gibberish, twaddle." As an adjective, *trumpery* means "worthless, trashy," describing things of no value, with the implication that the things so described are showy as well as worthless, as in *trumpery jewelry*, *trumpery arguments*. In Late Middle English, *trompery* was deceit, from Middle French *tromperie*, based on *tromper* (to deceive). Though the element of deceit is at the bottom of its etymological source, *trumpery*, in its literal sense of "rubbish, junk" or figurative sense of "stuff and nonsense," is simply one or the other, with hardly any reference to guile or duplicity, except that the showiness is, in a way, calculated to make a misleading impression.

turdine,   see **accipitrine**

tutelage,   see **tutelary**

tutelary   (TOOHT uh lair ee, TYOOHT-) *n.*, *adj.* *Tutelary*, as an adjective, describes someone acting as protector or guardian, like a *tutelary* angel or saint. As a noun, a *tutelary* is a saint or a deity, or a mere mortal in a *tutelary* position or relationship. The related noun *tutelage* (TOOHT uh lij, TYOOHT-) means "guardianship," the act or status of protecting or guiding, or "instruction," or the condition of being under a guardian. The Chinese revolutionary and political leader Sun Yat-sen (1866–1925) wrote of the three stages of revolution: "The first is the period of military government; the second, the period of political *tutelage*; and the third, the period of constitutional government." The words *tutor*, *tutorage*, and *tutorial*, as well as *tutelary* and *tutelage*, all go back to Latin *tutus*, past participle of the verb *tueor* (to look at, watch, and, by extension, to watch over, guard). *Tutus* (watched over), by extension, came to mean "safe, secure."

tyrannicide,   see **aborticide**

U, Non-U   (yooh, non yooh) *adj's.* This is primarily a matter of British sociolinguistics, but you may run into the terminology and
402

the liberty is taken to quote from Appendix I.C.6. of this author's *British English, A to Zed* (Facts On File, 1987):

> For the subtleties of variations in the vocabulary of spoken (and to a much smaller extent, written) British English based on class distinctions, the reader is referred to *U and Non-U, an Essay in Sociological Linguistics*, by Prof. Alan S. C. Ross, of Birmingham University (England) . . . , later in *Encounter*, and still later in *Noblesse Oblige*, a collection of articles edited by Nancy Mitford (1904–1973; Hamish Hamilton, London, 1956; Penguin Books, Ltd., 1959). His article was commented on by Miss Mitford in *Encounter*, in a piece entitled *The English Aristocracy* . . . She, in turn, was answered, still in *Encounter* by Evelyn Waugh in "An Open Letter to the Honorable Mrs. Peter Rodd (Nancy Mitford) On a Very Serious Subject." The Mitford and Waugh articles, too, are included in *Noblesse Oblige*. All these comments gave currency to the concept of U and Non-U as linguistic categories constituting "class-indicators." (The *U*, incidentally, doesn't stand for *You*, as in *While-U-Wait*, but for *upper class*.) It is felt that these distinctions would be lost on most Americans, whose ears are not attuned to English class differences based on accent or vocabulary and who suffer from a feeling of inferiority equally in the spoken presence of London cabbies and Oxford dons . . . It would be well to take the trouble to avoid some of the more glaring shibboleths, like *lounge* (for *living-room*), *serviette* (for *napkin*) . . . and *pardon!* (for *sorry!*).

Fowler says, of *U* and *Non-U*: "The English class system was essentially tripartite—upper, middle, and lower—and it was only by its language that the upper class (U) was clearly marked off from the others (Non-U)."

ubiety   (yooh BY ih tee) *n. Ubiety* is the quality or property of being in a definite place at any given time, "whereness," as it were, location. It comes from Middle Latin *ubietas*, based on Latin *ubi* (where), and should not be confused with *ubiquity* (yooh BIK wih tee), the property of being everywhere at the same time, from Late Latin *ubiquitas*, based on *ubique* (everywhere), from which we also get *ubiquitous* (yooh BIK wih tus), a familiar adjective. It may be said that the planets have *ubiety*, whereas, according to the British anthropologist Jacob Bronowski (1908–1974), man has *ubiquity*. In *The Ascent of Man*, Bronowski tells us that "Man is . . . the *ubiquitous* animal . . ."

ukase (YOOH kase, yooh KAZE) *n*. Originally, in imperial Russia, a *ukase* was an order or edict handed down by the Czar, which automatically acquired the force of law, but the term has now come to denote any peremptory proclamation issued by an absolute or arbitrary authority without right of appeal. The use of the term need not be confined to duly constituted government authorities. It can be said that certain party bosses never make suggestions or call for them; they simply hand out *ukases*. Hollywood moguls, old style, operated by *ukase*. We took the word from the French, who based it on Russian *ukaz*.

ullage (UL ij) *n*. *Ullage* is the quantity of liquid by which a container falls short of being full, i.e., the difference between the amount of liquid a vessel can hold and the amount it actually contains; from Old French *ouillage* or *eullage* (the amount of wine needed to fill a cask), related to *ouiller* or *oeiller* (to fill up). *Ullage* is used of a bottle of wine part of which has been lost by evaporation. In England, *ullage* was formerly used as a slang term for "dregs," and even more generally, "rubbish."

ulotrichous, see **cymotrichous**

ultramarine see **cisalpine**

ultramontane, see **cisalpine**

ululate (YOOHL yuh late, UL ool-) *vb*. Fowler suggests a different pronunciation: ūlūl-, i.e., OOH looh-, saying, ". . . the imitative effect got by repeating the same sound should not be sacrificed; *ulul-* suggests howling much more vividly than *ŭlūl-* [i.e., ul ool] . . ." In any event, to *ululate* is to howl, like a dog or a wolf, to wail, to lament shrilly, without words; also, to hoot or screech like an owl. *Ululate* is derived from Latin *ululatus*, past participle of *ululare* (shriek, yell, howl), and also a noun meaning "howling, shrieking, wailing"; and *ulula* is Latin for "owl," and is involved in the derivation. The noun, *ululation* (yoohl yuh LAY shun, ul-) implies repeated, rhythmic wailing. *Ululate* is an onomatopoeic word, i.e., it imitates the sound it describes. To hear wolves *ululate* in the darkness sends shivers down one's spine, but to hear the *ululations* of professional mourners can be worse.

ululation,   see **ululate**

umbrageous   (um BRAY jus) *adj. Umbrageous* has two entirely distinct meanings. Its principal meaning is "shady," in the sense of creating or providing shade, like the famous " . . . spreading chestnut tree . . ." (in the poem by the American poet Henry Wadsworth Longfellow, 1807–1882) under which " . . . the village smithy stands. . . . " An *umbrageous* tree, then, is a shade tree. But an *umbrageous* person *(umbrageous* here refers back to the word *umbrage*, a feeling of offense, resentment, and annoyance, usually found in the expression to *take umbrage*) is one quick to take offense. When *umbrageousness* reaches the point of mental disorder, it becomes *paranoia. Umbrageous* is from Latin *umbratus*, past participle of *umbrare* (to shade or overshadow), and it may be the feeling of being overshadowed that creates the *umbrage. Umbrageous* trees provide shade; *umbrageous* people feel overshadowed.

umiak   (OOH mee ak) *n.* This is a Greenland Eskimo word for an open boat constructed of a wooden frame covered by animal skins, with a number of seats placed abeam for the rowers, exclusively women, who sit on opposite sides of the boat, each paddling with one oar. Such cross-seats in a boat are known as *thwarts. Umiaks* are used to carry passengers and freight, and are quite different from *kayaks*, Eskimo hunting boats, which are covered by flexible closures that fit around the waists of the crew.

unicameral,   see **bicameral**

uninitiated   (un ih NEE shee ay tud) *n. pl.* The *uninitated* are those not in the know, the "innocents," perhaps. To *initiate* is, inter alia, to introduce (someone) into the knowledge and understanding of a subject, or into the secret rites of an organization, whether the Masons or a college fraternity. It comes from Latin *initiatus*, past participle of *initiare* (to initiate). There were various types of secret rites and "mysteries" in ancient Rome into which certain favored individuals were *initiated*. Those left out, the vast majority, were the *uninitiated*. What goes on behind closed doors in governments, large corporations, political organizations, etc., is not shared with the hoi polloi—the *uninitiated*—those in the dark and not privy to the inner workings, the wheels within wheels. In matters of art, the *uninitiated* are the opposite of the **cognoscenti**.

untoward (un TORD) *adj. Untoward* is not an antonym of *toward* (in the direction of) and doesn't mean "away from." *Toward* has a number of rarely used meanings, one of which is "propitious, favorable," and *untoward* as the negative of *toward* in that sense means "unfortunate, unfavorable." Thus it can be said that *untoward* circumstances led to the downfall of Oscar Wilde. *Untoward* can also mean "improper," and it is in that sense that *untoward* behavior can be said to make people socially unpopular. The relation of *untoward* to *toward* is like that of *unsavory* to *savory*, where *unsavory* has the common meaning of "morally offensive" while *savory* commonly means "tasty." *Savory* has the rarely encountered meanings of "agreeable, pleasant, attractive" and it is in reference to those senses that *unsavory* is its negative. These are cases where an *un-* word is an antonym of only a rare sense of the positive form.

uranology, see **genethlialogy**

uriticaria, see **urticate**

ursine, see **accipitrine**

urticate (UR tuh kate) *vb.* To *urticate* is to sting like a nettle. *Urtica* is *nettle* in Latin; the related Latin verb is *urticare* (to sting). *Urticaria* (ur tuh KAR ee uh) is an allergic condition of the skin causing severe itching similar to that produced by nettles. It is called *nettle rash* as well, or *hives*. *Urtication* (uh tuh KAY shun) is the development of that condition, and an extremely unpleasant one it is. There is a belief, as rampant in the English countryside as nettles and dock themselves, that the stinging sensation produced by contact with a nettle is promptly relieved by rubbing the affected part with a dock leaf. (These weeds grow in close proximity, and are particularly prolific.) This belief, from the author's own painful experience, is without foundation. Some say gentle pressing will help.

usufruct (YOOH zoo frukt, -soo-, YOOHZ yoo-, YOOSH-) *n. Usufruct* is a term used in law primarily, to denote one's right to enjoy the use and benefits flowing from the use of another's property, without the ownership of it and without the right to harm or waste or destroy it. The word is from Late Latin, based on two Latin words, *usus* (use) plus *fructus* (fruit), and indicates the "fruit of the use." If A makes an arrangement with B for B to use A's estate or other asset and retain the profits and benefits of that use, on condition that A keeps it intact, B is said to have the *usufruct* of that asset, or to have a *usufructuary* (yooh zoo FRUK chooh uh ree—same variations in pronunciation of first two syllables as shown above) right in it.

uxorial (uk SOR ee ul, ug-) *adj. Uxor* is *wife* in Latin, and *uxorial* means "wifely," describing the attitudes, devotion, responsibilities, and anything else pertaining to, befitting, or typical of wives. *Uxorilocal* (see **matrilocal**) and on a more somber note, *uxoricide* (see **aborticide**) are both based in part on *uxor*. Another *uxor* adjective, from Latin *uxorius* and not to be confused with *uxorial*, is *uxorius* (uk SOR ee us, ug-). The two words have nothing in common except the *uxor*. Whereas *uxorial* describes women in the marital role, *uxorious* applies only to the opposite sex, men who simply dote on their wives, are excessively and uncritically fond of them and lovingly submissive. *Uxorious* has the sense of overdoing it, and has a somewhat disparaging flavor. Sociological-cum-etymological note: There appears to be no Latin-derived adjective for a doting wife.

uxoricide, see **aborticide**

uxorilocal, see **matrilocal**

uxorious, see **uxorial**

vaccine, see **accipitrine**

vade mecum, see **ench(e)iridion**

valetudinarian (val ih toohd uh NAIR ee un, -tyoohd), also **valetudinary** (val ih TOOHD uh ner ee, -tyoohd-) *n.*, *adj.* A *valetu-*

dinarian or *valetudinary* is an invalid, particularly one who is unduly concerned about his poor health. Both words are adjectives as
well, describing the condition of one in poor health, or excessively anxious about it. These words are derived from Latin
valetudinarius (sickly), based on the noun *valetudo* (state of
health—good or bad), related to the verb *valere* (to be strong).
Valetudinarians differ from hypochondriacs, in that *valetudinarians* really do have something to worry about, and may do so to
excess, while hypochondriacs suffer from imaginary ills, and worry
about them just as excessively, like *Le Malade Imaginaire* (The
Imaginary Invalid) in the comedy by the French actor and comic
playwright Molière (1622–1673). Do not confuse *valetudinarian*
with *valedictorian*, the top student in a graduating class who deliv-
ers the *valedictory* address at commencement.

variorum   (var ee OR um) *n., adj.* A *variorum* edition of a work
is one that contains varying versions of the text, or annotations by
scholars, as in a *variorum* edition of *The Divine Comedy* or an early
Shakespearean printing. By itself, a *variorum* is a *variorum* edition.
The term is a **compendious** form of the Latin phrase *editio cum
notis variorum* (edition with notes of various people). The *variorum*
in that expression is the masculine genitive plural of the Latin adjective *varius* (various) used as a noun, so that *variorum* means "of
various people." *Variorum* is not the neuter nominative singular
that, in the words of Fowler. " . . . the bookseller took it to be
when he offered a *good variorum edition including variora from
MSS in the British Museum.*"

vatic,   see **vaticinate**

vaticide,   see **aborticide**

vaticinate   (vuh TIS uh nate) *vb.* This verb is defined as "to
prophesy" by dictionaries both American and British, but the admirable *Chambers Twentieth Century Dictionary* (W. & R. Chambers Ltd., Edinburgh) adds "(chiefly ironical)" and Fowler
comments, "The verb, formerly equivalent to *prophesy*, now usually connotes contempt . . ." One who *vaticinates* is a *vaticinator*
(vuh TIS in nay tur). The practice is *vaticination* (vat ih suh NAY
shun), and the related word *vatic* (VAT ik) means "prophetic, orac-
408

ular, inspired." The derivation is from Latin *vaticinatus*, past participle of *vaticinari* (to prophesy), based on *vates* (seer). (Incidentally, note the difference in the English spelling of *prophesy*, verb, and *prophecy,* noun, as well as the difference in the pronunciation of the last syllable. The noun comes from Greek *propheteia*, and the verb is simply a verb use in variant form.) There is an etymological connection between these *vatic-* words and the *Vatican*, the papal palace, which got its name from its location atop the *Vaticanus Mons* (Vatican Hill) of ancient Rome, the former headquarters of the Roman *vaticanitores* (soothsayers). Don't take the utterances of *vaticinators* too seriously: remember Delphic ambiguity and the double-talk of Nostradamus, the French physician and astrologer Michel de Nostradame (1503–1566), which could go either way.

velleity (vuh LEE ih tee) *n. Velleity* is mere inclination or wish, without the effort to accomplish it; the weakest form of volition, unlike **conation**, which combines striving with volition. *Velleity* is from New Latin *velleitas*, based on Latin *velle* (to be willing, to wish). Fowler contrasts *volition* and *velleity* this way: "Volition . . . an exercise of will-power for a specific purpose . . . *Velleity* . . . an abstract and passive preference." The English biographer and critic Lytton Strachey (1880–1932) wrote: "Every wish, every *velleity* of his (Prince Albert) had only to be expressed to be at once Victoria's." The English jurist and philosopher Jeremy Bentham (1748–1832) wrote, in *Scotch Reform*: "In your Lordship, will is volition, clothed and armed with power—in me, it is bare and inert *velleity*." (Good characterization of *velleity*: bare, inert.) Jean Jacques Rousseau, the French philosopher and author (1712–1778), in his *Prose Works*, wrote of mistaking ". . . emotion for conviction, *velleity* for resolve."

verbid (VUR bid) *n. Verbid* is a term used in grammar for a nonfinite verb form (infinitive—to say; gerund—saying; participle—saying or said) that has neither subject nor object, or a noun derived from a verb, also known as a *verbal*. To err is human, to forgive divine: *To err* and *to forgive* are used as nouns, subjects of *is* and are *verbids* or *verbals*. Parting is such sweet sorrow: *Parting* is in the same boat—a *verbid* or *verbal*. The noun *aesthete* (or *esthete*), a person sensitive toward the beautiful, especially in the arts, is from the Greek *aisthetes* (one who perceives), a *verbid* of *aisthanesthai* (to perceive—or, as they say in the jazz world, to *dig*.

verism (VEER iz um, VER-) *n. Verism* is realism in the arts, whether literary or graphic. It is also the name for the proposition that literal representation of reality and truth is of the essence in literature and art. *Verism* requires the resort to the ordinary, everyday material of life, even if ugly or sordid, in art. The novels of the Russian writer Feodor Dostoyevsky (1821–1881), the paintings of the German artist George Grosz (1893–1959), the caricatures of the French cartoonist and lithographer Honoré Daumier (1808–1879), all showed life in the raw, products of *verism*. It is a theory, called *verismo* in Italian, that influenced much of early 20th-century Italian opera like *La Bohème* of Puccini (1858–1924), *I Pagliacci* of Ruggiero Leoncavallo (1858–1919) and *Cavalleria Rusticana* of Pietro Mascagni (1863–1945). *Verism* comes from Latin *verus* (true), the source as well of a string of English words: *verify, verity, veritable*, etc.

verjuice (VUR joos) *n. Verjuice*, literally, is the sour juice of unripe fruits, especially crab apples and grapes. Figuratively, *verjuice* is sourness of temperament, disposition, or expression. It is the hallmark of a *curmudgeon*, itself an interesting word, generally described in dictionaries as of unknown origin though Samuel Johnson (the English lexicographer, 1709–1784) says in his *Dictionary*: "It is a vitious [the old spelling, based on Latin *vitiosus*] manner of pronouncing *coeur méchant* [French for *wicked heart*] . . ."

vernissage (ver nih SAJ) *n.* This French word (literally, varnish, or varnishing-day) has been taken over in art circles to mean the "private viewing" of an art exhibition, by invitation only. The meaning of *vernissage* in French, originally "varnishing," was extended to include "varnishing-day," a day reserved for the painters to apply a coating of varnish or put finishing touches to their works, a function sometimes attended by critics. The term was first applied to this ritual at the Paris Salon, the annual exhibition of painting and sculpture by living artists, and extended to include the private view at the opening of any art exhibition. *Vernissages* are attended by critics, **cognoscenti**, collectors, and those who are more interested (as at the opera) in being seen than in seeing.

410

veronica (vuh RON uh kuh) *n. Veronica* is not only the name of a plant and a girl's name, but also, as every aficionado of bullfighting knows, a classic movement with the cape, where the matador stands stock still and slowly swings the cape away from the charging bull. The original *Veronica* was a woman of Jerusalem who wiped Jesus's forehead with a kerchief while He was on His way to Calvary. It was found to bear His likeness and was called the "Vera Icon" (True Image) and the woman later became Saint *Veronica*. The kerchief is kept as a relic at St. Peter's in Rome. The matador's pass is called the *veronica* because the cape slowly swung before the face of the charging bull is like the kerchief of St. *Veronica* wiping Christ's brow.

vertiginous (vur TIJ uh nus) *adj. Vertigo* (VUR tuh go) is a fairly familiar word for "dizziness," a pathological condition in which a person feels that he or everything around him seems to be whirling around and that he is about to lose his balance. Not so well known is the adjective *vertiginous*, which some fail to relate to *vertigo* because the *g* is soft and the accent shifts from the first to the second syllable. *Vertiginous* can mean several things: "spinning" or "rotary," when it describes the movement of a top, or wind currents; "dizzy" or "giddy," of people affected with *vertigo*; "causing dizziness," like heights, a winding staircase, a rocking ship; or, figuratively, "unstable, subject to sudden change," in describing economic or social conditions. *Vertigo* was taken over from Latin, where it is related to the verb *vertere* (turn). *Vertiginous* comes from Latin *vertiginosus* (dizzy). In Latin, the accent of *vertigo* is on the second syllable (ver TEE go), and that used to be the pronunciation in English.

vespertine, see **acronical**

vespine, see **accipitrine**

viaticum (vye AT uh kum) *n.* According to Fowler, the use of *viaticum* for "provisions" is to be considered an example of "PEDANTIC HUMOR." The word is not often encountered, and when used seriously, denotes the funds and other necessities one takes along on a trip. The plural form is rare; some authorities supply the form *viaticals*, in the sense of "baggage." In ecclesiastical circles, *viaticum* has a special use: the Eucharist or Communion given to a dying person or one in danger of dying. In ancient Rome, *viaticum* was the travel allowance granted public officials sent out on a mission away from home, an advance "expense account." The word was taken intact from the Latin, where it means "money for a journey," and is the neuter form of the adjective *viaticus* (pertaining to a journey), based on *via* in the sense of "journey."

vigia (vih JEE uh) *n.* On a navigational chart, there are warning symbols called *"vigias"* indicating the approximate location of shoals or dangerous rocks. *Vigia* is a Spanish word meaning "look-out" or "watching"; in nautical parlance, "shoal"or "rock." Both Spanish and English are from Latin *vigilia* (keeping watch, guard; figuratively, watchfulness), from which we get *vigil, vigilance, vigilante*, etc. A chart full of *vigias* can make a helmsman quite nervous.

vinculum (VING kyuh lum) *n.* A *vinculum* is a bond or tie, denoting unity. *Vinculum* is Latin for "cord, chain, bond," primarily in the sense of "fetters," related to the verb *vincire* (to bind, fetter, restrain). It has a special use in mathematics, as the name of a line drawn over a group of quantities to signify that they are to be treated as a unit, with the same effect as a set of parentheses around the group. Thus, $\overline{a + b}$ is the same as (a + b). The *vinculum* comes in handy to denote a unit or units within a unit, thus: $(a + \overline{b + c})$ or $(\overline{a + b} + \overline{c + d})$. Brackets are used to show units within a unit, thus: $[(\overline{a + b} + \overline{c + d}) + (\overline{e + f} + \overline{g + h})]$. For units within units within units within units, use braces, thus: $\{[(\overline{a + b} + \overline{c + d}) + (\overline{e + f} + \overline{g + h})]\} + \{[(\overline{i + j} + \overline{k + l}) + (\overline{m + n} + \overline{o + p})]\}$. Incidentally, any of those plus signs, for the purpose of this discussion, could just as well have been minus signs. The *vinculum*, as used in mathematics, is still a tie or bond, serving a particular use.

viniculture, see **oenology**

viperine, see **accipitrine**

virgule, see **solidus**

viricide, see **aborticide**

virtu (vur TOOH, VUR tooh), *n.* This word, taken intact from the Italian, where it means, inter alia, "virtue" and "merit," stemming from Latin *virtus* (excellence, worth), covers a range of meanings, all connected with objects d'art: excellence in such items; such objects collectively; a taste for them; knowledge in that field; love of fine arts generally. *Objects of virtu* are of interest because of their workmanship, rarity or antiquity. They are collected by connoisseurs, dealers, and museums. The works of the Russian jeweler and goldsmith Carl Fabergé (1846–1920) housed in the Hermitage, a museum in Leningrad, are prime examples of *objects of virtu*. Except for their ancestry (Latin *virtus*), *virtu* has nothing to do with *virtue* in the sense of "moral excellence" or "chastity."

vituline, see **accipitrine**

viverrine, see **accipitrine**

viviparous (vye VIP uh rus) *adj.* Some animals give birth to living young. Others expel eggs which must hatch; still others produce eggs but instead of expelling them, hatch them inside the body so that the young are born alive. The first are *viviparous*; the second are *oviparous* (oh VIP uh rus); the third are *ovoviviparous* (oh voh vye VIP uh ruhs). Most mammals and some reptiles and fishes are *viviparous*. Birds, most reptiles, and a few species of mammals are *oviparous*. Certain reptiles and fishes are *ovoviviparous*. All these systems seem to work quite well. *Viviparous* is from Latin *viviparus* (giving birth to living young), based on the prefix *vivi-*, the combining form of *vivus* (alive) plus the suffix *-parus* (bearing), from the verb *parere* (to bear). *Oviparous* is from Latin *oviparus* (giving birth by means of eggs), based on prefix *ovi-*, the combining form of *ovum* (egg), plus the same suffix *-parus*. From the foregoing, the derivation of *ovoviviparous* is obvious.

volucrine, see **accipitrine**

voussoir, see **quoin**

vulpine,   see **accipitrine**

vulturine,   see **accipitrine**

widget   (WIJ it) *n.* *Widget* is a colloquial alteration of *gadget*, the name for any small mechanical device whose name the speaker or writer doesn't know or can't remember at the moment. Examples: a switch, a cogwheel, a coil, a washer, an insulator, all those little things we can't live without. When you walk into a hardware store, don't confuse *widget* with *widgeon* (WI jun), or you'll have the man looking for a duck with a reddish-brown head and a yellowish-tan crown, and he may be out of them.

xyster,   see **xystus**

xystus   (ZIST us), **xyst** (zist) *n.* A *xystus* or *xyst* is a long covered portico, especially one used by ancient Greek athletes for exercising in bad weather or during the winter. The Romans applied *xystus* to any open colonnade or tree-planted walk. This noun comes from Latin *xystus*, which in turn came from Greek *xystos*, based on the verb *xyein* (to scrape, polish), because the floor of a *xystos* was smooth and polished. These words are related to the noun *xyster* (ZIST ur), a surgical instrument for scraping bones, taken intact from the Greek, where it means "graving tool," and is likewise based on their verb *xyein.*

zarf   (zarf) *n.* A *zarf* is a cup-holder, usually a stand, for a cup without a handle. It is usually of decorative metal, sometimes precious, and usually richly ornamental. *Zarf* is an Arabic word for "vessel, container." The cup held by the *zarf* is called a *finjan* (fin JAN) or *fingan* (fin GAN). *Finjan* is Arabic, *fingan* Egyptian. The

414

cup in question is usually a small coffee cup containing the thick concoction popularly known as "Turkish coffee." *Zarfs* are never used without *finjans* or *fingans*. The arrangement is a little like the tea-glass held in a metal holder used by our Russian brethren, who otherwise wouldn't be able to hold the superheated glass—except that the Russian glass can stand up by itself, unlike the *finjan* or *fingan*, which, incidentally, is also sometimes spelt *findjan* or *fingian*.

zebrine, see **accipitrine**

zeitgeist (TSITE gyest) *n. Zeitgeist* is a German word, based on a combination of two nouns: *Zeit* (time, era, age, epoch) and *Geist* (spirit). [Note: All nouns are capitalized in German; *Zeigeist*, taken into English, may be spelt with either an upper or lower case *z*.] *Zeitgeist* (literally, time-spirit) is the spirit of the age, the typical attitude of the times, the characteristic moral or intellectual feeling of a particular era, the trend of culture and taste of a period in history. The *zeitgeist* of the Periclean age (c. 461–c. 431 B.C.) of ancient Greece was the attainment of greatness in the arts: architecture, sculpture, music, and drama. The *zeitgeist* of the Middle Ages operated against scientific investigation. The attempt to manage society through technocracy is part of the *zeitgeist* of the 20th century. The Women's Lib movement was definitely in tune with the *zeitgeist* of the 1970s.

zeugma (ZOOHG muh) *n. Zeugma* is a term used in grammar, rhetoric, or logic for a phrase in which one word governs or modifies two or more words not connected in meaning, as in the use of a verb with multiple subjects or objects, a preposition taking multiple objects, or an adjective modifying multiple nouns. In each case, the governing word is strictly applicable to one of the following words while the word appropriate to the other is omitted. The English novelist Charles Dickens (1812–1870) gives us a fine, jocular example in *Pickwick Papers*, when "Miss Bolo went home in a flood of tears and a sedan chair." The same *zeugmatic* situation occurs when, on a bitter, rainy day, a fisherman catches five fish and a cold, or funeral guests attend with weeping eyes and hearts, or a dinner party is spoiled by the host's bad wine and jitters, or an angry man leaves the house in high dudgeon and an overcoat. *Zeugma* is taken intact from the Greek, where it means "yoking," related to the verb *zeugnynai* (to yoke). (See also **syllepsis**.)